10.13.98

About Island Press

Island Press is the only nonprofit organization in the United States whose principal purpose is the publication of books on environmental issues and natural resource management. We provide solutions-oriented information to professionals, public officials, business and community leaders, and concerned citizens who are shaping responses to environmental problems.

In 1998, Island Press celebrates its fourteenth anniversary as the leading provider of timely and practical books that take a multidisciplinary approach to critical environmental concerns. Our growing list of titles reflects our commitment to bringing the best of an expanding body of literature to the environmental community throughout North America and the world.

Support for Island Press is provided by The Jenifer Altman Foundation, The Bullitt Foundation, The Mary Flagler Cary Charitable Trust, The Nathan Cummings Foundation, The Geraldine R. Dodge Foundation, The Charles Engelhard Foundation, The Ford Foundation, The Vira I. Heinz Endowment, The W. Alton Jones Foundation, The John D. and Catherine T. MacArthur Foundation, The Andrew W. Mellon Foundation, The Charles Stewart Mott Foundation, The Curtis and Edith Munson Foundation, The National Fish and Wildlife Foundation, The National Science Foundation, The New-Land Foundation, The David and Lucile Packard Foundation, The Surdna Foundation, The Winslow Foundation, The Pew Charitable Trusts, and individual donors.

About the Biodiversity Support Program

The Biodiversity Support Program (BSP) is a consortium of World Wildlife Fund (WWF), The Nature Conservancy (TNC), and World Resources Institute (WRI) funded by the United States Agency for International Development (USAID).

BSP's mission is to promote conservation of the world's biological diversity. We believe that a healthy and secure living resource base is essential to meet the needs and aspirations of present and future generations. To accomplish our mission, we support local communities, nongovernmental organizations, and governments to establish:

- Clear conservation priorities, goals, and objectives;
- Democratic social processes, dialogue, and partnerships that lead to conservation;
- Ethical valuation of nature;
- Favorable policies that promote conservation of biodiversity; and
- Enhanced awareness and knowledge about conservation.

BSP's approach focuses on the integration of conservation with social and economic development through implementation of projects, research and analysis of conservation and development approaches, and information exchange and outreach.

Partial support for the preparation of the manuscript was provided by the Global Bureau of USAID under the terms of project numbers DHR-5554-A-00-8044-00 and AEP-0015-A-00-2403-00. The opinions expressed herein are those of the authors and do not necessarily reflect the views of the Biodiversity Support Program, its consortium members (WWF, TNC, and WRI), or USAID.

Measures of Success

Measures of Success

Designing, Managing, and Monitoring
Conservation and Development Projects

RICHARD MARGOLUIS AND NICK SALAFSKY

Illustrations by Anna Balla

ISLAND PRESS

Washington, D.C. • Covelo, California

Any part of this book, including the illustrations, may be copied, reproduced, or adapted to meet local needs in developing countries provided:
    1. permission is obtained from Island Press;
    2. the parts reproduced are distributed free of charge or at cost—not
    for profit; and
    3. credit is given to the original work.

No part of this book may be reproduced in any form or by any means for
commercial ends without permission in writing from the publisher:
Island Press, 1718 Connecticut Avenue, N.W., Suite 300, Washington, DC
20009, USA.   *Fax:* (202) 234-1328.

ISLAND PRESS is a trademark of The Center for Resource
Economics.

Library of Congress Cataloging-in-Publication Data
Margoluis, Richard.
    Measures of success : designing, managing, and monitoring
conservation and development projects / Richard Margoluis and Nick
Salafsky ; illustrations by Anna Balla.
        p.   cm.
    Includes bibliographical references and index.
    ISBN 1–55963–612–2
    1. Biological diversity conservation.   2. Conservation projects
(Natural resources)   I. Salafsky, Nick.   II. Title.
    QH75.M328   1998   98–13588
    333.95'16—dc21   CIP

Printed on recycled, acid-free paper ✪

Manufactured in the United States of America
10 9 8 7 6 5 4 3 2 1

To our teachers past and present.

Contents

Preface

Audience for This Guide

Measures of Success is a guide to designing, managing, and monitoring the impacts of conservation and development projects. Some people believe that these are difficult tasks that only people with advanced academic training and degrees can do. We believe, however, that the people who are most qualified to do this work are the conservation practitioners and community stakeholders who are most familiar with local conditions. This guide is written for them.

If you are part of a conservation and development effort, then the systematic approach presented in this guide can help you design a new project or improve an existing one. If you are part of a group that supports field staff in project design, implementation, or evaluation, then this guide will provide you with some basic tools to assist you in your work. Other people who might find this guide useful include government officials, policy and decision makers, donors, researchers, and students.

Finally, although this guide was written for conservation and development projects, the approach can be easily adapted for use by projects in other related fields such as community development, public health, and education.

Roots of This Guide

In our jobs with the Biodiversity Support Program (BSP), we work closely with local project partners to help them design and implement monitoring strategies for their projects. In doing this work, we found that a common constraint to doing good monitoring is that the people responsible for actually carrying out monitoring activities are frequently not the people who designed the original project. Instead, design and management are often split apart from monitoring and treated as separate processes.

Our experiences convinced us, however, that project design, management, and monitoring cannot be separated. Thus, although we set out initially to write a guide focusing only on project monitoring, we realized that we could not do so without first discussing project design and management in a systematic fashion. And so we expanded our scope to cover these topics, finding a wealth of existing information that we could use as a starting point for our efforts. As shown in the diagram below, the approach presented in this guide is based on many different sources.

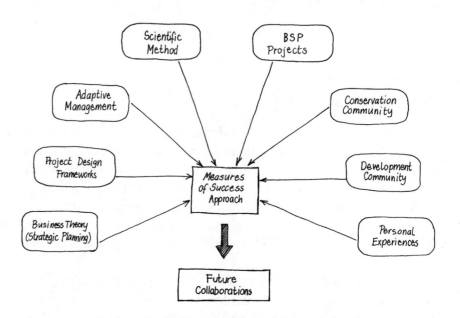

The theoretical sources for this guide lie in the extensive existing body of work on project design and management. The materials presented in this guide draw on many related project management approaches such as the "strategic planning" and "managing for results" techniques developed by business experts in the 1970s and 1980s. They also draw on a number of existing project design frameworks such as the "logframe analysis" used by many project developers, the "results framework" approach that has recently been established by the United States Agency for International Development (USAID), and the "ZOPP method" used by the German Gesellschaft für Technische Zusammenarbeit (GTZ). In addition, the approach also draws on the concepts of "adaptive management," a process originally developed to manage natural resources in large-scale ecosystems by deliberate experimentation and systematic monitoring of the results. All of these approaches themselves build on the "scientific method" that has been employed for centuries by researchers, public health practitioners, and engineers.

The practical sources for this guide are drawn from our field experience working with conservation and development projects. Our approach has been developed and field tested in conjunction with our colleagues from many different BSP supported projects in

Latin America, Africa, and Asia. Their experience and input have helped make this guide more practical and realistic. We have also greatly benefited from the experience, insights, and knowledge of our colleagues in BSP and the broader conservation and development communities. Their feedback has greatly helped to refine the guide. Finally, we have been able to draw upon our personal experiences in designing, managing, and monitoring projects.

Although some of the materials and techniques presented in this guide are not new, we hope it contributes a simple, clear, logical, and yet comprehensive approach to effectively integrating and applying these concepts to conservation and development projects. And we hope that as you use and improve on the approach presented in this guide you will let us know about your experiences. You can reach us at the following address:

"Measures of Success" c/o Island Press, Box 7, Covelo, CA 95428, USA.

Acknowledgments

We would like to thank the many individuals and organizations who have contributed to our work on this book.

Our approach to developing conceptual models and project management and monitoring plans was developed in conjunction with our BSP colleagues in preparation for a series of monitoring workshops. These colleagues include Hank Cauley, Bernd Cordes, Frank Hicks, Stacy Roberts, Diane Russell, Kathy Saterson, and Meg Symington of BSP and Doug Mason of USAID. This approach was greatly refined and enhanced by input and feedback from participants in workshops held for staff of projects supported by BSP's Biodiversity Convention Network (BCN) and Latin America and Caribbean (LAC) Program.

Subsequent versions of the approach have been field tested by project staff and community members at a number of projects in Asia, the Pacific, and Latin America. This book would not have been possible without their input. In particular, we thank Robert Bino, John Ericho, Arlyne Johnson, and the other staff of Research and Conservation Foundation of Papua New Guinea (RCF-PNG); Cosmas Makamet, Kurt Merg, John Sengo, and the other staff of the Foundation for the Peoples of the South Pacific, Papua New Guinea (FSP-PNG); Jane Larme and David Samson of PHF; and Andreas Lehnhoff, Oscar Nuñez, Estuardo Secaira, Marie Claire Paiz, and Eliseo Gálvez of Defensores de la Naturaleza, Guatemala.

For reviewing and commenting on various drafts of this guide, we thank the following: Joanne Abbot of the International Institute for Environmental Development (IIED), Janis Alcorn of BSP, Jane Bertrand of Tulane University, William Bertrand of Tulane University, Katrina Brandon, Michael Brown Bernd Cordes of BSP, Jan Crocker of The Nature Conservancy (TNC), Gretchen Daily of Stanford University, Barbara Dugelby of TNC, Eric Fajer of USAID, Ann Fitzgerald, Mark Freudenberger of World Wildlife Fund–United States (WWF–US), Lynne Gaffikin, Gary Hartshorn of the Organization for Tropical Studies (OTS), Rodney Jackson of The Mountain Institute (TMI), Nandita Jain of TMI, Diane Jukofsky of Rainforest Alliance, Agi Kiss of The World Bank, Claire Kremen of Stanford University, Virginia Ktsanes of Tulane University,

Evelyn Landry of AVSC International, Tom Lovejoy of the Smithsonian Institution, Leo Minaisian of the Florida Department of Environmental Protection, Bruce Moffat of TNC, Ruth Norris, Emilio Ochoa of University of Rhode Island Coastal Resources Center (URI/CRC), Pat O'Connor of USAID, Danyelle O'Hara of WWF–US, Walter Parham, John Parks of EcoTrack, Chuck Peters of the Institute of Economic Botany, Mark Renzi of the LIFE Programme, Alison Richard of Yale University, Don Robadue of URI/CRC, Johanna Rosier of Massey University, Diane Russell of BSP, Vance Russell of BSP, Kathy Saterson of BSP, John Sengo of FSP-PNG, Susan Shen of The World Bank, Meg Symington of BSP, Rod Taylor of BSP, Jim Tobey of URI/CRC, Bill Ulfelder of TNC, Linda Usdin, Anthony Willett of BSP, Barbara Wycoff-Baird, and Agnes Zeller, NGM.

Special thanks go to Janet Rice of Tulane University for commenting and advising us on Chapter 7. This chapter was one of the most challenging ones to write and her assistance and suggestions improved it immensely.

We would like to thank William Bertrand for his tireless insistence on developing conceptual models as the first step in project design. We thank Kathy Saterson and Hank Cauley for encouraging us to write and publish this book. We also thank Hillary Barbour, Connie Carrol, Jill Cheek, Norah Heckman, and Jennifer Jordan for their help in managing logistics. We thank Peter Cassat and Michael Goldberg for their good counsel. We thank John Parks for his help in reviewing the literature and compiling comments on earlier drafts. We thank Gretchen Daily for being a strong advocate for the publication of this book. We would also like to thank Barbara Dean and the staff at Island Press for their help in bringing this book to print. Finally, we wish to acknowledge Anna Balla for the long hours she put into creating the wonderful artwork found throughout this book.

The structure, layout, and tone of this book have been influenced by other guidebooks including: *Where There is No Doctor* by David Werner, *Anybody's Bike Book* by Tom Cuthbertson, *Mining Group Gold* by Thomas Kayser, *The Joy of Home Brewing* by Charlie Papazan, and *Sustainable Harvest of Non-timber Plant Resources in Tropical Moist Forest: An Ecological Primer* by Charles Peters.

Chapter 1
Introduction

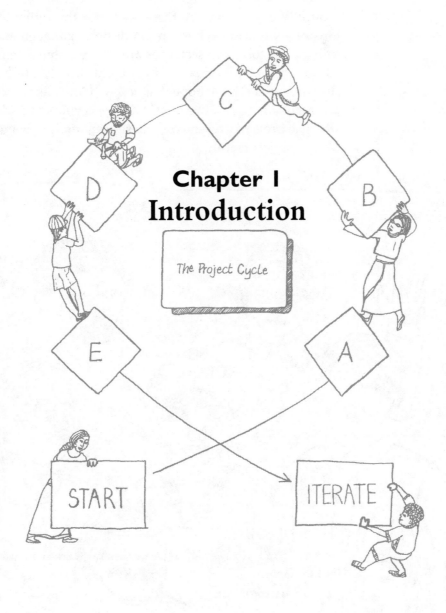

The Project Cycle

C

B

D

A

E

START

ITERATE

Four Project Scenarios

Measures of Success is structured around four scenarios that show the many challenges of managing conservation and development projects around the world. These projects are implemented by various types of groups, including nongovernmental organizations (NGOs), government agencies, local communities, and advocacy groups. We will draw on these scenarios throughout the guide to illustrate our approach to project design, management, and monitoring. The complete scenarios are also presented in Appendix A. Although the scenarios are hypothetical, they are based on real sites and projects. We hope that you will find elements of your project among them so that they may give you some ideas for your site. The projects presented in these scenarios are being carried out by our project team.

Tropical Forest Scenario

Suppose you are the manager of an NGO that is responsible for managing the Indah Biosphere Reserve. The core area of the reserve contains approximately 100,000 hectares of tropical moist forest which includes a mixture of primary and secondary forests. The 80,000 hectare buffer zone around the core area contains 30 small villages whose residents include native and migrant peoples. Residents of the villages are primarily subsistence farmers who grow grains, other food crops, and a few cash crops in small shifting agricultural plots in the forest. Residents also collect timber and non-timber forest products (NTFPs) which they use in their homes and sell in local markets. From what you can tell, it appears that the major threats to the forest include expansion of farms into forest areas, local overharvesting of forest products, commercial logging, expansion of cattle ranches, and the development of a large dam for hydro-electric power generation. At this point, the NGO that you are working for is planning a project that will involve working with community members to develop a few of the forest products for national and international sale and other interventions.

Savannah Scenario

Suppose you are a wildlife biologist working for the local office of the Government Park Service to coordinate a project to design and implement a conservation plan for Karimara National Park. The park is 750,000 hectares of savannah and grasslands in a semi-arid, subtropical setting with an additional 500,000 hectares of land in wildlife management areas (WMAs) around the park. Outside of the WMAs are a number of settlements inhabited by semi-nomadic livestock herders who graze their cattle in the WMAs and occasionally in the park. Residents of the settlements depend on their livestock and limited hunting and gathering of wild animals and plants for subsistence. Major threats to the park include overgrazing, overhunting, and poaching of large mammal species, and the effects of a rapidly increasing and unregulated for-eign tourism industry. The Government Park Service is consider-ing taking a number of steps to protect the park against these threats.

Coastal Scenario

Suppose you are the formally educated son or daughter of the traditional leader of a coastal village who has been chosen by your people to help them find the best way to maintain their resources for future generations. Your village is located at the mouth of a river flowing from upland forests through mangrove forests into Bocoro Bay. The residents of your village get most of their food from fishing and gathering shellfish in the river and coral reefs surrounding the bay. Residents cook their food and build their houses using wood from the mangrove forests growing along the coast. Over the past few years, you and your neighbors have noticed that residents of neighboring villages are increasingly coming into your village's traditional fishing grounds. In addition, large fishing boats from other countries have begun operating in the same area. The elders of the community have noticed over time that local fishermen have to go farther away from the community to catch enough fish to eat and sell and that they are catching smaller fish. In addition, silt and pollution coming down the river have ruined many of the reefs. Furthermore, it is becoming harder to find shrimp in coastal areas near small rivers where the mangroves have been cut down. The elders are now proposing to enhance your people's traditional resource management systems to conserve the plant and animal resources in the bay for future generations.

Wetlands Scenario

Suppose you are the manager of a local chapter of a conservation advocacy group whose members live near the Everson Watershed. The wetlands in the watershed serve as important habitats for migratory birds and for a number of fish and game species. These species support extensive recreational uses of the area including birdwatching, canoeing, fishing, and hunting. The wetlands are also part of the water supply system for major urban areas in the watershed. The wetlands are threatened by growing development and urbanization including road construction and dredging. They are also affected by water pollution (especially from agricultural chemicals) and invasions of exotic plant and animal species. You are planning to work with local landowners and governments to purchase or obtain conservation easements on lands containing critical wetland and upstream habitat. In addition, your organization is hoping to work to educate the public about the importance of the upstream habitats in maintaining the wetlands. Finally, you are hoping to devise a management plan to help control some of the impacts of exotic species.

Purpose of This Guide

A common challenge found in our scenarios and all other *conservation and development projects* is to be able to measure the success of project interventions. In order to ensure that desired conservation impacts occur, you need to know which actions work and which don't—and you need to know why. You also need to make sure that your project activities have a positive impact on the *stakeholders* the project is designed to benefit. Finally, if you are supported by outside organizations or are working with or for local communities, you need to be able to demonstrate to them that you are accomplishing the goals and objectives that were set out at the start of the project.

In response to the challenge of measuring *project* impact, an increasing number of *practitioners* are attempting to fully integrate *monitoring* into the design and management of their projects. These practitioners are faced, however, with a number of constraints in accomplishing this integration. For example, project staff are often so involved with day-to-day operations that they may feel that they don't have the time or money to invest in monitoring. Likewise, field staff may believe that monitoring can only be done by experts or scientists and that they are not qualified to do the job. Finally, and perhaps most importantly, people may simply feel that they don't know how to design comprehensive and useful management and monitoring plans.

Our motivation in writing this guide is a strong belief that, although these constraints are real, they can and must be overcome if conservation and development projects are ultimately to succeed. Although sound project design, management, and monitoring require an investment of time and money, we think that this investment will save resources in the long run by ensuring that the project is effective. Without adequate planning and monitoring, you have no sure way of knowing whether the project is making a positive difference or, worse yet, causing unintended negative impacts. In addition, we believe that the people who are most qualified to design, manage, and monitor projects are the field-based practitioners and local stakeholders who are most familiar with local conditions—not outside "experts" or "professionals." Finally, although every site has unique conditions making it impossible to develop a project design, management, and monitoring "cookbook," we feel that it is possible to come up with general guidelines that can help people determine what they need to do and how best to do it.

The purpose of *Measures of Success* is to demonstrate a simple, clear, and systematic approach to designing, managing, and monitoring projects that seek to conserve *biodiversity*. Whether you are a project manager, village leader, or researcher, it is our hope

Conservation and development projects have as their primary goal the conservation of natural ecosystems and species. They are based on the philosophy that, in order to maintain economic and community development, a healthy and viable natural resource base must be sustained. They operate by involving and addressing the needs of human *stakeholders*—the people who have an interest in the natural resources of the project site.

In this guide, the term *project* is not limited to referring to part of a formal, externally funded program. Instead, it is used to refer to any set of actions undertaken by any group of managers, researchers, or local stakeholders interested in achieving certain defined goals and objectives. For example, a project could include steps that community members take to revive traditional resource-harvesting customs.

Practitioners are managers, researchers, and local stakeholders who are responsible for designing, managing, and monitoring conservation and development projects.

In this guide, we use *monitoring* to refer to the periodic collection and evaluation of data relative to stated project goals, objectives, and activities. Many people often also refer to this process as monitoring and evaluation (M&E).

Biodiversity is the variety and variability of life on earth. It is an abbreviation for biological diversity.

that this guide will assist you in developing and implementing more successful conservation and development projects.

Principles Behind This Guide

Adaptive management is a process originally developed to manage natural resources in large-scale ecosystems by deliberate experimentation and systematic monitoring of the results. (See the references at the end of chapter 8 for more information about adaptive management.)

In this guide, we are using *project assumption* to refer to a causal chain of project activities and factors that affect a target condition. In scientific terms, it is equal to a hypothesis. We are using *underlying assumptions* to refer to the effects that other conditions and factors could potentially have on this causal chain. Although it is helpful to divide assumptions into these two categories, there is definitely a gray area between them—many underlying assumptions could actually be part of a project assumption.

A fundamental principle behind *Measures of Success* involves applying the concepts of **adaptive management** to conservation and development projects. In this context, adaptive management involves integrating project design, management, and monitoring to provide a framework for testing assumptions, adaptation, and learning.

Testing assumptions is about systematically trying different interventions to achieve a desired outcome. It is not, however, a random trial-and-error process. Instead, it involves first thinking about the situation at your project site, developing a specific **project assumption** about how a given intervention will achieve the outcome, and determining what **underlying assumptions** are behind this project assumption. You then implement the intervention and monitor the actual results to see how they compare to the ones predicted by your assumptions. The key here is to develop an understanding of not only which interventions work and which do not, but also why.

Adaptation is about systematically using the results of this monitoring to improve your project. If your project intervention did not achieve the expected results, it is because either your assumptions were wrong, your interventions were poorly executed, the conditions at the project site have changed, your monitoring was faulty, or some combination of these problems. Adaptation involves changing your assumptions and your interventions to respond to the new information obtained through your monitoring efforts.

Process Hint: See chapter 2 for a more detailed discussion of assumptions in the context of the project cycle and chapter 6 for examples of common project assumptions.

Finally, learning is about systematically documenting the process that your team has gone through and the results you have achieved. This documentation will help your team avoid making the same mistakes in the future. Furthermore, it will enable other people in the broader conservation and development community to benefit from your experiences. Other practitioners are eager to learn from your successes and failures so that they can design and manage better projects and avoid some of the hazards and perils you may have encountered. Through sharing what you have learned from your project, you will help conservation efforts around the world.

The *Threat Reduction Assessment* approach to project design, management, and monitoring is described in greater detail in chapter 3.

A second key principle behind *Measures of Success* involves taking a strategic **Threat Reduction Assessment** (TRA) approach to project design, management, and monitoring. Conservation and development projects typically involve complex mixtures of biological, social, economic, and institutional factors. The TRA process presented in this guide attempts to simplify project design and monitoring by directly identifying, addressing, and tracking the threats to biodiversity at a given site. In effect, threat reduction provides both a framework for developing the objective of the project and a framework for measuring conservation success. This strategy involves obtaining a mixture of social and biological data to measure project outcome—a fundamental shift from the traditional approach which involves only assessing the biological effects of project activities.

Style of This Guide

Measures of Success is written primarily with conservation and development practitioners in mind. For simplicity, we use the word "you" to refer both to the reader and the group that he or she is working with—this does not mean that we assume the reader is necessarily the leader of the group.

To meet the needs of this audience, this guide has been written to be as simple and as easy to use as possible. The first time that key words are used they are highlighted in **semibold italics** and defined in a sidebar or highlighted in *italics* and defined in the text. We also collect the terms and definitions in a glossary in Appendix B.

We have also scattered *Process Hints* in sidebars throughout the book that point out ideas that you may find helpful while using the approach presented in this guide. We also use many examples and drawings to illustrate the information being presented. These examples are drawn from the four scenarios that have been developed specifically to represent real-world conservation and development situations and projects.

Finally, you will notice that we spend a good deal of time defining words. In addition, our approach involves spending substantial time considering ways of phrasing goals, objectives, and other items in your Project Plan. We focus on definitions and language because we believe the success of this approach critically depends on everyone having a common and clear understanding of what the project is trying to accomplish. We hope that clear and specific definitions of terms will also facilitate cross-project learning by providing a common language for discussion.

Structure of This Guide

An overview of the general process described in *Measures of Success* is presented in the accompanying **project cycle** diagram. In addition to the starting and ending boxes, the diagram contains five diamonds, each of which represents a different stage in the overall cycle. These diamonds generally need to occur in the order represented by the letters A–E. The diamonds themselves,

Project cycle refers to the steps involved in developing and implementing a project and monitoring plan, and analyzing the results.

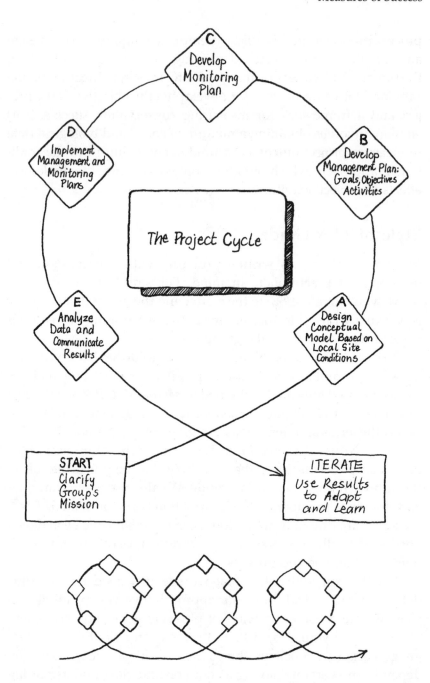

Iterative means repeatedly going through a series of steps in a process.

however, are part of an *iterative* process that involves going through the cycle numerous times as outlined at the bottom of the sketch.

Although *Measures of Success* is presented in a sequential and highly structured fashion, we realize that most people working on a project would not follow such a restricted step-by-step order. Instead, an experienced practitioner would "work the problem from both ends"—thinking first about the audiences for monitoring information and then about goals and maybe then about information needs and then maybe finally going back to the conceptual model. So, although for clarity we have presented the approach as a linear process in this guide, we would encourage you not to feel bound to it.

Start: Clarify Group's Mission

A mission statement provides a vision for the future of your group—your long-term desired outcome and the strategy for getting there. Before setting out to design a new project, you must have a clear understanding of your group's mission. If you plan to work with other groups on the new project, it is also important to understand their missions and how your mission relates to theirs.

Process Hint: Don't worry if you have trouble understanding any of the words used in the description of the contents of each step in the project cycle. Most of these terms are described in each specific chapter.

A: Design a Conceptual Model Based on Local Site Conditions

A *Conceptual Model* is the foundation of all project design, management, and monitoring activities. It is a diagram of a set of relationships between certain factors that are believed to impact or lead to your target condition. The model is first built to present a picture of the project area prior to the start of the project. It is next adapted to reflect local site conditions and then used to identify and rank the key threats to biodiversity that your project will address.

B: Develop a Management Plan: Goals, Objectives, and Activities

A *Management Plan* describes the explicit goals, objectives, and activities designed to address threats identified in the Conceptual Model. Goals are broad statements of the desired state toward which the project is directed. Objectives are more specific statements of the desired outcomes or accomplishments of the project. Activities are specific actions that project participants take to reach each of the project's objectives which in turn should lead to realization of the project's goal. All activities need to be linked to specific objectives that target critical threat factors identified in your Conceptual Model. These linked chains of activities and factors are your project assumptions.

C: Develop a Monitoring Plan

A *Monitoring Plan* describes how you will assess the success of your project interventions. The plan starts by outlining who your audiences are, what their informational needs are, what monitoring strategies you will employ to get the data needed to meet each of these needs, and the specific indicators you will measure. The remainder of the plan lists how, when, by whom, and where data for these indicators will be collected.

D: Implement Management and Monitoring Plans

The Project Conceptual Model, Management Plan, and Monitoring Plan taken together comprise a complete *Project Plan*. This stage involves implementing this Project Plan. From this point forward, however, it becomes more difficult for us to describe a specific process that you'll need to follow. Instead, in chapters 6 and 7, we provide reference material to assist you in determining what tools and techniques are best suited for implementing your particular Project Plan. We first discuss implementing your Management Plan and some of the common project assumptions that lie behind conservation and development projects. We then discuss several parts of your Monitoring Plan in more detail, including designing your monitoring strategy, selecting the specific units to monitor, and selecting the appropriate monitoring methods. Finally, we discuss implementing this plan, including preparing for field work, collecting data, and storing and handling data.

E: Analyze Data and Communicate Results

Once data have been collected, you need to analyze them and communicate the results to your internal and external audiences. In chapter 7, we discuss selected tools and techniques for analyzing data and for communicating the resulting information to various audiences.

Iteration: Use Results to Adapt and Learn

Iteration is the key step in adaptive management. It is where the work invested in monitoring can pay off by helping you incorporate the information to improve your project and move forward. In chapter 8, we discuss how to complete the process of testing assumptions and adapting your Project Plan based on your monitoring results. We also discuss why you should document and share the knowledge you have gained with others so that they can improve their conservation efforts.

Use of This Guide

As you read through and use *Measures of Success*, please keep the following points in mind. We've written this guide to cover design, management, and monitoring from the very beginning of the life of a project. So we assume that you will go through the entire process outlined in this guide from start to finish. This process, however, can be used almost as easily to redesign an existing project. You can use it to help think about your project in a structured fashion and develop and monitor successful interventions. You can even use this process to help you understand or evaluate another project that you are not directly working with.

A phrase that we use throughout *Measures of Success* is "project design, management, and monitoring are as much of an art as they are a science." By this we mean that there is no one right way to do things. Instead, many of the procedures involved in this approach require balancing guidelines with beliefs and experience. We encourage you to use the guide to help you think logically and systematically about the project you are putting together. We also encourage you to listen to and follow your own common sense. The art lies in combining the guidelines and your experience in appropriate proportions to produce a project that reaches your specific goals and objectives. Although we can provide you with the basic framework for developing a project, the artistic aspects of this process are difficult to teach in a book. You will have to rely on your experience and creative skills to make these decisions.

Finally, although you might be able to read this guide sitting in your home or office, it is best used by a team in conjunction with a real-life, field-based project. We encourage you to share *Measures of Success* with your project team and use it to discuss your project. The approach presented here can only be mastered by using it, experimenting with it, and above all, practicing it as much as possible.

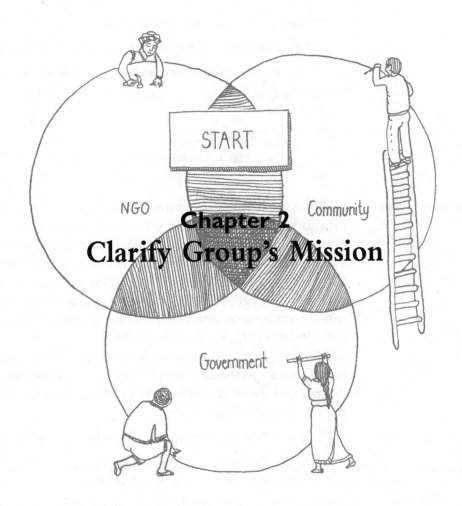

Chapter 2
Clarify Group's Mission

Before setting out to design a new project, you must have a clear understanding of your group's mission. If you plan to work with other groups on the new project, it is also important to understand their missions and how your mission relates to theirs. Without a clear sense of what you want to accomplish and an understanding of what your partners are trying to do, you will find it very difficult to design, manage, and monitor effective projects.

Using the information presented in this chapter, you should be able to:

• Define your group's mission (Step S1).

• Find common ground with your project partners (Step S2).

Define Your Group's Mission (Step S1)

Materials in this section are adapted in part from Espy (1986) and Support Center (1995).

"Would you tell me, please, which way I ought to walk from here?"

"That depends a good deal on where you want to get to," said the Cat.

"I don't much care where," said Alice.

"Then it doesn't matter which way you walk," said the Cat.

"—so long as I get somewhere," Alice added as an explanation.

"Oh, you're sure to do that," said the Cat, "if you only walk long enough!"

> — Lewis Carroll,
> *Alice's Adventures in Wonderland*

In this guide, we use the word **group** to refer to an organization or collection of people working to implement a project toward a common goal. We also use it interchangeably with **project team**.

Unlike Alice in the above example, your **group** probably has a clear idea of what it wants to achieve and where it wants to go. So it does matter which way you go. It also matters how you get there. The projects that a group develops are often the vehicle for getting the group to where it wants to go. Where your group wants to go, how it plans to get there, and what steps it will and will not take is called your *mission*, and it is generally presented in the form of a *mission statement*.

A mission statement provides a vision for the future. It does not focus on specific details or tactics but rather on your long-term desired outcomes and your general strategy for getting there. A mission statement describes:

- *Purpose.* What your group is seeking to accomplish.

- *Strategies.* The general activities or programs your group chooses to undertake to pursue its purpose.

- *Values.* The beliefs which the members of your group have in common and try to put into practice while implementing the group's strategies.

Process Hint: Many of the ideas presented in this section might seem as if they are more applicable to formal organizations like a nongovernmental organization (NGO) or government agency rather than to a group of community members. Nonetheless, although a group of community members may not go through these steps in a formal manner, it may be worth doing some level of strategic planning to define what it is that your group hopes to accomplish.

If your group already has a mission statement that covers these three parts, then you should review it before you begin to design your project. If you are satisfied with your mission statement, you can then choose to skip over the remainder of this section and go on to Step S2, "Find Common Ground with Your Project Partners." If your group does not have a mission statement, or you think it's time to revise the one you have, you should work with the other members of your team to develop one that adequately reflects the goals of your group.

Organize a Strategic Planning Meeting with Your Group

Most groups develop their mission through a process called strategic planning, which is a way of defining the general purpose of your group and then deciding what types of activities you will carry out to achieve your group's ends. It is useful for the following purposes:

- *Creating a Vision of the Future.* By identifying and analyzing different options, you can design the best possible approach to reaching your purpose.

- *Planning for the Use of Resources.* Usually, both financial and staff resources are limited in community-based or nongovernmental organizations. It is therefore crucial that you use resources efficiently and effectively.

- *Fundraising.* Most conservation and development organizations need to raise funds to support their programs through donors or other agencies. A strong strategic plan helps you present your group to potential funders in a convincing manner.

- *Team-Building.* Strategic planning gives all members of your team a chance to understand and work together toward common goals.

- *Coordinating Efforts with Other Groups.* A group's strategic plan provides a tool with which to negotiate partnerships, relationships, and agreements with other groups.

Strategic planning is most successful when it involves all levels of personnel, including administrative staff, project coordinators, upper management, and board members. Creative thinking is vital to a successful strategic planning process. Perhaps the best way to help you and your staff do this thinking is by organizing a special strategic planning meeting at a time and place when all relevant group members can attend. Make sure that you have a good *facilitator* for your meeting and that you work with this person to carefully plan in advance the activities that you will want to undertake.

Determine Your Group's Mission

In your strategic planning meeting, you should first discuss as a group each part of a mission: purpose, strategies, and values.

Purpose

The first part of developing your mission involves agreeing on your group's purpose—to decide what it is that you hope to accomplish and what types of problems you need to solve to get

Process Hint: If your group can afford it in terms of time and money, it is often helpful to hold a strategic planning meeting during a staff retreat held away from your normal working space. This retreat enables people to get away from their day-to-day activities and focus on long-term issues.

A *facilitator* is a person who helps members of a group conduct a meeting in an efficient and effective way, but who does not dictate what will happen. See Kayser (1990) for a description of what a good facilitator can do.

there. Are you trying to increase conservation of natural resources? To eliminate preventable childhood diseases? To enhance people's standard of living? To ensure that animals are treated humanely? To improve education levels?

As you can see from these examples, a purpose statement generally contains two key phrases. The first phrase contains a verb (in the form of an infinitive) that indicates a change in status (to improve, to prevent). The second phrase contains a noun that summarizes the problem or condition that needs to be changed (conservation of natural resources, education levels).

To determine your purpose, have the session facilitator ask different people in the meeting to state what they think the group's purpose should be. Hopefully, everybody will be in general agreement. The key here is to limit yourself to one main idea. Although all of the purposes listed earlier are both important and interrelated, one group generally will not be able to address more than one of them. For example, in the Tropical Forest Scenario, you and your co-workers might decide that your purpose is to enhance conservation of the country's tropical rainforests and that although it is important, you will not focus on community health or education.

If, however, there is wide disagreement in your group about what your purpose should be, it may be necessary to either have the leadership select it, or, in cases of intense disagreement, you may have to consider dividing your group into two or more separate groups. It sounds extreme, but if you can't agree on what you generally want to accomplish, then it will be very difficult for your group to function efficiently and effectively.

Strategies

Once you have settled on your purpose, you need to consider the broad strategies that you will use to move forward—what it is that you will actually do. For example, if your purpose is to enhance rainforest conservation, you could implement integrated conservation and development projects (ICDPs) at specific sites; or you could lobby the national legislature to change policies that affect forests; or you could educate local people about the importance of forests; or you could try to do applied research that could be used to train other groups doing similar work; or you could try to directly protect the Indah Biosphere Reserve by doing things like marking the reserve's boundaries and hiring and training guards; or finally, you could work to improve stakeholder institutions involved in the management of the reserve. As you can see from these examples, each strategy describes a specific set of actions that can be taken to achieve the stated purpose.

Although generally you can use many strategies to achieve a given purpose, in general, your group will want to employ only one or, at most, two strategies. To start the process of selecting a specific strategy or strategies that you will employ, have the facilitator ask the participants to brainstorm different ideas. Once you have written down these ideas, then either as a whole group or in smaller *breakout groups* you can discuss each strategy in relation to the following four criteria:

1. *What is the need for this strategy?* Is this approach important for solving the problems we have identified that stand in the way of achieving our purpose?

2. *Are other groups weak at it?* Are there other groups who are able to address these problems?

3. *Are we good at it?* Do we have the skills and expertise to do this type of work?

4. *Do we like doing it?* Do we enjoy doing this type of work?

Breakout groups are small subsets of the participants in a planning session that are given specific tasks to do. In most cases, once they have completed their tasks, they have to report the results back to the whole group. Breakout groups are useful when there are too many people in the meeting to enable all people to have a voice in discussions or when there are more tasks that need to be completed than there is time for the entire group to do them.

STRATEGY	CRITERIA				TOTAL SCORE
	Need for this Strategy	Other Groups Weak at it?	Are We Good at It?	Do We Like Doing It?	
Direct Protection	4	1	2	1	8
ICDP Implementation	5	4	3	5	17
Conservation Education	4	2	3	5	14
Institutional Development	4	3	2	2	11
Applied Research	4	1	1	1	7
Lobbying & Policy Development	5	4	3	4	16

It can be helpful to rank each potential strategy for each criteria on a scale of 1 to 5 as shown in the example above for the NGO in the Tropical Forest Scenario. A ranking of 1 means that the strategy does not fit the criterion at all, while a ranking of 5 means that it fits it very well. Once you have completed the rankings for all criteria, then you can add up the total score.

At the end of the exercise, you should be able to determine from both the total scores and from the discussion your group had in doing the rankings which strategies make the most sense for

Process Hint: Note that for the "other groups weak at it" criterion the rankings are backward. A score of 1 means that other groups are good at this while a score of 5 means that they are not. We use this backward ranking because we want a score of 5 to represent a gap that your group could potentially fill.

Process Hint: In general, the scores generated by a ranking technique like this are not very precise. This means that it is difficult to say that ICDP implementation with a score of 17 is ranked higher than lobbying and policy development with a score of 16. However, it is probably safe to say that both of these strategies are ranked higher than research with a score of 7.

you to pursue. In this case, you decide that you will focus on achieving conservation primarily by supporting site-specific ICDPs and secondarily by doing lobbying and policy development with appropriate governmental officials. Here again, if there is substantial disagreement over which strategy should be employed, either your group's leaders will have to make the final decision or you will have to consider dividing the group into two or more separate groups.

Values

Once you have agreed on your purpose and strategy, it's time to discuss your values—the beliefs that will guide your work. Are you going to try to include all local stakeholders in the work that you do? Are you going to maintain transparent relationships with all the people with whom you work? Are you going to attempt to achieve excellence? Are you going to follow the teachings of a certain religion? Are you going to strive to enhance the personal capacity of the members of your group? As you can see from these examples, each of these value statements outlines a belief that you hold that will influence what you will do or what you will not do to achieve your purpose.

To decide which values are important to you, have the facilitator ask the participants to suggest values that they think are important. For each suggested value, if there is general agreement regarding its importance, then you will probably want to include it in your mission. If there is not widespread agreement, it is probably less important that you keep it in. Unlike the purpose and strategy, you can include multiple values in your mission. The only constraint is that you may not want to have so many values that they clutter up your mission. It's generally better to leave out the more general and obvious values and focus on those that apply specifically to your purpose and strategy. For example, in the Tropical Forest Scenario, the group decides that its values will include maintaining open, clear, and democratic relations with its partners and with one another.

Finalize Your Mission Statement

Once you have agreed on your purpose, strategy, and values, you should write them into a formal mission statement. As a rule, it is best not to try to write the actual text of the mission statement as a group since writing is generally very difficult for groups to do. Instead, you should form a committee of one to three people who can take the results of the planning session and write them into a draft statement. This statement should then be circulated among all the members of your group for comment and revised as necessary.

For example, using the Tropical Forest Scenario, the group might use the results of its strategic planning exercise to develop as its mission statement the following:

> We seek to conserve our country's tropical forests [*purpose*] by developing long-term integrated conservation and development projects and supporting policies in partnership with the local community members who live in and around these forests and with appropriate government officials [*strategies*]. In doing so, we strive to maintain open, transparent, and democratic relationships with our partners and among ourselves [*values*].

Process Hint: The words in [brackets] are not part of the statement, but are only included to illustrate the three parts of the mission statement.

See the complete Project Plans in appendix A for examples of mission statements for the other scenarios.

Once everyone has agreed to the phrasing of the mission statement (or can at least live with it), you can post it where everyone can see it.

Find Common Ground with Your Project Partners (Step S2)

If you intend to collaborate on a project with other groups—which is almost always the case for conservation and development projects—you will need to discuss the similarities and differences of your respective institutions' missions. This discussion process is important as the specific actions a group will take will vary greatly depending on its mission. As outlined in the diagram that follows, it is unlikely that two groups participating in a project will have precisely the same set of purposes, strategies, or values in their mission. This difference makes it all the more important that each group explicitly spell out its mission so that it is possible to see where overlap exists (the shaded areas) and where the differences are (the unshaded areas).

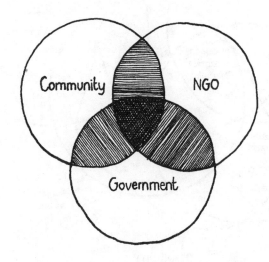

Negotiate Project's General Goal with Potential Partners

We will discuss how to develop a *goal* for your project in detail in chapter 4.

Before you enter into a partnership with another group for a new project, you must assess the similarity of your missions. If your missions are sufficiently compatible, you should come to a consensus on a broad definition of the project's *goal* before you progress. If there is not sufficient overlap between your missions, then you should probably not work together on this project. This includes not accepting money from a donor to do work that does not fit within your defined mission.

Returning to the Tropical Forest Scenario, suppose there are a number of groups and agencies that wish to collaborate with your NGO on a project in the Indah Biosphere Reserve. Equipped with your mission statement outlined earlier, you can discuss the potential project with the other institutions. Identify the appropriate people to talk to in each group and discuss with them their group's mission and their general ideas regarding the goal for the proposed project.

As outlined in the diagram that follows, another community-based NGO in the region has as its organizational mission to help communities gain tenure over traditional forest lands. Still another NGO has as its mission to promote the economic development of communities in forested areas through the provision of large-scale modern technologies to harvest timber. The provincial government in the region might want to increase production

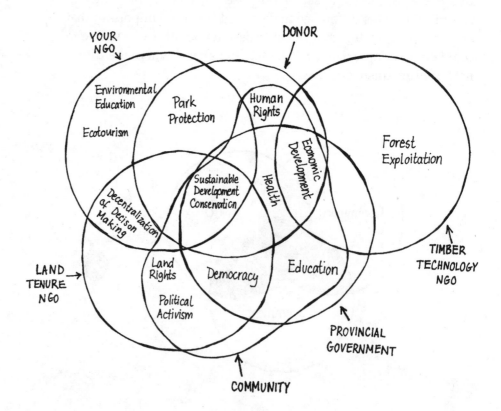

from lands that are currently economically underdeveloped. And finally, a multi-lateral donor in the region might want to improve the health of the residents of the area. All of the groups could potentially be interested in a project that involves developing community-run forest enterprises.

Although all the groups may be interested in the same project, they may take very different approaches to doing their work because of their different missions. For example, your group may wish to focus on keeping primary forest intact, but the NGO that promotes high-technology timber harvesting is looking to harvest primary forest. In this case, you may choose not to work with this high-technology timber harvesting NGO because its mission is too different from yours. You may decide, however, to work with the provincial government, the land tenure NGO, and the international donor to develop a project that helps local people to plant cacao in fallow and newly regenerated secondary forest areas in the Indah Biosphere Reserve buffer zone to generate increased income for participating households.

It is important that each group be explicit about what it hopes to achieve. It is all right if everyone doesn't agree on everything— but you do need to know where you have common interests and where you differ. In places where you differ, you can agree to disagree, negotiate mutually acceptable trade-offs, or decide you cannot move forward on the project.

Process Hint: See the Sources and Further Readings section at the end of this chapter for references to assist you in negotiation and conflict management.

Ensure Local Stakeholder Participation in the Project

One of the most important groups in any project are the *local stakeholders*. In developing your project, it is of the utmost importance that you ensure local stakeholder participation, that is, active involvement in the design, management, and monitoring of the project. It does not just involve notifying local community members about your new project. Instead, full participation requires active efforts on your part to ensure that representatives of all the stakeholder groups at the project site—men and women, young and old, rich and poor, those with power and those without power—become involved.

Full participation of stakeholders in conservation and development projects is essential because it:

- *Gives Stakeholders Control over How Project Activities Affect Their Lives.* Conservation projects are usually designed to support or modify human behavior that affects the status of some natural area or species. As these projects often directly affect those people whose livelihoods depend on access to or use of these resources, these stakeholders must participate in the decisions which will ultimately affect their own lives.

In a conservation and development project context, *local stakeholders* include residents of the project site who have a vested interest in the natural resources of the area (who are often called community members) as well as other people who potentially will be affected by project activities.

Although we often refer to local stakeholders as one group, in reality, they may be organized into many subgroups that have different or even opposing needs and desires.

Participation in this guide: Local stakeholder participation is a key element
to the successful completion of
each step in this guide. The exact
way in which you can ensure participation, however, depends on the
specific situation at your project site.

For example, in the Coastal and
Wetlands Scenarios, the projects are
designed, managed, and monitored
solely by the local stakeholders. In
the Tropical Forest and Savannah
Scenarios, by contrast, the projects
are implemented by representatives
of groups from outside of the project area who involve local stakeholders in project activities.

Each type of project requires a
different approach to ensuring full
participation. As a result, throughout
this guide, we have not made ensuring participation explicit in each step
but have assumed that project
teams will take the necessary steps
to do so.

- *Is Essential to Sustainability.* If a conservation project is designed and implemented exclusively by outsiders, those living in the project area are less likely to continue the project activities once the outsiders are gone. Full stakeholder participation in conservation efforts usually leads to a better understanding of the importance of conservation and inspires a greater commitment to long-term conservation goals.

- *Generates a Sense of Ownership.* As stakeholders become more actively involved in the design and implementation of conservation project activities, there is usually a corresponding growth in their conviction that they own and control the project. Stakeholder ownership in conservation activities usually means that they are more likely to support and defend the project when necessary.

- *Provides an Opportunity for Learning.* The active involvement of stakeholders in project design, management, and monitoring builds their capacity to carry out conservation activities. It also facilitates exchange of information between the stakeholders and project team members who are from outside the community, thus helping both sides to learn more about how to achieve conservation goals.

- *Leads to Responsibility.* When stakeholders participate fully in a conservation project, they accept the obligation to work hard for its success. True participation does not occur if stakeholders involve themselves in the project only when it is going well; they must be as involved in bad times as in good times.

- *Is Not Exclusive to or Controlled by One Group.* For there to be true participation in a conservation project, any stakeholder that is interested and willing to get involved in project activities should have equal access. One individual or group cannot exert undue power or influence—all stakeholders must have a voice in decisions.

- *Is Not a Guarantee of Conservation Success.* Although participation is important, no amount of local stakeholder involvement can save a poorly designed and implemented project from failure. Furthermore, although promoting local participation and conservation are both worthy goals, there are situations in which it may be difficult or impossible to design project interventions to achieve both of them. In these situations, actions that promote participation may come at the expense of conservation. As a result, if your goal is conservation, you should probably regard participation as a means to reach this end.

The exact way in which you go about ensuring local stakeholder participation in your project will depend on who you are and the conditions at your project site. As a rule, however, you will want to make sure that you consciously make an effort to (1) determine who all the stakeholders are at your site; (2) plan how to best approach them in the various steps of your project development and implementation; and then (3) follow through in implementing this plan.

Formalize Project's General Goal with Project Partners

Once you have found common ground and have negotiated the project's general goal with partner groups including local stakeholders, you should formally record this agreement. One way to do this is for all participating groups to sign an agreement or letter of understanding that broadly outlines what you hope to achieve and how you will set out to accomplish it. Whatever mechanism you choose, we strongly suggest that it be in writing. This may sound like an overly formal way of defining a partnership, but it provides clarity and can even help you and your partners resolve or avoid conflict in the future.

Sources and Further Readings

Bryson, John M., and Robert C. Einsweiler, eds. (1988). *Strategic Planning: Threats and Opportunities for Planners.* American Planning Association, Chicago, Illinois. An edited volume providing a general and theoretical discussion of the strategic planning process.

Espy, Siri N. (1986). *Handbook of Strategic Planning for Non-Profit Organizations.* Praeger Publishers, New York, New York. A discussion on strategic planning for nongovernmental organizations.

Fisher, R., W. Ury, and B. Patton (1981). *Getting to Yes: Negotiating Agreement Without Giving In.* Penguin Books, New York, New York. A good discussion of conflict resolution and negotiation techniques.

Kayser, Thomas A. (1990). *Mining Group Gold: How to Cash in on the Collaborative Brain Power of a Group.* Serif Publishing, El Segundo, California. An excellent guide to holding effective and efficient meetings.

Lederach, J.P. (1995). *Preparing for Peace: Conflict Transformation Across Cultures.* Syracuse University Press, Syracuse, New York. Another book on conflict resolution.

Support Center (1995). *Global Electronic Nonprofit Information Express (G.E.N.I.E.) Strategic Planning Help Files.* Support Center, San Francisco, California. Available on the Internet: http://www.supportcenter.org/sf/spgenie.html. An excellent summary of strategic planning and the development of mission statements that is focused on nonprofit groups.

Susskind, L., and J. Cruikshank (1987). *Breaking the Impasse: Consensual Approaches to Resolving Public Disputes.* Basic Books, New York, New York. A book on multi-party dispute resolution.

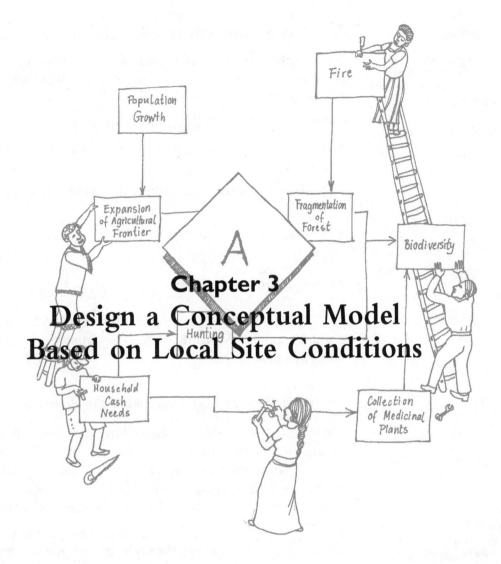

Chapter 3
Design a Conceptual Model
Based on Local Site Conditions

Now that you have developed your group's mission, it is time to turn to the specific project that you want to work on. The foundation of all project design, management, and monitoring activities is a Conceptual Model of the project. Your challenge now is to develop an Initial Conceptual Model for your project, ensure that this model reflects local site conditions, and then systematically identify and rank the key threats that your project will address. You will then complete your Project Conceptual Model, which we discuss in chapter 4.

Using the information presented in this chapter, you should be able to:

- Review and compile existing information about your project site (Step A1).
- Develop an Initial Conceptual Model of your project site (Step A2).
- Assess local site conditions to refine and improve your model (Step A3).
- Identify and rank threats at your project site (Step A4).

What Is a Conceptual Model?

A *Conceptual Model* is a diagram of a set of relationships between certain factors that are believed to impact or lead to a target condition. A good Conceptual Model:

The word *conceptual* refers to theoretical beliefs. The word *model* refers to a simplified representation of reality. A *Conceptual Model* is thus a representation of your theoretical beliefs about your project.

• Presents a picture of the situation at the project site.

• Shows assumed linkages between factors affecting the target condition.

• Shows major direct and indirect threats affecting the target condition.

• Presents only relevant factors.

• Is based on sound data and information.

• Results from a team effort.

Before getting to the steps involved in developing your conceptual model, it's worth discussing what these characteristics mean in a general sense.

Presents a Picture of the Situation at the Project Site

A good Conceptual Model shows how you think specific events, situations, attitudes, beliefs, or behaviors affect the status of some other situation that you are ultimately interested in influencing. There are four main building blocks of a Project Conceptual Model. They are represented by the following symbols:

An *outcome* or *dependent variable* is a function of other variables. For example, a child's health status (the dependent variable) is dependent on his or her diet and the presence of diarrhea and other diseases, among other factors.

> Target Condition

The *target condition* is the situation you intend to influence through your project activities. In your Conceptual Model, the status of the target condition is determined by the factors leading to it. The target condition is akin to the *outcome* or *dependent variable* in scientific analysis or evaluation research—it is the condition you are trying to explain, predict, or modify. As this guide focuses on biodiversity conservation, the examples we use all have something to do with the status of biodiversity as their target condition. In other situations, however, the target condition you wish to influence may be something else, such as the level of economic development, the health of women, or child nutrition in a particular area.

A *predictor* or *independent variable* is a variable that is used, possibly in conjunction with other variables, to describe a given outcome or dependent variable. In the example, the child's diet and the presence of diarrhea and other diseases are the independent variables.

> Factor

Factors are the specific events, situations, conditions, policies, attitudes, beliefs, or behaviors that you believe affect the target condition. Some of the most important factors that you must consider in model building for conservation and development projects are direct and indirect threats to biodiversity. Factors correspond roughly to *predictors* or *independent variables* in evaluation research. They are what determine the outcome or status of the dependent variable.

Activities are the actions you plan to take to modify particular factors which in turn will influence the status of the target condition. In evaluation research, a project activity can be equated to an event, treatment, or exposure that will cause a change in specific factors and the target condition. Project activities will be covered in chapter 4.

Relationships in the Conceptual Model are represented by arrows. These arrows usually point in one direction. One factor leads to another or one activity influences one or more factors. You find arrows between individual factors, leading from one factor to multiple other factors, leading from your activities to factors, and from factors to the target condition. As we will see later on in this section, getting the target condition, factors, and activities arranged with the arrows connecting them so that the model makes sense is as much an art as it is a science.

What does a Conceptual Model look like? As illustrated below, in a general sense, a Conceptual Model contains a target condition on one side of the drawing and a number of factors and activities linked to this target condition.

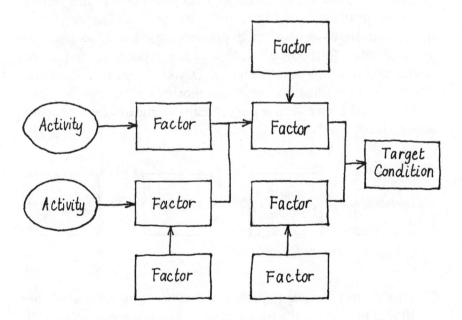

The process of constructing your Conceptual Model can be divided into two general phases. The first phase involves creating an *Initial Conceptual Model* that shows what is going on at your project site before you begin the project. This model describes the site's target condition, factors, and relationships prior to the start of your project. The second phase, which we discuss in chapter 4, involves treating your Initial Conceptual Model as a base and adding on the project activities that you will carry out to reach your project goals and objectives. Once you complete this second phase, you will then have a complete *Project Conceptual Model* that shows how you expect your project will influence the situation at your site.

Shows Assumed Linkages Between Factors Affecting the Target Condition

Process Hint: See chapter 6 for a more in-depth discussion of some of the major project assumptions in conservation and development projects.

A Conceptual Model is the basis of good project planning and allows you to explicitly see how different factors are linked together and thus how best to plan and manage your project. It also shows likely obstacles or difficulties you may encounter along the way and it illustrates (as we will see later) how your planned interventions may affect the target condition. A good model also makes project assumptions and underlying assumptions obvious and evident to everyone involved in the project. Finally, a good Conceptual Model permits you to identify the appropriate and necessary data you need for efficient and effective project monitoring.

Developing a Conceptual Model is similar to generating a hypothesis in basic scientific research. As you connect some factors to others, project activities to factors and factors to the target condition, you are assuming (or hypothesizing) that these relationships are true. The model provides you the opportunity to formally state relationships you believe affect your target condition and that you will later test with your monitoring efforts. For example, in the Coastal Scenario, the project team might develop a project assumption:

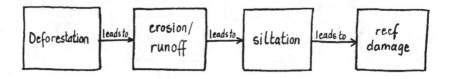

This project assumption shows that we assume that deforestation of the hills in the project area causes erosion of soil which runs off into rivers and causes the water to become full of dirt which gets washed into the ocean, smothering and killing the reef. So, a Conceptual Model allows you to show well-established relationships between factors and the target condition and to exhibit relationships that you believe exist. The model also provides the framework for you to be able to test the validity and accuracy of your assumptions as shown in the box that follows.

A good Conceptual Model will help you determine why a project succeeds or fails.

1. *Success:* If the conceptual model truly shows how your project activities will influence the target condition, then implementation of the project will lead to the desired results.

2. *Theory Failure:* If your model is inaccurate, then initiating the proposed project will probably not lead to the desired results.

3. *Program Failure:* If your model is accurate, but the implementation of the project activities is faulty, then it is likely that you will not reach the desired results.

4. *Absolute Failure!:* Finally, if you have an inaccurate conceptual model and project activities are poorly carried out, then it is highly unlikely that you will have any positive results.

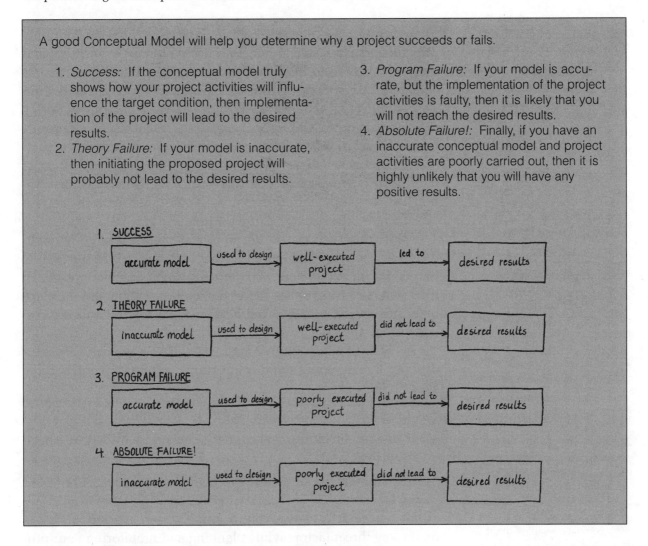

Shows Major Direct and Indirect Threats Affecting the Target Condition

In recent years, conservation and development practitioners have found it increasingly difficult to demonstrate the impact of the projects they manage. Why is this? One possible reason is that conservation projects have become much more complex in their design and implementation. Only a few decades ago, the most often used approach to conservation was park establishment and management. In theory (although not necessarily in practice) this approach seems easy and basic—declare a park, put up a fence, and keep people out. Measuring conservation success was fairly straightforward—having no one inside the park engaged in illegal activities equaled conservation success. The negative social consequences on the people living around the park were not taken into consideration by outside project managers.

Now, however, most conservation projects strive to incorporate local people into the management and conservation of

Direct threats are those factors that immediately impact biodiversity or physically cause its destruction.

Indirect threats are those factors that underlie or lead to the direct threats.

For example, the cutting down of forest by migrants to plant crops might be considered a direct threat to the biodiversity of the region. Poverty and lack of knowledge of the migrants who are cutting the trees are examples of indirect threats.

Common direct threats to biodiversity include habitat loss and fragmentation, overexploitation of living resources, introduction of exotic species, and pollution. Common indirect threats include human population growth, poverty, and social and economic policies that cause insecurity in local economies.

Some factors that may be classified as threats at one site, may not be threats at another. For instance, "hunting" is a factor that is found in two of our scenarios; it is classified as a threat in the Savannah Scenario but not in the Wetlands Scenario.

In fact, a factor like hunting can even be simultaneously a threat to and an opportunity for conservation at a given site in the sense that it may currently occur at unsustainable levels and yet, if managed properly, could serve as a strong incentive to sustainably manage forest habitats.

A common criticism of a threat-based approach to project design and monitoring is that it focuses on negative problems rather than positive opportunities. While we endorse the concept of creating more positive views of conservation (using a technique called "Appreciative Inquiry"), we believe that this is not sufficient to define effective projects. We believe a threat-based focus is a more practical way of overcoming constraints to achieving specific objectives.

natural resources. Conservationists have found that it is not only difficult and expensive to maintain parks but also impractical and even unethical to forbid local residents from having at least some access to the resources within the park boundaries. What the conservation field has gained in equity, it has lost in simplicity. Social, economic, and political forces become the major factors that must be addressed in order to ensure the long-term security of natural areas. Finding a balance between conservation and utilization of natural resources has become the primary challenge—conservation and development projects must be designed with the accomplishment of this balance as their ultimate aim.

Most conservation and development projects are designed to decrease the pressure people place on natural resources—to reduce the *direct threats* and *indirect threats* to biodiversity. It thus stands to reason that success of a conservation and development project can be measured by the extent to which these pressures are reduced.

The Threat Reduction Assessment (TRA) approach to project design, management, and monitoring operates under three assumptions:

• Almost all biodiversity destruction is human induced.

• All human threats to biodiversity can be identified at a site-specific level.

• Actual reduction of threat to biodiversity can be measured.

Using the TRA allows you to simplify your work by focusing on the key threat factors while planning and monitoring your project. If you can be confident that you have identified all the threats to biodiversity at a site and that you have addressed all of these threats, then you can assume that conservation has occurred or will occur in the future.

To implement this approach, a Conceptual Model for a conservation and development project must include direct and indirect threats to biodiversity as factors in the model. You will then be able to measure your success in meeting these threats over time. By accurately identifying the threats, measuring their status before your project begins, designing and implementing appropriate project activities, and monitoring the impact of your activities over time, you can determine the extent to which your project has been successful and make whatever adjustments are necessary.

Presents Only Relevant Factors

A good Conceptual Model does not attempt to explain all possible relationships or contain all possible factors that influence the target condition but instead tries to simplify reality by containing only the information most relevant to the model builder. One of the difficulties in building models is to include enough information to explain what influences the target condition without containing so much information that the most critical factors or relationships are hidden. Too much information can conceal important aspects of the model, while too little information in the model leads to oversimplification which in turn leads to a higher likelihood that the portrayal is not accurate. So, a perpetual challenge to building good models is to find a balance between presenting too much and too little information.

Drawing a Conceptual Model is as much an art as it is a science. You first need to get good and reliable information (the science) that you'll arrange in a diagram (the art) to represent your interpretation of the situation at your site. Whatever you do, don't downplay the artistic aspect of developing your Conceptual Model—it's often the hardest part to do. Like a big puzzle, the easy part is getting your hands on the pieces (the different bits of information composed of the target condition, factors, and activities). The difficult part is putting those pieces together in some semblance of order. Even more challenging than a true puzzle that has only one correct final arrangement, a Conceptual Model can have multiple correct arrangements. Furthermore, the model is only a best guess—one that must be changed and revised as you get more information and develop new insights.

Based on Sound Data and Information

Ultimately, a Conceptual Model is only as good as the **data** and **information** upon which it is based. Conceptual models are composed of **existing information** and **primary information**. As we will see in the next section of this chapter, the first step in developing your model is to review all available existing information. Existing information is useful because it has already been compiled and in many instances can be easily accessed. You may find, however, that in some cases existing information is difficult to obtain because, for example, original documents no longer exist or people are unwilling to share materials with you. Existing information is usually most helpful as background material.

Once you have developed a first draft of your Conceptual Model, you will then need to go to the field to collect primary information to further develop your model. Collecting primary data allows you to design the format, approach, and tools to obtain information directly from residents of the project site, relevant experts, or your own observations. With primary data you have more control over the type and quality of the information you collect. If you are not a resident of the area where the project is taking place, then gathering primary data requires visiting local communities and spending time with residents to understand firsthand the situation in the field. For conservation projects, it also demands

Strictly speaking, **data** are collected through monitoring and research efforts while **information** is drawn from these data through analysis. For simplicity, however, we use the phrase "collecting information" as a shorthand way of saying "collecting data and analyzing it to extract information."

Existing information is data that have already been collected for some purpose other than designing and monitoring your project.

Primary information is data that you specifically collect while designing and monitoring your project.

visiting the natural areas that are to be conserved to observe their biological composition, dynamics, and importance and to see how they are related to the people that live in or around them.

Results from a Team Effort

Developing a Conceptual Model can be a helpful activity for a project team. While you build your model, team members can share ideas about important factors at your site and how they think these factors influence the target condition. This kind of discussion can help your team come to some mutual agreement or consensus about what factors are important or which threats need to be addressed immediately. By explicitly showing the perceived relationships in diagram form between activities, factors, and the target condition, your team reaches a better understanding of the situation at the site. As a result, it will be easier for them to understand how best to devise project activities that will directly help them reach project goals and objectives.

A Conceptual Model is not only helpful when you are starting a new project but can also serve as an important tool that you can use to orient new staff. Many projects have difficulties with a lack of continuity as project staff composition changes over time. New staff members often fail to see the connections between project activities and the intended impact. Furthermore, personnel who design a project are often not the same as those responsible for carrying it out. A final Conceptual Model can help new staff understand why your team has chosen specific project activities. Of course, with the addition of new staff comes new ideas, perspectives, and strategies. The Conceptual Model thus provides an excellent means for your team, new and old, to be able to reevaluate and revise your perceptions of what is going on at the project site. To help keep your team focused on the task at hand, put your model up where everyone can see it.

Process Hint: Going into a Conceptual Model building exercise, team members may tend to think that they hold similar views regarding the major factors affecting the target condition. In many cases, however, they soon find that they have widely differing views. The model building exercise thus becomes an opportunity to discuss these differences and reach a common and clear understanding.

How Do You Develop a Conceptual Model?

A complete Project Conceptual Model is developed in five basic steps. We'll go through the first four steps in this chapter and cover the fifth one in chapter 4. We delay describing this last step because the complete Project Conceptual Model includes your project activities, which we will introduce in chapter 4.

Review and Compile Existing Information About Your Project Site (Step A1)

Building a Conceptual Model requires the same basic background review as any kind of scientific or evaluation research. Unfortunately, one of the most common mistakes made by researchers and program planners alike is a failure to review existing information—in doing so, they overlook a great, readily available resource. The more you know about previous work related to your field site or project, the better your Conceptual Model and project will be. By reviewing existing information, you will increase the odds that your project is well rooted in reality and does not duplicate previous work or other projects' mistakes.

Most of the time, you will find that there is a wealth of available information waiting to be uncovered that will help you (1) begin to identify the important factors at the project site, (2) develop project assumptions, and (3) determine what project activities might work best—in other words, help you to construct your Conceptual Model.

Collect Existing Information

Whether your project team is composed of local residents or outsiders, the first task involves collecting all available existing information about the project site. The trick here is not to be shy about getting any information you can get your hands on. You can get existing information from a variety of sources.

Process Hint: If you are having trouble finding any existing information about your project, don't let this stop you from starting to develop your model. Do the best you can with the information you have and then make sure to collect sufficient primary information while working with the local stakeholders.

Some of the best information may already be close by in the heads of the people with whom you work or live. Sit down with your team members and discuss their knowledge, perceptions, and insights about the project site and potential project activities. You may also find that there are some individuals who are particularly familiar with the area where you intend to work or the local populations living there. Talk to these people and see what they know.

Other sources of existing information are government records and statistics. You can find these records at ministry offices in the capital city or in provincial or district offices. You can often find good records and statistics at health posts, extension offices, and park headquarters. You can also usually get information from non-governmental organizations working in or near your project site. Sometimes you will find that there are university researchers who have worked in your area and have published potentially helpful reports. Perhaps the organization you work for has conducted previous surveys or studies at the project site. Make sure you draw on these sources to complete your review of existing information.

Process Hint: Many national or local governments maintain libraries that are open to the public. In addition, you will find that most universities, research institutions, and some local NGOs have good publicly accessible libraries where you can also find an abundance of information.

If you are new to your project site, the easiest place to start your search for information may be a local library if one exists. Not only do libraries have books, magazines, and journals but most also keep archives of local and national newspapers, which can be an excellent source of existing information. Another rapidly expanding source of information is the Internet, a global network of computers in which you can (with some know-how and practice) rapidly find information on a variety of topics.

Compile Information in a Standard Format

As you collect information from all these sources, make sure that you do it in a standardized format as illustrated in the example below. Although existing information can often represent a sizable, economical, and diverse source of facts and figures, it does have some drawbacks. Sometimes the difficult part of using existing information is deciding where to start your search for relevant sources. Existing information is rarely in the exact form you need it, and you often have to go through piles of documents to pull out the pieces you want. Also, because someone else collected the information, it is difficult to assess its reliability. Finally, existing information that is relatively old may be out of date and no longer valid.

Example: Collecting Information in a Standardized Format

As you collect existing information, make sure you record it in a standardized way in your notebook, in some other written format, or in your computer. That way, it will be easier to share with your colleagues and refer back to when you begin to develop your model. Also, if you record the source of the information, it may help you to evaluate the quality of the information at a later date. As you collect existing information make sure you include:

- *Your name:* So someone else reading your notes knows who collected the information
- *Date:* Date you collected the information
- *Location:* Where you got the information
- *Source:* From whom you got the information
- *How to gain access to the information in the future:* Who you need to speak to or what steps you have to go through to get to the information so that the next time you or your colleagues go to get information from the same source it will be easier
- *Information:* The relevant information you collected

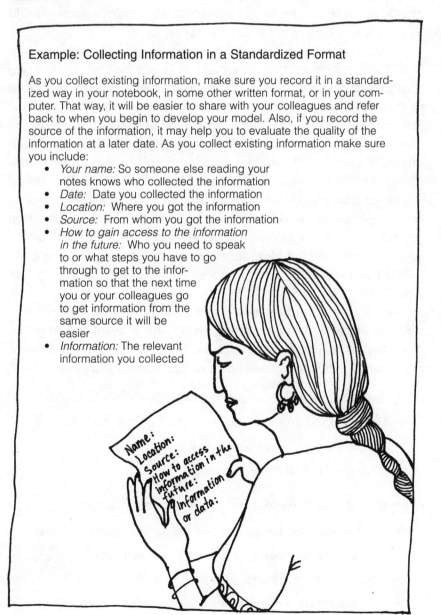

Develop an Initial Conceptual Model of Your Project Site (Step A2)

Once you have collected all readily available information, you are now ready to begin developing your Conceptual Model.

Identify Target Condition

The first task is to identify your target condition—the situation you intend to influence through your project. Your target condition should be related to the starting point in the project cycle—your group's mission. If you work for a conservation organization, then the target condition for all of your projects should involve biodiversity conservation. If you work for a community development organization, then the target condition for your projects should involve improving human quality of life.

Process Hint: As a rule, the success of your project will be easier to determine if you limit yourself to one simple target condition.

Some organizations may have broader missions relating to both conservation and development. If that's the case, these organizations may be tempted to include two or more target conditions in their Conceptual Model. Alternatively, they may try to define one complex target condition that contains all their goals. Be aware, however, that if you attempt to address multiple target conditions in one project, you may find it difficult to plan project activities that will simultaneously address them all. We would therefore strongly recommend that you try to limit your model outcome to one simple target condition. If you are involved in a conservation project, by excluding community development from your target condition you will not necessarily be ignoring it—it can be brought into the model as one or more factors that influences your target condition.

A *state* in this context is used in the sense of an object or system at one point in time.

The target condition is a *state* that you want to influence through some activity or intervention. As a result, it must be described as a situation that occurs independent of your project. For example, the target conditions of our scenarios include:

- Tropical forests and fauna in the Indah Biosphere Reserve
- Grassland and savannah ecosystems in Karimara National Park
- Marine biodiversity in Bocoro Bay
- Wetlands in the Everson Watershed

Examples of poorly worded target conditions include:

- To conserve the biodiversity of the Indah Biosphere Reserve
- To maintain the habitat of Karimara National Park
- To protect the marine resources in Bocoro Bay
- To preserve the wetlands in the Everson Watershed

Notice that our examples of poorly worded target conditions include action words like "conserve," "maintain," "protect," and "preserve." As we will see later, however, these action words will be used when it's time to take action and the target condition is transformed into the project goal. The target condition merely describes the existing situation we will be trying to change with our project activities.

Identify and List Factors That Influence the Target Condition

Based on the extensive review of existing information you've just conducted and what you already know about your field site, you should now be able to identify three main categories of factors:

- *Direct Threats*. Factors that immediately affect biodiversity (the target condition) or physically cause its destruction.

- *Indirect Threats*. Factors that underlie or lead to the direct threats.

- *Contributing Factors*. Factors that are not classified as indirect or direct threats but that somehow affect the target condition. **Opportunities** are included in this category.

As you and your team go through the existing data you have collected, list the major direct and indirect threats and contributing factors that you believe somehow affect the target condition at your site. For now, don't worry about how they all fit together, just list them.

For the remainder of this chapter, we will use the Savannah Scenario as an example of how you might develop a Conceptual Model and rank threats. After a review of existing information, you might initially conclude that the following factors are the most important ones affecting the target condition which is:

Grassland and savannah ecosystems of Karimara National Park

Direct Threats
- Hunting
- Cattle grazing in Karimara National Park
- Fire
- Diseases from cattle and dogs transmitted to wildlife

Indirect Threats
- Poverty
- Lack of knowledge of national park hunting restrictions

Contributing Factors
- Weather
- Social/cultural values

Opportunities are factors that potentially have a positive effect on your target condition. As we stated before, sometimes threats can also be opportunities.

Process Hint: The key to developing both the target condition and factors is not to think of them in either positive or negative terms but as neutral states that do not show direction. For example, you would not talk about "increased clear-cutting." Instead you would call it "commercial timber harvesting."

Arrange Factors and Target Condition in Diagram Format

A picture of the project team arranging the factors in their Conceptual Model in diagram format can be seen below. The general procedures to complete this task are:

1. Place the target condition off to one side of your work space.

2. Take the direct threat factors and place them just off to one side of the target condition. As you do this, draw arrows to show how you believe, based on your team's knowledge and the existing information, the various direct threats relate to each other and the target condition.

3. Include and arrange the indirect threats in a way that shows how they lead to or influence the direct threats and the target condition. Make sure you continue to include the arrows.

4. Add the contributing factors to show how they influence the other factors (direct and indirect threats) and the target condition.

5. Reexamine your new model to see if it represents your field site to the best of your knowledge given the information you have. Refine it if you think you need to do so.

Process Hint: The best way to arrange the factors and target condition in a diagram is to cut out small pieces of paper (self-sticking memo notes work very well for this) and write the factors and target condition on them. Lay them out on a table or on the ground. It is best if you do this over a very big piece of paper so that you can draw the arrows that connect them together.

The following shows an example of the use of this procedure in creating a model diagram.

1. Place the target condition off to one side of your work space.

Grassland
and
Savannah
Ecosystems in
Karimara
National Park

Comments: Target condition is "Grassland and Savannah Ecosystems in Karimara National Park."

Process Hint: We are using "Comments" to explain this process—you don't need to include them.

2. Take the direct threat factors and place them just off to one side of the target condition. As you do this, draw arrows to show how you believe, based on your team's knowledge and the existing information, the various direct threats relate to each other and the target condition.

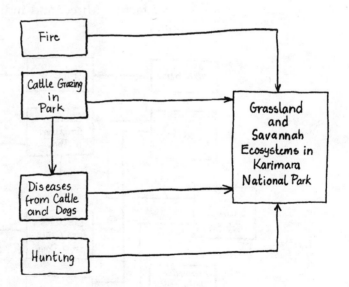

Comments: (1) "Hunting," "Cattle grazing in the park," "Diseases from cattle and dogs," and "Fire" all directly affect the target condition. (2) "Cattle grazing in the park" also affects the transmission of disease to wild animals. (3) "Disease from cattle and dogs" causes hoof-and-mouth disease in wild grazing animals and distemper in wild dogs.

3. Include and arrange the indirect threats in a way that shows how they lead to or influence the direct threats and the target condition. Make sure you continue to include the arrows.

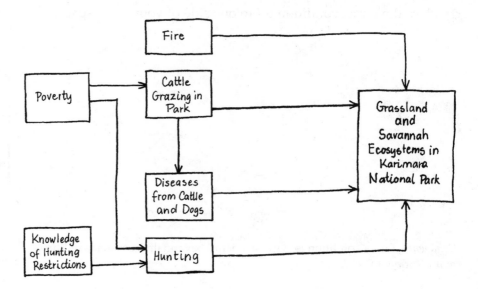

Comments: According to local sources (1) "Poverty" influences both "Cattle grazing in the park" and "Hunting" as local people raise cattle and hunt to cover basic family needs. (2) "Lack of knowledge of hunting restrictions" in the park affects "Hunting."

4. Add the contributing factors to show how they influence the other factors (direct and indirect threats) and the target condition.

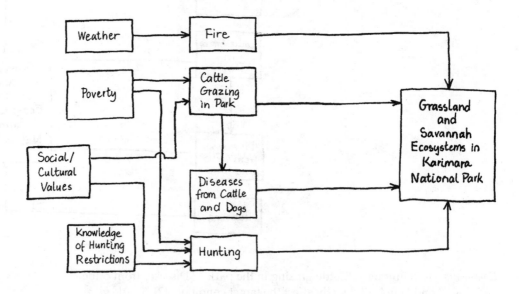

Process Hint: Try to avoid crossing lines whenever possible. If it is unavoidable, use the bridge symbol ∩ to show where the lines cross.

Comments: (1) "Weather" affects the conditions which lead to "Fire." (2) "Social/cultural values" affect both "Cattle grazing in the park" and "Hunting" practices. In the communities around the park, having a lot of cattle gives the owner greater social status.

5. Reexamine your new model to see if it represents your field site to the best of your knowledge given the information you have. Refine it if you think you need to do so.

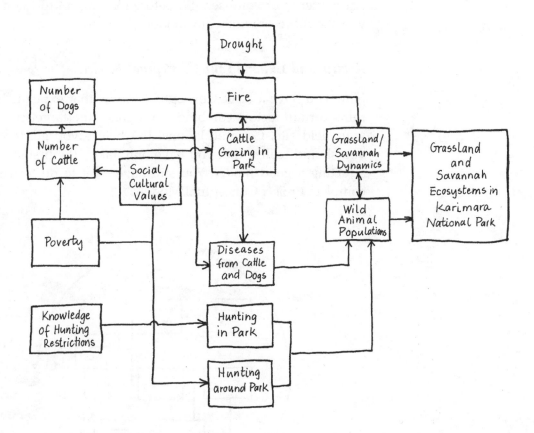

Comments: (1) To make the factor more specific, "Weather" was changed to "Drought" as it is a lack of rain that leads to dry conditions and fire. (2) Also to be more specific, we added the factors "Grassland/savannah dynamics" and "Wild animal populations." (3) We also added the factors "Number of cattle" and "Number of dogs," as it is believed the more cattle and dogs there are, the more likely they will infect wild animals with domestic diseases. (4) We added an arrow between "Cattle grazing in the park" and "Fire," as herders set fire to grasslands to encourage new growth of pastures for their cattle. (5) We divided "Hunting," to be more specific, into "Hunting in the park" and "Hunting around the park," as these are very different effects with different legal status. (6) We modified the effects of "Social/cultural values" to show that it indirectly affects "Cattle grazing in the park" through the "Number of cattle." (7) We similarly modified the relationship between "Poverty" and "Cattle grazing in the park," as the economic status of residents determines how many head of cattle they have.

This process of arranging your Conceptual Model might sound easy at first, but as you will see when you try it, it in fact takes a lot of thought and hard work. As you begin to construct your model, have your team discuss how the model comes together and what the relationships between the factors and target conditions are. As you go through the process, you may want to rearrange the

Process Hint: You may at times want to combine the relationship arrows of two (or more) boxes that lead to a common third factor—for example, "Number of cattle" and "Number of dogs" leading to "Diseases from cattle and dogs," as shown in the diagram.

factors, add some new ones, combine them, or remove others. Again, this is where the art of Conceptual Model building applies. You want your model to be relatively simple and well organized, not cluttered or confused. So before moving on to the next step, you should reexamine your model as shown earlier.

Review and Expand Your Conceptual Model

Now you have a basic Conceptual Model that explains how you think certain factors combine to influence the target condition at your field site. Congratulations! But before you get too excited, you should realize that you have only taken the first step to constructing a good model. You still have a lot to do to reach your complete Project Conceptual Model.

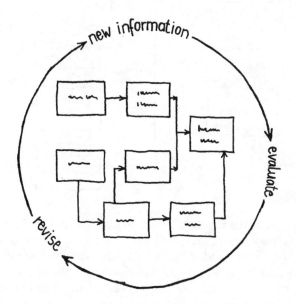

The next task is to review your model. Throughout this entire process, whenever you get new information about your site, make sure it fits into your model and determine whether you have to update your model to make use of any conclusions you draw based on the new information. You want to try to keep your model dynamic and flexible—adaptable to any new information you obtain and insights you may gain. The challenge is to keep your model alive.

For instance, returning to the Savannah Scenario, as you review your model with your co-workers, you will probably find that it looks a little like a puzzle with some missing pieces. You may find yourself asking, "What is it that causes a given factor to appear as it does in the model?" If you determine that a broader understanding of this factor is critical to understanding and interpreting the Conceptual Model itself, you need to look into it further. You may find the answer in the information you have already collected. On the other hand, you may find that you need to investigate a little more—consult key informants again or review more existing information to get your answers. As you uncover the essential information, expand your Conceptual Model as necessary as shown in the following.

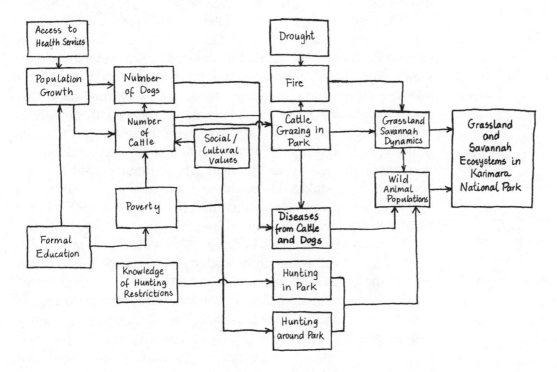

Comments: Based on conversations with key informants, we added the factors "Formal education," "Population growth," and "Access to health services." "Formal education" affects the socioeconomic status of families. "Population growth" affects the number of cattle and dogs—the more people, the more domestic animals. "Access to health services" has a direct bearing on population growth as inadequate health care may lead to premature death and tends to influence women to have more children because they are unaware of the health benefits (for both mothers and children) of adequate child spacing.

Assess Local Site Conditions to Refine and Improve Your Model (Step A3)

You may be wondering why we have not yet formally involved local stakeholders in the Conceptual Model development process—or if your project team is made up of community members, why you haven't yet discussed your ideas with your neighbors. Before talking to local stakeholders, you first must have a fairly good idea of what you want to talk to them about. You don't want to be asking a lot of basic or irrelevant questions that waste their time and make you look like you don't know anything.

Therefore you need to be as prepared as possible so that you can be focused and clear during your conversations with local stakeholders. Hopefully, through the process of developing the first draft of your Conceptual Model, you now have a better idea of what you think is happening at the project site. Now it is time to see just how accurately it reflects reality and to modify it to incorporate local stakeholders' viewpoints.

Working with local stakeholders is perhaps the most critical stage in constructing your Conceptual Model. It is during this stage that you consult with local stakeholders to understand their views, knowledge, attitudes, and behaviors so you can refine and improve your Conceptual Model. It is at this stage that you evaluate the accuracy of any social, biological, or natural resources–related information you may have gathered while building your draft model. If you fail to take this step and assume you know the reality at the field site without consulting and involving local stakeholders, chances are good that your model will be missing some key factors. Indeed, your whole model may be completely wrong and misleading.

As you assess local site conditions, you will want to talk to official and unofficial community leaders. At the same time, do not neglect those residents who do not normally have a "loud voice" in community affairs. Make sure you talk to women, children, old people, poor residents, families with lots of children, and newly arrived migrants. Their perspectives are as important as the leaders' ideas. It is often the marginalized groups in a community that have the greatest impact on the use or conservation of natural resources. When you're gathering information from local stakeholders, it is important to talk to enough people that you are confident that the information you collect is representative of the entire community.

By the time you have completed the construction of your Initial Conceptual Model, you must have identified the major direct and indirect threats that affect the target condition. And you must begin to develop a sense of what opportunities exist to counter these threats.

Consult with Local Stakeholders Regarding Threats

Key informant interviews (also called informal interviews) are semi-structured in-depth consultations with knowledgeable individuals. Instead of using a formal survey questionnaire, an informal topic guide is generally used. *Matrix ranking* is the use of tables to determine the relative importance of particular factors, threats, or preferences.

One way to get good information at your field site is to conduct a series of *key informant interviews*. This approach is very useful to generate lists and understand the importance of the various threats and opportunities that exist at the field site. Another tool that is often very useful and relatively quick and easy to use is *matrix ranking*. Matrix ranking can be done in a variety of ways, but one that is best suited for ranking the relative importance of threats and opportunities on a community-wide scale is *preference ranking*. This method allows you to incorporate the viewpoints of a number of local stakeholders in your assessment. It is very similar to voting but is done individually as you talk to different residents.

Preference ranking is a very useful tool for determining the relative importance of direct threats as they are perceived by the community. In the following section, we illustrate the application of this tool by returning to the Savannah Scenario to rank the threats in Karimara National Park.

1. As you talk to people in the community about the various threats they perceive as important, record them in your notebook. According to the residents, the major direct threats include the following:

   - Big game hunting
   - Hunting by foreign poachers
   - Community hunting
   - Tourism
   - Fire

   Notice that community residents identified four threats that were not immediately apparent after reviewing existing information: Big game hunting, Foreign poachers, Community hunting, and Tourism. Although the threat Hunting is in your Conceptual Model, it was not subdivided into the three types of hunting perceived by the community.

2. When it seems as though you have recorded all of the major threats that community members perceive, add to your list the ones you determined were important after your review of existing information but that were not mentioned by community members. According to your initial analysis and the existing information you gathered, this includes the addition of:

   - Cattle grazing in the park
   - Diseases from cattle and dogs

3. Next, at the top of a blank piece of paper or in your notebook, set up a blank matrix (table) that includes: the title of the preference ranking exercise, the name of the community, and the date. On the left side, list the threats down the page (you may want to abbreviate to save space—just make sure you record what each entry means). Across the top, include columns with a letter representing each informant (including room for his or her age and sex—you do not need to include names), a column for the total score, and a column for the final ranking.

4. Count the number of threats you have in your list. This total number will represent the highest possible score each respondent will be able to give any particular threat. The score of "1"

Preference ranking allows the field team to quickly determine the main problems or preferences of individuals in a given site and enables the priorities of different individuals to be easily compared. See chapter 6 for more details on using all three of these techniques.

Process Hint: Most of the threats that are listed in this ranking are direct threats. In general, in terms of identifying the threats that are most important, you will want to look at direct threats.

When it comes time to design interventions to counter these threats, however, you will focus primarily on the indirect threats that underlie these direct threats. It is more effective over the long run to deal with indirect threats than direct ones, as it is the indirect threats that are generally the root of the problem.

If you arrest one person who is illegally hunting wild game to sell in local markets, there are dozens of other people who will take his place. If, however, you can find an alternative, secure, profitable, and legal source of income for the hunters in the area, it is more likely that they will reduce or cease their poaching.

Community-Perceived Threats to Karimara National Park, Karibu Village, 30 February 1996

Threat	Respondent (_/_ = Sex/Age)						Total Score	Rank
	A (_/_)	B (_/_)	C (_/_)	D (_/_)	E (_/_)	F (_/_)		
Big Game Hunting								
Foreign Poachers								
Community Hunting								
Tourism								
Fire								
Cattle Grazing								
Diseases from Cattle and Dogs								

will be the lowest score a respondent can give a particular threat. The more important a respondent thinks that a given threat is, the higher the score of the threat. In this example, the highest score a threat can get is "7," as there are seven threats.

Process Hint: As each respondent ranks the threats, it may be helpful to write each possible choice on a slip of paper (or draw a picture for people who can't read) and ask him or her to arrange the threats from most to least critical. Another technique is to have the person use stones or beans to represent the number they wish to assign to each threat.

5. Now, talk to as many residents as you can or as many as you need to before it appears a clear pattern in the responses is emerging. Be sure to record the sex and age of each respondent so that you can later see if responses differ between men and women or younger and older residents. Ask each respondent to rank the threats you have in your list, starting with the greatest threat. Give them a choice of all the threats and ask them to choose the most critical one. Record the highest possible score for their first choice. Then ask them to choose the next most important threat from the remaining ones and give that one the next highest score. Continue this way until you finish the list.

For our example, you begin by asking: "Between Big game hunting, Foreign poachers, Community hunting, Tourism, Fire, Cattle grazing in the park, and Diseases from cattle and dogs, which is the one that causes the most damage to Karimara National Park?" If the first respondent (Respondent A) answers "Foreign poachers," then this threat gets a score of "7."

Next you ask (leaving out "Foreign poachers"): "Between Big game hunting, Community hunting, Tourism, Fire, Cattle grazing in the park, and Diseases from cattle and dogs, which is the one that causes the most damage to Karimara National Park?" If Respondent A answers "Tourism," then this threat gets a score of "6." After you have gone through your list of the seven threats with Respondent A, your preference ranking table might look like the figure that follows:

Community-Perceived Threats to Karimara National Park, Karibu Village, 30 February 1996

Threat	Respondent (_/_ = Sex/Age)						Total Score	Rank
	A (M/23)	B (_/_)	C (_/_)	D (_/_)	E (_/_)	F (_/_)		
Big Game Hunting	3							
Foreign Poachers	7							
Community Hunting	2							
Tourism	6							
Fire	4							
Cattle Grazing	5							
Diseases from Cattle and Dogs	1							

Continue to interview other residents until the table is filled in. Continue with additional tables as needed to include as many community residents as is necessary.

6. When you have completed a table, you need to analyze the results. To calculate the "Total Score," simply add across the row for each threat. (If you have more than one sheet or table, add up the total scores from each.) To calculate the relative ranking of each threat (the last column), rank the threat with the highest total score as "a," the threat with the next highest score "b," and so on.

After you have gone through your list of the seven threats with all respondents and tabulated the results, your preference ranking table might look like the figure that follows:

Community-Perceived Threats to Karimara National Park, Karibu Village, 30 February 1996

Threat	Respondent (_/_ = Sex/Age)						Total Score	Rank
	A (M/23)	B (F/56)	C (M/18)	D (M/31)	E (M/68)	F (F/23)		
Big Game Hunting	3	4	1	2	3	1	14	f
Foreign Poachers	7	2	5	6	5	7	32	b
Community Hunting	2	5	4	7	4	2	24	e
Tourism	6	7	6	4	6	6	35	a
Fire	4	3	7	5	2	4	25	d
Cattle Grazing	5	6	3	3	7	5	29	c
Diseases from Cattle and Dogs	1	1	2	1	1	3	9	g

So as you can see, the most important threat according to these respondents is Tourism, the second most important is Foreign poachers, the third most important is Cattle grazing in the park, and so on.

Consult with Local Stakeholders Regarding Opportunities

While assessing local site conditions, in addition to evaluating threats, it is also a good idea to evaluate the opportunities that exist in the communities where you'll be working. In our scenarios, opportunities are those conditions or factors that are supportive of conservation. These opportunities can include community leaders or elders that are keenly aware of the need for conservation, a particularly interested and engaged village, or funds from some other project that can be used to help you achieve your project goals and objectives.

In addition to matrix ranking, there are a variety of other ways you can get data about local site conditions. In chapter 6, we describe in detail a few selected methods that are particularly suited to monitoring conservation and development projects—many of these methods can also be used during this initial site assessment phase.

For example, in the Savannah Scenario, the project team conducts a participatory mapping exercise with some of the community members to outline how different lands are used. They learn that the community members have heard that there are some legal restrictions to grazing their cows in the park, but they are unsure of what they are. The team members also attend a local community meeting and are able to directly observe that the local leadership is strong and seems to be respected by most people. Finally, while walking along a trail leading to the park, the team conducts informal interviews with some hunters that they find coming back with game they have killed. They learn that the hunters are concerned about foreign poachers and that they are also worried about regulating local hunting practices to avoid overhunting certain species.

Revise Your Conceptual Model

After you have assessed local site conditions, what should you do? It is time again to review and revise your model. In many cases, it may be helpful to review your Conceptual Model with the local stakeholders at your project site. Sit down with key people from the community and show them your model and see what they think about it. Or you may want to work with them to build a new model and then see how it compares to the one that your team put together.

Taking your model out into the field and seeing how accurately it reflects local site conditions is a way of *pre-testing* your Conceptual Model. Once you have gathered and analyzed the data from the local site, you may find that your model is a reasonably good picture of the present situation and that it requires only minor revision. On the other hand, you may find that your model really does not adequately describe the local situation or that you failed to include some major threat or other factor. It's good if you discover that your model is not completely accurate before you have proceeded and designed your project activities. That way, you still have time to modify your model before you start. Simply change your Conceptual Model to incorporate the new insights you gained from the local stakeholders. By being open to modifying and adapting your model, you will increase the likelihood that your project will be successful.

For example, returning to the Savannah Scenario, after assessing local site conditions, we find that we have some important new information that we failed to include in our model. Results of the local site assessment include:

Direct Threats

- Tourism and poaching by foreigners are the most important threats to Karimara National Park according to community members.

- Community hunting occurs on a much more limited scale than originally estimated.

- Most community hunting is for subsistence, but community members claim that foreign poachers hunt to sell bush meat to urban areas and animal parts to international traders.

- According to community members, disease transmission from their cattle and dogs to ungulates and wild dogs, respectively, is not as big a problem as it was 10 years ago.

Indirect Threats

- Most community residents explain that their greatest need is cash to purchase goods, such as food, and services, such as medical attention. Community members express an expectation that some of the funds generated from tourism should go to the communities.

- There are almost no economic opportunities in the region for community residents. About the only activity they can do to earn some money is selling milk from their cattle or a little bit of bush meat to neighbors.

Contributing Factors (Including Opportunities)

- Community members understand that there are some legal restrictions to grazing their cattle inside the park, but they

Pre-testing involves trying your ideas to see how accurately they reflect actual conditions. In this case, it is simply comparing the model you first developed to the one you develop after assessing local site conditions.

are not clear as to what they are. They are open to having the Park Service come to their villages to explain park policies.

- The communities around the park have strong community leaders and councils that can be effective in maintaining community participation and communication.

- There is high interest in the communities in self-policing hunting practices and in working with the National Park Service to reduce poaching by foreigners.

Our next task is to incorporate this new information into our model. You can now produce an Initial Conceptual Model as shown below.

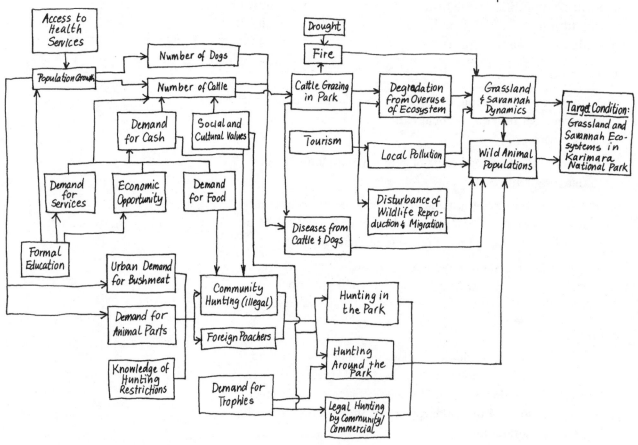

Savannah Scenario:
Initial Conceptual Model

Describe Your Conceptual Model in Writing

Finally, to capture all the hard thinking that you put into your Initial Conceptual Model so that you and other staff can review it later, it's a good idea to describe in words what all the factors are and how they relate to each other. The best way to do this is to start with the target condition and work to the other end of the model. A description of our Savannah Scenario Initial Conceptual Model is:

> In Karimara National Park, our target condition is grassland and savannah ecosystems. It can be described in terms of grassland and savannah dynamics and the animal populations that are found in the park. The grasslands and savannah are degraded by tourism, cattle grazing, and fire.
>
> As Karimara is a popular tourist destination, commercial tour hotels and tour operators are usually booked to capacity. Large numbers of tourists and the vehicles they use for game viewing damage extensive areas of fragile grasslands and savannah. Vehicle traffic also disturbs the normal reproductive and migration cycles of many of the animal species found in the park. Tourism is also responsible for polluting the park because of improper disposal of sewage and solid wastes.
>
> The intensity of cattle grazing in the park is influenced by the number of cattle owned by herders who reside in the communities around the park. At the end of the dry season, herders burn large tracts of grasslands to promote growth of new pasturage for their animals. Fires occur more frequently and with greater intensity during drought years.
>
> Cattle and the dogs that are used to herd them have been known to transmit diseases to wild ungulates and wild dogs, respectively, in the past. The number of cattle (and correspondingly the number of dogs) families own is a function of their economic situation. As milk production is one of the only sources of income in the area and social status is determined by the number of animals a family owns, most families strive to have as many cattle as possible. Increasing human population around Karimara has caused a parallel increase in the population of cattle.
>
> The demand for cash is a function of the need to cover expenses such as food and basic services (for instance, school and medical services). It is also related to how many other economic opportunities exist in the region. Formal education influences these economic factors as well as population growth in the area. Family heads with more formal education tend to have fewer children. Access to health services for women and children also has an impact on family size.
>
> Wild animal populations in and around the park are directly affected by hunting. Cash demands force some community members to hunt in and around the park, although this does not appear to be significant at the moment. Poachers from the neighboring country also hunt highly prized animals to sell their meat in urban markets and parts to international traders. Big game trophy hunting is also present around the park. Community members complain that they have little knowledge of hunting restrictions in and around the park and have expressed a willingness to cooperate with the National Park Service to curb illegal hunting in and around Karimara National Park.

Identify and Rank Threats at Your Project Site (Step A4)

So now you have this beautiful diagram—your Initial Conceptual Model. Your model shows how a series of factors—direct and indirect threats and contributing factors—combine to influence some target condition. But how do you figure out which factors need to be addressed or modified in order to have some impact on the status of the target condition? In order to develop your Management Plan, you must first determine which of the direct threats in your model you will seek to address.

Develop Criteria for Ranking Threats

Direct ranking helps the team identify lists of criteria by which to judge the relative importance of identified threats.

To rank direct threats in order of importance, you can use a variation of matrix ranking called *direct ranking*, an activity the entire project team should take part in because it requires a lot of discussion and careful thought to determine which threats are the most important.

Unlike preference ranking, which allows you to compare and add up different respondents' perceptions of the relative importance of various factors, direct ranking allows you to evaluate factors against specific criteria or attributes. The criteria you and your project team use to rank the relative importance of each threat is up to you, but we suggest using the following ones at a minimum:

- *Community Perceived Importance.* How did the community members rank the threats during the time you assessed local site conditions?

- *Area.* How wide an area does the threat affect? Is it going to affect your whole project site or just a small part of it?

- *Intensity.* How strong is the impact of the threat on a given piece of habitat or animal population? Will it destroy it completely? Or will it cause only minor damage?

- *Urgency.* How important is it that immediate action take place to deal with the threat? Is the threat occurring now? Or is it only likely to be important 10 years from now?

- *Political Feasibility.* Given the local, national, or international political situation, how realistic is it for you or your organization to attempt to address the threat? For example, can you stop an army from destroying forest during a civil war?

- *Social Practicality.* Given local or national social conditions, how sensible is it for you or your organization to try to deal with the threat? For example, is it realistic to stop hungry residents hunting for subsistence?

- *Organizational Ability.* How capable or prepared is your organization to combat the threat? Do you think you have enough financial and human resources to effectively address the threat?

Rank Threats

Draw a table like the one below. Make sure you title it, record the names of the team members who participated in the exercise, and include the date. Using the threats you included in the preference ranking exercise you did with community members, list them from top to bottom in the first column. Along the top, list the criteria you intend to use to compare and rank the direct threats.

Process Hint: For a more detailed description on how this direct ranking is done, see chapter 6.

Direct Ranking of the threats to Karimara National Park
Team members present: _____
Date: _____

Threat	Criteria							Total Score	Rank
	Community Perceived Importance	Area	Intensity	Urgency	Political Feasibility	Social Practicality	Organizational Ability		
Big Game Hunting									
Foreign Poachers									
Community Hunting									
Tourism									
Fire									
Cattle Grazing									
Diseases from Cattle and Dogs									

Now rank the threats with your team. The highest score that any threat can get for each criterion is equal to the total number of threats in the matrix. As before in our example for the preference ranking exercise, this is "7." The lowest score is always "1."

Start by recording the results of the community-perceived preference ranking exercise. Then for each of the other criteria, discuss with your team the relative ranking of each threat. The higher the rank, the greater the score it gets. After ranking the threats by each of the criteria, the matrix might look like the figure that follows.

Direct Ranking of the threats to Karimara National Park
Team members present:_____
Date:_____

Threat	Criteria							Total Score	Rank
	Community Perceived Importance	Area	Intensity	Urgency	Political Feasibility	Social Practicality	Organi- zational Ability		
Big Game Hunting	2	2	2	3	3	4	6	22	f
Foreign Hunters	6	4	4	5	5	5	5	34	b
Community Hunting	3	3	3	4	4	2	4	23	e
Tourism	7	5	7	7	1	1	7	35	a
Fire	4	6	5	2	6	6	3	32	c
Cattle Grazing	5	7	6	6	2	3	2	31	d
Diseases from Cattle and Dogs	1	1	1	1	7	7	1	21	g

So, according to the direct ranking exercise, your team ranked the threats affecting Karimara National Park in the following order: (1) Tourism, (2) Foreign poachers, (3) Fire, (4) Cattle grazing in the park, (5) Community hunting, (6) Big game hunting, and (7) Diseases from cattle and dogs.

Some interesting conclusions can be drawn from this final threat analysis. First of all, note that the order of the ranking that you and your team did came out almost identical to the order of the threats based on the local stakeholder assessment. This kind of consistency usually means that addressing the highest priority threats will be relatively easy, as the stakeholders agree with (or at least are aware of) what your team concluded were the most significant threats. Second, although there is a clear order to the ranking of the threats, there is also a definite cut-off between the top four and the bottom three threats. It is clear that you will want to address the problems that Tourism is causing. Also, according to your analysis, Foreign poachers must be addressed. Third, notice how the next two factors, Cattle grazing in the park and Fire, received very similar scores; as we mentioned before, these two factors are closely related, as herders set fire to grasslands to encourage new growth of pasture for their cattle. In all likelihood, you will be able to address both of these threats together. Fourth, Community hunting and Big game hunting did not come out as major threats to Karimara National Park. You may decide, however, to address them if you feel that it is the responsibility of the National Park Service to keep them under control. Finally, although according to the review of existing data, the spread of

Disease by cattle and dogs was once a significant threat, it no longer appears to be something that must be immediately addressed.

So now you have a fairly good idea of the priority issues for which you need to begin to develop project objectives and activities. Which threats you actually choose to address is ultimately up to you and the local stakeholders you are working with, but at least you have a relatively objective assessment of the importance of each threat.

Sources and Further Readings

Byers, Bruce (1996). *Understanding and Influencing Behaviors in Conservation and Natural Resources Management*. Biodiversity Support Program, Washington, D.C. A guide to assessing local site conditions.

GTZ (1990). *ZOPP: An Introduction to the Method*. Deutche Gesellschaft für Technische Zusammenarbeit (GTZ), Frankfurt, Germany. A description of the conceptualization process used by GTZ, a German development agency.

McNeely, Jeffrey A., Kenton R. Miller, Walter V. Reid, Russell A. Mittermeier, and Timothy B. Werner (1990). *Conserving the World's Biological Diversity*. International Union for the Conservation of Nature and Natural Resources (IUCN), Gland, Switzerland. A good general discussion of the various threats to biodiversity.

Ostrom, Elinor (1995). "A Framework Relating Human 'Driving Forces' and Their Impact on Biodiversity." Paper presented at the Smithsonian/Man and the Biosphere Program "Measuring and Monitoring Forest Biological Diversity," Washington, D.C., May 23–25, 1995. A conceptual analysis of factors affecting human incentives and behavior as they relate to biodiversity.

Salafsky, Nick, and Richard Margoluis (1998). The Threat Reduction Assessment (TRA) Approach to Measuring Conservation Success: A Practical and Cost-Effective Framework for Evaluating Project Impact. Manuscript submitted to *Conservation Biology*. A detailed explanation, with multiple examples, of the TRA approach.

Chapter 4
Develop a Management Plan: Goals, Objectives, Activities

At this point, you have created an Initial Conceptual Model for your project and you and your team hopefully have a good understanding of the factors that influence the target condition. You have also identified and ranked the importance of the threats to your target condition. Your challenge now is to design a Management Plan that will enable you to address these threats. Developing a complete Management Plan includes coming up with goals, objectives, and activities for your project.

Using the information presented in this chapter, you should be able to design a Management Plan that includes the following steps:

- Develop a goal for your project (Step B1).
- Develop objectives for your project (Step B2).
- Develop activities for your project (Step B3).

Develop a Goal for Your Project (Step B1)

A *goal* is a general summary of the desired state that a project is working to achieve. A good goal meets the following criteria:

- *Visionary.* Inspirational in outlining the desired state toward which the project is working.

- *Relatively General.* Broadly defined to encompass all project activities.

- *Brief.* Simple and succinct so that that all project participants can remember it.

- *Measurable.* Defined so that changes in the target condition upon which the goal is based can be accurately assessed.

Write a Draft Goal Using Your Target Condition

As you might have guessed by now, goals are generally fairly easy to create. Take the target condition from your Conceptual Model and convert it into an action phrase that describes the general impact that you hope to have on it. Although in some instances a project can have multiple goals, it is usually easier to have just one. For example, in the Tropical Forest Scenario, the target condition is "primary forest in the Indah Biosphere Reserve." A draft goal for the project is:

> *Draft Goal.* To preserve primary forest in the Indah Biosphere Reserve.

Apply the Criteria and Modify the Draft Goal as Necessary

In this book, we are using *criteria* (the singular is criterion) to refer to attributes of various parts of management and monitoring plans.

Process Hint: It may be helpful to write each criterion on a small card and to hold up the cards one at a time as you review your goal.

Review each *criterion* and ask yourself whether the goal meets it. If the goal does not, then modify the goal so that it does meet the criterion. If it does, then go on to the next criterion.

A good goal should provide all project members with a visionary picture of what the project is hoping to accomplish. Goals are what you rely on to motivate you and your project partners during difficult times. For example, suppose you are working in the Tropical Forest Scenario. You are trying to map forest areas and you drop your notebook while standing knee deep in muddy water as you are being bitten by flies and mosquitoes during a fierce rain storm. It probably would not be too inspirational to remember at that moment that the goal of the project is:

> *Draft Goal.* To preserve primary forest in the Indah Biosphere Reserve.

Preservation of forest is undoubtedly something that the project should hope to attain. It can, however, be worded in a more inspirational way, such as:

Goal. To conserve the forests in the Indah Biosphere Reserve for future generations.

Most steps in the project-design process require careful measured thinking. When it comes to goals, however, you get a chance to be a bit more expressive. Goals are also more inspirational when written in a positive sense. For example, in the Wetlands Scenario, it is not very inspirational to have a negative-sounding goal like:

Draft Goal. To stop wetland habitat destruction.

Instead, it is more motivating to have a positive statement such as:

Goal. To maintain healthy wetlands in the Everson Watershed to provide water to nearby urban areas and wildlife-based recreational opportunities for residents and visitors.

Notice that this second goal is basically advocating the same vision as the first one (stopping the loss of wetlands) but is stated in a more positive way.

Relatively General — A goal should be a fairly general statement of what you want to accomplish. Leave the specifics for the objectives and activities, which will come later. You don't want to have dozens of goals for a project—one will usually do, and at most you might have two or three. At the same time, however, you don't want to be so general that the goal becomes meaningless. Here again, it's an art and not a science to determine the appropriate balance. For example, in the Savannah Scenario, it is a bit too specific to have as your goals:

Draft Goal 1. To reduce cattle grazing in Karimara National Park from Salaka Village.

Draft Goal 2. To reduce goat grazing in Karimara National Park from Karibu Village.

Draft Goal 3. To reduce sheep grazing in Karimara National Park from Raitan Village.

As we will see later, this level of detail is more appropriate for activities. Instead, it is probably better to have a more general goal that integrates these draft goals and many others as well, such as:

Goal. To conserve the grassland and savanna ecosystems of Karimara National Park.

This last goal is much broader and more comprehensive. It basically covers all of the other goals. However, you don't want to be too general and unspecific. So it is probably not such a good idea to merely say:

Draft Goal. Save Karimara National Park.

This goal is too general. Once again, it is an art to develop goals that are not too specific and yet not too broad.

Brief

The third criterion for a good goal is that it is brief. It should be a statement that you can easily memorize. You should be able to write your goal on a sign in your office so that you can see it and be reminded by it everyday. In the Coastal Scenario, an example of a goal that is too wordy is:

Draft Goal: To develop sanctuary areas for marine life, taboo fishing periods for critical species, nondestructive fishing technologies, catch-size limits, enhanced relations with neighboring villages, reduction of fishing by foreign operators, substitution of other materials for current uses of mangrove wood in housing and cookstoves, and promotion of family planning.

As we will see later, this draft goal is basically a mixture of objectives and activities. A better goal for this project is:

Goal. To ensure the availability of marine resources for our grandchildren and our grandchildren's grandchildren.

Measurable

The final criterion for a good goal is that it is measurable. As we will see in the next section, you can partially measure your project's success by measuring the extent to which you have met your project's objectives. However, as success is ultimately determined by whether or not you achieve your goal, you need to be able to measure whether you have achieved it. If you can show that you have both met your objectives and achieved your goal, then you can justly claim that

```
┌─────────────────────────────────────────────────┐
│   Karimara National Park - Management Plan        │
│ ┌───────────────────────────────────────────────┐│
│ │                                               ││
│ │ Project Goal: To conserve the grassland and savannah ecosystems │
│ │              in Karimara National Park         │
│ │ Objective 1.                                   │
│ │ Factor in Conceptual Model Targeted by Objective: │
│                                                   │
└───────────────────────────────────────────────────┘
```

your project is a success. Returning to the Savannah Scenario, one of the draft goals that we wrote down is relatively unmeasurable:

Draft Goal. Save Karimara National Park.

It is hard to figure out how we might measure the concept of saving a national park. Since we can measure changes in savannah and grassland habitat, a more measurable goal is:

Goal. To conserve the grassland and savannah ecosystems of Karimara National Park.

Place the Goal in Your Management Plan and a Prominent Spot

Put the goal in your Management Plan. You may also want to put it in a prominent spot where all the members of the project team can see it on a regular basis and be inspired by it, as shown in the drawing on the preceding page.

Practice Examples: Goals

Determine which of the following meet the criteria for goals. For those that don't, see if you can figure out how they fall short.

1. Improve community health standards in the Wildlands Region.
2. To save Wildlands National Park.
3. To support the Department of Parks in its efforts to enforce hunting regulations in Wildlands National Park.
4. To hold planning workshops with government officials.
5. Develop sustainable livelihoods based on careful use of the natural resources from the Wildlands project area.
6. To assist local NGOs in implementing conservation-based development projects in the Wildlands Region.

Meets All Criteria?
1. Yes.   But not a conservation goal.
2. No.   Too general and not measurable.
3. No.   Too specific and not inspirational—sounds more like an activity.
4. No.   Too specific—sounds more like an activity.
5. Yes.
6. No.   Not very visionary—sounds more like an activity as well.

Develop Objectives for Your Project (Step B2)

Objectives are specific statements detailing the desired accomplishments or outcomes of a project. If the project is well conceptualized and designed, realization of a project's objectives should lead to the fulfillment of the project's goal. A good objective meets the following criteria:

- *Impact Oriented*. Represents desired changes in critical threat factors that affect the project goal.

- *Measurable*. Definable in relation to some standard scale (numbers, percentages, fractions, or all/nothing states).

- *Time Limited*. Achievable within a specific period of time.

- *Specific*. Clearly defined so that all people involved in the project have the same understanding of what the terms in the objective mean.

- *Practical*. Achievable and appropriate within the context of the project site.

A commonly used system of criteria for objectives states that they should be Specific, Measurable, Attainable, Realistic, and Time Limited (which spells out the acronym SMART). Although the criteria we use are similar, there are some key differences including, in particular, the focus on making them impact oriented.

Select a Factor from Your Conceptual Model

As a rule, you will want to start with a factor corresponding to the most important direct threat that you identified in chapter 3. You can then use your Conceptual Model to help you determine what interventions you can take to address this threat factor. This may either involve developing interventions that are directly related to this direct threat or developing interventions to address associated indirect threat factors.

Process Hint: Although you generally start with a factor linked to the highest ranked threat, if you are doing this for the first time, for practice you may wish to start with a simple example.

Write a Draft Objective or Objectives Related to This Factor

For the chosen factor, write down one or more draft objectives. A given factor can have more than one objective associated with it, depending on what you want to accomplish. There are the usual trade-offs, however, between not having enough objectives and having too many of them. In general, if you find that your objectives are getting to be long and complex, it may make sense to start dividing them. On the other hand, you also don't want to have a hundred different objectives. A good general rule is to have between one and three objectives for each factor that you want to address in your Conceptual Model.

For example, suppose you are coordinating the project in the Coastal Scenario. Based on the Conceptual Model that you and your team developed, you determine that a major threat to the long-term health of the marine resources in the project site is the current local practice of harvesting immature (undersized) fish and shellfish, which damages the reproductive potential of these marine populations. You plan to work with community leaders to

Process Hint: To help draft project objectives, ask yourself the questions: (1) What do we need to accomplish to have the desired effect on our target condition? and (2) What information do we need to be able to show that we have accomplished what we set out to do?
It may help to imagine yourself at the end of your project having to explain to local stakeholders and outside donors why the project you just completed should be considered a success.

define size limits for harvesting fish and shellfish, produce measuring devices that fishermen can take with them in their boats, and hold a number of meetings with community members to explain the size limits and the rationale behind them. Your first attempt to develop an objective might be:

> *Draft Objective A.* Hold two sessions with community elders to determine size limits for harvesting fish and shellfish, produce 200 measuring devices, and hold six meetings with community members to explain the size limits.

Apply the Criteria and Modify the Draft Objective as Necessary

Review each criterion and ask yourself whether the draft objective meets the criterion. If it does not, then modify the objective so that it does. If it does, then go on to the next criterion.

| Impact |
| Oriented |

Perhaps the most important criterion for any objective is that it must have some relevance to the factor in the project (shown in your Conceptual Model) that you are trying to affect. A good objective will be written in such a way that attaining the objective will guarantee that the project will change the desired factor and thus ultimately affect the project's target condition. It also provides the target against which you will measure the success of your project's interventions. One of the most common mistakes that is made in writing project objectives is to confuse *impact* with *process*. As a result, many project objectives mix impact and process and end up sounding like draft objective A.

Is this objective impact oriented? At first glance, it may seem okay. But if we think about it, does it really matter whether the elders have attended one or two decision-making sessions or whether the village has produced 200 or 2000 measuring devices or whether the project has held one or six or twenty-three meetings with community members? Not really. These are all activities with unknown impact. What does matter (according to our Conceptual Model) is how the fishermen's behavior has changed—are they harvesting fish below the size limit or not? Thus, an "impact-oriented" objective for the same project might be:

> *Draft Objective B.* Reduce incidents of harvesting of undersized marine resources.

This does not mean that the decision-making sessions, production of measuring devices, and community meetings are not important—these interventions are necessary for us to achieve our objective. They fit into the Management Plan as activities, which will be described later in this chapter. Completing these activities, however, is not sufficient to ensure that we have had our desired impact on the factor we are hoping to affect. We thus need to explicitly

Process Hint: Again, as was the case with goals, it may be helpful to write each criterion on a small card and to hold up the cards one at a time as you review your objective.

Impact refers to "what" you are trying to accomplish; **process** refers to "how" you are going to achieve this impact.

In any project, objectives describe your intended impact, while activities describe the process you plan to undertake to reach these objectives and thus ultimately your goal. In the case of the conservation and development projects that are the focus of this guide, good objectives are generally linked to reducing key threats to conservation.

state an objective that represents this desired impact. Some additional examples of draft objectives that do and do not meet the impact-oriented criterion are presented in the following table.

Do Not Meet the "Impact-Oriented" Criterion	Meet the "Impact-Oriented" Criterion (but not all others)
Establish a nontimber forest product harvesting enterprise.	Add value to standing forest by establishing a nontimber forest product harvesting enterprise that will increase income of all families by 25 percent.
Hold a series of community meetings.	Increase knowledge of local community members about the importance of reefs for maintaining fish populations.
Work with park officials to patrol park boundaries.	Reduce illegal hunting in the park area by 50 percent over a three-year period.

A *scale* is a set of evenly spaced numbers like markings on a ruler or rankings between 1 and 10.

Measurable

Another important criterion for an objective is that you are able to measure at any point in time at least roughly how close you are to achieving the objective. In effect, for each objective you need a *scale* against which you can measure your project's progress in achieving the objective.

Although draft objective B is impact oriented as it states that you want to reduce incidents of harvesting undersized marine resources, it says nothing about reducing incidents by how much. Accordingly, the objective could be rewritten as:

Draft Objective C. Reduce incidents of harvesting of undersized marine resources to fewer than two per month.

With this revised objective, at any given point in time, you can monitor the behavior of fishermen in the community and determine how well you are doing in attaining your objective. For instance, you may find at the start of the project that there are on average 200 incidents of harvesting undersized marine resources per month. After initially meeting with the elders, producing the measuring devices, and holding three community meetings, the number of incidents drops to 175 per month. At this point, you know you still have a way to go to achieve the objective. And after another meeting with the elders to redefine the limits and another two meetings with the community members in which you present revised materials, the number of incidents drops to 37 per month.

With this information, you decide that your interventions are not completely working and that you have to work with the elders to develop a community policing and fine system to provide sanctions against fishermen who don't observe the size limit regulations. Six months later, you find that there are now only four incidents per month. At this point you may decide that you have come sufficiently close to achieving your objective. The key is that with a measurable scale, you can determine how close you are and take corrective actions if necessary.

Process Hint: By measuring the incidents of violations, you will learn which intervention is most effective. In the future, you may wish to avoid the visual materials that you used in the first set of meetings that only resulted in a small drop in the number of violations (200 to 175 per month) and focus instead on the materials in the second set of meetings, which resulted in a much larger drop (175 to 37 per month).

Typical ways of making objectives measurable include:

- *Absolute Amounts.* Infractions reduced to two incidents per month. Average family income raised by $50 dollars per year.

- *Percentages.* Infractions reduced by at least 90 percent. Average family income raised by a minimum of 5 percent per month.

- *Fractions and Multiples.* Infractions reduced by 4/5. Average family income doubled annually.

- *Verbal Words Such as "All" or "Nothing."* No infractions occur. No buildings in the village made from mangrove wood. In this case, it is best to restrict the use of verbal descriptions to "all," "nothing," or "a majority"—saying "a few infractions" or "some buildings" is too vague.

> Time
> Limited

Another criterion for a good objective is that it is achieved within a defined time limit. If the objective is written without defining the date by which you expect to accomplish it, then you will have no idea of when to judge if your project is a success. If, however, you have specified a time limit and by the end of this period you have not reached your objective, then you know that you must either revise your time schedule or change your project objective or interventions.

With draft objective C, it's not clear whether reduction of infractions is supposed to occur in a day, a month, a year, or even a decade. A better way to state this objective would be:

Draft Objective D. By the end of the third year of the project, reduce incidents of harvesting of undersized marine resources to fewer than two per month.

At the end of the three-year period you should be able to see whether you have achieved your objective. If you have, great. If not, then you need either to revise the time frame for the objective

or to revise the activity so that you can achieve the desired impact. Typical ways of making objectives time limited include:

- *Absolute Time*. Within three years from now . . . , After six months . . . , By March 2003 . . . .

- *Relative Time*. At the project half-way point . . . , Within two months of the signing of the agreement . . . , By the end of the seventh year of the project . . . , By the end of the project . . . .

Specific

Yet another important criterion for a good objective is that it is specific so that it can be understood by everyone involved in the project. If an objective is too general—for example, to reduce cutting trees—then you might not know at any given point if you have or have not achieved it. If, however, the objective is more specific—for example, to reduce by one-third the amount of mangrove firewood used by households in Samak Village—then it is easier to see whether the objective has been met.

In draft objective D, it is not particularly clear what is meant by size limits or marine resources. If at the end of the project it could be shown that some species of very small inedible fish were being released, would that constitute success for the project? Probably not, given that your goal is to maintain critical food resources for future generations. It would be better if defined limits were set for specific species. Therefore, an improved objective would be:

Draft Objective E. By the end of the third year of the project, reduce incidents of harvesting snappers, groupers, and conch in violation of community agreed upon size limits to fewer than two per month.

| Practical |

The final criterion for a good objective is that it is something practical that can actually be accomplished. This criterion is difficult to describe without reference to local site conditions. Furthermore, as is often the case in project management, there is a fine line between writing an objective that is too easy to obtain (and therefore meaningless) and one that it too difficult or even impossible to obtain (and therefore also meaningless). Making an objective practical is one more example of where the art of project management comes into play.

For example, in draft objective E, it may not be possible to reduce the number of violations to only two per month. A more realistic and practical objective might be to state:

> *Objective.* By the end of the third year of the project, reduce incidents of harvesting snappers, groupers, and conch in violation of community council defined size limits to fewer than 15 per month.

Record Factor to Be Influenced, Project Assumptions, and Underlying Assumptions

Once you have written your objective, it is often helpful to write down a few notes outlining why and how you came up with the objective. These notes will be helpful to other people who may read your management plan. They will also assist you in the future when you revisit your management plan and need to remember why you developed each objective. As illustrated below using the Savannah Scenario, write down the objective that you have developed. In addition, write down the factor in your Conceptual Model that you hope this objective will influence.

Next, write down the project assumptions that describe why you developed this objective. The project assumptions should capture the discussions that you and your colleagues have had in developing the objective. They should in particular outline (1) what information you collected that led you to write this objective and (2) how meeting the objective will enable you to address the factor you targeted in your model.

Finally, write down all other underlying assumptions that relate to this objective. These assumptions include your predictions as to what conditions must exist in order for you to be able to meet the objective.

Karimara National Park - Management Plan

Project Goal: To conserve the grassland and savannah ecosystems in Karimara National Park.

Objective 1. Household Demand for Cash: To provide 20% of the gross revenue from park entrance fees to the 7 communities that surround Karimara National Park by the end of the third year of the project (dispursement to Community Conservation and Development Committees (CDCs) provided on per capita basis).

Factor in Conceptual Model Targeted by Objective: Demand for Cash

Project Assumption: 1) During initial visits of the project team to the communities bordering the National Park, discussions revealed that their need for cash was a major factor causing them to keep large herds of livestock, one of the major threats to the wildlife of the Park. 2) The Park is currently generating substantial revenues from foreign and domestic tourists who come to see wildlife in the Park. 3) Community members are aware of the large amounts of cash being generated. 4) The National Government is currently undertaking a series of initiatives to devolve control over local issues from the national level to the local level. 5) Project staff have thus decided to affect the local demand for cash by providing for revenue-sharing of funds from tourism in the National Park with

Underlying Assumptions: 1) 20% of gross revenue from the park will be sufficient to motivate community members to protect the Park. Funds will be tranferred from NPS accounts to the community accounts on timely basis. 2) Communities find it acceptable to have CDCs receive, manage and use the money. 3) Communities will spend the money equitably and wisely.

Practice Examples: Objectives

Determine which of the following meet the criteria for objectives. For those that don't, see if you can figure out where they fall short and how you could rewrite them to make them better using the key criteria.

1. To promote community well-being and health in the area surrounding Indah Biosphere Reserve.
2. To establish a sustainable enterprise-based conservation and development project that meets the needs of local people while protecting biodiversity in the region surrounding Indah Biosphere Reserve.
3. By the end of the project, household income for all families participating in nontimber forest product harvesting enterprises has increased by at least 20 percent.
4. Within three years, support the Department of Parks in its efforts to enforce hunting regulations in the Indah Biosphere Reserve.
5. To reduce the amount of illegal hunting in the Reserve by 30 percent in two years.
6. Within three years, less than two incidents per month occur in which residents of the villages bordering the Indah Biosphere Reserve are found hunting illegally in the reserve.
7. By the end of the third year of the project, NGO staff members provide technical assistance to five local communities that wish to begin their own natural resource-based enterprises.
8. By the second year of the project, two-thirds of the secondary school children in the community of Orosus understand the importance of conserving the rainforest to ensure sustainable yields of nontimber forest products in the future.

9. To increase sales of woven baskets by each participating family by 30 percent from the beginning of year one to the end of year three.
10. By the end of the project, have at least one community-managed butterfly enterprise that shows a profit.

Meets the Criteria?

1. No.   It is not impact oriented, measurable, time limited, specific, or practical. Sounds more like a goal.
2. No.   Again, it doesn't meet many of the criteria. It is too vague and not impact oriented. It sounds more like an activity.
3. Yes.
4. No.   Not impact oriented or specific. This is an activity.
5. Yes.
6. Yes.   This is a good objective provided that there is adequate surveillance by NGO staff or community members.
7. No.   This is an activity, not an objective.
8. Yes.
9. Yes.
10. Yes. Generally meets the criteria ("showing a profit" is measurable as income less expenses.)

Repeat Process and Write Objectives for All Identified Factors

Once you have written an objective for the first factor, continue developing objectives for the other factors that you identified as being important for the project. For each objective, make sure that you go through the criteria for objectives and then write down the factor that you are targeting, your project assumption, and any underlying assumptions that you may have.

Develop Activities for Your Project (Step B3)

Activities are specific actions or tasks undertaken by project staff designed to reach each of the project's objectives. A good activity meets the following criteria:

- *Linked*. Directly related to achieving a specific objective.

- *Focused*. Outlines specific tasks that need to be carried out.

- *Feasible*. Accomplishable in light of the project's resources and constraints.

- *Appropriate*. Acceptable to and fitting within site-specific cultural, social, and biological norms.

Select an Objective and Develop Activities Using the Criteria

The starting point for developing activities is your Conceptual Model and list of objectives. Generally, you will start with your most important objective, although if you are new to this process and your most important objective is complex, then you may wish to start with a relatively simple and concrete one.

Write down an initial list of the major activities that you think will help you achieve the objective. Try to arrange the activities in the sequence in which they need to occur to achieve the task. Next, apply the four criteria to each activity on the list. If you find the activity does not meet the criteria, either modify it or drop it and develop another activity.

| Linked |

Activities should always be linked to specific objectives—you don't want to have random activities that are unrelated to what you are trying to accomplish. Generally, as shown in the example in the sidebar, there will be a sequence of activities that needs to take place to achieve an objective. It should be readily apparent why each activity is being undertaken.

| Focused |

Unlike objectives which need to be impact oriented, activities should be clearly process oriented. Activities should be written as focused statements of actions that the project is going to undertake. They must include information on how you are going to do the activity (which tasks need to be undertaken), who is responsible for carrying out these tasks, when these tasks will be completed, and where the tasks will be undertaken.

In writing down activities and their component tasks, the artistic aspects of project design come into play as you try to determine at what level of detail you need to describe your activities. For instance, in the Coastal Scenario, the first objective is:

Process Hint: A general outline of how a project's goal, objectives, and activities fit together in a management plan looks like:

GOAL
Objective 1
- Activity 1
- Activity 2
- Activity 3

Objective 2
- Activity 1
- Activity 2

Objective 3
- Activity 1
- Activity 2
- Activity 3
- Activity 4

Objective 1a. During the second year of the project there are no incidents of community members fishing in sanctuary areas.

For this objective, you don't want to have a general activity like:

- *Draft Activity A.* Designate sanctuary areas where fishing is forbidden.

This activity is not easy to accomplish in a day, a week, or even a month. On the other hand, you also don't want to list every last task in minute detail. For example, it becomes a bit counterproductive (not to mention boring) to have a list of micro-level activities like:

- *Draft Activity B.* Call first Houseline Chief to organize meeting Monday three weeks from now.

- *Draft Activity C.* Call second Houseline Chief to organize meeting Monday three weeks from now.

- *Draft Activity D.* Make sure that meeting house will be free for meeting.

- *Draft Activity E.* Prepare coffee for meeting Monday three weeks from now.

The happy medium here is to write a series of activities as shown in the following list:

Objective 1a. During the second year of the project, there are no incidents of community members fishing in sanctuary areas.

- *Activity 1.* Hold meetings with community members to discuss declaring parts of the traditional fishing grounds as sanctuary areas.

- *Activity 2.* Convene meeting of Council of Elders to designate, map, and mark sanctuary areas based on traditional fishing practices.

- *Activity 3.* Develop and implement the policing mechanisms that will be used to enforce the sanctuary policies.

As we will see later, you can put some of the detail into your description of tasks for each activity.

Resources can include things like staff time, managerial time, local knowledge, money, equipment, the presence of trained personnel, and sociopolitical opportunities.

Constraints are generally the flip side of resources—lack of time, lack of money, lack of trained personnel, and lack of sociopolitical opportunities.

| Feasible |

As you start to develop activities, you might notice that for any given objective there are practically an infinite combination of activities that could be undertaken to achieve the objective. You need to select the ones that are most feasible. In particular, you need to select the activities that make the most sense given the project's *resources* and *constraints*.

When designing project activities, it is important to consider how to best allocate resources to meet objectives while facing real-world constraints. The ideal is to maximize impact while minimizing costs (monetary and otherwise). Each activity thus needs to be considered both for its feasibility by itself (is it doable?) and, more importantly, relative to other potential activities (does it provide more or less impact given its cost?).

For example, in the Savannah Scenario, if you had no time or money constraints, you might develop activities as follows:

Objective 4. To reduce by 90 percent incidents of illegal hunting inside the park and wildlife management areas (WMAs) by the end of the project.

- *Draft Activity 1.* Conduct daily mounted patrols around the border of the park.

- *Draft Activity 2.* Build armed guard stations at one-half km intervals around the park.

- *Draft Activity 3.* Conduct hourly helicopter overflights over the park area.

If we think about these three activities, we might begin to realize that they are not particularly suited to the constraints of our situation. For example, the Park Service may not have sufficient staff time to devote to carrying out daily mounted patrols as outlined in draft activity 1. Likewise, it's probably not politically or socially acceptable to build armed guard stations as outlined in draft activity 2. Finally, the Park Service probably will not have the financial resources to fund hourly helicopter overflights as outlined in draft activity 3—and even if it could afford the expense, there are probably much more ***cost-effective*** ways in which that money could be spent. It makes more sense to have the following activities:

Cost-effectiveness refers to the ratio of impact to cost. For example, an activity that is highly cost-effective will have a high degree of impact relative to the amount of money required.

Objective 4. To reduce by 90 percent incidents of illegal hunting inside the park and wildlife management areas (WMAs) by the end of the project.

- *Activity 1.* Hold meetings with local trophy game hunting operators to clarify park boundaries, hunting restrictions (both inside the park and in WMAs around the park), and penalties for unlawful hunting.

- *Activity 2.* Provide National Park Service guards to accompany and monitor all trophy game hunts.

- *Activity 3.* Hold community meetings to discuss hunting restrictions in the park and WMAs and penalties for unlawful hunting.

- *Activity 4.* Take all community men on field visits to learn the park and WMA boundaries.

- *Activity 5.* Work with local community leaders to develop a community-based self-policing system for monitoring illegal hunting in the park and WMAs.

Determining which activities are cost-effective and fit within project constraints is not always easy. In some cases it may be fairly clear which activities should be undertaken to reach the project objectives. In other cases, however, difficult choices need to be made. If necessary, matrix ranking as described in chapter 3 may be a helpful tool to determine priorities.

Finally, it is of course important to make sure that activities are appropriate within the local context. Although setting up a fishing enterprise in a local river may seem like a good idea in theory, it won't work if there are no fish in the river (it is biologically inappropriate), if there is no market for excess fish (it is economically inappropriate), if local cultural taboos prevent people from handling fish (it is culturally inappropriate), or if local people just don't want a fishing enterprise (it is just plain inappropriate).

In particular, when you are looking at cultural appropriateness, it is important to focus on all elements of the society so that you take into account the needs and desires of all subgroups of the community (e.g., poor castes, women, minority religions).

Write Down Details About the Activities

Once you have developed your activities, it is helpful to write down details about them so that you and the other members of your project team will have a clear understanding of how and why you are doing them. Specific bits of information that are helpful to write down for each activity include:

- *Why do this activity?* Explain how this activity links to the objective.

- *How will the activity be carried out?* List the tasks that need to be completed to achieve the activity.

- *Who is responsible for the activity?* List who is responsible for undertaking the activity.

- *When will the activity take place?* Describe the target date for completing the activity tasks.

- *Where will the activity take place?* Describe where the activity will take place.

- *Underlying assumptions.* List any assumptions underlying the activity.

- *Prerequisites.* List the tasks and events that need to occur before the activity can be undertaken.

Karimara National Park - Management Plant

Objective I. Household Demand for Cash: To provide 20% of gross revenue from Park entrance fees to the communities that surround Karimara National Park by the end of the third year of the project (disbursement to community conservation and development committees (CDCs) provided on capita basis).

Factor in conceptual Model Targeted by Objective: Demand for Cash

Project Assumptions: 1) During initial visits of the project team to the bordering communities of the National Park, discussions with residents revealed that their need for cash was a major factor causing them to keep large herds of livestock, on of the major threats to the wildlife in the Park. 2) The park is currently generating substantial revenues from foreign and domestic tourist who come to see wildlife in the Park. 3) Community members are aware of the large amounts of cash being generated. 4) The National Government is currently undertaking a series of initiatives to devolve control over local issues from the national to the local level. 5) Project staff have thus decided to affect the local demand for cash by providing for revenue-sharing of funds from tourism in the National Park with local people.

Underlying Assumptions: 1) 20% of gross revenue from the park will be sufficient to motivate community members to protect Park. Funds will be transferred from NPS accounts to the community accounts on timely basis. 2) Communities will find it acceptable to have CDCs receive, manage and use the money. 3) Communities will spend the money equitably and wisely.

- **Activity I. Produce Revenue Sharing Accord:** Produce an official Government accord that provides for communities to share the revenues generated by national parks, and gives the National Park Service the authority to manage such arrangements.
Why do this activity?: In order to communities to receive revenues generated from National Parks, National legislation must be enacted to permit this type of revenue sharing arrangement.
How will this activity carry out? NPS negotiates with ministries of tourism, natural resources
Who will be responsible for this activity?: National Park Service Director.
Where will the activity take place? Central offices of NSP in the capital.
When will the activity take place? By the end of the first year of the project.
Assumptions: 1) Support for this type of legislation exsist in the National Government 2) Passage of this legislation will be relatively easy.
Prerequisites: NSP Director contacts key government officials.

Complete information for one activity from the Savannah Scenario is illustrated above.

Repeat Process for Other Objectives

Once you have developed activities for your first objective, you need to repeat the process for your other objectives. Writing out all the details for three or four objectives worth of activities can take a lot of time and effort. However, it is also extremely important—otherwise, how will you know which interventions to undertake and how and when to do them? So make sure you take the time to think and plan.

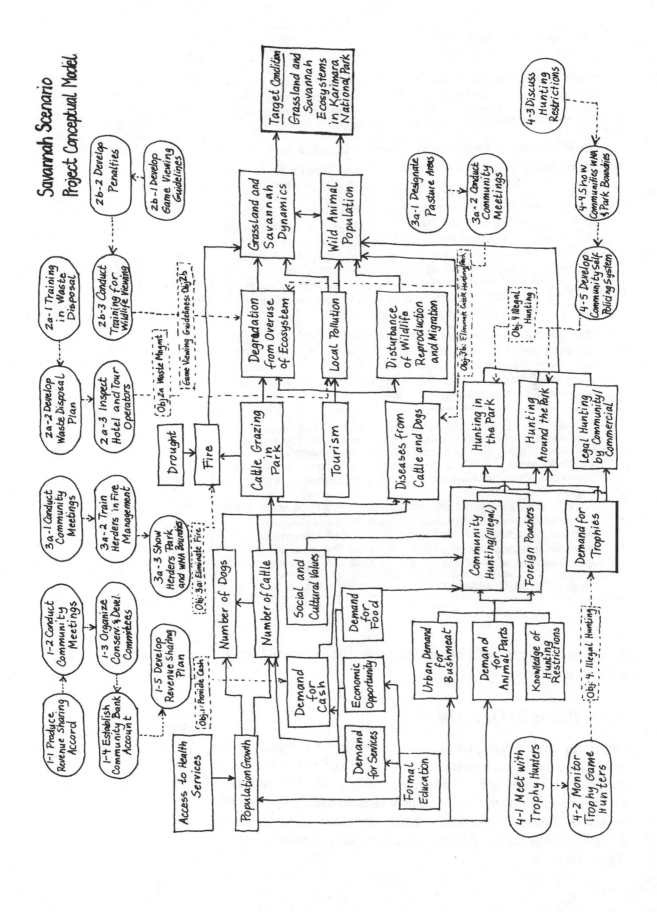

Savannah Scenario
Project Conceptual Model

Put Activities into Your Conceptual Model

Once you have developed activities for all your objectives, it's time to revisit your Initial Conceptual Model—remember the model that you spent so much time on in chapter 3? As we said in chapter 3, your Project Conceptual Model is not complete until you have shown how you anticipate your project activities will enter the model and influence certain factors and threats which will ultimately lead to a change in the target condition.

For each factor that you targeted with your objectives, add the activities that you developed. You may want to include your activities in the model using another shape, such as an oval. If the direct effect on the factor is not clear, you may wish to include additional factors that make this connection explicit. These additional factors should be entered in the model using rectangles since they are not activities but merely extensions of your Conceptual Model.

Using our Savannah Scenario example, the Final Project Conceptual Model is now shown on the previous page. The process of putting your management plan into your Conceptual Model is very important. As illustrated by the tree below, successful project design is completely dependent on your understanding of a series of precise and specific linkages: between the Conceptual Model and project goals, between goals and objectives, and between objectives and activities.

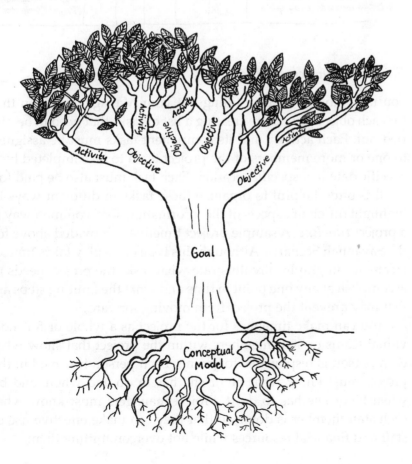

Monitoring Task	Year 1 Q1	Q2	Q3	Q4	Year 2 Q1	Q2	Q3	Q4	Year 3 Q1	Q2	Q3	Q4	Year 4 Q1	Q2	Q3	Q4	Year 5 Q1	Q2	Q3	Q4	People Responsible
Goal: To conserve the grassland and savannah ecosystems of Karimara National Park.																					Project Coordinator
01. Demand for Cash																					
—A1. Produce revenue sharing accord		X																			Project Coordinator
—A2. Conduct community meetings...	X	X			X	X															Project Coordinator
—A3. Organize CDCs						X															Project Coordinator
—A4. Establish community bank accounts						X			X												Project Coordinator
—A5. Develop revenu sharing plans						X			X												Project Coordinator
02a. Tourism Waste Management																					
—A1. Training in waste disposal					X				X				X				X				Project Assistant
—A2. Develop waste disposal plans				X																	Project Assistant
—A3. Inspect hotel and tour operators					X	X			X	X			X	X							Park Inspector
02b. Tourism Game Viewing																					
—A1. Develop game viewing guidelines					X																Project Coordinator
—A2. Develop fines					X																Project Coordinator
—A3. Conduct training for wildlife viewing					X				X				X				X			X	Project Coordinator
03a. Eliminate Escaped Fires																					
A1. Conduct community meeting to explain benefits	X	X			X	X			X	X			X	X			X	X			Project Coordinator
—A2. Train herders in fire management		X			X																Project Coordinator
—A3. Show herders the Park and WMA boundries		X																			Project Coordinator
03b. Cattle Herding Inside Park																					
—A1. Designate pasture areas		X																			Project Assistant
—A2. Conduct community meeting to explain boundries.	X	X			X	X			X	X			X	X			X	X			Project Coordinator
04. Reduce Illegal Hunting																					
—A1. Meet with trophy hunting operators		X																			Project Coordinator
—A2. Monitor trophy game hunts		X			X				X				X							X	Project Coordinator
—A3. Meet with communities to disccuss...		X																			Project Coordinator
—A4. Develop community policing system		X																			Project Coordinator

PROJECT MONITORING TIMELINE– KARIMARA NATIONAL PARK

Finalize Management Plan

You may have noticed in filling out your Management Plan that for each objective you are creating a list of tasks that need to be carried out. Each activity and its component tasks must be assigned to one or more members of the project team to be completed by a specific date in a specific location. Each task must also be paid for.

It is often helpful to organize these tasks in different ways to highlight different aspects of the information. One common way is a project *timeline*. A sample project timeline is provided above for the Savannah Scenario. Although this type of display takes time to create, it can graphically illustrate what tasks the project needs to accomplish at any one point in time and what the limiting steps are that may prevent the project from moving forward.

You can make timelines for the project as a whole or for individual teams or staff members within the project that show what each person is responsible for doing. Each person involved in the project must know what he or she has to do and where and by when he or she has to do it. Project managers must know what each staff member is doing so that they can make effective use of staff and financial resources while not overcommitting them.

A *timeline* (also known as a Gantt Chart) is a bar graph which lists the major activities and tasks involved in the project. It also shows how long the various activities are supposed to last and the relationship between different activities.

Sample Budget – The Savannah Scenario, Year 1 of Project Only

Item	Unit	Cost per Unit	Amount	Total
EXPENSES				
O1. Household Cash Demand				
Salaries				
Project Coordinator (salary)	days	50	40	2,000
Project Assistant (salary)	days	35	40	1,400
NPS Director (expenses)	days	10	10	100
Travel				
To 7 communities	2 way per person	15	14	210
To district capital	2 way per person	35	14	490
Supplies				
Notepads and flipcharts	1 set	5	7	35
Subtotal for this Objective				4,235
O2a. Tourism Waste				
Salaries				
Project Coordinator (salary)	days	50	20	1,000
Project Assistant (salary)	days	35	30	1,050
Park Staff (expenses)	days	5	30	150
Travel				
To major hotels	2 way per person	15	5	75
Supplies				
Notepads and flipcharts	1 set	5	5	25
Meeting expenses	1 meeting	50	5	250
Subtotal for this Objective				2,550
———— [Other objectives left out of example] ————				
Project Overhead				
Salaries				
Project Coordinator (salary)	days	50	50	2,500
Project Assistant (salary)	days	35	30	1,050
Accountant	1 week/month	50	12	600
Other Expenses				
Office Rent	month	100	12	1,200
Copier	month	20	12	240
Postage	month	15	12	180
Printing	month	20	12	240
Subtotal for Overhead				6,010
Total Project Costs				12,795
INCOME				
Grant from Donor				11,000
Park Service Contributions				2,000
TOTAL PROJECT INCOME				13,000

It is also helpful to create a **budget** for your project. There are many ways in which you can organize the items in your budget and you should use a system that makes sense to you. One such way is to organize it under project objectives as outlined in the example above. For each objective, you list the staff required, any other expenses such as travel or lodging that the staff will incur,

A **budget** is a table that outlines the predicted expenses for the project.

Project overhead in this context refers to items that are not directly attributable to any one objective of the project. It includes things like the time that staff spend planning the project and administrative costs like supplies and rent.

and any supplies or equipment that your staff will need. You also need to have a separate section for *project overhead* that cannot be assigned to any one objective. For each item in the list, you then determine what unit you will use to measure the amount of the item needed, the price per unit, and then the number of units that you will need over the time period being considered in the budget table. You can then multiply the number of units needed times the cost per unit to get the total cost for that item. It is generally a good idea to calculate the subtotal cost for each objective as well as the total project cost. You probably will want to compare this cost against your income for the same time period to make sure that your project is remaining financially stable.

Your timeline and budget are very helpful tools to use with your Conceptual Model. In developing your Management Plan, you should select the threat factors that you identified as being the most important ones to address. When creating the timeline, however, you may find that addressing one or more of these factors will take two times as many staff members as you currently have. Or in doing the budget, you may find that it requires three times as much money to address the factors as you currently have. If this situation occurs, you have basically three choices: (1) Find a more time-efficient or cheaper way to address the factor that will still be effective, (2) find new sources of money to hire new staff or to pay for your activities, or (3) select a different factor to address. The best management plan in the world will not work if you do not have the staff time or funds to carry it out.

Sources and Further Readings

Several references describe processes for project design that are roughly similar to parts of the procedure outlined in this chapter. These include:

GTZ (1990). *ZOPP: An Introduction to the Method*. Deutsche Gesellschaft für Technische Zusammenarbeit (GTZ), Frankfurt, Germany. A description of the project design process used by GTZ, a German development agency.

Larson, Patricia, and Dian Sesler Svendsen (draft 1996). *Participatory Monitoring and Evaluation: A Practical Guide to Successful ICDPs*. World Wildlife Fund, Washington, D.C. A step-by-step guide to developing monitoring workplans for Integrated Conservation and Development Projects (ICDPs).

Lewis, James P. (1997). *Fundamentals of Project Management*. American Management Association, Washington, D.C. A business-oriented guide to developing projects.

USAID (1996). *Re-Engineering USAID NRM Programs in Africa*. United States Agency for International Development (USAID), Washington, D.C. A manual describing the "results framework approach" being developed by USAID for its overseas projects.

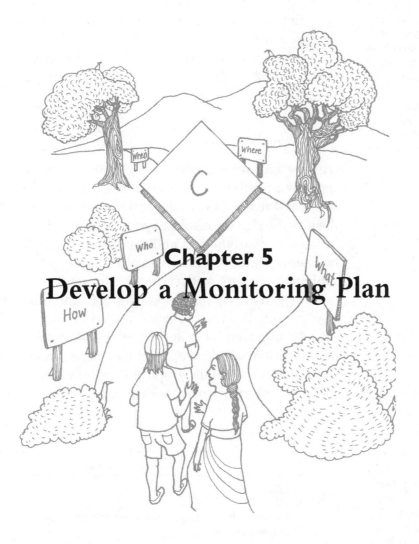

Chapter 5
Develop a Monitoring Plan

Now that you have created your Project Conceptual Model and designed the Management Plan, the next step is to develop a Monitoring Plan. The Monitoring Plan is the outline for the steps you will undertake to ensure that the project is on track. If you do not monitor your project's interventions, then you will have no way of knowing whether you have achieved your goal and objectives or what you need to do to improve the project. Taken together, your completed Project Conceptual Model, Management Plan, and Monitoring Plan are your Project Plan.

Using the information presented in this chapter, you should be able to:
- Determine audiences, information needs, monitoring strategies, and indicators (Step C1).
- Select methods and determine tasks necessary to collect data (Step C2).
- Determine when, by whom, and where data will be collected (Step C3).
- Develop a Monitoring Plan for project activities (Step C4).

Determine Audiences, Information Needs, Monitoring Strategies, and Indicators (Step C1)

In this chapter, we present these steps in this order. You should keep in mind, however, that in reality you need to undertake the first three of these steps more or less simultaneously. For example, there is no point in developing an indicator if there are no appropriate methods to measure it, or there are no project staff members trained in using a chosen method.

The first step is to determine who will be using the information that you will be collecting and what it is that they would like to know. You may have collected the best information in the world, but if nobody cares about it or it is in a form that people can't or won't use, then all your hard work will be wasted.

Determine Your Audiences

Almost any project will have multiple audiences. To begin the process of selecting your audience, sit down with your project team and make a list of the various groups who you think might be interested in the results of your project and monitoring work. In almost all cases the first audience listed should be your own project team. Other possible *internal* audiences include the local community members with whom your project is working, other groups that are collaborating with you, and other stakeholders in the project. Potential *external* audiences include donors, policy makers in government and other agencies, other members of the conservation and development community, and the broader public. For example, in the Tropical Forest Scenario, a list of the audiences for information about the project and its results might be:

Process Hint: It is important to consider your audience throughout the entire process of designing, managing, and monitoring your project. In particular, you should always make sure to provide results to the community members and other stakeholders at your project site who were involved in your monitoring process.

Audience	General Information Needs
INTERNAL	
Project Team	
Management Staff	How to improve project & its impact
Other Community Members	
Leaders	Impact of project on community members
NTFP Harvesters	How to improve harvesting returns
Other Members	Income potential of project enterprise
Collaborating Partners	
University Faculty	Impact of project on plants and animals
EXTERNAL	
Government Agencies	
Ministry of Infrastructure	Local perceptions of planned dam
Ministry of finance	Amount of taxes generated by enterprises
Ministry of Agriculture and Forestry	Impact of sustainable farming programs on forests and NTFP harvesting practices
Donors	
Multi-Lateral Banks	Feasibility of enterprise based approach
Others	
General Public	Impact of and lessons learned from project
Foundations	Feasibility of enterprise based approach
Conservation Agencies	Impact of and lessons learned from project

Determine Your Audiences' Specific Information Needs

The next step in developing a Monitoring Plan involves determining your audiences' specific *information needs*. Any project will have hundreds of possible questions that could potentially be asked about it. Your primary challenge in designing a monitoring plan is to focus on only the most important ones. If you were just now starting to develop a Monitoring Plan, it would be very difficult to figure out what information you need to track. But don't worry. At this point you have a good head start on this whole process. The hard work and thinking you have invested in developing a Project Conceptual Model and Management Plan for your project will make it much easier to determine what you need to monitor.

Information Needs

◇ **Goal.** To conserve the grassland and savannah ecosystems of Karimara National Park. (Based on Target Condition)

◇ **Objective 1.** To provide 20•/• of the gross revenue from park entrance fees to the 7 communities that surround Karimara National Park by the end of the third year of the project. (Demand for Cash)

◇ **Objective 2a.** By the end of the project (December 2001), all local commercial hotel and tour operation dispose of wastes in ways that do not contaminate the park and its surrounding areas. (Localized Pollution; Commercial Tourism)

◇ **Objective 2b.** By the end of the project, all local commercial hotel and tour operators adhere to Karimara National Park guidelines for game viewing and other park use. (Disturbance of Wildlife Reproduction and Migration; Degradation: overuse of Ecosystem.

◇ **Objective 3a.** By the end of the project, there will be no more uncontrolled fires set by local residents within the Wildlife Management Areas (WMAs) around the Park to generate pasture for Cattle inside the park boundries. (Disease from Cattle and Dogs; Degradation; Overuse of Ecosystem)

◇ **Objective 3b.** Within the last two years of the project, there are no reported incidents of herders grazing their cattle inside of the Park boundries. (Disease from Cattle and Dogs; Degradation: overuse of Ecosystem)

◇ **Objective 4.** To reduce by 90•/• incidents of illegal hunting inside the Park and WMAs by the end of the project. (Hunting in the Park, Hunting Around the Park; Community Hunting-Legal and Illegal)

The obvious starting points for monitoring are the goal and objectives that have already been developed in your Management Plan. As we've said before, your goal is what you are ultimately trying to achieve. Furthermore, your objectives have been designed so that achieving them leads to the realization of the goal. You will therefore want to monitor the project's progress in achieving your goal and objectives. So the first information needs that you can write down are simply your goal and your objectives from your Management Plan.

Once you have listed your goal and objectives, you need to think about what your and your audiences' other information needs might be. To do so, it's time to go back and revisit your Project Conceptual Model. Each objective is linked to a specific threat factor in the Project Conceptual Model. There are, however, other factors in the model that clearly affect your target condition that you chose not to include in your project because either (1) they were not sufficiently important threats or (2) you could not realistically hope to change them. But do you need to monitor them to measure the impact of your project activities? By all means.

For example, in the Savannah Scenario, other factors in the model include:

- Drought
- Urban demand for bush meat
- International demand for animal parts
- Population growth
- Social cultural values

These other factors are not being directly addressed by the project because, based on the threat-ranking exercise, the project staff determined that they were of lower priority or not possible for the project to address. This decision not to deal with these factors makes sense—indeed it is hard to imagine how a local project could address things like drought or the international demand for animal parts. At the same time, however, these factors clearly have an impact on both the target condition and the ability of the project to meet its stated objectives.

When project impacts are *confounded*, this means that it is hard to distinguish the cause or effect of one impact from another.

For example, even if the project staff succeed in meeting their objective of eliminating illegal hunting by community residents and trophy hunters, the wildlife populations in the park may still decrease if there is a severe drought or if hunting by foreign poachers increases as a result of greater demand for bush meat in the cities. So, even though the project will not be carrying out activities related to drought or the demand for bush meat, it is still important that the project staff collect information about their influence on the target condition. This information can be used to (1) ensure that planned project impacts are not *confounded* by changes in these other factors and (2) monitor these other factors to see if it becomes necessary to design interventions to deal with them.

Accordingly, project staff add to their list of information needs:

Additional Information Need 1. Relative importance of number of cattle in determining social status. (Related to social cultures values Factor)

Additional Information Need 2. Price for a kilogram of bush meat in the provincial capital. (Related to Urban Demand for Bush Meat Factor)

Additional Information Need 3. Number of people living in villages in the project area. (Related to Population Factor)

Additional Information Need 4. Comparison of rainfall levels in the region to the historical record. (Related Drought Factor)

In addition to information needs related to factors in the Project Conceptual Model, it is also important to keep your mind and model open to new changes that might occur at the project site. Accordingly, as you monitor your project over time, you may want to keep on your information needs list:

"New Factors" Information Need. What new factors have emerged at the site that may affect the project's success?

Design a Monitoring Strategy for Each Information Need

Once you have determined what it is that you would like to know, the next step is to design a monitoring strategy for getting the data needed to meet each of these information needs. This monitoring strategy should describe the specific *comparison* that you will be making with your monitoring efforts.

For example, in the Savannah Scenario, one of the objectives is:

Objective 1. Demand for Cash. To provide 20 percent of the gross revenues from park entrance fees to the seven communities that surround Karimara National Park by the end of the third year of the project (disbursements to community conservation and development committees provided on a per capita basis).

In this case, the team wants to know whether this objective is being met, so they decide on a monitoring strategy:

Monitoring Strategy. Measure the change over time in park revenues flowing to the seven communities receiving benefits.

In this example, the monitoring strategy involves comparing the group of communities receiving benefits to themselves over time.

Another objective in the Savannah Scenario is:

Objective 4. Reduce Illegal Hunting. To reduce by 90 percent incidents of illegal hunting inside the park and WMAs by the end of the project.

Here again, the team wants to know if this objective is being met. Because, however, there are several different types of hunting taking place in the park, the team needs to develop multiple monitoring strategies for this objective:

Monitoring Strategy 1. Compare the number of elephants and rhinos killed before and after project interventions.

Monitoring Strategy 2. Measure the change in the number of encounters with hunters inside the park over time.

Monitoring Strategy 3. Compare the levels of illegal hunting by trophy hunting operators in Karimara National Park to a neighboring park.

By definition, all monitoring efforts involve making *comparisons* between your project's impacts and some defined benchmark. As described in more detail in chapter 6, there are two main types of comparisons that you can make: (1) comparing a group affected by your project to itself over time and (2) comparing a group affected by your project to a group not affected by your project over time.

Each of these three monitoring strategies involves making a different comparison.

Develop One or More Indicators for Each Information Need

Once you have determined what it is that you would like to know and your general monitoring strategy, the next step is to develop specific *indicators* for each information need that you will follow throughout the life of the project. An indicator is a unit of information measured over time that documents changes in a specific condition. A given goal, objective, or additional information need can have multiple indicators. A good indicator meets the following criteria:

- *Measurable.* Able to be recorded and analyzed in quantitative or qualitative terms.

- *Precise.* Defined the same way by all people.

- *Consistent.* Not changing over time so that it always measures the same thing.

- *Sensitive.* Changing proportionately in response to actual changes in the condition or item being measured.

To develop an indicator, look at the goal, objective, or additional information need that you are considering and think about what type or types of data you need to collect to assess it. For instance, if in the Tropical Forest Scenario your goal is as follows:

Goal. To conserve the forests in Indah Biosphere Reserve for future generations.

Then you may want an indicator such as:

Indicator 1. Area (hectares) of forest in the reserve core area.

Similarly, if one of your objectives is:

Objective 2. Within three years, current Ministry of Infrastructure plans to build a hydroelectric dam immediately adjacent to the Biosphere Reserve have been abandoned.

Then you may want an indicator such as:

Indicator 1. Dam construction plans status.

Process Hint: When trying to develop indicators, it is easy to make things more complex than necessary. Often, appropriate indicators for goals and objectives will be both obvious and simple—don't make the process harder than it needs to be.

In both of the preceding examples, the indicators that were selected were directly contained within the goal or objective—it is fairly obvious what the indicator should be. In other cases, however, it may require a bit more thought as to what indicator or set of indicators is appropriate.

One case in which it is necessary to develop additional indicators is when you know that your interventions may be affecting the system (described in your Conceptual Model) in which they are taking place. In the goal mentioned earlier, for instance, in addition to wanting to know about the area of forest in the reserve, the team might have indicators about other aspects of biodiversity that potentially will be impacted by the project's nontimber forest product (NTFP) harvesting activities such as:

Indicator 2. Density of rattan species (canes/ha).

Indicator 3. Regeneration of rattan species (seedlings/ha).

Indicator 4. Density of bamboo species (plants/ha).

Another case in which it is necessary to develop additional indicators is when the situation that you are assessing is complex and requires several pieces of data to be fully understood. For example, if your objective is:

Objective 1. By the end of the fifth year of the project, 10 percent of the families in the buffer zone cover 25 percent of their annual cash needs from NTFP harvesting and processing enterprises.

Then there is no one indicator that you can measure to assess this entire objective. You can, however, develop the following set of indicators:

Indicator 1. Percentage of families in the project area (buffer zone) earning income from NTFPs.

Indicator 2. Amount (pesos/year) earned by households involved in the project from NTFPs.

Indicator 3. Annual cash needs per household.

Once you have collected the data for these three indicators, you can combine the information to assess your success in meeting the objective.

In both of these cases it is clearly necessary to develop more than one indicator to assess the goal or objective. Unfortunately, there is no set formula to determine if additional indicators are necessary, or what they should be. As usual, it's more of an art than a science to determine the appropriate indicators for a given information need.

Apply the Criteria and Modify Indicators as Necessary

Once you have developed a draft indicator, you need to make sure that it meets the criteria for a good indicator. If it does not, then modify the indicator so that it does.

Process Hint: The best indicators are those that are linked as tightly as possible to both your goal and objective so that assessing them helps you to measure reduction of threat to your target condition.

Process Hint: Here again, it may be helpful to write each criterion on a small card and to hold up the cards one at a time as you review your indicator.

We use the same "measurable" criterion for goals, objectives, and indicators because in order to be able to monitor them, we have to measure them. A measurable goal or objective should, by definition, have a measurable indicator associated with it.

Measurable

Perhaps the most important criterion for an indicator is that it must be measurable in either quantitative or qualitative terms. Both goals and objectives should be written to be measurable. In general, it therefore should be fairly easy to create measurable indicators for these information needs. For instance, in the Coastal Scenario, one of the objectives states:

Objective 1c. By the end of the second year of the project no fishermen are using either cyanide or bombs for capturing fish.

One potential indicator that could be developed for this objective would be:

Draft Indicator 1. Numbers of incidents of fishermen using cyanide or bombs.

Unfortunately, this indicator is not very measurable. Fishermen in the community know that using cyanide or bombs is illegal and therefore would only use these techniques secretively. You might be able to hear a few bombs going off close to the village, but it's almost impossible to measure the number of times fisherman are using bombs or cyanide. It is much better to use as indicators:

Indicator 1. Reef area damaged by cyanide fishing.

Indicator 2. Reef area damaged by bomb fishing.

These indicators are much easier to measure by doing regular surveys of reefs to assess the damage caused by cyanide or bombs.

Precise

Another important criterion for an indicator is that it is precisely defined. It is generally the case that a variety of individuals will be collecting data to measure a certain indicator. This involvement of different individuals occurs when data are being collected over a wide area (for example, by trained local observers in 30 villages). It also occurs when data are being collected over a long time period (as is usually the case in monitoring efforts). There is often substantial turnover in project staff and new people become responsible for data collection and analysis. In either case it's important that everyone collecting data is measuring the same thing.

For instance, in the Wetlands Scenario, the project goal is:

Goal: Maintain healthy wetlands in the Everson Watershed to provide water to nearby urban areas and wildlife-based recreational opportunities for residents and visitors.

One potential set of indicators that could be developed to help measure this goal involves looking at populations of key water birds that depend on wetlands for feeding and breeding habitat:

Draft Indicator 1. Numbers of wading bird nests per hectare of wetland habitat.

Draft Indicator 2. Densities of fish eagles in wetland habitat.

The first of these draft indicators is not very specific because it does not define which wading bird species are included in the indicator. One biologist doing a survey of the wetlands on the east side of the watershed might count members of three heron species and one stork species, whereas another biologist doing a survey on the west side might count only sightings of one heron species. As a result, there is no precise estimate of wading bird abundance.

The second of these draft indicators is more specific in terms of listing just one species of bird, but it still does not specify what constitutes a record of a fish eagle sighting. One biologist doing a baseline survey of eagle populations might count free-flying adults and come up with an average of eight birds per square kilometer. Another biologist who is resurveying the area a year later might count both adults and nesting chicks and come up with an average of 16 birds per square kilometer. It would therefore seem that the population has substantially increased, but in reality it has probably stayed about the same—each pair of adult birds just has two chicks. Finally, a third biologist who is resurveying the area three years later counts nesting pairs of birds and comes up with an average of four pairs per square kilometer. He might think the population had now dropped, but again in reality it has stayed the same. The preceding examples may seem a bit extreme, but it is clearly important for indicators to be carefully specified. Improved indicators for these examples might be:

Indicator 1. Numbers of green and blue heron nests per hectare of wetland habitat.

Indicator 2. Densities (nesting pairs/sq. km) of fish eagles in wetland habitat.

Yet another important criterion for an indicator is that it is consistent over time. If an indicator is going to provide a reliable measurement of change in a factor, then it is important that observed effects be due to changes in the actual condition, not to changes in the indicator. Note that this criterion generally applies only to *proxy indicators* as opposed to indicators that measure something directly.

For example, in the Tropical Forest Scenario, one potential objective might be:

> Consistent

Proxy indicators are used as a substitute for an indicator that cannot be directly measured or assessed. For example, in some cultures where people invest their income in cattle, the number of cattle that a household owns can serve as a proxy indicator for household wealth.

Draft Objective. By the end of the fifth year of the project, 10 percent of the families in the buffer zone receive an increase of 50 pesos per year from nontimber forest product (NTFP) harvesting and processing enterprises.

Two potential indicators that you could develop for this objective are:

> *Draft Indicator 1.* Percentage of families in project area earning income from NTFPs.

> *Draft Indicator 2.* Amount of income (in pesos) per household per year from NTFPs.

Let's assume that household cash needs are initially about 500 pesos per year. The project team goes out and measures income at the start of the project and finds that 2 percent of families in the project area receive income from harvesting NTFPs and that they get an average annual income of 50 pesos per family from this work. Five years later, the project team goes out and measures average annual NTFP income for the families in the project area and finds that now 12 percent of the families receive income from harvesting NTFPs and that they now get an average of 125 pesos per year from this work. It seems obvious that the project has been successful in meeting its objective of raising income by 50 pesos—indeed this objective has been exceeded by 25 pesos. Can you and the other project team members congratulate one another on a successful effort?

At first glance, you might think so. But wait. What if during this five-year time period the peso has been devalued by 200 percent and now only buys one-third as much as it did five years ago? In other words, what the community members could buy with 500 pesos now costs them 1500 pesos. In this case, even if household income has been raised by 75 pesos, the families are in reality getting proportionately less income from NTFPs than they were getting at the start of the project. Initially they could meet 10 percent of their annual cash needs (50 out of a total of 500 pesos needed), but now they can only meet 8.3 percent of their needs (125 out of a total of 1500 pesos needed) with their earnings from NTFPs.

This problem occurs because (strange though it may sound) pesos are not a consistent measure of income. Instead, as explained in the sidebar, you need to measure income in pesos that are standardized to one year. The project team could solve this problem by keeping the draft objective the same but changing the second indicator to:

> *Draft Indicator 2.* Amount of income (in 1996 pesos) per household per year from NTFPs.

Alternatively, the team could rephrase the objective and indicators to:

> *Objective 1.* By the end of the fifth year of the project, 10 percent of the families in the buffer zone cover 25 percent of their annual cash needs from NTFP harvesting and processing enterprises.

Process Hint: To compare absolute monetary values across two time periods it is necessary to adjust for inflation and devaluation of the currency. The easiest way to do this is to multiply all values by a price index to convert values in future years to a standard year. This index should generally be available from government agencies. Note that this conversion is only necessary for absolute values (net profits, gains in income) and not for relative values (the ratio of profits to sales or income to expenses).

Indicator 1. Percentage of families in project area (buffer zone) earning income from NTFPs.

Indicator 2. Amount (pesos/year) earned by households involved in the project from NTFPs.

Indicator 3. Annual cash needs per household.

In this case, the indicator no longer has to be in 1996 pesos since the objective is to cover 25 percent of family cash needs, which will automatically adjust with the devaluations of the currency. Here, however, the team will have to measure total household income need and income from NTFPs.

| Sensitive |
The final criterion for an indicator is that it is sensitive. A sensitive indicator will change proportionately and in the same direction as changes in the condition or item being measured. Similar to the consistency criterion, this criterion also only applies to proxy indicators where the effect is not being directly measured.

For instance, in the Savannah Scenario, the first objective states:

Objective 1. To provide 20 percent of the gross revenue from park entrance fees to the seven communities that surround Karimara National Park by the end of the third year of the project (disbursement to conservation and development committees provided on a per capita basis).

The project team might decide that although the main indicator for this objective will be the revenue provided to the local communities, it may also make sense to add an additional indicator that measures changes in overall household income. At this site, owing to the existence of a substantial noncash economy and cultural taboos, it is very difficult to measure household income directly. The project staff thus decide to use monthly household rice consumption as a proxy indicator for household income because, in this society, when people have extra cash they spend it on rice, which is considered a luxury good. The indicator that the project team proposes is:

Draft Indicator 1. Average per capita household rice consumption (kg/month).

The first graph below shows a case where, if we could actually know the true change in household income over time, rice consumption serves as a sensitive indicator in that as income rises, rice consumption increases proportionately.

Basically, rice consumption is a sensitive indicator as long as when households get more money, they continue to buy more rice. The next graph, however, shows a case where rice consumption increases with the amount of income received up to a point but then remains constant, as household members can only eat so much rice per month.

Process Hint: Although a given indicator should be consistent in what it measures over time, this does not mean that you have to keep the same indicator throughout the life of your project—if three years later you find an indicator is not sensitive, then you need to find a better one. The cost here, however, is that you may not have previous information on the new indicator.

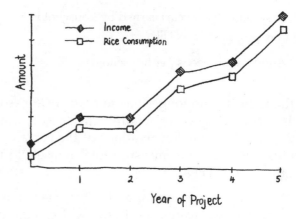

Rice Consumption as a Sensitive Indicator for Income

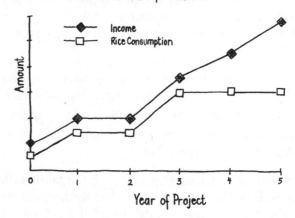

Rice Consumption as Non-Sensitive Indicator for Income

Once they no longer need to buy more rice, the household members then use their additional income to buy something else (perhaps tinned fish) and so rice is no longer a sensitive indicator. As a result, you need to monitor tinned fish consumption as well at this particular site or find another way of indirectly measuring income.

Place Information Needs, Monitoring Strategies, and Indicators in Monitoring Plan

Once you have developed your information needs, monitoring strategies, and indicators, it is helpful to put them in a table out-lining your monitoring plan as shown in the example that follows from the Savannah Scenario. Each information need should get its own page—write the goal, objective, or additional information need as shown in the example. Next, beneath this record the mon-

---

Goal, Objective, or Additional Information:

Objective 1. Demand for Cash: To provide 20% of the gross revenue from the park entrance fees to the 7 communities that surround Karimara National Park by the end of the project (disbursement to community conservation and development committees (CDCs) provided on per capita basis)

Monitoring Strategy: Measure the change over time in Park revenues flowing to the 7 communities receiving benefits.

WHAT (Indicators)	HOW (Methods and Tasks)	WHEN	WHO	WHERE	Comments
% of gross park revenues going to communities					

Activities for Objective 1.				Person Responsible for Monitoring the Activity	Target Date(s) for Obtaining Information

---

itoring strategy. Finally, in the open lines on the bottom, write the various indicators that you plan to measure.

Select Methods and Determine Tasks Necessary to Collect Data (Step C2)

Select a Range of Methods for Each Indicator

Once you have identified indicators for each information need, the next step is to select the *methods* that you will use to collect data to measure them. We will discuss details about a select group of methods that we feel are most useful for monitoring conservation and development projects in the next chapter. In this section, however, we will discuss some of the general principles that are involved in selecting methods to measure indicators.

There is usually a wide range of methods that can be used to collect data to assess a given indicator. In most cases you or the other people you are working with will have some degree of familiarity with the range of methods available. If, however, this is a completely new field to you, then you can learn about various methods by talking to experienced people, reviewing other field manuals and materials on the subject, taking courses, or scanning through the list of methods discussed in chapter 6.

As an example, in the Tropical Forest Scenario, two indicators that the project team is planning to measure to assess the goal are:

Indicator 1. Area (in hectares) of forest in the reserve core area.

Indicator 2. Density of rattan species (canes/hectare).

Process Hint: To clearly demonstrate the potential scope of methods, in these examples we have listed a wide range of methods. In your project it will probably be more obvious what methods are appropriate for your indicators and you may only need to consider a couple of methods.

To collect data on Indicator 1, the project ecologist has identified the following range of possible methods:

Potential Method 1. Work with community members to develop sketch maps of the forest habitat in the reserve.

Potential Method 2. Use a compass and tape measure to map various forest areas on existing topographic base maps.

Potential Method 3. Use a *Global Positioning System (GPS)* and aerial photography to collect coordinates of forest areas which will be entered into a computer-based *Geographic Information System (GIS).*

To collect data on Indicator 2, the project ecologist has identified another set of methods:

Potential Method 1. Use published rattan densities from the literature to estimate rattan densities in the forest at the site.

Potential Method 2. Monitor amounts of rattan collected by harvesters.

Potential Method 3. Use randomly positioned 5×500 meter transects in rattan habitats to sample rattan densities.

Potential Method 4. Count every rattan plant in the core area of the reserve.

In addition, to assess Objective 1 (which is related to income generation) the project team is planning to measure another indicator:

Indicator 1. Annual cash needs per household.

To collect data on this indicator the project enterprise coordinator has identified the following range of methods:

Potential Method 1. Estimate household cash needs based on purchases at stores.

Potential Method 2. Conduct systematic random household surveys of cash needs.

Potential Method 3. Interview all households in the region about their cash needs.

Select Appropriate Method According to the Criteria

Once you develop a range of methods, you need to select the specific ones that you will use. The criteria that you need to consider in selecting a method to measure a given indicator are:

Global Positioning System (GPS) receivers are hand-held devices that use signals from a network of satellites to automatically calculate precise geographic coordinates. Data from GPS receivers can be entered into a computerized *Geographic Information System (GIS).* A GIS generally refers to computerized maps that can store and display data in reference to geographic coordinates.

- *Accuracy and Reliability.* How much error exists in data collected by using the method? To what degree will results be repeatable?

- *Cost-Effectiveness.* What does the method require in terms of resource investment? Are there cheaper ways to get the same data?

- *Feasibility.* Does the project team have people who can use the method?

- *Appropriateness.* Does the method make sense in the context of the project? Is it culturally suitable?

The concepts behind these criteria for selecting a method are perhaps best explained by using a non–conservation and development project example. Consider a vendor at a marketplace who is trying to sell 10-kilogram bags of a certain fruit. The vendor has a number of different tools available for weighing the bags of fruit. These options include guessing at the weight by just putting fruits in bags, comparing the weight by holding the bag in one hand and a measured 10-kilogram bag in another, using a simple mechanical balance (scale with weights), and using a high-tech computerized balance. Her challenge is to select the appropriate method to use to weigh out the fruit.

| Accuracy and Reliability |

The first criterion that the vendor has to consider is how precise she needs her measurements of the bags of fruit to be. Precision has two components: accuracy and reliability.

Accuracy refers to the degree of *error* inherent in the measurement. For example, guessing at the weight of fruit in a bag will result in a fairly inaccurate measurement—it is not hard to imagine that the bags that the vendor fills up using this method could end up being somewhere between 7 and 13 (10 ± 3) kilograms. If she compares the weights to a standard by hand, she could end up with bags that weigh somewhere between 9 and 11 (10 ± 1) kilograms. Using the mechanical balance, the bags that she weighs might end up being somewhere between 9.5 and 10.5 (10 ± 0.5) kilograms. And finally, using the computerized balance, the final weights might end up being somewhere between 9.99 and 10.01 (10 ± 0.01) kilograms. Clearly some of the methods available are more accurate than others.

Reliability refers to the degree to which results obtained by using the method will be repeatable. For example, if the vendor fills the bags by estimating the weights, each bag will likely have a different amount of fruit in it. If she uses the computerized balance, however, it is far more likely that each bag will have the same amount of fruit in it. Reliability of a given method is, to some degree, related to its accuracy. However, if the method has a

Error refers to the uncertainty in a measurement made using a given method. In the case of the fruit seller, we have basically guessed what the error is for each method. Strictly speaking, however, error needs to be experimentally determined. To do so in this case, we would have to use each tool to repeatedly measure a known weight and then calculate the error from the measurements. This process is known as calibrating the method.

Bias refers to a tendency to produce results that are systematically lower or higher than the true value. In the fruit example, if the mechanical balance is slightly rusted or damaged, then using it may produce bags of fruit that are consistently biased toward being too light.

systematic *bias,* then it's possible for it to be reliable without being accurate.

Let's now look at the ranges of methods identified in the previous section for the Tropical Forest Scenario. Using rattan density data from the literature to estimate the rattan densities at the forest site is probably going to be less accurate than the other methods. On the other hand, counting every rattan plant is going to be very accurate (assuming that you could actually do it).

At first glance, estimating household cash needs based on purchases seems like it will be less accurate than interviewing all households in the region. However, when dealing with people as subjects, we always need to guard against the chance of bias in interview responses. Thus, as we will see, if people in a particular culture find it very offensive to be interviewed about their income or they are ashamed about their perceived poverty, they might actually give biased answers.

Cost - Effectiveness The second criterion that the vendor needs to consider is cost-effectiveness, the trade-off between how accurate and reliable she needs her measurement to be and how much money and other resources she has to spend on making the measurement. If the product that she is selling is very valuable (if for example, she was selling gold instead of fruit), then accuracy is important—both the vendor and her customers have a strong interest in making sure that the weights are precise. In this case the computerized balance may make sense, even if it is the most expensive. Furthermore, if the vendor is dealing in gold, she will also probably be able to afford the expensive computerized balance. If, however, she is selling ordinary fruit, then accuracy is less important. It is also unlikely that the vendor will have enough money to spend on the fancy computerized balance. But even if she had the money, it would not make sense to spend it on such a sophisticated balance. The mechanical balance or even the estimation process is sufficiently accurate and the vendor could use her savings to lower her prices for the fruit (thus charging less than her competitors) or to buy needed items for her household.

Looking at the range of methods proposed in our example from the Tropical Forest Scenario, there are clear differences in terms of cost and effectiveness. Working with community members to develop sketch maps of the forest or using a compass and line to map forest areas on existing topographic plots may produce less technically accurate maps, but they will also be relatively inexpensive. Using a GPS/GIS-based system, however, will produce very accurate maps in theory but will require massive financial investments in computer software and hardware, and more importantly, in staff time and energy.

Feasibility | The third criterion that the vendor needs to consider is the feasibility of using each method. A given method is only as effective as the person using it. If the vendor has no idea how to use the fancy computerized balance, then she could end up with a wildly inaccurate result, or not use it all, thus losing her investment. She would have been better off with simpler technology such as the mechanical balance, even though it is theoretically less accurate.

As a general rule in projects, it's best to try to keep methods as simple as possible. Reliance on complex methods will often impede a project from moving forward. For example, if a project plans to use a GPS/GIS system to map forest habitats, it is important that project staff know how to use and maintain all the equipment. Likewise, whether the project is conducting transects to measure rattan densities or household surveys to measure cash needs, it is important that the project team has someone who knows how to ensure that sampling is done correctly. If it is not done so, substantial error or unreliable measurements could result.

Appropriateness | The fourth criterion that the vendor needs to consider is the appropriateness of the method to the task. There are two kinds of appropriateness. The first is whether the method is the most effective one for the task at hand. For example, it is conceivable that the vendor could measure the bags by weighing each piece of fruit on a tiny mechanical scale and then add up the results to get 10 kilograms. If she were very careful, she could produce a measurement that was both accurate and reliable. Furthermore, assuming her salary is not that high, this method could be very cheap and could thus be considered cost-effective. Nonetheless, this is not a very appropriate method—it makes much more sense to consider one of the other ones.

The second type of appropriateness is related to environmental and cultural contexts. For instance, suppose the vendor is selling her wares from a boat moored in the village harbor. The harbor is often very wavy and this makes it difficult to use a mechanical balance. It therefore may make most sense to estimate the weights of the bags, even though this is a less accurate method.

The concept of appropriateness is a bit difficult to illustrate in the context of the vendor. But appropriateness is very important in considering monitoring methods to use in a project. For example, as mentioned earlier regarding the example from the Tropical Forest Scenario, it may be socially unacceptable in the communities in the project site to ask people directly about their income or financial status. In this case, estimating cash needs based on purchases at stores may be the best available method. Similarly, it may be impossible to use GPS monitors under a thick forest canopy or it may be inappropriate to use aerial photography because dense cloud cover at the site makes it hard to get pictures of the forest.

List Tasks for Each Method in the Monitoring Plan

Once you have decided on a method for measuring a particular indicator, enter it in the Monitoring Plan as shown in the example that follows from the Savannah Scenario. For each method you should list the tasks that need to be completed to collect data. *Tasks* are the specific actions that need to be undertaken to implement each method. They include planning for data collection, collecting data at different intervals, and following up as necessary.

In writing a list of tasks there is the usual tension between not showing enough detail and showing too much. If the members of your team are very familiar with the method, then you only need to list aggregated tasks. For instance, in the Savannah Scenario for an indicator looking at the "Number of hotel and tour operators disposing of sewage in compliance with accepted disposal plan," for which you will use the direct observation method, you might list:

Task 1. Inspect sewage disposal systems at hotels and tour sites.

If, however, your team is not very familiar with a method, it may be helpful to list more specific tasks. For example, the task in the above example could be subdivided into:

Task 1. Train park inspectors in sewage monitoring.

Task 2. Notify hotel and tour operators of proposed inspection timing, protocol, and objectives.

Task 3. Make inspections.

Task 4. Write reports and discuss with hotel owners and tour operators.

Task 5. Follow up with violations.

Goal, Objective, or Additional Information:

Objective 1. Demand for Cash: To provide 20% of gross revenue from the Park entrance fees to the 7 communities that surround Karimara National Park by the end of the third year of the project (disbursement to community conservation and Development Committees (CDCs) provided on per capita basis).
Monitoring Strategies: Measure the change over time in Park revenues flowing to the 7 communities receiving benefits.

WHAT (Indicators)	HOW (Methods and Tasks)	WHEN	WHO	WHERE	Comments
% of gross park revenues going to 7 communities	Review of Records - Determine gross revenue and disbursment to communities from National Park Service Records (NSPs) Key informants, interviewers - Interview CDC members				

Activities for Objective 1.			Person who is responsible for Monitoring Activity		Target Date (s) for Obtaining Information

This detailed list of tasks will hopefully enable your project team to know exactly what they have to do.

Determine When, by Whom, and Where Data Will Be Collected

Once you have identified the tasks involved in collecting data, you need to decide when, by whom, and where these data need to be collected. In figuring out these parts of the Monitoring Plan, it is important to be as specific as possible in listing dates, personnel, and places.

Decide When Data Will Be Collected

For each method it is necessary to determine the frequency and timing of data collection. The most commonly used monitoring strategies involve collecting data on the same indicator over time. So in these cases, at a minimum you will have to collect *baseline* and *final data* for each indicator to measure the success of your project. In many cases, however, you may wish to collect data on a more frequent basis.

Baseline data are collected at the beginning of a project. They provide a benchmark against which change that occurs during the project period can be assessed. *Final data*, as the name implies, are collected at the end of the project. They are used to assess the ultimate impact of the project.

As you might have guessed, it is an art and not a science to determine exactly how often data need to be collected. It depends not only on your internal and external audiences' needs but on the type of data you are collecting. As you are considering the timing of data collection, it is especially important to consider seasonality. For example, in a project looking at fruit harvesting, it makes sense to measure indicators of fruit availability only during the season in which the fruit is available—there is no point in monitoring fruit production when you know there will be no fruit on the trees. Likewise, there may be seasons in which it is difficult to do household surveys in a given village if, for instance, people are away from the village in remote farming camps during these periods or if the rainy season makes it impossible to travel to the village.

Decide by Whom Data Will Be Collected

Just as in the Management Plan where all tasks had to be assigned to a project team member, in the Monitoring Plan tasks also have to be assigned to the people who will be responsible for carrying them out. For each task it is necessary to determine who on your team is responsible for (1) directly collecting data and (2) overseeing data collection.

In assigning tasks it is important to make sure that team members have the necessary qualifications and training to undertake the tasks. You also need to make sure that the workload for any one individual is not too heavy. Monitoring can require extensive

Process Hint: Don't be surprised by the cost of monitoring—in many cases, it may require anywhere from 10 to 30 percent of your project budget.

resources, especially commitments of project team members' time. When faced with a multitude of tasks that need to be accomplished as well as time and budget constraints, it can be tempting to pull people away from monitoring or assign the work to less qualified team members. We trust that by now, however, you understand how important it is to invest in monitoring. Without this investment, you'll never be able to get the information you need to assess your project's success or make necessary adaptations to your project's Management Plan.

Decide Where Data Will Be Collected

Finally, for each monitoring task you need to determine where the task will be carried out. It is hard to give general rules for determining where you should be monitoring—these decisions are method and site specific. When you are deciding where to undertake these tasks, you need to be as specific as possible. For instance, it is better to say that surveys will be conducted in a "sample of 30 households in Orosus Village" as opposed to just saying "in villages."

Complete List of When, by Whom, and Where Data Will Be Collected for Each Task

Once you have determined when, by whom, and where data will be collected, enter this information in the relevant boxes in the Monitoring Plan for each task. It may also be helpful to use the

---

Goal, Objective or Additional Information:

Objective 1. Demand for Cash: To provide 20% of the gross revenue from entrance fees to the 7 communities that surround Karimara National Park by the end of third year of the project (disbursement to community conservation and development commetees (CDC's) provided per capita basis.)

Monitoring Strategy: Measure the change over time in Park revenues flowing to the 7 communities receiving benefits.

WHAT (Indicators)	HOW (Methods and Tasks)	WHEN	WHO	WHERE	Comments
% of gross revenue going to 7 communities	Review the records: -Determine gross revenue and dispursement to communities in National Park Service (NSP) records.	Every 6 months	Project Assistant	Village Governments	
	Key informant Interviews - Interview CDC members	Every 6 months	Project Assistant	Park Headquarters	

Activties for Objective 1. | **Person Responsible for Monitoring the Activity** | **Target Date(s) for Obtaining the Information**

Activity 1: Produce revenue sharing accord. — Project Coordinator — By the end of first year of project
Activity 2: Conduct community meetings to explain benefits. — Project Coordinator — Every 6 months in 1st 2nd years of project
Activity 3: Organize Conservation and Development Commitees. — Project Coordinator — At end of 2nd year and 3rd years of project
Activity 4: Establish community bank accounts — Project Coordinator — At end of 2nd year and 3rd years of project
Activity 5: Develop revenue sharing plan — Project Coordinator — At end of 2nd year and 3rd years of project

"comments" column to list any explanations necessary for all members of the team to understand what the plan entails.

As was the case for your Management Plan in the previous chapter, once the plan is completed, you should develop timelines and budgets for your monitoring work. These should be constructed in a similar fashion to the ones described earlier for the Management Plan.

Process Hint: See the scenarios in Appendix A for examples of timelines for monitoring plans.

Develop a Monitoring Plan for Project Activities

In the preceding three steps, we've primarily focused on developing a monitoring plan for collecting data related to your project goals and objectives to measure the impacts of your project activities. This type of monitoring (impact assessment) is critical because meeting your project's goals and objectives are ultimately what the project is all about. However, it's also important to track your progress in accomplishing your project activities (process assessment). You need to monitor activities to ensure that they are getting done—if they are not, then there's little chance that you will be able to have the impact that you desire in terms of reaching your project goals and objectives.

Assessing whether an activity has been completed is generally easier than monitoring a goal, objective, or additional information need indicator. In most cases it merely involves developing a checklist for recording when activities are completed. On the bottom of the Monitoring Plan for objectives you will see a space to list your project activities as outlined in your Management Plan. For each activity, list the person responsible for making sure the activity is completed and the target date(s) for acquiring information confirming the completion of the activity. Be as specific as possible. The column "person responsible" does not refer to the person actually doing the activity but to the person responsible for verifying that it gets done. This list should also be reviewed by the project manager on a periodic basis.

Sources and Further Readings

The following references can be used to obtain information about monitoring:

ACVAFS (1983). *Evaluation Sourcebook for Private and Voluntary Organizations.* American Council of Voluntary Agencies for Foreign Service, New York, New York. A general resource for monitoring work.

Buzzard, Shirley, and Elaine Edgcomb, eds. (1992). *Monitoring and Evaluating Small Business Projects: A Step by Step Guide for Private Development Organizations.* PACT, Washington, D.C. A general overview of the monitoring and evaluation process focused on small businesses.

Kosecoff, Jacqueline, and Arlene Fink (1982). *Evaluation Basics: A Practi-*

tioner's Manual. Sage Publications, Beverly Hills, California. A good overview of monitoring and evaluation.

Rossi, Peter H., and Howard E. Freeman. (1993). *Evaluation: A Systematic Approach*. Sage Publications, Newbury Park, California. A textbook that provides extensive detail about the evaluation process by two gurus of the evaluation field.

Rugh, Jim (1992). *Self-Evaluation: Ideas for Participatory Evaluation of Rural Community Development Projects*. World Neighbors, Inc., Oklahoma City, Oklahoma. A general overview of the evaluation process.

Theis, Joachim, and Heather M. Grady (1991). *Participatory Rapid Appraisal for Community Development: A Training Manual Based on Experiences in the Middle East and North Africa*. International Institute for Environment and Development, London, United Kingdom. Although written as a training guide, this is one of the best basic references on using Participatory Rural Appraisal techniques for monitoring.

U.S. Environmental Protection Agency (1994). *Volunteer Estuary Monitoring: A Methods Manual*. U.S. Environmental Protection Agency, Office of Water, Oceans and Coastal Protection Division, Washington, D.C. A user-friendly overview of the monitoring process focused on wetland areas.

Weiss, Carol H. (1972). *Evaluation Research: Methods of Assessing Program Effectiveness*. Prentice-Hall, Englewood Cliffs, New Jersey. An excellent, clearly written primer on program evaluation.

Chapter 6
Implement Management and Monitoring Plans

Until now, we have been going through a step-by-step process designed to help you develop a complete Project Plan, including a Project Conceptual Model, Management Plan, and Monitoring Plan. The next step is to implement these plans. From this point forward, however, it becomes more difficult for us to describe a specific process that you'll need to follow. Instead, in this and the next chapter, we provide reference materials to assist you in determining how to implement your project and deciding what tools and techniques are best suited for your particular project and how best to apply them.

Using the information presented in this chapter, you should be able to:

• Implement your Management Plan (Step D1).
• Implement your Monitoring Plan (Step D2).

Implement Your Management Plan (Step D1)

Putting Your Plan into Action

Implementing your Management Plan is probably the single most important step in the entire project cycle. You may have developed the best plan in the world, but unless you follow through and put it into action, you will have no hope of achieving your project's goals and objectives. At the same time, however, there is very little advice that we can give you about implementing this except for:

If you start to feel overwhelmed and think that you will not be able to accomplish your project goals and objectives, don't worry. Trust your plan, trust your colleagues and partners, and trust your instincts. Your plan may not be perfect—plans never are—but the whole point of the process outlined in this guide is to help you learn from your successes and failures. The only way you can move forward is to put your plan into action and then monitor the results.

Common Project Assumptions in Conservation and Development Projects

Although you should not hesitate to implement your Management Plan, you should also never forget the project assumptions inherent in it. By formally stating and testing your assumptions, you will be better able to measure the impacts of your project's activities and adapt them to ensure that they are having the desired impact.

To get you started in this process of stating and testing assumptions we present a few of the most common assumptions inherent in conservation and development projects. These are:

- Systematic organizational adaptation and learning through careful project design, management, and monitoring will lead to conservation success.

- Income generation from small-scale commercial natural resource-based enterprises will lead to conservation success.

- Environmental education will influence people to act to conserve natural resources.

- Control and ownership of natural resources by local stake holders will lead to a greater chance of conservation success.

- Strict policing and enforcement of conservation legislation will bring about conservation.

- Intensification of agriculture through the use of sustainable agricultural practices will lead to the conservation of biodiversity.

- Training of conservation project personnel will lead to greater conservation.

These assumptions are drawn from the projects illustrated in the four scenarios presented in this guide. However, they are by no means a complete list of all possible assumptions. For each assumption, we illustrate how it might be represented in your Conceptual Model, describe the chain of cause and effect in general terms, show an example from our scenarios, and examine particular questions that may be raised by the assumption that may need to considered.

Systematic Organizational Adaptation and Learning Through Careful Project Design, Management, and Monitoring Will Lead to Conservation Success

General Description of the Assumption

In keeping with our own rule about making assumptions explicit, we have chosen to start off by examining one of the major assumptions underlying *Measures of Success*. This assumption is that by following a systematic approach to designing, managing, and monitoring conservation projects, implementing groups can more effectively test assumptions and determine the extent to which their activities are reaching stated goals and objectives (adaptive management). By following this approach, individuals and organizations can learn about successes and failures and can apply these lessons to future conservation activities. Incorporating these learnings into these future project activities will lead to a greater likelihood of future conservation success.

Example of Assumption from the Scenarios

The Project Conceptual Models for each of the four scenarios in appendix A set the stage for designing effective projects based on

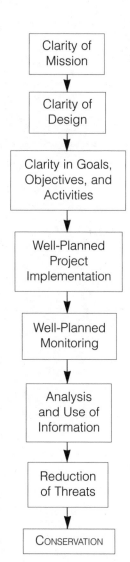

local site conditions. The scenarios also provide examples of sound Management and Monitoring Plans that will ensure the effective implementation and tracking of project activities. Of course, we'll have to wait and see just how well the field team and community members do in implementing their projects.

Questions Raised by the Assumption

- How do institutions learn from their successes and failures and apply these lessons to future activities?

- Is an adaptive approach to project design, management, and monitoring the best approach to take? If not, what is?

- Are good project design, management, and monitoring necessary and sufficient to reach conservation objectives?

- Is this level of structure in this process necessary to objectively and accurately measure and document impact?

- Is this approach cost-effective?

Income Generation from Small-Scale Commercial Natural Resource–Based Enterprises Will Lead to Conservation Success

General Description of the Assumption

At present, one of the most popular forms of simultaneously promoting conservation and community development objectives is through the support of community-based commercial enterprises based on the sustainable use of natural resources. Activities that fall into this category include ecotourism, nontimber forest product (NTFP) gathering, processing and marketing, and community-based selective logging. Promotion of these types of activities is grounded in the underlying assumption that by providing sustainable nature-based employment alternatives to community residents, they will use the cash they earn to buy needed goods and services (such as food, clothing, and health services) which will improve their standard of living. Most importantly, once residents see that the ecosystem-linked activities provide cash, they will value the natural resource base more and will act to protect it.

Example of Assumption from the Scenarios

In the Tropical Forest Scenario, community-based resin and bamboo enterprises will increase family income by at least 25 percent for those harvesters involved in the enterprise activities. This increase will directly benefit residents by providing them greater access to goods and services which will, in turn, influence residents to place a higher value on natural resources. Once residents see the importance of maintaining the natural resources found around their community, they will act to conserve them and counter identified threats.

Questions Raised by the Assumption

- Who benefits from nature-based income-generating activities? Who benefits within the household? Within the community? Within the region?

- Is the amount of cash income that is generated from nature-based enterprises sufficient to provide significantly more access to goods and services than already occurs?

- Does more cash at the household level mean that people will spend it on goods and services that will improve their standard of living, or will they spend it on other things that may not fit with conservation?

- Just how much additional income is required to increase a family's standard of living? Can the activity produce this threshold amount?

- Does the nature-based commercial activity take participants away from other nonnature-based income-generating activities?

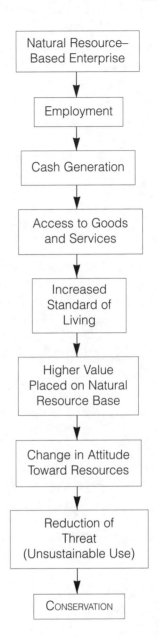

- Does involvement in such activities change residents' attitudes toward nature? Does it cause them to take action to conserve biodiversity?

- Does this type of activity act as an economic "magnet" that attracts more people to an area?

Environmental Education Will Influence People to Act to Conserve Natural Resources

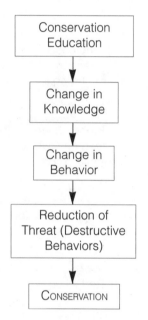

General Description of the Assumption

This assumption is that by educating people on a given conservation-related topic by either formal or nonformal means, a change will occur in their knowledge which will lead to a change in behavior so that they act to conserve natural resources.

Example of Assumption from the Scenarios

In the Wetlands Scenario, community outreach sessions that are held in towns throughout the Everson Watershed to explain the importance of and threats to the habitats in the area will lead to a greater understanding among community residents of the importance of the watershed and, thus, will prompt them to act to conserve it.

Questions Raised by the Assumption

- Do conservation education activities cause a change in knowledge? How do we know?

- To what extent is the success of conservation education based on its connection to other conservation activities?

- Is a change in knowledge about some conservation issue sufficient to promote a change in behavior?

Control and Ownership of Natural Resources by Local Stakeholders Will Lead to Improved Conservation Success

General Description of the Assumption

This assumption is that stakeholders who have control over or ownership of natural resources will see that it is in their best interest to save those resources for their own future use. This perceived need to protect resources will lead to enhanced stewardship of natural resources and thus biodiversity conservation.

Example of Assumption from the Scenarios

In the Coastal Scenario, community residents are fully responsible for the design, management, and monitoring of all project activities. Through the Bocoro Bay conservation project, community residents are gaining increasing control over the use of marine and coastal resources and they recognize the importance of maintaining these resources for future generations. Conservation of these resources is ensured as the community is willing to take action to develop lasting self-policing and sustainable use strategies.

Questions Raised by the Assumption

- What are the conditions under which increased local control over natural resources leads to sustainable conservation?

- How are local resource needs reconciled with conservation needs?

- Does complete control over and access to natural resources by local populations necessarily lead to conservation?

- Who must participate in the design, management, and monitoring of conservation activities for the project to be successful?

- Can participation by some stakeholders work against conservation?

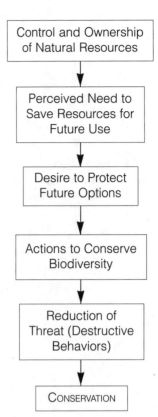

Strict Policing and Enforcement of Conservation Legislation Will Bring About Conservation

General Description of the Assumption

This assumption holds that enacting and enforcing (for example, through guarding or fencing of protected areas or levying fines) strict legislation that is protective of biodiversity will prevent people from destroying natural resources and thus will lead to its long-term conservation.

Example of Assumption from the Scenarios

In the Savannah Scenario, National Park Service guards work with communities to uphold legislation regulating hunting within Karimara National Park. Enforcement of hunting restrictions in and outside of the park will prevent illegal poaching and thus lead to enhanced biodiversity security.

Questions Raised by the Assumption

- How effective is enforcement in conservation success compared to other activities?

- In some countries where law enforcement staff is limited or where there is extensive corruption, is it possible to actively protect natural resources from being destroyed?

- What are the potential outcomes of attempts by enforcement agencies to force people to do or not do certain things?

- Is it cost-effective to invest in enforcement activities?

Intensification of Agriculture Through Sustainable Agricultural Practices Will Lead to the Conservation of Biodiversity

General Description of the Assumption

Intensification of subsistence agriculture increases household crop production and thus provides greater food security and economic resources to the household. This approach reduces the total

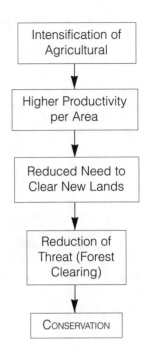

Intensification of
Agricultural

↓

Higher Productivity
per Area

↓

Reduced Need to
Clear New Lands

↓

Reduction of
Threat (Forest
Clearing)

↓

CONSERVATION

amount of family labor required to produce a unit of food and serves to increase the family's standard of living. Increased production per hectare of land reduces farmers' needs to clear new crop lands and thus drives them to shift from traditional swidden agricultural practices to permanent plots. This in turn leads to diminishing pressure on natural areas and works to conserve biodiversity.

Example of Assumption from the Scenarios

In the Tropical Forest Scenario, project activities that teach local farmers about soil erosion control, intercropping, and integrated pest management will increase crop production per hectare. Initial investment of labor in permanent plots and the increase in production levels will decrease the need to clear more primary forest from the Indah Biosphere Reserve.

Questions Raised by the Assumption

- To what extent does the intensification of household-level agriculture produce greater output?

- Is the added output from intensification sufficient to decrease the demand for more land?

- Will increased productivity per unit of land act to prompt people to grab more land to increase their wealth?

- What role does family size and increasing population play in agricultural encroachment and expansion?

Training of Conservation Project Personnel Will Lead to Greater Conservation

General Description of the Assumption

This assumption is that training of personnel promotes a better understanding of conservation issues and leads to greater capacity to plan and manage projects. This increase in knowledge and

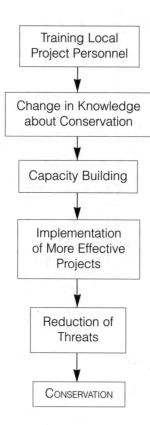

skills, and the resulting increased capacity, will lead to enhanced staff performance and thus improved conservation.

Example of Assumption from the Scenarios

In the Wetlands Scenario, local NGO chapter staff are trained in monitoring the habitats in their areas. This training provides these on-site personnel with the enhanced capacity necessary to identify potential threats to the wetland habitats and take appropriate actions.

Questions Raised by the Assumption

- How much training needs to be done to accomplish conservation objectives?
- How is the best type of training determined?
- Are the right people included in the training?
- Are there people qualified to do the training?
- Is training cost-effective?

Implement Your Monitoring Plan (Step D2)

While you are implementing your Management Plan, you also have to implement your Monitoring Plan. Unlike the previous section on implementing your Management Plan, where there was not much guidance that we could provide, there is a lot to discuss in this section. We first provide a more in-depth discussion of three aspects of your monitoring plan that were briefly covered in the previous chapter: designing your monitoring strategy, selecting the specific units to monitor, and selecting the appropriate method. We also then discuss implementing this plan, including preparing for field work and collecting, storing, and handling data.

Designing Your Monitoring Strategy

Monitoring enables you to do an *impact assessment* of your project's interventions—to determine whether you have achieved your goals and objectives and what you need to do to improve the project. The core of an impact assessment lies in developing a monitoring strategy for each information need. In the previous chapter, although we discussed the importance of developing these strategies, we didn't really give you any guidance as to how you should go about doing so. So now we would like to revisit this concept.

In order to be able to measure the impact of each of your project interventions, you need to be able to compare the results of your project interventions to some benchmark. These comparisons involve *groups* of individual monitoring *units* that are drawn from a defined *population*. There are basically two types of comparisons that you can make in monitoring projects:

- *Comparing a Group Affected by Your Project to Itself Over Time.* This comparison involves measuring how a given factor changes as a result of project activities. This type of comparison does not necessarily establish causal relationships.

- *Comparing a Group Affected by Your Project to a Group Not Affected by Your Project Over Time.* This comparison involves measuring how a given factor changes in a group affected by the project relative to a similar group that is not influenced by the project. This type of comparison can help establish causal relationships.

Within each of these two categories, you can make comparisons that are simple and comparisons that are more complex. As you might expect, the more complex comparisons can—if done correctly—give you more accurate information about the success of your project. Unfortunately, the more complex comparisons also tend to be more difficult and expensive to implement. As a result, you need to select a monitoring design that balances the accuracy of the information that you will obtain against the feasibility of using the design and the amount of resources it will take to carry it out.

Comparing a Group Affected by Your Project to Itself Over Time

There are two main ways in which you can make this comparison: (1) pre-test/post-test monitoring design and (2) time-series monitoring design.

Pre-Test/Post-Test Monitoring Design

The simplest way to make this comparison is to use a same group *pre-test/post-test* monitoring design. The pre-test/post-test design

A *unit* is a single item or individual that you are interested in observing. Depending on the type of monitoring that you are doing, units can be such things as a community, a household, a person, a garden plot, or a tree.

The collection of all units that you could potentially observe is called a *population*. All units in a population must share at least one characteristic—for example, households in a community, rattan collectors, trees of a certain species.

A *group* is a specific subset of the population that you choose to consider in your monitoring efforts—for example, households participating in a project, rattan collectors not participating in the project. Groups can be selected in different ways depending on the monitoring strategy that you are using.

involves measuring your group of units before your intervention to establish a baseline, implementing your intervention, and then remeasuring the group to see how it has changed as part of a follow-up. This process is illustrated in the following drawing:

Group Influenced by the project : T_1 --------⊗-------T_2

T_1 = The time when baseline data are collected
T_2 = The time when follow up data are collected
⊗ = Implementation of project activity

This design is relatively straightforward to understand—you are merely looking at how things have changed over time as a result of your project.

In this example, the monitoring unit is a household and the population is composed of all households in the village during a given assessment period.

Process Hint: See the description of paired t-tests in chapter 7 for a discussion of how to analyze data from this type of comparison.

Example: Pre-Test/Post-Test Monitoring Design

This example is drawn from the Coastal Scenario.

One of the project's objectives is:

Objective 3a. By the end of two years, all households will use one-third less mangrove firewood (measured by weight) than they did at the start of the project.

To meet this objective, the project team will work with residents of the village to develop improved cooking stoves. The team develops a monitoring strategy in which they will:

Monitoring Strategy: Compare the amount of mangrove wood used by households at the start of the project to the amount of mangrove wood used at the end of the project.

To implement this strategy, the team plans to conduct a household survey to measure the average kilograms of mangrove wood used by households in the first year of the project to establish the baseline measurement and then plans to do a similar survey of the same group of households in the second year of the project as the follow-up measurement.

Time-Series Monitoring Design

A more complex way of comparing a group of units to itself over time is with a *time-series* monitoring design. As illustrated in the following drawing, a time-series design involves collecting data multiple times before and after your project intervention:

Group influenced by project: T_1----T_2--T_3--⊗--∹--T_4--T_5--T_6
T_1 - T_6 = Times when monitoring data collected.
⊗ = Implementation of project activity.

It can also involve collecting data around a series of interventions as shown in the following:

Group influenced by project T_1- ⊗-T_2---⊗--T_3--⊗---T_4

T_1 - T_4 = Times when monitoring data are collected.
⊗ = Implementation of project activity.
|--+--| Continuous or periodic implementation of project activities.

The choice of whether you should use a pre-test/post-test or a time-series monitoring design is largely a function of the type of data you have, how accurate you need the results to be, and how much time and money you have to spend on monitoring. Because it tracks trends, the time-series monitoring design can provide more reliable results than the pre-test/post-test monitoring design. The time-series design is also more expensive, however, since it requires collecting and analyzing greater amounts of data.

Example: Time-Series Monitoring Design

This example is drawn from the Coastal Scenario.

Another objective of the project is:

Objective 1d. By the end of the third year, for snappers, groupers, and conch there are no incidences of harvesting in violation of size limits as defined by the community council for each species.

To meet this objective, the project team will work with community members to decide on minimum size limits for each species and produce measuring devices for the fishermen and women to use. The team will also get the elders of the village to inspect boats coming into the village in the evening. The team develops a monitoring strategy in which they will:

Monitoring Strategy: Compare the number of undersize snappers, groupers, and conch in boatloads of fish brought to shore over time.

To implement this strategy, the team plans to record the number of undersized fish in boatloads of fish brought in on a daily basis.

In this example, the monitoring unit is a fish and the population consists of all fish brought into the village during a given assessment period.

Process Hint: See the description of chi-squared tests in chapter 7 for a discussion of how to analyze data from this type of comparison.

Comparing a Group Affected by Your Project to a Group Not Affected by Your Project Over Time

Although the monitoring designs comparing your project to itself can be very useful, they have a key weakness in that they do not enable you to determine *cause and effect*. In either the pre-test/post-test or time-series monitoring designs, if you observe a

Cause and effect refers to the extent to which one factor influences another.

change in an indicator over time, you can't know for sure if your interventions or some other event caused this change or whether it occurred on its own by chance. To solve this problem, the second way of assessing the impact of your project involves comparing two groups of units, one of which is influenced by your project activities and the other of which is not. By examining changes in the indicator between the two groups, you can tell whether or not your activities have made a difference. Here again, there are two main ways in which you can make this comparison: (1) strict-control monitoring design and (2) comparison-group monitoring design.

Strict–Control Monitoring Design

The most complex and rigorous way to make this comparison is by setting up *strict controls*. A strict-control design, also referred to as "experimental design," involves taking all units in the population and randomly dividing them into two groups. Individuals in the **treatment group** will be subject to the project intervention, whereas individuals in the **control group** will not. The monitoring involves comparing the treatment group with the control group to determine whether the project had an effect, as shown in the following drawing:

Group influenced by project (treatment): T_1 - - - - ⊗ - - - - - T_2

Group not influenced by project (control): T_1 - - - - - - - - - - - T_2

T_1 = The time when data are collected.
T_2 = The time when follow-up data collected.
⊗ = Implementation of project activity.

To do a true strict-control monitoring design, you must plan your project interventions (your Management Plan) to fit within your monitoring design. In effect, you can only implement project activities with the treatment group. Furthermore, you cannot change your project's activities midway through the experiment—even if it seems that they are not having the desired result. You must wait until the end of the monitoring period (at T_2) before making any changes so as not to confound the experiment.

The advantage of doing a strict-control monitoring design is that (at least in theory) it can give you a very accurate assessment of what the extent of the impact of your project intervention has been—it enables you to determine true cause-and-effect relationships. This advantage is usually outweighed, however, by a number of ethical and practical disadvantages to using a strict-control monitoring design. In particular, if your monitoring units involve people or communities, there can be problems in assigning some people to the treatment group and others to the control group. Projects can greatly affect people's lives and it is often neither ethical

A **treatment group** is composed of randomly selected units that have been subjected to project activities.

A **control group** is composed of randomly selected units that have not been subject to project activities.

Because of the theoretical accuracy of strict-control experiments, this technique is often used to evaluate the results of medical treatments.

nor feasible to direct project activities toward the treatment group and withhold them from the control group.

Example: Strict Control Monitoring Design

This example is drawn from the Wetlands Scenario.

One of the project's objectives is:

> *Objective 2.* Within 10 years, levels of inorganic pesticides in water and wildlife in the Everson Watershed are reduced by 75 percent.

To meet this objective, the project team will work with farmers in the watershed to reduce or eliminate pesticide use. Because the team is unsure of whether this approach will work, they decided to initially experiment using a strict-control monitoring design. They develop a monitoring strategy in which they will:

> *Monitoring Strategy:* Compare tributary stream watersheds in the overall Everson Watershed.

To implement this strategy, the team makes a list of the 24 tributary streams in the Everson Watershed. They then randomly assign 12 stream watersheds to the treatment group and 12 to the control group. The team will implement the project activities in the watersheds in the treatment group and will do nothing in the watersheds in the control group. The team will then monitor the levels of pesticides in animal tissues and in water and sediment samples in both the treatment and control watersheds every year for five years.

In this example, the monitoring unit is a tributary stream watershed and the population is composed of the 24 tributary watersheds in the overall Everson Watershed.

Process Hint: See the description of two-sample t-tests in chapter 7 for a discussion of how to analyze data from this type of comparison.

Comparison-Group Monitoring Design

Although a strict-control design for impact assessment is usually not feasible for conservation and development projects, there are similar and yet less restrictive monitoring designs that can be used to compare groups affected by the project to those not affected. Perhaps the next best option is using *comparison groups*. Here, instead of forming randomized treatment and control groups, a group of units is deliberately selected and "matched" to the treatment group influenced by the project (which in this case does not have to be randomly selected). The monitoring involves comparing the treatment group with the comparison group to determine whether the project had an effect as shown in the following drawing:

Group influenced by project (treatment): T_1 ---- ⊗ ---- T_2

Group not influenced by project (comparison) T_1 ---------- T_2

T_1 = The time when baseline monitoring data are collected.
T_2 = The time when follow-up monitoring data are collected
⊗ = Implementation of project activity.

Process Hint: Most of the examples in the scenarios presented in *Measures of Success* use either pre-test/post-test or time-series monitoring designs since they are generally most appropriate for monitoring conservation and development projects. The control and comparison group designs are generally only used in cases where documenting cause and effect is of particular importance.

In this example, the monitoring units are individual residents and politicians and the population is composed of all residents and all politicians in the Everson Watershed.

Process Hint: See the description of two-sample t-tests in chapter 7 for a discussion of how to analyze data from this type of comparison.

In the comparison group design, you cannot be absolutely sure that if the politicians show improvements in their knowledge relative to the comparison group, that this is due to your intervention. It might occur because the politicians in your treatment group are naturally more interested in environmental issues.

The comparison-group design does not fulfill the strict requirements of true experimentation and thus cannot be used to determine true cause-and-effect relationships. It can, however, provide good indications of what the effects of your project have been. Furthermore, the comparison group design is both ethically and practically easier to implement in the context of monitoring conservation and development projects.

Example: Comparison Group Monitoring Design

This example is drawn from the Wetlands Scenario.

Another objective of the project is:

> *Objective 4.* Within three years, 15 percent of the community members and 45 percent of relevant government officials in the Everson Watershed have knowledge about the importance of and threats to upstream forest areas that support wetland habitats.

To meet this objective, the project team will hold a series of community outreach sessions with the general public and a series of meetings with town councils. The team develops a monitoring strategy in which they will:

> *Monitoring Strategy:* Compare the knowledge of people in the watershed who have attended the sessions with the knowledge of people who haven't.

In reviewing the knowledge of community members, the team decides to do a strict-control monitoring design by sampling 100 community members and randomly assigning half of them to 5 treatment groups of 10 people each who attend a session in which information about the watershed is presented and the other half of them to 5 control groups that attend a presentation about astronomy. Both the treatment and control groups are then tested before and after the presentation to see how their knowledge about the environment has changed.

In looking at the knowledge of the politicians, however, the team decides that they cannot afford to pass up a chance to influence the relevant politicians on the town zoning boards—that it would be a lost opportunity to put half of them in control groups. As a result, the team decides to do a comparison-group monitoring design. All of the relevant politicians are placed in treatment groups and asked to attend the information sessions. The team matches the targeted politicians with comparison groups of other politicians in the watershed who serve on boards that do not deal with environmental issues and who do not attend the information sessions. Both the treatment and comparison groups are then tested to see how their knowledge has changed.

Selecting the Specific Individuals to Monitor

Once you have determined your monitoring strategy, you still need to decide which specific individuals (units) in the population you will use to collect data. There are basically two ways in which you can select these individuals:

- *Censusing.* This involves counting all individuals in the population.

- *Sampling.* This involves measuring a subset of individuals in the population.

Censusing

In some projects, you can easily monitor all the individuals in a population. For instance, if you are interested in using a formal survey to monitor change in household income for a village of 18 households, it probably will be fairly easy to collect data for all the households. Likewise, if you are interested in measuring the number of fruit trees in a small agroforestry plot, you can count all the trees in the plot. When you measure all of the units in a given population, this is called a *census*. Using a census has the inherent advantage that you know your monitoring data will adequately represent the entire population since you have collected data for all individuals.

> ### Example: Censusing
>
> This example is drawn from the Wetlands Scenario.
>
> One of the project objectives is:
>
> > *Objective 1:* Within five years, 80 percent of identified privately owned priority wetland and adjacent natural habitat areas have been legally protected against conversion.
>
> To monitor this objective, the project team will make a list of all the priority areas and then census them on an annual basis to see which ones have been protected.

Sampling

Suppose, however, that in the previous examples, the populations that you are interested in monitoring are much larger—perhaps you want to know about income changes in 20 villages that each have about 100 households. Or say that you are interested in knowing how many trees of a certain species are in a 500,000 hectare forest. In both of these cases, given enough time and money, you could conceivably survey every household about their income or count the number of trees of a particular species in every hectare of the forest. But why would you want to? Is it necessary?

Doing all this counting would be a waste of time and money. Instead, it is far better to try to identify and measure a subgroup of households within the villages or a few hectares of forest that you think will represent the whole population. This subgroup is known as a *sample* and the procedure involved in selecting this group is called *sampling*. If your sample is truly representative of your population, then you can monitor the indicator that you are interested in the sample and **extrapolate** the results to the broader population.

The main advantages of sampling over censusing lie in the reduced cost and greater speed of measurement made possible by collecting data on a subset of individuals rather than on an entire population. In many cases, it may not be possible to conduct a census—sampling will be the only choice that you have. For example, in the Wetlands Scenario, you will not be able to test every drop of water in the Everson River for pollutants. Instead, at best you will only be able to test selected samples. The disadvantage of sampling is that it requires using **statistics** to determine to what extent your sample data represent the population. There are three main considerations in selecting a sample.

The first consideration is the size of the sample that you choose. Generally speaking, the larger your sample size, or in other words, the closer it approaches the total population size, the more likely it is that your results from the sample will truly apply to the overall population. As a rule, as the variance of your sample increases, the size of your sample should increase.

The second consideration is what sampling frame you will use to select the sample that will be interviewed, studied, or measured. A sampling frame is a description of the set of all the possible individuals that you could sample. For example, if you are interested in interviewing 20 percent of the households in a village, your sampling frame might consist of all the households in the village. If you are interested in measuring the density of a certain tree species in a forest, your sampling frame might consist of all the possible plots in a defined forest area that you could measure. Ideally, your sampling frame will describe your population either as specific units (each household in the village) or in general terms (the boundaries of the forest that you will study).

The third consideration is how you select your sample. A sample must be selected in a way that ensures that it adequately represents the larger population from which it was drawn and avoids any bias. There are two basic ways of selecting samples: (1) probability sampling and (2) nonprobability sampling.

To **extrapolate** is to take the results from a sample and apply them proportionately to the overall population.

Statistics is the science of analyzing data drawn from samples to make inferences about populations. See chapter 7 for a broader discussion of statistical techniques.

Process Hint: There are a number of technical procedures you can follow to calculate what sample size you collect given the parameters of your population and the types of questions you are interested in asking. Consult any good statistics book for details about making these calculations.

Probability Sampling

Probability sampling is associated with quantitative data collection and analysis. In this type of sampling every individual in the population has an equal chance of being selected for the sample. Two of the most commonly used types of probability sampling are *simple random sampling* and *stratified random sampling*.

In simple random sampling the group of individuals is selected randomly from a list of the population. Stratified random sampling is similar, except the population is first divided into different subgroups, or *strata*, based on some characteristic (such as age, sex, tribal group in a household survey, or habitat type in a botanical survey) and then a random sample is selected within each stratum.

An advantage of the stratified approach is that you get a more accurate representation of the different subgroups within the population as you are assured an adequate sample with which to do your analysis. The cost, however, is that you have to have sufficient information about the population at the start of the monitoring to accurately assign all members to the appropriate strata.

In determining whether to use stratified sampling, you need to pay particular attention to how you define the individual unit you will be sampling. For example, as shown in the first of the following diagrams, if you are interested in determining the density of a

Process Hint: Although probability sampling is always used with strict-control monitoring designs, it can also be used with pre-test/post-test and time-series designs.

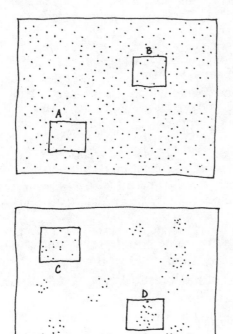

tree species that is randomly distributed in a forest, you can use randomly chosen one-hectare plots as your sample unit. Each plot will contain roughly the same number of trees and so simple random sampling will be fine. If, however, as shown in the second diagram, the trees are not randomly distributed and are instead clumped (perhaps because the trees only grow in abandoned farm sites), then you could potentially bias your sample by using random plots as your sampling frame. In this case, you might want to stratify the area into old farm and nonfarm sites.

Examples: Simple and Stratified Random Sampling

These examples are drawn from the Coastal Scenario.

One objective for the project involves promoting family planning efforts. The team plans to use a formal survey in a pre-test/post-test monitoring design to measure the percentage of women and men who are knowledgeable about family planning options. Based on village records, the team knows that there are 126 households in the village. The team determines that they want to survey about 30 percent of these households.

Simple Random Sample

To do a simple random sample we can merely write the name of each head of household on a slip of paper, put all the slips into a hat, mix them up, and choose (without peeking!) 38 names (30 percent of 126 households).

Stratified Random Sample

Let's say that village residents earn their living by doing one of three primary activities: fishing, agriculture, or commerce. In fact, most families are fishing families and very few are farmers or merchants. We want to be sure we have included the minority farmers and merchants in our sample in order to have a stratified random sample. To do this, we look at the distribution of the families between the three categories and find that there are 77 fishing families, 29 farming families, and 20 merchant families.

We still want an overall sample of 30 percent so we take 24 fishing families (30 percent of 77), 9 farming families (30 percent of 29) and 6 merchant families (30 percent of 20) for a total of 39. (This is slightly higher than our sample for the simple random sampling example because whenever you calculate a fraction of a sampling unit—for instance 30 percent of 77 is really 23.1—you should always round up.) You then select a random sample within fishing, farming, and merchant families of 24, 9, and 6 families, respectively, to get your total sample for the village.

A commonly used variation of random sampling involves systematically selecting houses at a predetermined interval—say every third house (126/38 = about 3). This systematic sampling is not truly random and it can produce biased results.

Nonprobability Sampling

Nonprobability sampling is most often associated with qualitative data collection and analysis. In this type of sampling the chance of a given individual within the population being selected is not known or is unequal compared to the chance of other individuals being selected. Nonprobability sampling is frequently used because it is usually less time consuming, costly, and complicated than probability sampling. Two popular forms of nonprobability sampling are *purposeful sampling* (also known as convenience or judgmental sampling) and *quota sampling*.

Purposeful sampling involves deliberately selecting information-rich cases or key informants for your monitoring work. For instance, in the Savannah Scenario, you might want to understand why cattle herders use certain areas of Karimara National Park for pasturage at specific times of the year. Instead of doing a census or random sample of all the herders around the park, you may wish to select only a few of the biggest herders in the area to get in-depth data about their herding practices.

Process Hint: Purposeful sampling is generally only used with pre-test/post-test and time-series monitoring designs.

One variation of purposeful sampling is **sentinel site** sampling. In this form of sampling, you purposefully select a small and manageable number of individuals who you think will be especially sensitive to some factor of particular importance as outlined in the example below.

A **sentinel site** is a sampling unit that is selected based on some characteristic of particular importance to your monitoring. A sentinel site is also particularly sensitive to some condition in which you are most interested. Examples of important characteristics may include a community's proximity to a particular area, a household's vulnerability to a particular disease, or a natural area's vulnerability to a particular type of natural disaster.

Example: Sentinel Site Sampling

This example is drawn from the Savannah Scenario.

One objective for the project involves eliminating escaped fires. Based on previous experience, the monitoring team knows that fires almost always start in the areas that are most purely grassland and that the savannah areas where more trees are found are usually the last to be affected by fire. The team learns from village residents and observations over the past decade that during the driest years and during the driest seasons, fires almost always start near two villages in the park. Therefore, it makes more sense for the team to select these two villages as sentinel sites and recruit some community volunteer monitors who are responsible for contacting the park headquarters as soon as they see signs of fire.

Process Hint: Quota sampling is generally only used with comparison group monitoring designs.

Quota sampling involves selecting a fixed and predetermined number of units that possess some particular characteristic of interest to be included in the monitoring work. These cases are compared to an equal number of units that are similar except in that they lack the particular characteristic of interest. This approach is particularly useful when you want to isolate and monitor one particular aspect of the individuals in a population. These samples, however, can potentially be extremely biased.

Example: Quota Sampling

This example is drawn from the Tropical Forest Scenario.

One objective of the project is to increase income of participants in NTFP harvesting enterprises. The project team wants to measure the economic impacts of resin harvesting on participants in the project enterprise using a comparison group monitoring strategy. They employ a quota sample by selecting 50 resin collecting families and comparing them to 50 similar families that do not collect resin. Using the data collected on household income from various sources including the resin enterprise, the team assesses the extent to which income from resin impacts household economics. In this case, families that do not collect resin act as the comparison group.

Selecting Monitoring Methods

The techniques presented in this section are by no means a complete list of all possible monitoring methods—they are merely the methods that we have found to be most helpful.

Process Hint: The methods presented in this section are all for collecting primary data. As discussed in Step A1, however, you should also make use of whatever existing information you can find about your project. Existing information is particularly useful in providing a background for deciding which methods to use and what questions to ask. Existing information is therefore most needed during the initial stages of monitoring plan design, including instrument development and pre-testing. Existing information may also be useful in establishing a baseline. Sometimes you can start with

At this point in the project cycle you should have already selected the methods that you will use for monitoring in Step C2. In our description of that step, we discussed the basic principles of selecting monitoring methods. In this section, we provide a brief overview of a few different methods that we feel are particularly effective for monitoring conservation and development projects.

For any type of monitoring activity the choice of methods for collecting data is determined by what information you need, what information is available to you, the skill of your project team, and how much time, money, and other resources you have to invest in monitoring.

There are many methods for collecting data. These methods are often subdivided by academic disciplines. For example, there are certain methods that biologists use, other methods that anthropologists use, and still other methods that economists use. From a project monitoring perspective, however, it does not necessarily make sense to subdivide methods in this fashion.

Instead, in this guide, we integrate different types of methods because we believe that most conservation and development projects require integrated monitoring. For example, you may wish to collect data on the fruiting behavior of a certain species of tree. You can do this by directly observing the trees yourself during the course of the year, or you can interview a few key informants (like fruit collectors, hunters, or forest guards) to get the data. Likewise, you can collect data on the fruit collecting behavior of local residents by directly observing them or by speaking with the chosen key informants. As we can see from this example, both of these methods—direct observation and key informant interviews—can be used to collect both biological and social data.

Another illustration of the crossover between social and biological techniques is the use of formal surveys to collect monitoring data. Using the same example, say we wish to monitor fruit production of the tree species we are studying. We can select a sample of trees—using either transects or plots—and we can survey the amount of fruit they produce over time. Likewise, we can select a sample of fruit collectors and survey them using an indepth formal questionnaire to determine fruit production levels.

Instead of subdividing methods into disciplines, we have divided them based on the type of data that they are designed to collect:

- *Quantitative Methods.* These methods produce data that are easily represented as numbers, such as answers to formal surveys and enterprise financial records. Quantitative data generally describe formal measurements of variables like income, crop production, or animal population densities.

- *Qualitative Methods.* These methods produce data that are not easily summarized in numerical form, such as minutes from community meetings and general notes from observations. Qualitative data normally describe people's knowledge, attitudes, or behaviors.

The relative advantages and disadvantages of qualitative and quantitative methods have been debated for a long time. We do not intend to try to resolve this debate here. Instead, we wish to stress that we believe that these two approaches are not incompatible with one another but are completely complementary. In fact, we believe that almost every monitoring plan should include both quantitative and qualitative methods. Combining quantitative and qualitative approaches in monitoring will help ensure that the data you are collecting will give you as complete a picture as possible of your project site.

Furthermore, like the crossover we mentioned earlier between social and biological data collection methods, there is a similar crossover between quantitative and qualitative techniques. Carefully conducted qualitative methods can produce quantifiable results and well-designed quantitative studies can provide insight into typically qualitative topics like attitudes and opinions. Using our fruiting tree example again, you may be able to get a reason-

baseline data that were collected by someone else and follow-up by collecting primary data. For example, if you are planning to measure changes in forest cover, your baseline might be a map prepared by the government forest service fifteen years ago.

We are using "quantitative methods" as shorthand for "methods for collecting quantitative data" and "qualitative methods" as shorthand for "methods for collecting qualitative data."

ably precise estimate of the amount of fruit production from a specific group of trees from key informant collectors who have been harvesting these trees for years. Likewise, you can learn a great deal about the collectors' beliefs regarding what factors most influence a tree's fruit production from data you gather during a formal survey.

Quantitative Methods

There are two quantitative methods that are particularly useful for monitoring conservation and development projects: tracking project records and formal survey.

Tracking Project Records

What is it? Tracking project records involves designing a form that is used to systematically collect quantitative data like a business's profit and loss, levels of community participation, and production figures. Sometimes, records are automatically tracked as a part of routine project management.

What are its advantages? Tracking records can be a relatively easy form of capturing important data. It can also require a minimal amount of staff time.

What are its disadvantages? None.

What does it cost? Tracking records is generally fairly inexpensive.

What other resources or special skills are needed? Staff with knowledge of entering, compiling, and analyzing numerical data.

Example: Tracking Records

This example shows part of the record collection form taken from a study of fish harvesting from the Coastal Scenario.

Record Tracking Form for Fish Catch
  Species: Red Snapper

	Number of individuals		
Weight (kg)	*1/23/03*	*3/26/03*	*6/18/03*
0–1	67	89	75
1.1–2.5	41	58	60
2.6–5	35	40	38
5+	22	15	17

Formal Survey

What is it? A **formal survey** is frequently used to collect social and biological data. One of the most common methods for collecting social data involves using a household survey. Most biological data are also collected through formal surveys using transects, botanical plots and belts, and wildlife surveys. A formal survey is, at its core, a standardized approach to the collection of data on individuals (including people, plants, and animals) or groups (households or organizations) through structured measurement or questioning of systematically identified samples. The real power of a formal survey is that you obtain not only a measurement of the data you are trying to collect but also an assessment of how accurate that measurement is.

During a formal social survey, monitoring team members interview respondents by asking a series of questions that are listed on a questionnaire and recording answers using a predetermined list of possible responses. When designing a social questionnaire, careful consideration must be given to each of the questions. Most people tend to include too many questions in their questionnaire. You want to be sure to collect only necessary data because asking inessential questions wastes time and obscures the meaningful ones. When you're developing a formal social survey questionnaire, keep the following points in mind:

* When you're ready to write down a question, think about what data it will provide and how this relates to measuring indicators of your project's goals and objectives. Every time you write down a question, ask yourself: "Why do I want to know this?" Your answer must be: "To provide me the data I need according

A **formal survey** is also sometimes referred to as a *formal census*. Strictly speaking, as discussed in the previous section, a census involves assessing all units in the population while a survey involves sampling a subset of the population.

to my monitoring plan." "It would be interesting to know" is not an acceptable answer.

✳ Make sure the question is appropriate to the situation. If it offends or threatens potential respondents, don't use it. Use vocabulary that is appropriate to the area.

Phenology refers to the timing of plant cycles.

During a formal biological census or survey, monitoring team members record carefully defined data about the plants, animals, or habitats that they are studying. Data on plants and stationary animals (such as coral reef species) are generally collected by monitoring randomly positioned plots, belts, or transects in a given habitat. The specific measurements that are taken on the organisms in the plots, belts, or transects depends on the monitoring needs—these techniques can be used to study questions of species density, distribution, *phenology*, and regeneration.

Absolute density refers to how many individuals there are per unit area. *Relative density* refers to the number of individuals in one area or time period compared to another.

These techniques are drawn from van Schaik (1994). Refer to this source, Rabinowitz (1996), or any other good ecological methods textbook for more information as to how to use these techniques.

Data on mobile animals are generally collected by conducting wildlife censuses and surveys. These techniques can be used to look at species density and habitat preferences. As illustrated in the table that follows, there are a number of specific techniques that can be used depending on the type of information needed (for example, *absolute density* versus *relative density*), the type of organism being studied, and the habitat. As is the case with social surveys, here again it is important to collect only data that are linked to key indicators in your monitoring plan.

Different Biological Techniques for Measuring Wildlife Density

Absolute Density	Relative Density	
Census Techniques	*Survey Techniques*	*Index Techniques*
Absolute Counts	Line Transects	Camera Trapping
Concentration Counts	Variable Radius Point Samples	Track Counts
Sweep Samples/Drives	Capture-Mark-Recapture	Sighting per Unit Effort
Range Mapping		

What are its advantages? Formal surveying relies on censuses or probability sampling and thus the results are, in theory, representative of the population being surveyed. Furthermore, as discussed earlier, formal surveying gives you both a measurement and an estimate of the accuracy of the measurement. This means that you can generally be confident of how closely your results reflect the realities at your site.

It is fairly easy to train field staff in conducting formal surveys. Skill levels for this technique are usually less than what are required to carry out effective key informant interviews or focus group discussions, although analysis of the data requires a high level of skill.

What are its disadvantages? Formal social surveys use standardized written questionnaires that should not be altered during the course of the exercise. This lack of flexibility means that you must be especially careful to get the questionnaire, sampling scheme, and interview protocol right from the start. Respondents can get annoyed with the interviewers if the questionnaire is too long or if sensitive questions are being asked. In a similar fashion, it is also hard to adjust the format for collecting biological data midway through the study.

Both social and biological surveys are usually very costly and time consuming because many individuals must be sampled. Sampling frameworks are often complicated and rigid and must be strictly followed to produce the most accurate results. If a formal survey is conducted without proper pre-testing of the questionnaire or proper staff training, the results will likely be unreliable. In many instances, discrepancies emerge between standard and local units for measuring parameters—it is often necessary to do a short study to establish the equivalency between local units (for example, baskets of rice) and international ones (kilograms of rice).

What does it cost? The cost of conducting an effective formal survey is relatively high. Of the methods we cover in this chapter, it is usually considered to be the most expensive. In particular, analysis of formal survey data requires a high level of skill which usually translates into higher project costs. Because computers are usually needed for data entry, cleaning, and analysis, this also represents an additional cost to the project.

What other resources or special skills are needed? Management and analysis of formal surveys requires staff who are well trained in using these techniques and who have some knowledge of basic statistics. If a computer is necessary, someone must be skilled in the software programs that will be used for data handling and analysis.

Example: Formal Social Survey

This is part of a questionnaire drawn from the Tropical Forest Scenario.

Household Survey: Female Head of Household
Date: _____
    1. Name of interviewer: _____
    2. Name of community: _____
    3. Name of respondent: _____
    4. How old are you? ____years
    5. How many family members are living with you presently?
      Total ___
        How many children less than or equal to 6 years old? ___
        How many children older than 6 and less than or equal
          to 16? ___
        How many children older than 16 and less than or equal
          to 21? ___
        How many people older than 21? ___
        [Calculate total: Total   ___]
    [*If calculated total different from respondent's preliminary
      answer, figure out why with respondent*]
    6. How much fuelwood does your family use on a daily
      basis?
    (*Have respondent show you how much and weigh with
      Salter scale*) ___ kg
    7. How long does it take you to walk to where you collect
      fuelwood? ___hours
    8. Five years ago, how long did it take you to walk to where
      you collected fuelwood? ___hours
    9. Who in your family makes bamboo baskets to be sold in
      the market? (circle all mentioned individuals)
      (A) Respondent
      (B) Father
      (C) Male children   How Many : ___
      (D) Female children   How Many : ___
      (E) Other (Specify) _____

(continues)

10. How many baskets does your family make each week?
   (A) Small # ___
   (B) Medium # ___
   (C) Large # ___
   (D) Other (specify)._____ # ___
11. How much do you sell each of your baskets for?
   (A) Small L$ ___
   (B) Medium L$ ___
   (C) Large L$ ___
   (D) Other (specify) _____ L$ ___

Example: Wildlife Survey Using the Line Transect Method

This is part of a line transect survey procedure for the Wetlands Scenario. The procedure outlined is adapted from van Schaik (1994).

A line transect involves determining a fixed area within which you measure the numbers of one or more wildlife species. In this method a line of known length is traveled and the number of animals encountered as well as the perpendicular distance from the line are recorded. In effect, you are measuring a strip through the habitat whose width is different for each species you encounter—the width is calculated when you do your analysis based on how easy it is to detect a given species at a given distance.

Before transects can be conducted, you must first mark a series of trails that will be walked. Trails should in theory be randomly positioned with respect to terrain and habitat, but in steeply sloped areas they will have to follow ridges or other natural features. Trails should be measured and the distances marked at regular intervals (every 25 or 50 meters).

You should then walk alone along the trail at a consistent slow pace. When an animal is encountered, you do the following:

1. Upon detection, mark and record your position on the trail and the time that you encountered the animal.
2. Identify and record the species and its activity at the time of contact.
3. Determine and record the location of the animal. If it is a group of animals, determine and record the location of the closest and farthest animals and estimate the size of the group.
4. Using a compass, measure and record the angle between the trail and the animal.
5. Using a tape measure, measure and record the distance from the initial observation point to the animal or the shortest distance from the animal to the line of the trail.
6. Record how you detected the animal (such as by seeing it, hearing it move, hearing a vocalization).
7. Record any other relevant information about the encounter.

Qualitative Methods

There are five types of qualitative methods that are most applicable to monitoring. These include: key informant interviews, focus group discussions, matrix ranking, direct observation, and mapping.

Before going into the details of these techniques, it is worth mentioning that a variety of qualitative social methods are sometimes arranged together and presented as a package known as *Rapid Appraisal*. Rapid Appraisal techniques are designed to encourage maximum community involvement and consultation in data collection, analysis, and use. They can be effectively used to help make informed and timely decisions regarding conservation and development projects.

Rapid Appraisal techniques are especially useful for assessing local site conditions (see chapter 3). Because these techniques can provide in-depth and extensive descriptive information, they can be used to develop a comprehensive depiction of local communities that allows you to design and implement appropriate projects. Generally, however, most Rapid Appraisal techniques are too descriptive and open ended in nature to be used as the only tool for rigorous and long-term project monitoring efforts.

Key Informant Interview

What is it? Key informant interviewing is a form of interviewing in which only some of the questions are predetermined. Interviews are conducted one-on-one between the respondent and a fairly well-trained and highly skilled interviewer. Although you can develop a questionnaire to be followed by the interviewer, most often a topic guide, a list of topics to be covered in the key informant interview, is used in *probing* the respondent. Questions are generally open ended, meaning that they leave space for the respondent to answer in different ways.

What are its advantages? A key informant interview is useful when you want to quickly gain some insight into a particular subject or you are collecting data on a highly complex subject matter and there are particularly knowledgeable respondents whom you can interview. It is also useful when you must collect data on a highly sensitive subject matter, when respondents are widely dispersed over a large area, or when peer pressure may influence a respondent's answer in a group.

What are its disadvantages? A major theoretical disadvantage of a key informant interview is that it can be very difficult to gauge the extent to which responses from a given individual represent the population as a whole. Analysis and comparison of the results is thus often difficult because a typical key informant interview produces respondent-specific data.

The family of *Rapid Appraisal* approaches includes Rapid Rural Appraisal (RRA), Participatory Rapid Appraisal (PRA), and Participatory Rural Appraisal (also PRA). All of these approaches use a similar set of data collection methods. The main difference between them is the degree of community participation in data collection and analysis processes.

Useful Rapid Appraisal tools include:
- Community maps
- Community transects
- Seasonal calendars
- Venn diagrams of institutional relations
- Community histories
- Community event calendars
- Daily routines
- Matrix ranking
- Direct observation lists
- Informal group discussions

Probing involves following up on a specific point and asking as many questions as necessary to get a good understanding of the issue. In this and all other qualitative methods, it is especially important that the person collecting the data have a good understanding of the project's goals, objectives, and activities so that he or she can probe effectively.

Technically speaking, key informants are respondents who have special knowledge of a particular issue or subject. We use the term key informant interviews as a synonym with informal and semi-structured interviews and have chosen to do so because most of the time this form of individual in-depth interview is done with a key informant as the respondent.

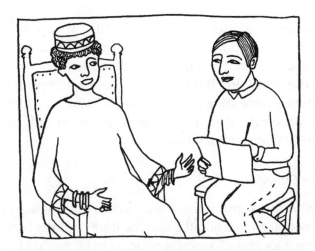

One practical disadvantage of the technique is that some responses may not be accurately recorded by the interviewer as there may be a large gap between the respondent's knowledge and that of the interviewer. In addition, the potential for providing supervisory feedback is limited as *debriefing* is time consuming. Finally, the interviewer often has little control over the setting in which the interview is conducted, so it is often difficult to avoid interruption.

What does it cost? Conducting a key informant interview is relatively inexpensive. You interview fewer respondents and thus the cost of employing this method will be substantially less than conducting a formal social survey.

What other resources or special skills are needed? Conducting a key informant interview properly requires a very high level of skill. If you intend to use this method, you must invest fully in adequate training and supervision of your monitoring team. Unlike formal

Debriefing involves having the person collecting the data discuss his or her findings with other members of the monitoring team.

Example: Key Informant Interview

This is part of a key informant interview topic guide from the Coastal Scenario.

Key Informant Topic Guide: Bocoro Bay

Interviewer: _____   Date: _____
  1. Name of key informant:
  2. Position in the community:
  3. How many families fish in Bocoro Bay?
  4. What kinds of fish do they usually catch?
  5. How do people generally catch fish in Bocoro Bay?
  6. Have you noticed a change over the past 10 years in the amount of fish people catch?
6a. If the answer is "yes," ask: How has the amount changed over the past 10 years? and Why do you think it has changed this way?

surveys where the interviewer merely fills in or checks off responses, key informant interviewing requires quick and creative thinking and the ability to understand and process the data provided by the informant. It is important that the interviewer be able to accurately receive data, accurately recall data, critically evaluate data, and act on the data as they are received in order to control and properly manage the interview.

Focus Group Discussion

What is it? A focus group discussion involves bringing together a group of people to talk about a specific topic. It takes advantage of group dynamics and allows respondents to be guided by a skilled moderator into increasing levels of depth on key issues included in the monitoring plan. Focus groups are ideally fairly *homogenous* groups of between six to eight participants.

Determining the number of focus groups you need to discuss a particular subject is dependent on a variety of issues. You should consider the following points when planning your monitoring:

* Conduct at least two focus groups for each subset of the population from which you want data (such as women of child-bearing age or rattan collectors).

* Conduct focus groups until the data obtained are not new.

* Conduct focus groups in each geographic region where you feel a meaningful difference exists.

The composition of the focus groups can be determined by such factors as:

* Socioeconomic class

* Type of resource user (such as resin collectors, fishermen, hunters)

* Level of expertise (such as familiarity with sustainable agriculture techniques, years hunting)

* Demographic data (such as age, marital status, or gender)

* Cultural or ethnic differences

The moderator conducts the focus group using a topic guide similar to the one described for key informant interviewing. The topic guide is an extremely important element of the focus group method. It serves as a summary statement of the issues and objectives to be covered in the focus group. Preparing the topic guide is an exercise that forces both the moderator and the project manager to organize their thoughts and to review the monitoring plan thoroughly. A loosely constructed topic guide generally means that

Much of the material in this section is drawn from Debus (1995).

Homogenous means that all members of the group are similar

the subject has not been thought through in enough detail to get good results from the focus group sessions. The topic guide also serves as a road map and as a memory aid for the moderator. A good moderator will have the flexibility and skill to stay on course and to cover all of the objectives of the session and yet allow the discussion to flow naturally and spontaneously from respondents. The moderator will also pursue new issues raised by respondents if they are relevant to the topic.

The moderator is assisted by an observer who watches the reactions and body language of the participants in the focus group. One of the main functions of the observer is to operate a tape recorder that records the entire focus group session. At the beginning of the focus group, the moderator explains the importance of accurately capturing what the respondents have to say and thus the use of the tape recorder. If any of the participants are unhappy with the use of the tape recorder, then it can be removed and the observer will have to take good and complete notes.

What are its advantages? A focus group provides the opportunity for group interaction which will generally stimulate richer responses and allow new and valuable thoughts to emerge. It also enables project managers to observe discussions and gain first-hand insights into the respondents' behaviors, attitudes, language, and feelings. Finally, it can be completed more quickly and generally less expensively than a series of key informant or formal social surveys.

What are its disadvantages? Conducting a truly effective and useful focus group requires a high level of skill. Managing the discussion group is rarely problem free. Often group dynamics will work against the moderator. Participants may be reluctant to speak out in public and for this reason you may not get much variation in the response and input. Likewise, you may get a dull group which lacks interest in the subject matter. In addition to problems that occur across an entire group, there are often problems associated with individual respondents. Some of the most frequently encountered problematic participants in focus groups are dominating, shy, overly talkative, angry, disruptive, or questioning respondents.

Transcription refers to the process of typing or writing out the results of recorded focus group sessions.

In addition, from a practical perspective, analyzing focus data is a difficult and time-consuming task. As focus group sessions are generally tape recorded, they must be transcribed before they can be analyzed. This *transcription* process takes a considerable amount of time and effort. Furthermore, once discussions have been transcribed, an analysis strategy must be developed and the data must be reorganized, compiled, and evaluated before a final report can be produced.

What does it cost? Like a key informant interview, a focus group is generally less expensive than a formal social survey. However, since it requires a high level of interviewer skill and lots of time for analysis, the cost can still be quite high.

What other resources or special skills are needed? A focus group is perhaps the most difficult qualitative method to do well. In addition to the moderator, an additional monitoring team member is need-

---

Example: Focus Group

This is part of a focus group topic guide drawn from the Wetlands Scenario.

Topic: Threats to the Everson Watershed

Moderator: Observer: Location: Date:
(Warm-up, personal introductions, and introduction to the topic)

1. Theme: Pollution
Do you think that pollution from the cities affects the Everson Watershed? What are the major sources of pollution? What do they produce that pollutes the watershed? How does pollution affect the watershed? (*Probe:* How does it affect water quality? Wildlife? Plant life?) Does pollution of Everson affect the human populations that live around the watershed? How so? What can be done to reduce the amount of pollution that occurs? (*Probe:* Can ordinary citizens do anything to curb pollution? What would you do personally to help stop pollution?)

2. Theme: Hunting
Do you think that hunting is a problem in the Everson Watershed? Are you aware of any benefits of hunting in the watershed? What types of animals are most affected by hunting in the watershed? Does the hunting of specific species affect other animals living in the watershed? How so? Do you think there should be tighter control of hunting in the Everson Watershed?

ed to record the discussion. Small portable tape recorders, often expensive in many countries, are needed to record the sessions. Adequate training and supervision are essential.

Matrix Ranking

What is it? Matrix ranking is a convenient and highly effective tool for monitoring. Matrix ranking involves ordering various items, conditions, or perceptions in an objective manner. There are four basic type of matrix ranking:

Much of this section is derived from Theis and Grady (1991).

✳ *Preference Ranking (or Ranking by Voting).* This is used to quickly determine the main problems or preferences of individuals in a given site and enables the priorities of different individuals to be easily compared.

✳ *Pairwise Ranking.* This is used to determine the main problems or preferences of individual community members, identify their ranking criteria, and easily compare the priorities of different individuals.

✳ *Direct Ranking.* This is used to identify lists of criteria for a certain object. It allows the team to understand the reasons for local preferences for such things as a certain tree or fish species. These criteria are likely to change from group to group.

✳ *Wealth Ranking.* This is used to determine the relative socioeconomic level of community members within a project area. For monitoring, wealth ranking is most useful to see whether the socioeconomic status of project participants improves over time compared to those who do not participate in the project.

Relative order (or ordinal rankings) refers to ranking one point as being higher or lower along some scale than another point without referring to how much distance is between them. For example, we might state that one person earns a higher wage than another.

Absolute order (or cardinal rankings) refers to ranking points and specifying where they are located along the scale. For example, we might state that one person earns 20 pesos per day while the second earns 30 pesos per day.

Aggregated refers to combining data from many respondents.

What are its advantages? Matrix ranking complements other forms of data collection by generating basic information which leads to more direct questioning. Ranking is useful for sensitive information, especially for income and wealth. Often, informants tend to be more willing to rank preferences or income sources in a *relative order* rather than *absolute order*. Ranking scores are usually easier to obtain than absolute measurements and they can be *aggregated*.

Preference ranking provides you with the opportunity to quickly survey a small sample of respondents. Pairwise ranking allows respondents to compare preferences or problems two at a time so that they don't get confused by having to sort out their preferences for many different things simultaneously. Direct ranking, which uses a list of criteria developed by the respondent, provides the interviewer the opportunity to reach a deeper understanding of why the respondent selects his/her preferences in the order he/she does. Wealth ranking can be used to monitor changes in socioeconomic status over time. It can also be used as means to determine income strata to be targeted for monitoring.

What are its disadvantages? Ranking can sometimes be a long process. Respondents sometimes get bored quickly and begin to loose their concentration during the exercise. It's important to keep the numbers of items being ranked to between four and eight to avoid confusion (except when doing wealth ranking, in which case you have to include as many community members as necessary). You will also want to have between four and eight criteria (except in wealth ranking where you want to have at most four). It's also important to avoid mixing radically different types of items that are being ranked so as to avoid confusion. Matrix ranking requires some training and a good deal of practice.

What does it cost? Matrix ranking is also a relatively inexpensive way to collect good quality data. Its costs are similar to those of direct observation. Matrix ranking requires some training, but not extensive amounts.

What other resources or special skills are needed? None.

Example: Preference Ranking Matrix with Multiple Respondents

This matrix is drawn from the Tropical Forest Scenario.

Preference ranking involves the following steps:

1. Choose a set of problems, opportunities, or choices (preferences) to be ranked (in our example this is "Constraints to Agriculture").
2. Talk to a couple of residents to get an idea of the range of possible preferences or options.
3. Make a matrix as shown below and list the above preferences down the left column.
4. Ask each respondent (shown by the letters A–E) to order their preferences from first to last. The first preference gets the highest score, which equals the total number of preferences.
5. Add up the scores from each respondent in each row of the matrix to get the total score for each preference. Rank these totals from highest to lowest using letters as shown in the example.

In this example, "Insects" are viewed as the biggest constraint.

Constraints to Agricultural Production in the Indah Biosphere Reserve

| | Respondent (__/__ = Sex/Age) | | | | | | |
Factor	A (M/23)	B (M/53)	C (F/48)	D (M/16)	E (M/31)	Total	Rank
Bad weather	2	1	1	2	3	9	e
Poor soil	3	2	2	5	1	13	d
Animals	1	3	4	3	4	15	c
Insects	4	5	5	4	2	20	a
No fertilizer	5	4	3	1	5	18	b

The instructions for doing the various matrix rankings in this example are adapted from Theis and Grady (1991).

See Step A3 for another example of a preference ranking matrix.

Example: Pairwise Ranking Matrix with a Single Respondent

This matrix is drawn from the Wetlands Scenario.

Pairwise ranking involves the following steps:

1. Choose a set of problems, opportunities, or choices (preferences) to be ranked (in our example "Destructive Impact of Recreational Activities").
2. Choose, with the help of the respondent (or based on previous input from key informants), six or less of the most important items or answers in this set.
3. Record each of the items on separate cards (or you can use pictures).
4. Place two of the choices in front of the respondent and ask him or her to choose the biggest problem (or preferred item). Record the answer in the matrix (for example, between birding and canoeing, this respondent believes canoeing has a greater destructive impact). Ask the respondent to explain why he or she made the choice and record the answer in the second table.
5. Present the next pair of choices and continue to do so until the table is complete.
6. Tabulate and score the response by counting the number of times each preference was chosen.
7. Cross-check the results by asking the respondent what he or she thinks is the biggest problem (or preference). For our example, you could ask "Of these recreational activities that you mentioned, which is the most destructive to the Everson Watershed?" Chances are the answer to this response will correspond to the highest ranked preference in the matrix.
8. Repeat the exercise for a number of respondents and tabulate.

Destructive Impact of Recreational Activities on the Everson Watershed

Hunting	Fishing	Birding	Canoeing	Camping		Total	Rank
	Hunting	Hunting	Hunting	Hunting	Hunting	4	a
		Fishing	Fishing	Camping	Fishing	2	c
			Canoeing	Camping	Birding	0	e
				Camping	Canoeing	1	d
					Camping	3	b

For this example, the respondent thinks that hunting has the most destructive impact on recreational activities.

Reasons for Choice by Preference

	Positive	Negative
Hunting	- Brings revenue to residents living in the watershed area - Controls animal overpopulations	- Kills and scares away many animals - Works against tourism
Fishing	- Brings revenue to residents living in the watershed area	- Boaters leave lots of trash in the wetlands - Boat wakes erode waterway banks
Birding	- Brings revenue to residents living in the watershed area - Promotes appreciation of wildlife without destruction	
Canoeing	- Brings revenue to residents living in the watershed area - Promotes appreciation of wildlife with little destruction	- Disrupts roosting and nesting birds
Camping	- Brings revenue to residents living in the watershed area	- Campers leave lots of trash - Disrupts wildlife

Example: Direct Ranking Matrix with Single Respondent

This matrix is drawn from the Coastal Scenario.

Direct ranking involves the following steps:

1. Choose a set of problems, opportunities, or choices (preferences) to be ranked (in our example this is "Preference for Fishing Techniques").
2. Choose, with the help of the respondent, six or less of the most important items or answers in this set and six or less criteria on which you would like to evaluate the items. Make sure all criteria are positively phrased (for example, change "it is unsafe to use" to "it is safe to use."
3. Create a blank matrix. On the left side, list the identified items. Across the top, list the criteria that you have identified.
4. Rank the items under each criterion. The highest score that any item can get for each criterion is equal to the total number of items in the matrix. The lowest score is always 1. To do this, for each criterion ask the respondent: "Which item is best, next best?" and "Which item is worst, next worst?"
5. Ask: "Which criterion is most important and why?" and "If you could select only one of these items, which would it be?" This will help you validate the results from step 6.
6. To calculate the "Total Score" simply add up the row for each item. (If you have more than one sheet or table, add up the total scores from each.) To calculate the relative ranking of each item (the last column), rank the item with the highest total score as "a," the item with the next highest score "b," and so on.

For this example, 'Set' line came out as the most preferred fishing technique.

Preference for Fishing Techniques in Bocoro Bay

			Criteria				
Item	Easy to use	Catches most fish	Catches best fish	Safe to use	Environmentally friendly	Total Score	Rank
Hand-line	3	1	3	4	6	17	d
Gill net	4	4	6	3	4	21	b/c*
'Set' line	5	3	5	5	5	23	a
Trap	6	2	4	6	3	21	b/c*
Cyanide	1	5	1	2	2	11	f
Bomb	2	6	2	1	1	12	e

* b and c came out with equal scores and are thus tied in ranking.

Example: Wealth Ranking Matrix with Multiple Respondents

This matrix is drawn from the Savannah Scenario.

Wealth ranking involves the following steps:

1. List all the households and assign each a number. Each household head is listed on a card.
2. Select and ask a number of key informants (scorers) who have lived in the community for a long time to sort the names into as many baskets (which represent wealth categories) as they perceive necessary using their own criteria. For illiterate key informants, read out the name on the card and have them place it into whatever basket they deem appropriate. It helps to use different baskets to help keep the categories straight.
3. After the scorer has ranked all of the cards, ask him or her to explain his or her wealth criteria for each category.
4. Repeat the exercise for each additional scorer. You will want to shuffle the cards between the scorers to keep the original order random.
5. To tabulate the results, for each scorer take the total number of categories (baskets) that he or she identified and divide this number into 100 percent to get the scores assigned for each category. If the scorer identifies four baskets, then you would divide four into one hundred to get categories of 25, 50, 75, and 100. If the scorer identifies three baskets, then you'd get categories of 33, 67, and 100. Assign the appropriate score to each household.
6. Total up the score for each household based on all scorers' responses. Use this score to rank the households from lowest to highest. Determine categories by looking at where natural divisions lie in the ranking.

Wealth Ranking: Karibu Village, Karimara National Park

Household #	Scorer A	B	C	D	Score	
5	25	20	25	33	25.75	Poorest
17	25	20	25	33	25.75	
19	25	20	25	33	25.75	
2	50	20	25	33	32	
11	50	40	25	33	37	
9	25	20	50	67	40.5	
16	50	20	50	67	46.75	Poor
15	50	20	50	67	46.75	
7	50	20	50	67	46.75	
13	50	20	50	67	46.75	
6	50	40	50	67	51.75	
8	75	40	50	67	58	
18	75	20	75	67	59.25	
20	75	40	75	67	64.25	Medium
14	75	40	75	67	64.25	
4	75	60	75	67	69.25	
10	100	80	100	100	95	Wealthy
12	100	100	100	100	100	
# of categories	4	5	4	3		

Direct Observation

What is it? Direct observation is a technique in which you systematically observe individuals, groups, animals, plants, objects, events, processes, or relationships and record your observations. We include *participant observation* in this category. Results of direct observation can be recorded by using a checklist based on a formal outline that guides your observations or by taking extensive notes in your field notebook.

What are its advantages? Direct observation is a vital tool for collecting biological and social data. Many biological field studies rely heavily on this approach for observing animals. Direct observation is also a useful tool for *validation* in monitoring because it can be used to cross-check respondents' answers. This tool is extremely easy to learn—in fact, we do it in our everyday lives. The only difference is that to use direct observation as a monitoring tool, you need to record your observations systematically.

What are its disadvantages? For collecting data about social issues and conditions, direct observation should not be used as the sole monitoring method, especially if the members of your monitoring team are not from the project area. Interpretation of observational findings is necessary and usually the only way to do this accurately is to consult with or interview local residents. Similarly, for biological monitoring, direct observation should generally be employed in conjunction with other techniques.

What does it cost? This approach is one of the lowest cost techniques we'll discuss. As training needs are in many cases minimal and most people can record their direct observations relatively easily,

Participant observation is when community members and other stakeholders in the project conduct observations.

Validation is the process of cross-checking to ensure that the data obtained from one monitoring method are confirmed by the data obtained from a different method. See the discussion of triangulation later in this chapter to see one way in which to validate your findings.

little investment needs to be made to get monitoring team members ready to use this technique. In some biological monitoring situations, however, direct observation requires training and special skills, such as the ability to identify bird species.

What other resources or special skills are needed? None.

Example: Direct Observation

This data form is from the Savannah Scenario.

Park Guard Observation Checklist: Karimara National Park

Guard: _____   Date: _____
Evidence of hunting:
Number of carcasses encountered _____
Carcass 1: Species_____ Cause of death _____ Location _____
Carcass 2: Species_____ Cause of death _____ Location _____
Carcass 3: Species_____ Cause of death _____ Location _____
Carcass 4: Species_____ Cause of death _____ Location _____
Carcass 5: Species_____ Cause of death _____ Location _____
Evidence of illegal vehicle travel:
Sighting of vehicle? __Yes __No
If "Yes," Make_____ Model _____
Owner_____
Driver_____ License #_____
Citation issued? __Yes __No
If "Yes," Citation # _____
If "No," Describe evidence of vehicle travel:
Coordinates: _____

Mapping

What is it? A map records information in the form of a drawing, picture, or image that references data according to geographical locations. There are many ways of producing maps that are useful for monitoring. These range from simple sketches drawn by community members to complex computer-generated images. Maps are particularly useful for measuring changes in land-use patterns over time.

Map data can be obtained by actually surveying, measuring, or observing things on the ground. Alternatively and more expensively, data can be collected using *aerial photography* or *satellite imagery*. Increasingly, technology such as the *Global Positioning System (GPS)* is being used to assist in the production of highly accurate maps. Community members and field researchers alike can use hand-held GPS receivers to determine the exact latitude and longitude of their location. Maps can be drawn in the sand, on paper, or stored electronically in a computer using a *Geographic*

Aerial photography is the process of taking pictures of an area from an airplane. *Satellite imagery* is the process of taking similar photos from space. Many government agencies will have aerial photographs or satellite images on file which can be a good source of historical land-use data.

A *Global Positioning System (GPS)* receiver is a device that receives signals from a network of satellites. The receiver references its position with respect to these satellites, thus giving an accurate measurement of the observer's geographical coordinates. Note that the observer still has to separately record information about the location to go with the coordinates.

Information System (GIS) program. Some of the most common forms of mapping include:

* *Social (or Participatory) Mapping.* This involves having community members draw or assist in drawing maps. These maps are drawn from a "bird's-eye" or aerial perspective and may or may not be drawn to scale. Depending on the field conditions, some practitioners prefer to have community members draw maps on the ground using sticks, stones, and any other objects that can be used to represent different features. These maps must always be recorded on paper if they are to be used for monitoring.

* *Social Transects or Land-Use Profiles.* These involve drawing cross-sections of human or natural landscapes. These maps are drawn from a side-view perspective and may or may not be drawn to scale. These maps can be made by walking a straight line transect with community members and asking them to describe important land-use features encountered or by having project team members make observations at regular intervals.

* *Habitat Mapping.* This involves combining biological, ecological, and physical data to form maps illustrating natural area and human land-use pattern boundaries. In monitoring, this technique is used most often to determine the impacts of different human activities on natural areas and to represent changes over time of species distribution and density.

A *Geographic Information System (GIS)* commonly refers to a computer-based mapping program that can display data in reference to geographical coordinates.

What are its advantages? A map is very visual and can be used to turn complex concepts into easily understood images. People generally enjoy and respond to seeing data presented in map form. Most maps can be grasped by a wide range of people with different backgrounds and for this reason maps make an effective communications tool. Generating basic social and habitat maps requires little training and can be accomplished with most communities. Generating more complex maps using GPS and GIS technology can be extremely powerful but requires a much greater investment in training and equipment.

What are its disadvantages? If maps are to be used for monitoring, special care must be given to ensure that they are produced in the same way over the course of the monitoring cycle. Standardization of information included in the maps must be carried out at the beginning of monitoring to ensure that different map elements are recorded in the same way by all participants.

As we have mentioned, maps are easy to read and people generally prefer to see data presented in a spatial format. This advantage, however, can also be a problem as users sometimes accept maps as being accurate without taking into consideration the quality of the data that are used to produce them. Sometimes maps oversimplify conditions found in the field. Even very limited and inaccurate data can be represented in map form. As a result, maps can be very misleading if the quality of the data used to produce them is inadequate.

There also can be problems associated with using GIS technology to monitor typical conservation and development projects as documented by the study described in the sidebar. These techniques should only be used if the project can justify the cost and the team members are comfortable with the technology that is required.

What does it cost? Social mapping and social transects require relatively few financial inputs. Habitat mapping requires greater amounts of financial resources as it usually requires more skilled staff to make accurate measurements. And finally, GIS programs

Computer-based mapping is generally fairly difficult to manage by most monitoring teams. One study (Poole, 1995) found that a high proportion of those organizations that have GIS technology cannot take full advantage of the system. This is attributed to a lack of such things as adequate training, follow-up by technology providers, skilled personnel, and adequate funds to maintain software, hardware, and technicians.

Example: Social Map

This example of a social map is from the Savannah Scenario.

and the use of satellite and aerial photography can be very costly if you must purchase the images yourself. These types of data and systems are also expensive as they require computer hardware, software, and highly trained staff.

What other resources or special skills are needed? As we mentioned, using GPS and GIS technology requires a high degree of skill.

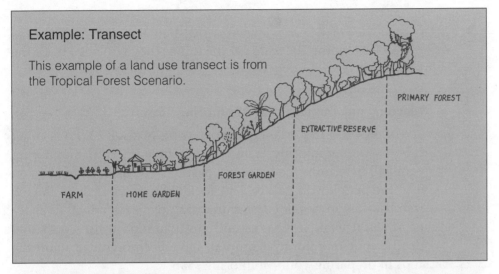

Example: Transect

This example of a land use transect is from the Tropical Forest Scenario.

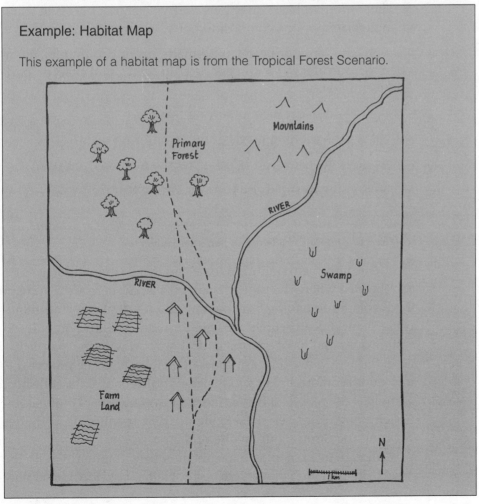

Example: Habitat Map

This example of a habitat map is from the Tropical Forest Scenario.

Preparing for Monitoring Field Work

By now, you should have developed your complete Monitoring Plan. To implement it, you need to think about:

- *Selecting and Training Your Monitoring Team.* This involves choosing and preparing the people who will do the monitoring work.

- *Assembling the Material Resources That Your Team Will Require.* This involves helping the team get the things they will need to do the work.

Selecting and Training Your Monitoring Team

One of the most important questions you can ask is "Who is going to be on the monitoring team?" The people on your monitoring team will determine the types of questions you ask, the places you visit, the people you talk to, and the quality of your data. In fact, even before you develop the monitoring plans described in chapter 5, you'll want to give careful consideration to this question. Ideally, your monitoring team will have been involved in all the steps in preparing your Monitoring Plan.

There are five basic questions that you need to keep in mind when determining the composition of your monitoring team:

✴ Should the monitoring team be made up of community members or outsiders? Volunteers or paid staff? Full-time or part-time employees?

✴ How do you select the monitoring team?

✴ What are the training needs of the monitoring team?

✴ How does the team you select affect the methods you use?

✴ Who is going to supervise the monitoring team?

Should the monitoring team be made up of community members or outsiders? Volunteers or paid staff? Full-time or part-time employees?

Candidates for the monitoring team can come from within or outside the area where the project is taking place. There are a number of advantages to having local community residents on your monitoring team. Local people are usually more sensitive to cultural complexities and have a more natural rapport with the people living in the area. Since they are knowledgeable about the project site, they may be more able to judge the accuracy of data collected. Training local people to be monitoring team members builds local capacity and increases the likelihood that monitoring activities will continue throughout the life of the project.

Although local monitoring team members' familiarity with the project site may help, it can create problems. Local residents may find it difficult to ask probing questions of their neighbors. The neighbors may be less likely to talk about personal beliefs, attitudes, or behaviors with someone they know. Local monitoring team members may be less *objective* than outsiders because they may believe they know the "right answers." The way they ask questions in interviews with community members may bias responses.

In some monitoring programs—especially those that are a part of community managed projects—volunteers are responsible for collecting monitoring data. Having an all-volunteer monitoring team will usually mean that the cost of monitoring will be substantially less than having a paid staff. Volunteers, however, are usually not bound to the monitoring activity by any type of contract. They usually earn their living from some other activity and it may be more difficult to keep them to the monitoring schedule. On the other hand, paid staff are usually contracted to do specific work. This formal arrangement usually means paid staff are more legally and professionally obligated to perform the duties of their job.

Depending on the extent and intensity of the monitoring you intend to do, you'll want to consider how much of a commitment you'll need from the monitoring team. If the monitoring is going to be very straightforward and require relatively little field work (for example, based primarily on reviewing records), you may want to consider hiring staff on a part-time basis. In this situation, it may also be appropriate to use volunteers that help only at specific times during the monitoring process.

If, however, monitoring is much more intense and you'll need to collect a lot of data over an extended period of time, you may want to consider hiring full-time monitoring staff. As you decide which way you want to go, you should think about two important factors: cost and sustainability. Having to hire a paid full-time monitoring team will be more expensive than using a group of volunteer part-time workers. On the other hand, hiring temporary outside staff instead of making an investment in building the capacity of local monitoring team members will mean that monitoring will probably stop as soon as the team members' contracts are completed.

How do you select the monitoring team?

Finding the right people to help you collect data as part of your project monitoring is not an easy task. Data collection is often a difficult and demanding activity. You want to make sure your monitoring team is physically and mentally capable of doing the job. Remember, the monitoring team members are going to be representatives of your group while they are out in the field. It is important to get people you feel will do a good job representing your group.

Objective in this sense refers to collecting and analyzing data without having preconceived notions that influence how the data are interpreted.

The composition of the monitoring team you select should reflect the diversity of the population where you will be working. For example, if your monitoring plan calls for collecting data in an area where there are indigenous people and migrants, then your monitoring team should be made up of members of both groups. As almost all monitoring of social data requires talking to women, it is critically important that your monitoring team include women. In most cases monitoring teams should be roughly equally divided between men and women. Monitoring team members must have at least some basic formal education—they will be expected to do a lot of writing while collecting and compiling data.

Characteristics of a good team member include that he or she is:

* *Patient.* Maintains his or her composure even when things are not going as planned.

* *Attentive.* Listens to a respondent without interrupting, judging, or lecturing.

* *Humble.* Is not class conscious and doesn't put himself or herself above others.

* *Respectful.* Shows regard for community members and fellow team members.

* *Friendly.* Is easy to work with and gets along well with others.

* *Enthusiastic.* Is eager and animated.

* *Thorough.* Completes tasks as instructed.

* *Creative.* Is dynamic and shows flexibility in thinking.

* *Curious.* Shows genuine interest in what people have to say.

* *Strong.* Can handle difficult field work schedules, long hikes, and uncomfortable conditions.

* *Self-Motivated.* Takes the initiative to do needed tasks on his or her own.

A review of these characteristics may lead you to believe that monitoring team members need to be super-human. In fact, being a good monitoring team member is a very difficult task, as illustrated in the quote in the sidebar.

What are the training needs of the team?

Once your team has been identified, you'll need to determine how much they'll have to be trained to prepare them for field work. Most new conservation and development project monitoring teams will need at least to be introduced to the project—the social, cultural, biological, and physical context of the site—and the selected monitoring methods you intend to use. If monitoring

A field-worker should be able to sweep the floor, carry out the garbage, carry in the laundry, cook for large groups, go without food and sleep, read and write by candle light, see in the dark, see in the light, cooperate without offending, suppress sarcastic remarks, smile to express both pain and hurt, experience both pain and hurt, spend time alone, respond to orders, take sides, stay neutral, take risks, avoid harm, seem confused, care terribly, become attached to nothing. The nine-to-five set need not apply.

—Patton (1990)

team members will also be responsible for preparing data for analysis or conducting the analysis itself, they need to be trained in these subjects too. It is a good idea to decide with the team how they want to present themselves to a community upon arriving for the first time. Honest, consistent, and clear presentations will build trust with community members and will pave the way for smooth entry into the community.

How does the team you select affect the methods you use?

Selecting your monitoring team and the methods you use for monitoring influence each other. If your monitoring plans call for the use of sophisticated methods for data collection, then the monitoring team should be highly skilled. If your team doesn't have a lot of skills, then you will have to make sure that you select methods that they can use. For instance, if you cannot find monitoring team candidates who will be able to conduct a focus group discussion effectively, you'll have to use another method such as a formal questionnaire or a key informant interview.

Who is going to supervise the monitoring team?

As we saw earlier, monitoring a conservation and development project can be a full-time job for an entire team. Whether you hire paid full-time staff or organize a volunteer part-time team, you must have someone who is responsible for supervising the monitoring team and coordinating efforts. The supervisor must clearly understand the purpose and approach of the monitoring activities and must have a good understanding of the areas where the monitoring will take place. In addition to sharing the characteristics described earlier for good monitoring team members, the supervisor must be well organized, a good leader, and able to handle a variety of social and political situations. If the monitoring team is to be divided to cover a wide area, it may be useful to have more than one supervisor so that monitoring team members can be accompanied at all times.

Assembling Necessary Resources and Materials

Before you begin monitoring, you will also need to assemble necessary resources and materials. There are three basic questions that you need to keep in mind while doing so: What will the monitoring cost? What materials and equipment will you need to do the monitoring? What permissions do you need to get before you start your field work?

What will the monitoring cost?

You are probably wondering why we didn't ask this question first. After all, it seems to be an important one for so many aspects of monitoring. In addition to the benefits of monitoring, the cost is something that conservation and development practitioners must always consider closely. Although monitoring provides the means to better manage and measure the impacts of your project, some practitioners are concerned that money spent on monitoring could be better spent on other project activities. There is a balance that must be reached between too little and too much monitoring. It is unavoidable that at least some financial, technical, and human resources be devoted to data collection and analysis. The success of your project depends on it. Items you may need to include in your monitoring budget are staff salaries, field expenses, transportation, training, equipment, and materials.

What materials and equipment will you need to do the monitoring?

There are a number of items you will need to consider getting to help carry out monitoring activities. Your monitoring team members may need notebooks, pens, pencils, and paper. They may also need, among other things, small backpacks, rain gear, water bottles, sleeping bags, and flashlights. Your team will also need whatever equipment is required by the monitoring techniques that you are using. For example, if you are going to be conducting focus group discussions, you'll need to purchase an adequate number of small battery-operated cassette tape recorders and plenty of spare batteries and blank tapes. If you are doing animal census work, you will need binoculars and a good compass. Chances are, if you don't have one already, you'll need to buy a computer for data entry, processing, and analysis, and for writing up reports. Finally, how are you and your monitoring team going to get around? You may have to rent or buy a vehicle or bicycles.

What permissions do you need to get before you start your field work?

Before you and your team go to the field to begin your monitoring activities, you need to think about clearances or authorizations that are required to work in the project area. Usually, if permission is required by local authorities to work in the project site, you and other people responsible for implementing the project have probably already gotten it. If you haven't, now is the time to do it. In many countries, you'll need to get permission from local, regional, and, in some cases, national civilian authorities. Furthermore, in some countries it is essential to consult and receive written permission from the military to travel freely and conduct project and monitoring activities. Whatever the requirements of the country

where you're working, don't overlook this seemingly trivial detail. A little investment of time now may save you a lot of trouble in the future.

Applying Methods and Collecting Data

Although each method needs to be applied in its own way, there are a few general concepts involved in the application of almost all of these methods. In particular, we discuss:

- *Collecting and recording data systematically*, which involves making sure that you obtain data in a standard format.

- *Pre-testing your methods and instruments*, which involves trying your techniques before fully implementing them.

Collecting and Recording Data Systematically

Once you determine what methods you will use to gather the data and your sampling frame, the next step is to draft your *data collection instruments*. A data collection instrument is the standardized format that you will use for obtaining data, such as a questionnaire, topic guide, checklist, or record form. A carefully designed instrument will make data collection and analysis much easier and will reduce the potential for error. Because data are the raw material that you will collect to monitor your project's impact and ultimate success, it is particularly critical that data collection be carried out with extreme care.

A general principle to follow when designing field monitoring instruments is that the needs of the respondents, monitoring team, and data analysts must be considered simultaneously. It is important, however, to pay the greatest amount of attention to the first two groups—the respondents, or the people from whom you will collect data, and the monitoring team—a poorly designed instrument will create confusion, misunderstandings, and discomfort during interviews.

Specific approaches to collecting and recording data depend on the method being used to obtain the data. For example, you may be recording responses directly onto a formal survey questionnaire. Or you may be recording sightings of wildlife in a field notebook. No matter which method you use, one of the most important skills monitoring team members can develop is the ability to collect and record data in ways that are systematic, standardized, and accurate.

Systematic Data Collection and Recording

The term *systematic* refers to collecting and recording the same data for each individual observation that you are making. For both quantitative and qualitative data, this is best achieved by using a

structured data collection sheet. As a rule, the outline for your data sheet will depend on the method that you are using and the types of analyses that you hope to complete.

For example, in the Tropical Forest Scenario you might conduct a formal survey to look at cash needs and adoption of sustainable agricultural practices. You would want to develop a standardized questionnaire that has space for writing answers to questions about such things as household type and size, annual income, socioeconomic status, sustainable agricultural methods currently employed, and other types of data required for your analyses. Even if you end up writing your answers in a notebook instead of on the sheet, having the list of questions will help ensure that you collect your data in a systematic fashion.

Likewise, in the Wetlands Scenario you might conduct an animal census to look at population densities in different habitats. You might put a list in your notebook to remind yourself to collect data systematically about the time of sighting, on which trail the sighting occurred, your location along the trail, distance from trail, numbers of individuals, species, behavior, and how you first noticed them. If you are conducting a key informant interview with birdwatchers, then you can put a list into your notebook to remind yourself to ask them about their previous birdwatching experience, the places where they birdwatch, and the habitats that they think are important for birdwatching.

Standardized Data Collection and Recording

The term *standardized* refers to collecting and recording data in the same way for each observation. In particular, for both quantitative and qualitative data, all members of the monitoring team must collect and record data in the same way compared to one another and over time. On your instrument, you should make sure that entries are made in the same standardized way.

For example, in the household survey from the Tropical Forest Scenario described earlier, you want to make sure that households are defined the same way by the person doing the monitoring in each community. Are elderly grandparents living with their sons and their families considered part of the household? Are they a separate household? It doesn't matter which, as long as everyone in the project uses the same definition. You also want to make sure that all monitoring team members use the same lists of response choices. For instance, for a question about economic activities undertaken by the household, you don't want one person writing down "farming" while another writes down "subsistence agriculture" and a third "cash cropping."

In a similar fashion, in the animal census in the Wetlands Scenario, you want to make sure that groups of birds are counted in the same way (either by numbers of free flying individuals or by numbers of nesting pairs) and the data for distance from the observer are recorded in the same manner by all people (distance in meters along a perpendicular line from the trail). In the key informant interview from the Wetlands Scenario, it is important that all project staff doing interviews use the same topic guide.

Accurate Data Collection and Recording

The term *accurate* refers to collecting and recording data with a minimum of error. For both quantitative and qualitative data, it is vital that data be as close to their true value as possible. There are dozens of ways in which errors can be introduced into a data set. The most common sources of error include interviewer, respondent, data recording, and data coding errors. For example, field researchers can make mistakes (misinterpret statements during the household interview, misidentify a bird species during a census), get incorrect data from a respondent (the respondent makes up an answer because he is too embarrassed to acknowledge he doesn't know the real answer), miss observations (skip certain questions during the interview, not see a group of birds flying overhead), or write down the wrong data (write down monthly income instead of weekly income, write down that the birds are north of the trail instead of south).

Errors are an unavoidable part of doing research. However, all project staff involved in monitoring need to maintain a constant guard against sources of error. It is important to realize that, as a monitoring team member, if you don't know or can't get the data—don't make it up! It is better to have no data than fictitious data. It is okay to be unsure about a particular data entry—as long as the uncertainty is noted.

Ensuring data accuracy is a job in which everyone involved in

Process Hint: Use question marks when taking notes or recording data to show uncertainty. A common convention is to use the question mark directly after the piece of data that is uncertain (this helps eliminate problems in sorting the data in a computer). For example, in the Wetlands Scenario, a sample data record for an animal census might read:

0645, Trail 3, 535m, N50
3? Crows calling, heard
0715, Trail 3, 605 m, S100?,
2 Hawks flying, saw

In the first record, the question mark indicates that the observer is uncertain about how many crows she heard. In the second record, the question mark indicates that the observer is uncertain about how far south of the trail the hawks were sighted.

data collection should participate. If you are a monitoring team member collecting data, then you should review your notes, questionnaires, observations, or other completed instruments as often as possible to make sure they are complete. If you are the person responsible for managing monitoring activities in your project, a major part of your job should be to check and cross-check collected data to make sure that they are as accurate and consistent as is possible.

Pre-Testing Methods and Instruments

When designing a field data collection instrument, it is essential to do it properly from the start—you don't want to have to substantially revise your instrument half-way through the monitoring process, making all the work that you've done up until that time meaningless.

It is difficult to plan data collection without having some familiarity with the monitoring subject matter, the population you are sampling, the way people will react to questions, and even the answers they are likely to give. It is also difficult to determine how long data collection will take, how many interviews or field visits you'll have to do, and which questions are best for getting the information you need. The best way to deal with these issues is to *pre-test* (or field test) the methods you designed in the previous step.

This pre-testing process involves taking a draft of your instrument or instruments to the field and trying them out on a small sample of the population. It is best to divide up your pre-testing activities into a number of small portions where you try out different specific techniques or approaches. Eventually, you'll want to test your entire approach to make sure all the component pieces fit together and your overall monitoring strategy is effective and appropriate.

Pre-testing will help you to determine the adequacy of your sampling design, the range and variability of potential measurements, the suitability of the methods of data collection, the adequacy of the instruments, the efficiency and effectiveness of the instructions and training given to the monitoring team, and (specifically in the case of social data) the number of *nonresponses* and *noncontacts* you can expect.

Pre-tests can range in size from measuring just a few to hundreds of your sampling units depending on the methodology. In the case of social monitoring, for example, it usually takes no more than 10–15 interviews to get a good idea whether or not a method or approach is working. It is best to pre-test with a representative group of respondents who are most like the ones you expect to encounter during the actual monitoring—but not the same. For instance, you may pre-test your methods and approach in a com-

Nonresponse is when a person being interviewed refuses to give an answer to a particular question.

Noncontact is when a potential respondent refuses to be interviewed at all.

Pre-testing allows you to estimate the effectiveness of different ways of reducing nonresponse and noncontact. As a result, one method may be chosen over another; some questions may be excluded or altered, or the timing and duration of the interview may be changed.

munity adjacent to but not included in your project area. It is important to discuss the pre-test process and results thoroughly with the monitoring team to capture their perceptions and thoughts.

After completing the pre-testing phase, you must take the results and modify your methods and approach as needed. You can make adjustments to the wording, order, and format of questionnaires and other instruments depending on the results of the pre-test. You may want to modify or eliminate some of the data you will collect. You may even need to modify one or two of the indicators you included in your monitoring plan if they prove not to be feasible to measure or to be inaccurate gauges of the condition you are trying to assess.

Handling and Storing Data

Once you've pre-tested your instruments and revised them as needed, you are now ready to use them to collect data. Many projects get to this point and then become overwhelmed with the shear amount of data coming in and thus are unable to use them. While we hope that the preceding steps in this guide have helped you focus your monitoring efforts on only the key information needs, even so, you will undoubtedly be generating lots of data. Your challenge now is to organize the data coming in. In this section we describe:

- *Coding Data.* This involves defining how you want to represent and record them.

- *Reviewing Coding Data.* This involves checking for obvious recording errors and gaps.

- *Transcribing Data.* This involves recording your data in a systematic format.

- *Entering and Organizing Data.* This involves setting up a database.

- *Backing Up Data.* This involves making duplicate copies for storage.

- *Cleaning and Preparing Data for Analysis.* This involves going over data to catch any errors introduced during any of the previous steps.

Coding Data

Data coding is the process of defining how you want to represent and record your data. Each piece of data you collect should be recorded using a consistent and specific code that represents each characteristic you are measuring. Coding should be fully integrated with instrument design and should be field tested along with your methods as described earlier.

The data that you collect during monitoring activities will come in many forms. Questions in a formal survey are usually *closed* or *open ended*. Closed questions have a predetermined range of possible answers. For instance, in the example we used in the section on methods for the formal survey, we ask: "Who in your family makes bamboo baskets to be sold in the market?" Possible allowable responses include: (1) respondent (female head of household); (2) father; (3) male children; (4) female children; and (5) other. The interviewer is asked to circle those individuals who are mentioned by the respondent. In this closed question example, the interviewer has only five options to choose from.

Open-ended questions are left for the respondent to answer without having predetermined expected outcomes. For instance, using our key informant questionnaire example from the section on methods we see that that we include the question: "How has the amount [of fish people catch] changed over the last 10 years?" There is nothing on the questionnaire to suggest that we expect any particular answer—the question is left open for the respondent to answer as he or she wishes and for the interviewer to record the answer as it is given. Open-ended questions are generally used when there are many possible answers, the interviewer wants to get more than one simple response to the question, or the interviewer has no way of knowing what answers to expect.

It is often during the field testing phase that you can determine if questions should be closed or open ended and how you should code the responses. During this phase, you can purposefully leave questions open ended with the idea that the range of responses will become clear from the answers received during the field test. You can then choose to transform some of your open-ended questions into closed questions for the final version of your instrument.

Specific data coding techniques can be subdivided into those used for quantitative data and qualitative data.

Quantitative Data

Quantitative data are usually classified in one of two ways. They may be recorded as a number, as in "the number of fish caught in a net." This type of numerical data for which there are an unlimited number of possible outcomes is referred to as a **continuous variable**. Data can also be classified, as in "house with a thatch roof" or "house with a tin roof." This type of data for which there is a limited number of possible classifications is referred to as a **categorical variable**.

When coding continuous variables (numbers, distances, weights, incomes), it is generally best to enter the variable directly, making sure that it is in a common unit (like meters, kilograms, or

A *continuous variable* is measured along a scale.

A *categorical variable* is recorded in discrete intervals or as groups.

pesos). At this point you should not group values into categories. When coding categorical variables, it is important to make sure that the same categories are used consistently for each respondent. As we'll see in chapter 7, you may wish to group data into meaningful categories during data analysis. This is particularly useful for open-ended questions for which you can determine appropriate categories after you've collected the data.

As you develop the codes for your responses and data, you'll want to keep a record of these codes and what each value means. To do this you should create a *codebook* for each data collection instrument you use. Codebooks are generally developed for questionnaires and checklists that are comprised primarily of closed questions. A codebook is simply a reference guide that lists each question or piece of information you're collecting, the possible responses for each question or piece of information, and the codes you have assigned to each possible response. The codebook serves as a record of how you coded your data so that you or anyone else can code and interpret the same instrument in a standard manner in the future. Even if entries seem obvious, writing the codebook ensures that everyone who uses the data will have a common understanding of what form the data should be in. It is also a good idea to include a specific code for *missing data* for each question in your codebook.

The following two examples show how you can turn your data collection instruments into codebooks based on data collected from a formal household survey and a biological survey, respectively. These examples show both a sample of the instrument with which data are collected in the field and the accompanying codebook. Each codebook specifies what the acceptable format and range of entries are for each question or piece of information.

Missing data refers to places in your instrument where, for some reason, you did not collect the necessary data. This problem can be the result of the interviewer forgetting to record a response or observation or where a respondent refused to answer the question. You will want to keep missing data to a minimum. A convention for recording missing data is the use of the number "9" to fill coding spaces left for the response.

Example: Developing a Codebook for a Household Survey

This codebook is from the household survey in the Tropical Forest Scenario.

Household Survey: Indah Biosphere Reserve
(1) Respondent's name:_____
(2) Date:_____
(3) Interviewer:_____
(4) Location of house (describe):
(5) Household type: (Direct Observation)
  (A) Immediate
  (B) With elderly parents
  (C) Two or more households together
  (D) Single parent
  (E) Other (specify:_____)

(6) How many people are permanent residents of this house (live here full-time)? ___
(7) How do you and the others in your household earn a living?
   (circle all mentioned responses)
      (A) Traditional slash and burn agriculture
      (B) Permanent plot agriculture
      (C) Own small trade store
      (D) Receive money from relatives outside village
      (E) Government salary (teacher, health post)
      (F) Other (specify: _____)
(8) What is the total amount of cash you earn from all sources (include entire
   household) per year? _____ pesos/year
(9) Do you hold title to any of your agricultural land? ___Yes ___No
(9a) If "Yes," How many hectares of land do you hold title to? _____ ha
(10) Do you use any of the sustainable agriculture techniques that
   have been promoted here in the past? ___Yes ___No
(10a) If "Yes," Which techniques do you use? (circle all responses)
      (A) Soil erosion control techniques
      (B) Intercropping techniques
      (C) Integrated Pest Management (IPM)
      (D) Enhanced use of fire
      (E) Other (specify: _____)

Codebook: Indah Biosphere Household Survey

Q #	Question	Description	Range and Codes
1	Respondent's name	Respondent's first and last name	001-998: Each respondent is assigned a number in sequential order that is the questionnaire number 999: Missing Data
2	Date	Date of interview in month-day-year	01-12: Month 01-31: Day 96-99: Year
3	Interviewer	Name of interviewer	1: Ernesto 2: Baba 3: Hank 4: Phyllis 9: Missing Data
4	Location of house	Description of location of house for follow-up	Not coded
5	Household type	Composition of the household according to direct observation of interviewer	1: Immediate 2: With elderly parents 3: Two or more households together 4: Single parent 5: Other 9: Missing Data

(continues)

Codebook: Indah Biosphere Household Survey (*continued*)

Q #	Question	Description	Range and Codes
6	How many people are permanent residents of this house?	Total number of people (including infants & children) living full-time in the household	01-25: Actual number of people 99: Missing Data
7	How do you and the others in your household earn a living?	Major economic activities of those who earn income in household	1: Traditional slash and burn agriculture 2: Permanent plot agriculture 3: Own small trade store 4: Receive money from relatives outside village 5: Government salary (teacher, health post) 6: Other 9: Missing Data (Multiple Response: Can code up to 4 techniques)
8	What is the total amount of cash you earn from all sources per year?	Total annual household cash income from all sources: Interviewer must add all sources of income provided	0001-9997: Actual number of pesos earned 9998: Greater than or equal to 9998 pesos earned 9999: Missing Data
9	Do you hold title to any of your agricultural land?	Ownership of title to land	1: Yes 2: No 9: Missing Data
9a	How many hectares of land do you hold title to?	Amount of land owned by household if answer was "Yes" to Question 9.	001-500: Actual number of hectares of titled land 999: Missing Data or answer was "No" in Question 9
10	Do you use any of the sustainable agriculture ideas promoted here in the past?	Utilization of any sustainable agriculture techniques	1: Yes 2: No 9: Missing Data
10a	Which techniques do you use?	Types of sustainable agricultural techniques currently employed if the answer was "Yes" in Question 10	1: Soil erosion control techniques 2: Intercropping techniques 3: Integrated Pest Management (IPM) 4: Enhanced use of fire 5: Other 9: Missing Data or answer was "No" in Question 10 (Multiple Response: Can code up to 4 techniques)

Example: Developing a Codebook for a Wildlife Survey

This record form and codebook are taken from the Wetlands Scenario.

Transect Record Form: Everson Watershed

Record	Obs	Date	Time	Location	Distance	Number	Species	Behavior	Register

Codebook: Everson Watershed Transect Record Form

Item	Description	Range and Codes
Record	Sighting number: A coding number assigned to each sighting	001-600: In sequential order, one per observation 999: Missing Data
Obs	Observer: Name of person collecting data	1: Ernesto 2: Baba 3: Hank 4: Phyllis 9: Missing Data

(continues)

Codebook: Everson Watershed Transect Record Form (*continued*)

Date	Observation date: month-day-year	01-12: Month 01-31: Day 96-98: Year
Time	Observation time: Recorded in 24 hour time	0000 - 2359 (Midnight - 11:59 pm) 9999: Missing Data
Trail	Trail name: Name of trail from which observation was recorded	1: North River Trail 2: South River Trail 3: Marsh Trail 4: East Bog Trail 5: West Bog Trail 6: Valley Trail 9: Missing Data
Location	Location on trail: Distance along the trail in meters	01-50: This first number (2 digits) refers to 50 meter marked trail intervals (1 = 50m, 5 = 250m, etc.) 01-49: Second number (2 digits) refers to distance in meters from marked 50m interval (e.g. 0835 refers to a point 435 meters along the trail ((8 x 50m) + 35m = 435m) 999: Missing Data
Distance	Approximate distance from trail: Perpendicular distance in meters from the trail to the location of the animal	001-300 meters: Approximate distance from trail 999: Missing Data
Number	Number of animals: The number of free traveling animals observed (immobile juveniles are not counted)	01- 50: Actual number of animals observed 99: Missing Data (Includes hearing animals but not knowing how many there are)
Species	Species observed	01: Common crow 06: Large goose 02: Deer 07: Red duck 03: Fish eagle 08: Unidentified Raptor 04: Marsh hawk 09: White Heron 05: Muskrat 99: Missing Data
Behavior	Behavior of animal at first observation	1: Flying 4: Stationary 2: Calling 5: Feeding 3: Hunting 6: Other 9: Missing Data
Register	How observer noticed animal	1: Visual sighting 2: Heard vocalization 9: Missing Data

Qualitative Data

Qualitative data are usually recorded as a verbal statement as in the response: "I think that pollution is the major threat to the habitats in the watershed." Coding qualitative data is a bit different from coding quantitative data. In this case you do not design a database and codebook but instead try to organize the transcribed statements from conversations, focus groups, and informal interviews as well as other notes that were collected. Since qualitative data tend to be collected in words and not in numbers, it makes them in some ways harder to compile and work with. In addition, most words are meaningless without the context around them. The key in coding qualitative data is thus not to extract the words from their surroundings but rather to identify and extract key concepts that are relevant to your monitoring work. To do so you need to develop a coding guide that enables you to organize your data in preparation for analysis.

The following example illustrates coding of qualitative data from a focus group interview. This example shows parts of the topic guide and the transcribed data, the first portion of the coding guide (really an outline of how we want to organize the data), and then a sample of how you might disassemble the original text and reassemble it using your coding guide.

Example: Developing a Coding Guide for a Qualitative Data Set

This focus group guide, transcript, and coding guide are from the Wetlands Scenario.

Focus Group Topic Guide

Topic: Threats to the Everson Watershed

1. Theme: Pollution

Do you think that pollution from the cities affects the Everson Watershed? What are the major sources of pollution? What do they produce that pollutes the watershed? How does pollution affect the watershed? (*Probe:* How does it affect water quality? Wildlife? Plant life?) Does pollution of Everson affect the human populations that live around the watershed? How so? What can be done to reduce the amount of pollution that occurs? (*Probe:* Can ordinary citizens do anything to curb pollution? What would you do personally to help stop pollution?)

Transcript of tape recording: Focus Group Topic Guide

Topic: Threats to the Everson Watershed: Pollution

Group: Women between the ages of 20 and 65 in the town of Omokalee

Number in Attendance: 7

Moderator: Phyllis   *Observer:* Amy   *Location:* Omokalee

Date: 6/30/03

[*Moderator first welcomes everyone, has each woman introduce herself, and introduces the theme of the focus group*]

(continues)

The materials presented in this example are only partial excerpts of the full versions.

Moderator: Do you think that pollution from the cities affects the Everson Watershed?

Woman 1: Oh, of course! Can't you just smell all the pollution in the water when you're driving down the main highway? It all comes from the city. Too many people there. So much garbage they don't know what to do with it. You know they don't even have a sewage treatment plant in the city. Yup. All that dirty water just flows right into the canals.

Woman 2: Yeah, lots of water pollution comes from the city, but the really bad stuff comes from right here around our own town. You should see the amount of pesticides and chemical fertilizers the farmers around here use. When it rains, it all just washes right into the watershed. I remember about 20 years ago, we had a particularly dry summer but with lots of pests affecting the crops. People were out there spraying just about every day. When it finally did rain, so much poison washed into the canals that it killed all the fish. You should have seen it. And oh did it smell. . . .

Woman 3: Oh, I remember that. It was horrible. We couldn't eat the fish for months. . . .

Woman 4: I really think that very little pollution from the city gets out here. My son is studying engineering at the university and he told me that in one of his classes they're studying Everson. He told me that almost everything that gets dumped into the water in the city flows out to the ocean and not back into the Everson.

Woman 1: Yeah. I guess you're right. Most of the water pollution comes from around here. But what about the air pollution? Have you seen when that brown air blows over here on cold humid days? It's disgusting. I tell you, it's not good for Everson and it is definitely not good for us.

Woman 4: You're right about that.

Woman 2: I know that's right.

Moderator: So it sounds like chemical pesticides and fertilizers are a major source of pollution in the Everson Watershed. What are other major sources of pollution?

(The focus group interview continues)

Coding Guide

From the data we gathered simply asking the one question, "Do you think that pollution from the cities affects the Everson Watershed?," we can begin to develop a coding guide. Reviewing the transcript we might decide on the following preliminary outline (of which an excerpt is shown):

I. Pollution in the Everson Watershed
    I.A. Pollution from urban area
        I.A.1. Water pollution
        I.A.2. Air pollution
    I.B. Pollution from rural area
        I.B.1. Water pollution
            I.B.1.a. Agricultural run-off
                I.B.1.a.1. Effects on people
                I.B.1.a.2. Effects on ecosystem

We can then use this coding guide to disassemble the transcript and reorganize it as follows in preparation for analysis:

I. Pollution in the Everson Watershed

I.A. Pollution from urban area

I.A.1. Water pollution
Woman 1: Oh, of course! Can't you just smell all the pollution in the water when you're driving down the main highway? It all comes from the city. Too many people there. So much garbage they don't know what to do with it. You know they don't even have a sewage treatment plant in the city. Yup. all that dirty water just flows right into the canals.
Woman 1 later says: Yeah. I guess you're right. Most of the water pollution comes from around here.
Woman 4: I really think that very little pollution from the city gets out here. . . . He *[Woman 4's son is an engineering student at the university]* told me that almost everything that gets dumped into the water in the city flows out to the ocean and not back into the Everson.

I.A.2. Air pollution
Woman 1: . . . .but what about the air pollution? Have you seen when that brown air blows over here on cold humid days? It's disgusting. I tell you, it's not good for Everson and it is definitely not good for us. *[Women 2 and 4 agree with this statement]*

I.B. Pollution from rural area

I.B.1. Water pollution

I.B.1.a. Agricultural run-off
Woman 2: Yeah, lots of water pollution comes from the city, but the really bad stuff comes from right here around our own town. You should see the amount of pesticides and chemical fertilizers the farmers around here use.

I.B.1.a.1. Effects on people
Woman 3: It *[the fish kill due to pesticide and fertilizer run-off 20 years ago]* was horrible. We couldn't eat the fish for months. . . .

I.B.1.a.2. Effects on ecosystem
Woman 2: When it rains, it *[pesticides and chemical fertilizers]* all just washes right into the watershed. I remember about 20 years ago, we had a particularly dry summer but with lots of pests affecting the crops. People were out there spraying just about every day. When it finally did rain, so much poison washed into the canals that it killed all the fish. You should have seen it. And oh did it smell. . . .

Reviewing Data

Your first opportunity to *review* your data and check them for any obvious recording errors and gaps will be immediately after collection in the field. For example, if you look over your formal questionnaire data, you may find blanks where you forgot to write down answers. Be careful, however, not to infer too much and make errors by assuming that you know the answer to a question and writing in a response. If you have a blank in your responses and you can't go back to the source of the data to fill in the gap, it is better to record it as missing data.

Transcribing Data

For many methods, *transcribing* data is a necessary step in preparation for analysis. This process involves systematically, consistently, and clearly recording your data in some predetermined format. It is especially useful for organizing field notes and open-ended responses. Some methods like formal surveys, however, may not require this step as responses are recorded directly onto the instruments themselves. Transcription of focus group, key informant, and other qualitative data is particularly important as it allows you to begin to assemble data in an ordered and systematic fashion. Transcribing focus group data often involves listening to the recorded tapes of each of the sessions and typing them word for word into a computer or onto paper (this actually occurs before you develop your coding guide). It is also important to transcribe field notes and informally collected data so that you have a secure record of the data.

By taking the time to transcribe your data, you get the added benefit of providing yourself with a back-up copy of your valuable data. One of the worst feelings in the world is to realize that the data that you've collected that represents hundreds or even thousands of hours of work is missing. If you transcribe your data, then you are less vulnerable to losing your hard work if you drop your notebook in the river or forget your backpack with all your surveys in it on a bus.

Entering and Organizing Data

Once you have transcribed your data, you are ready to enter them into your data handling system. It is often easier to deal with data in small batches than to wait until all the data have been accumulated. However, in many cases you may have to wait, if, for example, data are being collected by members of a monitoring team posted in distant villages. Data entry is generally not that exciting, but it is very important that it be done accurately and that you cross-check your entries when possible. We will review this cross-checking process when we talk about data cleaning later. When entering data, take your time and make sure to take frequent breaks. Sometimes it can be effective to have one person reading the data and the other typing or writing the entries.

Specific data handling techniques can be subdivided into those used for quantitative data and qualitative data.

Quantitative Data

Most quantitative data collected using questionnaires or checklists are entered or archived in some kind of database, which is a table or archive that contains all the data that you have collected. This

archive can be kept on paper or in computer files using a ***spreadsheet, database program***, or ***statistical package***.

As shown in the example that follows from the Tropical Forest Scenario, a database is generally divided into records (rows) and fields (columns). Its structure is drawn directly from the instrument codebook that we discussed earlier. Each record or row represents a new sample unit, such as an interview, family, community, questionnaire, or animal sighting. Each field in a database contains one specific type of data. This corresponds to the data we saw in the "Range and Codes" sections of the codebooks we developed in previous examples.

Let's continue to use the same examples we used earlier to develop our codebooks. In the database presented below for the Tropical Forest Scenario formal survey, note that our fields (columns) include:

- Respondent's name (interview number)
- Date
- Interviewer
- Household type
- Number of people living in the household
- Sources of income
- Total household income
- Ownership of land (title)

A *spreadsheet* is a table designed to help manage numbers. Most computer spreadsheet programs contain lettered columns and numbered rows that form cells into which data can be entered. Computerized spreadsheets also contain various functions that help you manipulate numbers. Some of the more advanced programs will also help calculate statistics and draw basic graphs. Common brand name spreadsheets include Microsoft Excel, Lotus 1-2-3, and Quattro Pro.

A *database program* is designed to help you enter and manage data. Common brand name programs include Microsoft Access, dBase, and FoxPro.

A *statistical package* is a more advanced computer program specifically designed to help you do statistical analyses.

- Amount of land owned (in hectares)
- Use of sustainable agriculture techniques
- Type of sustainable agriculture techniques used

These fields correspond directly to the questions in the codebook except for the question on the location of the household. This field is not included in the database because, as you can see in the codebook, it is not coded. This bit of information is written down not as a piece of data to be analyzed but as reference information in case the household must be revisited. What you see below is the data entered into the database using the codes from the codebook we developed for the Tropical Forest Scenario earlier.

Example: Database for a Quantitative Data Set

This portion of a database is from the household survey in the Tropical Forest Scenario.

Formal Survey Database

Name	Date	Inter-viewer	HH Type	HH Size	Economic Activities*	Annual Income	Titled Land Yes/No	ha	Sustainable Agriculture Yes/No	Technique
001	030797	3	1	06	1230	1250	2	9	2	9999
002	030797	3	1	06	1300	2100	2	9	2	9999
003	030797	1	1	05	1245	4000	1	3	1	1200
004	030897	2	3	08	1000	2300	1	1	2	9999
005	030897	1	2	12	1200	3050	2	9	2	9999
006	031197	4	1	05	9999	3500	1	9	1	1000
007	031297	3	9	03	1200	2000	2	9	2	9999
008	040197	2	2	15	1500	5050	2	9	2	9999
009	040197	1	1	06	3000	2000	1	6	1	4000

* For these fields, remember that there can be multiple responses. Therefore, each of the 4 numbers corresponds to one of the possible choices found in the codebook. "0" means there were no additional responses

---

A similar example is shown with part of a database drawn from the wildlife survey in the Wetlands Scenario example. In this example, we show you how a monitoring team member actually filled in the instrument and then show you how it looks in the coded database format. Here fields include the same categories of data that were recorded earlier, including the following:

- Sighting number
- Observer
- Observation date
- Observation time
- Trail name

- Location on trail
- Approximate distance from trail
- Number of animals
- Species sighted
- Behavior of the individual
- How observer noticed animal

Data in these fields are entered into the database as shown in the following example.

Example: Database for a Quantitative Biological Survey Data Set

This form and database are from the wildlife survey in the Wetlands Scenario.

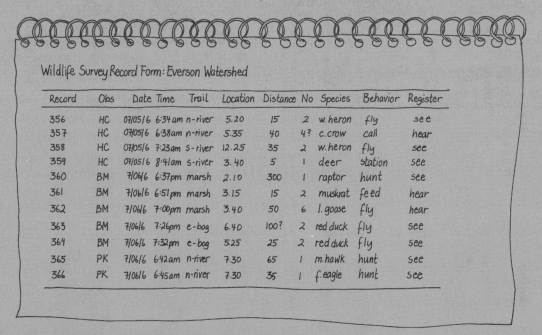

Wildlife Survey Record Form: Everson Watershed

Record	Obs	Date	Time	Trail	Location	Distance	No	Species	Behavior	Register
356	HC	07/05/6	6:34 am	n-river	5.20	15	2	w. heron	fly	see
357	HC	07/05/6	6:38am	n-river	5.35	40	4?	c. crow	call	hear
358	HC	07/05/6	7:23am	s-river	12.25	35	2	w. heron	fly	see
359	HC	07/05/6	8:41am	s-river	3.40	5	1	deer	station	see
360	BM	7/06/6	6:37pm	marsh	2.10	300	1	raptor	hunt	see
361	BM	7/06/6	6:51pm	marsh	3.15	15	2	muskrat	feed	hear
362	BM	7/06/6	7:00pm	marsh	3.40	50	6	l. goose	fly	hear
363	BM	7/06/6	7:26pm	e-bog	6.40	100?	2	red duck	fly	see
364	BM	7/06/6	7:32pm	e-bog	5.25	25	2	red duck	fly	see
365	PK	7/06/6	6:42am	n-river	7.30	65	1	m. hawk	hunt	see
366	PK	7/06/6	6:45am	n-river	7.30	35	1	f. eagle	hunt	see

Coded Database for Wildlife Survey Record Form: Everson Watershed

Record	Obs	Date	Time	Trail	Location	Distance	No	Species	Behavior	Register
356	3	070596	0634	1	0520	015	02	09	1	1
357	3	070596	0638	1	0535	040	04	01	2	2
358	3	070596	0723	2	1225	035	02	09	1	1
359	3	070596	0841	2	0340	005	01	02	4	1
360	2	070696	1837	3	0210	300	01	08	3	1
361	2	070696	1851	3	0315	015	02	05	5	2
362	2	070696	1900	3	0340	050	06	06	1	2
363	2	070696	1926	4	0640	100	02	07	1	1
364	2	070696	1932	4	0525	025	02	07	1	1
365	4	070796	0642	1	0730	065	01	04	3	1
366	4	070796	0645	1	0730	035	01	03	3	1

There are a number of computer programs that you can use to manage text data. One that we use and like very much is a shareware program called Zoot, available on the World Wide Web at http://www.zootsoftware.com. Although Zoot can be difficult to use at first, it provides a great utility for managing text information from many different sources.

Qualitative Data

Qualitative data collected through techniques such as focus groups or unstructured key informant interviews are usually not entered into a database as we saw in the previous examples. Nonetheless, organization of the data generated from these types of techniques is vital. As we explained in the section on coding, you should review your focus group or key informant data and develop a detailed outline of how you will want to organize and collate the data. With this outline and your coded data, you can go through your focus group or key informant results again, pull out and group relevant information, and rearrange it so that it follows your outline. You can do this with the assistance of a computer or you can use scissors and glue—what the pros call "cutting and pasting."

Backing Up Data

Once you code, transcribe, enter, and organize your data, store the originals in a safe place, separate from revised versions. It is best to put your filled-in data collection instruments in plastic-lined boxes and put them in a cool dry place. As soon as possible and at regular intervals thereafter, make at least two backup sets of your most recent versions. Depending on how your data were collected, you may want to do this as files in a computer or by photocopying relevant forms and documents. When traveling with data, leave one backup set behind with a colleague or friend and send one

backup set in the mail in case your boat sinks or someone steals your suitcase. Backing up your data may cost a little bit of money in terms of photocopying charges and postage, but it'll give you peace of mind.

Cleaning and Preparing Data for Analysis

Finally, *cleaning data* is the process of going over your data to catch any errors that were introduced during the coding and entering process. For quantitative data, look at the data in each field of your database. If you are using a computer, sort the file on each field (first making sure the records are numbered so that you can also return to the original order). Are there obvious **outliers**? If so, go

Outliers are data points that are outside of the expected range for the particular variable. They are not necessarily errors, but should be carefully checked to ensure that they represent true values.

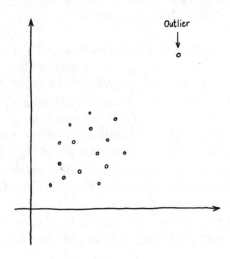

back to the original source of the data and check the data point. Was it a mistake in entry or coding? If so, change it. If not, then decide whether it is a mistake in collection or represents a true value. Add row and column totals and make sure they work out across and down. In some cases it may even be worth entering data twice and then using special software packages to compare them. For qualitative data, review the information that you have pulled out and organized. Does it all make sense? Have you left anything out? If so, go ahead and make necessary changes.

Remember, once you have completed your data files, make photocopies of the paper tables or print-outs and back-up any computer files you may have. Store them in separate places (perhaps one at home and one at the office).

Sources and Further Readings

The sources that we used most and recommend for additional information about the topics in this chapter include:

Cintrón, Gilberto, Jorge Reni García, and Francisco Geraldes (1994). *Manual de Métodos Para La Caracterización y Monitoreo de Arrecifes De Coral.* World Wildlife Fund, Washington, D.C. In Spanish—a basic overview of techniques for monitoring coral reefs.

Davis-Case, D'Arcy (1990). *The Community's Toolbox: The Idea, Methods and Tools for Participatory Assessment, Monitoring, and Evaluation in Community Forestry.* Food and Agriculture Organization (FAO), Community Forestry Field Manual, Number 2, Rome, Italy. A basic introduction to Rapid Appraisal techniques.

Debus, Mary (1995). *The Handbook for Excellence in Focus Group Research.* Academy for Educational Development, Washington, D.C. One of the best available guides to doing and analyzing focus group research.

Hall, Pamela, and Kamaljit Bawa (1993). "Methods to Assess the Impact of Extraction of Non-Timber Tropical Forest Products on Plant Populations." *Economic Botany* 47: 234–247. An overview of different techniques for monitoring the impact of product extraction on plant populations.

Kalton, Graham (1983). *Introduction to Survey Sampling.* Sage Publications, Newbury Park, California. A technical guide to different kinds of sampling.

Kruger, Richard (1994). *Focus Groups: A Practical Guide for Applied Research,* 2nd edition. Sage Publications, Thousand Oaks, California. A technical guide to collecting and analyzing focus group data.

Mack, Andrew L. (1996). *Training Manual for Field Survey Techniques: The Rapid Assessment Program (RAP) for Papua New Guinea.* Conservation International, Washington, D.C. A hands-on overview of techniques for conducting biological surveys of different types of organisms.

Patton, Michael Quinn (1990). *Qualitative Evaluation and Research Methods,* 2nd edition. Sage Publications, Newbury Park, California. An excellent resource guide for qualitative research.

Peters, Charles M. (1994). *Sustainable Harvest of Non-Timber Plant Resources in Tropical Moist Forest: An Ecological Primer.* Biodiversity Support Program, Washington, D.C. A basic guide to methods for monitoring the impacts of product harvesting on plant populations.

Pretty, Jules, Irene Guijt, Ian Scoones, and John Thompson (1995). *A Trainer's Guide for Participatory Learning and Action.* IIED Participatory Methodology Series, International Institute for Environment and Development, London, United Kingdom. A handbook for trainers and facilitators in using Rapid Appraisal tools.

Rabinowitz, Alan (1993). *Wildlife Field Research and Conservation Training Manual.* Wildlife Conservation Society, Bronx, New York. A user-friendly guide to ecological monitoring methods.

Rossi, Peter H., James D. Wright, and Andy B. Anderson (1983). *Handbook of Survey Research.* Academic Press, New York, New York. A comprehensive guide to survey research.

Rothman, Kenneth (1986). *Modern Epidemiology.* Little, Brown, and Company, Boston, Massachusetts. An introductory textbook to analytical methods in the field of public health.

Russell, Tim (1997). "Pairwise Ranking Made Easy." *PLA Notes* 28: 25–26. A basic description of the pairwise ranking matrix technique.

Schoonmaker-Freudenberger, Karen (1995). *Tree and Land-Tenure: Using Rapid Appraisal to Study Natural Resource Management.* Food and Agriculture Organization (FAO), Community Forestry Case Study Series, Number 10, Rome, Italy. A basic introduction to Rapid Appraisal techniques.

Theis, Joachim, and Heather M. Grady (1991). *Participatory Rapid Appraisal for Community Development: A Training Manual Based on Experiences in the Middle East and North Africa.* International Institute for Environment and Development, London, United Kingdom. Although written as a training guide, this is one of the best basic references on Rapid Appraisal techniques that we have found. Especially useful discussions of key informant interviews, matrix ranking techniques, and direct observation.

van Schaik, Carel (1994). *Censusing and Surveying Sumatran Rain Forest Animals (Birds and Mammals): A Brief Guide.* Duke University, Durham, North Carolina. An excellent overview of wildlife census and survey methods.

The following are other sources that we used in writing this chapter that you might find useful.

GreenCOM (1996). *Starting with Behavior: A Participatory Process for Selecting Target Behaviors in Environmental Programs.* GreenCOM, Washington, D.C.

Kleinbaum, David G., Lawerence L. Kupper, and Hal Morgenstern (1982). *Epidemiologic Research: Principles and Quantitative Methods.* Lifetime Learning Publications, Belmont, California.

Levy, Paul S., and Stanley Lemeshow (1980). *Sampling for Health Professionals.* Lifetime Learning Publications, Belmont, California.

Marshall, Catherine, and Gretchen B. Rossman (1989). *Designing Qualitative Research.* Sage Publications, Newbury Park, California.

Mausner, Judith S., and Anita K. Bahn (1974). *Epidemiology: An Introductory Text.* W.B. Saunders, Philadelphia, Pennsylvania.

Miles, Matthew B., and A. Michael Huberman (1984). *Qualitative Data*

Analysis: A Sourcebook of New Methods. Sage Publications, Newbury Park, California.

Moser, C.A., and G. Kalton (1972). *Survey Methods in Social Investigation.* Basic Books Publishers, New York, New York.

Poole, Peter (1995). *Indigenous Peoples, Mapping, & Biodiversity: An Analysis of Current Activities and Opportunities for Applying Geomatics Technologies.* Biodiversity Support Program, Washington, D.C.

Sudman, Seymour, and Norman M. Bradburn (1988). *Asking Questions: A Practical Guide to Questionnaire Design.* Jossey-Bass Publishers, San Francisco, California.

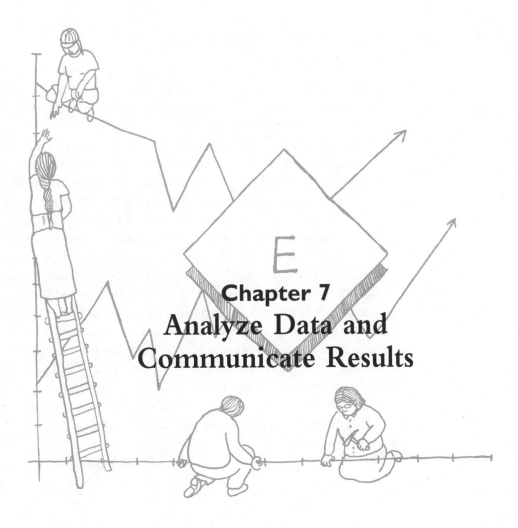

E

Chapter 7
Analyze Data and
Communicate Results

We have seen in previous chapters how to develop and implement a Project Plan. In the last chapter we examined specific monitoring methods and discussed how to collect and organize project data. Your challenge now is to turn these data into useful information and then communicate your results to your project partners, other stakeholders in and around the project site, and outside audiences.

There is no point in collecting data unless you know how and by whom they will be analyzed and used. As we said in the introduction, you must consider the steps involved in this chapter as early as possible in your project. Although the concepts and materials presented in this chapter are complex, we believe that these types of analyses are necessary for effectively monitoring projects, and that anybody who can follow the steps in other sections of this book can also do most of the analyses presented in this chapter.

Using the information presented in this chapter, you should be able to:

- Analyze data (Step E1).
- Communicate results to your internal and external audiences (Step E2).

Analyze Data (Step E1)

Analysis is a continuous process of reviewing data as it is collected, classifying it, formulating additional questions, verifying data, and drawing conclusions. Analysis is the process of making sense of the collected data. It should not be left until all data have been collected.

—Theis and Grady (1991)

Once data have been collected, entered, and cleaned, the next step is to analyze them. Analysis should not be left until the very end. Instead, as we can see in the quotation in the sidebar, analysis is a continuous and ongoing process.

If at all possible, analysis should take place while you are collecting data and as close to the field as possible. There are several reasons for doing this. First, the sooner you do your analysis, the less likely you are going to forget the context in which you gathered your data. Second, as is the case for all parts of your project, the more that you involve the project stakeholders in the analysis and verification of data, the more likely it is that they will understand and use the results. Finally, doing analysis during the data collection process enables you to *triangulate* your results and cross-check them if necessary. Triangulation is accomplished by using a variety of sources, methods, or field team members to collect the same data. As you cross-check your data, the more consistent they are, the more likely it is that they are valid. Triangulation is especially important when using qualitative monitoring methods which do not employ rigorous sampling techniques. Some examples of triangulation from our scenarios include:

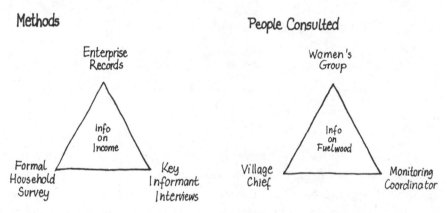

We are using "quantitative methods" as shorthand for "methods for collecting quantitative data" and "qualitative methods" as shorthand for "methods for collecting qualitative data."

Analysis is not a magical procedure that automatically gives you crystal clear results containing absolute truths about your project. Instead, it is simply a tool which you can use to extract information from your data. Ultimately it is up to you and your project team to take the results and interpret them in a way that enables you to manage your project better and document your success.

It is far beyond the scope of this book to go into a detailed discussion of the hundreds of techniques available for data analysis. Instead, we will discuss a few general concepts involved in analysis and provide a brief description of some of the specific techniques for analyzing different types of data generated by the quantitative and qualitative methods discussed earlier in chapter 6.

Quantitative data can be divided into two types, categorical and continuous, and we will explore analysis techniques for each of these data types.

Before getting into the specifics of the different analytical techniques, let's look at the two general kinds of analysis for using quantitative and qualitative data:

- *Describing Your Data.* Almost all analytical efforts start by taking the raw data that you have and summarizing them into a manageable form. This process involves organizing and characterizing observations about a set of **units** drawn from a specific **population** or **sample**. These characterizations include measuring typical or representative values, the degree of variability among the values, or the number of times which certain values appear.

- *Testing Hypothesis About Your Data.* Once you have described your data, the next step is to use them to examine the success of your project's interventions. This process involves examining how two or more **variables** differ or how they are related to one another. We also sometimes need to measure and predict how changes in one or more variables are associated with or lead to changes in another.

An Important Warning

In the following sections we present a number of different statistical analyses. When many people hear the word "statistics," their immediate response is something like:

> "Oh no, statistics!"

> "Statistics are boring and not useful."

> "I can't do statistics."

While we understand these reactions, we also feel that these types of analyses are both vital for monitoring and that anybody who can follow the previous steps in this guide can also do some, if not most, of the analyses presented in the following section.

To help you decide which of the following analyses to use, we have marked them according to their degree of difficulty. If you are new to this type of work, you may at first wish to focus on the basic ones. Once you gain some experience, you may then move on to the more advanced ones. It is perfectly okay, however, to use only the simpler techniques—often the basic ones are the best ones to use. Furthermore, if you don't fully understand a more advanced analysis technique and use it improperly, you may actually be worse off than if you had used a more basic one. The most important thing is that you are comfortable with the analysis that you are doing and that it provides the information that you and your audiences need.

As stated in the previous chapter, a *unit* is a single item or individual that you are interested in looking at. Depending on the type of monitoring that you are doing, units can be, for example, a community, a household, a person, a garden plot, or a tree. The collection of all units that you could potentially observe is called a **population**. All units in a population must have at least one characteristic in common—for example, households in a community, rattan collectors, or trees of a certain species. A **sample** is the portion or subset of a population that you measure. Samples are used to represent the entire population or some specific subgroup within the population—for example, the set of households included in the survey is a sample that we hope represents the households in the project site.

A *variable* is a particular characteristic of a unit that we are interested in observing or measuring—for example, household size or crop production per year.

In the following sections, the degree of difficulty of the various techniques are marked:
● = basic analysis
■ = intermediate analysis
◆ = advanced analysis

Analyzing Quantitative Data

Describing Quantitative Data

As a reminder, *categorical data* are recorded in discrete intervals or as groups. These groups can either be ordered or unordered. An example of ordered categorical data is household income measured in categories (rich, middle, poor). An example of unordered categorical data is the gender of respondents (male or female).

Continuous data are those that are measured along a scale. Examples of continuously measured data include household income measured in pesos/year or age of the male and female heads of the household measured in years.

Note that while continuous data can be converted into categorical data (dividing income into three categories as shown in the above example), categorical data cannot be converted into continuous data. Thus, if you have a choice, it is generally better to record data as continuous rather than categorical because you can always convert it if the need arises.

As stated earlier, the first step in analysis is to organize and characterize the data set that you have collected. For instance, in the formal survey example from the Tropical Forest Scenario, you might want to know how the use of various sustainable farming methods (for example, intercropping, composting) varies across different income categories or education levels. You also might want to come up with one number that is characteristic of household size or household income in the community. Finally, you might want to look at how household size or income varies across the community.

One technique that is most useful for describing *categorical data* is grouping data with similar characteristics. Techniques that are most useful for describing *continuous data* include measuring the central tendency of data, and measuring the variability of data.

Categorical Data: Grouping Data with Similar Characteristics (●)

A common technique used to look at grouping data is to construct a *frequency table*. A frequency table is the best descriptive technique to use with categorical data. It can also be used, however, with continuous data if you divide the data points into classes and show the frequency by which observations fit into each class. Data from a frequency table can then be displayed in a *histogram* (often called a bar graph) which visually displays the data in the table. Frequency table data can also be expressed in terms of proportions (percentages) of the total number of observations or sub-categories. Finally, data can also be arranged into a contingency table (often called a cross tabulation) which displays how two variables are related to one another. A general *contingency table* looks like:

| | *Variable A* | | |
Variable B	Category A1	Category A2	Total
Category B1	a	b	a+b
Category B2	c	d	c+d
Category B3	e	f	e+f
Total	a+c+e	b+d+f	n=a+b+c+d+e+f

The letters "a–f" represent measured observations.
The letter "n" represents the total sample size.

If a data set is small, it is generally fairly easy to inspect it to see patterns among the variables. As the data set gets larger and larger, however, it becomes more difficult to merely look at it and see a pattern. This is when frequency tables and histograms become more useful. For instance, in the formal survey example from the Tropical Forest Scenario, you might want to group residents in a village by income levels into rich, middle-income, and poor households. Contingency tables are useful to help determine relationships among different variables in the data set. In the above example, you might look at the frequency of the use of different sustainable farming methods in the community or do a cross tabulation of household income and type of farming methods used.

Example: Creating Frequency Tables, Histograms, and Contingency Tables

In your formal survey from the Tropical Forest Scenario, you have sampled 120 households and you have asked them about their annual income. Looking at the data, you are able to construct a frequency table as follows:

Income (pesos/year)	Frequency
Poor (0–1999)	42
Middle (2000–3999)	58
Rich (4000+)	20
Total	120

(continues)

A given data set can be organized into many different and equally valid frequency tables. For instance, you could have divided your data in this example into four categories (very poor, poor, middle, and rich). General guidelines to follow in choosing the classes that you will divide the observations into include:

1. The first interval should contain the smallest observation and the last should contain the largest one.
2. Class intervals should not overlap; every observation should be included in one class.
3. If possible, classes should be of equal length (although the above example does not completely follow this guideline because the final category is unbounded).
4. Class separations should reflect natural boundaries in the data if possible.

The same data can also be represented in a histogram as follows.

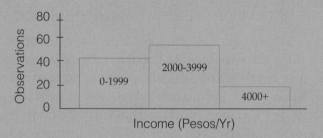

Finally, as part of your survey you have also ranked each of the 120 households according to their degree of adoption of sustainable farming techniques (full, partial, or none). To show household income in relation to adoption of sustainable techniques, the data are placed in a contingency table as follows:

Household Income vs. Sustainable Technique Use				
(Pesos/Year)	None	Partial	Full	Total
Poor (0-1999)	18	13	11	42
Middle (2000-3999)	24	14	20	58
Rich (4000+)	7	7	6	20
Total	49	34	37	120

Continuous Data: Measuring the Central Tendency of Data (●)

In this context, *location* refers to the distance along a numerical scale used to measure the variable in question.

One way in which the *location* of a population can be described with respect to a given variable is through various measures of *central tendency*. These are used to describe one representative value for a given group of observations. In effect, measures of central tendency answer the question "If we could use only one number to describe a group, what would it be?"

As shown in the example below, the *average* or *mean* is calculated by adding all the observations in a group and dividing by the total number of observations. Another useful measure of central tendency is the *median,* which is the middle value in a set of observations ordered by size. Measures of central tendency are good for quickly describing a sample or a population. For instance, in the household survey example from the Tropical Forest Scenario, you might want to describe household income or household size in the sampled population as shown below.

Example: Calculating Averages and Medians

The average, or mean, is calculated by adding all the observations in a population or sample and dividing by the total number of observations. For example, household sizes recorded in a sample during the formal survey described above are:

6, 6, 5, 8, 12, 5, 3, 15, 6
6 + 6 + 5 + 8 + 12 + 5 + 3 + 15 + 6 = 66

The average is 66 ÷ 9 = 7.3.

The median is calculated by arranging the observations in order of size and taking the middle one. For the same example, rearrange the data:

3, 5, 5, 6, *6*, 6, 8, 12, 15

The median is the fifth observation which equals 6 (if there are an even number of observations, you can merely average the middle two).

In a *normally distributed* population, the average and median should be identical. When they differ, this is an indication that the population is *skewed*. In this example, the average is higher than the median. This occurs because the average is sensitive to extremes (the household with 15 members) whereas the median is not. The average is biased by the fact that in two of the sampled households, there are multiple families living together.

Process Hint: If you are using a Microsoft Excel spreadsheet, you can easily use its "functions" to calculate the average and median for a data set. Enter your data in a column or row. Go to the cell where you want to display the average and enter =Average(Data Range) where "Data Range" equals the cells containing your data. To calculate the median, use the same data set, but enter =Median(Data Range).

Other software programs have similar types of functions—consult the manual for specific instructions.

A *normally distributed* population is one that follows a traditional bell-shaped curve with a peak in the center and two equal tails on either side as shown in the following drawing.

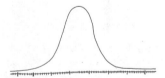

A *skewed* population is not centered but is biased to one side, as shown in the following diagram.

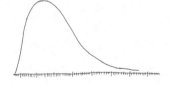

Continuous Data: Measuring the Variability of Data (■)

Differences between members of a group are most commonly described using measures of *variability*. A group's *range* is the difference between the smallest and largest observations. *Variance* is a more technical calculation of variability that involves calculating the average difference between each observation and the average for the group (with the differences being squared to avoid problems with positive and negative signs). Finally, *standard deviation* is the square root of the variance.

Measures of variability are good for describing the differences in a population. For instance, in the household survey example, although the average income is 2788 pesos/year, incomes range between 1200 and 5000 pesos/year. Furthermore, it may be the case that in future years the project finds that although the average income has stayed about the same, the variance may have dramatically increased (meaning the rich are getting richer and the poor are getting poorer) or decreased (meaning the gap between rich and poor is narrowing).

Between the different measures, range is useful because it is easy to calculate. It deals with the extremes, however, and not with the majority of observations which tend to be located around the mean. Variance is harder to calculate (unless you are using a computer spreadsheet or software package) but is a better measure of overall differences among individuals in the sample. Standard deviation is sometimes used instead of variance because it is expressed in the same units as the variable being measured and can therefore be used to show the average plus or minus the standard deviation.

Process Hint: If you are using a Microsoft Excel spreadsheet, you can use its variance and standard deviation functions. Enter your data in a column or row. Go to the cell where you want to display the variance and enter =Var(Data Range) where "Data Range" equals the cells containing your data. To calculate the standard deviation, use the same data set, but enter =Stdev(Data Range). Other software programs have similar types of functions—consult your software's manual for specific instructions.

If you are calculating the variance for a population instead of a sample, you divide the total sum of squares by the number of observations without subtracting 1.

Example: Calculating Range, Variance, and Standard Deviation

The range is calculated by subtracting the smallest observation in a population or sample from the largest one.

For example, for the household survey described above, the household sizes are:

6, 6, 5, 8, 12, 5, 3, 15, 6

The range is 15 – 3 = 12.

The variance is calculated for a sample according to the following procedure illustrated in the table below.

1. List each observed data point in the sample as shown in column A.
2. Put the average for the data sample in each row of column B. In this example, as calculated above, the average is 7.3.
3. Subtract the average from each data point as shown in column C.
4. Take each number in column C and square it (multiply it by itself) as shown in column D.
5. Add up all the squares in column D to get the total sum of squares. In this case, the Total sum of squares is 116.01.
6. Take the number of observations in the sample and subtract 1 from it. In this case, the total number of observations is 9 and 9 – 1 = 8.
7. Divide the (total sum of squares) by (number of observations – 1) to get the variance. In this case, the variance is 14.5.

Finally, the standard deviation is simply the square root of the variance, which in this case is $\sqrt{14.5}$ = 3.8. So you could say that in this case, the average household size in our sample is 7.3 ± 3.8 people (the average plus or minus the standard deviation).

A Data	B Average	C (Data Point- Average)	D (Data Point- Average)^2
6	7.3	−1.3	1.69
6	7.3	−1.3	1.69
5	7.3	−2.3	5.29
8	7.3	0.7	0.49
12	7.3	4.7	22.09
5	7.3	−2.3	5.29
3	7.3	−4.3	18.49
15	7.3	7.7	59.29
6	7.3	−1.3	1.69
Total Sum of Squares			116.01
Number of Observations − 1			9 − 1 = 8
Variance		116.01 ÷ 8 = 14.5	

Testing Hypotheses with Quantitative Data

Once you have described your data, the next step is to use them to examine the success of your project's interventions—to test your project assumptions. For instance, in the formal survey example from the Tropical Forest Scenario, you might want to see whether rich or educated households adopt sustainable agriculture techniques more readily than poorer or less-educated ones. You might also want to compare the average income in a village located near the forest to the average income in a village located away from the forest. Or you might want to see how average income in each of the two villages has changed over time. Or you might want to look at the relationship between household education levels and income. Finally, you might also want to try to predict how people's income levels will change as a result of their having a higher level of education.

To answer each of these questions, you need to use what is called in statistics a *hypothesis testing process*. This process involves using the various techniques outlined below to support or reject a certain **hypothesis** about your project. These hypotheses can involve comparing the same variable in one population over time or between two or more populations or looking at the relationships between two or more variables in a given sample or population. Hypothesis testing can be done with both quantitative and qualitative data, but the specific analysis you can do varies according to the type of data that you have and the type of problem you are attempting to analyze.

A *hypothesis* is a formal statement proposed about the population or populations being sampled, such as "Average income of Umoja Village is greater than average income of Bikuna Village" or "Increasing income leads to adoption of sustainable farming techniques."

Hypothesis testing is straightforward if you include all the units in all populations being measured—all you need to do is directly compare the measurements of the variable. For example, in the Tropical Forest Scenario, suppose your hypothesis is:

> Average income of households from Umoja Village participating in the enterprise at the end of the project is greater than average income for these households during the initial year of the project.

Assuming you can survey every household in the village, then you can simply measure average incomes at the start and the end of the project and compare them. If, for example, you find that at the start of the project average income was 1843 pesos/year and at the end of the project average income is 3123 pesos/year (and you can assume that your measurements are accurate), then you can conclude that your hypothesis is true. In order to determine if there is a significant change, all you need to do is decide how large a difference is meaningful.

Hypothesis testing is not as straightforward, however, when you are using samples to make comparisons between the overall populations. In this case, in addition to the problem of determining whether the overall hypothesis is true or false, you also need to consider a second problem of whether or not the samples you are working with truly represent the populations that you are trying to measure. For example, suppose you sampled 10 percent of the households at the start of the project and found that the average income in your sample was 2036 pesos/year. You then go back at the end of the project and sample a different 10 percent of the households and find that the average income in your sample is 2845 pesos/year. At first glance, it may seem like you have proved your hypothesis. But what if by pure chance, in your first sample you mainly interviewed poor families while in your second sample you mainly interviewed rich families? In this case, you may be stating that your hypothesis is true when in fact it is not—in effect, claiming that your project was successful when in fact it wasn't.

To solve this second problem, you need to use a technique referred to as *statistical inference*. Statistical inference involves using different techniques to assess the probability that a hypothesis about an association between two or more populations (that is based on samples of these populations) is true or false. For a given set of samples, an *association* can be a comparison of one or more variables or causal linkages between variables.

There may be many reasons for an apparent association but only one reason that no association occurs—it is simply not present. For that reason, it is easier to test the hypothesis when there is no association. A statement of no association is called the ***null hypothesis.*** To test the null hypothesis, you assume that there is no

---

Note that although you may have proved this hypothesis "true," it does not necessarily mean that you have achieved your stated management objective—you may have needed to increase income by 1500 pesos/year to get households to stop their overharvesting, which is a threat to the forest.

A *null hypothesis* describes the opposite effect to the one you are trying to demonstrate. Using the example from above, you may be trying to prove a hypothesis: Average income of households

association (that the null hypothesis is true) and then ask the question: "Do our data support this assumption?" Thus, you are in a position of wanting to reject the hypothesis of no association if you want to see an effect. If your data make the null hypothesis of no association look unreasonable, then you can reject the null hypothesis and thus accept your original hypothesis of association. If, however, your data support the null hypothesis, then you must reject your original hypothesis. We know that this sounds backward and strange, but it is the way that statistical tests are done.

If you are doing this statistical inference step by step, the basic procedure is:

- Develop a hypothesis.

- Formulate the opposite null hypothesis.

- Calculate a *test statistic* from the data.

- Compare this test statistic to a standard distribution to develop a measure of probability or *p-value* that indicates the likelihood of the null hypothesis being false—how "unreasonable" it is.

- Either reject or accept the null hypothesis thus proving or disproving the original hypothesis at the given level of significance.

If you can reject the null hypothesis, you have solved the problem of whether your sample represents your population and can state with a defined level of confidence that there is a statistically *significant* effect. You still need, however, to go back and see whether this effect is meaningful in the context of your project's objectives.

The process of testing statistical hypotheses can seem difficult if you have never done it before. Like anything, however, although it can be hard the first time, it gets easier with practice. If possible, find someone who has done this type of analysis before and work with them. Once you have done it a few times, it will become much easier to do.

Hypothesis testing with data collected using quantitative methods can also be divided into categorical and continuous techniques. For categorical data the technique most often used is comparing expected and observed values in grouped data. For continuous data, those techniques that are most useful include comparing averages with census data drawn from all units in a population, comparing averages from samples drawn from a single population over time, and comparing averages from samples drawn from two different populations. We then present two techniques for testing hypotheses about relationships between variables. These include graphical analyses of correlations between variables and statistical analyses of causal relationships using linear regression.

from Umoja Village in the enterprise at the end of the project is greater than average income for these households during the initial year of the project.

The null hypothesis (no effect) that you actually test is:

Average income of households from Umoja Village in the enterprise at the end of the project equals average income for these households during the initial year of the project.

If you can show that there is a strong likelihood that the null hypothesis is false, then you can "reject" it and thus accept your original hypothesis.

A *test statistic* is a number calculated according to a certain formula based on the sample data. No sample reflects the population perfectly. There is always the chance that the sample will be atypical and cause you to incorrectly conclude that there is a real association. A *p-value* is the probability that your test statistic represents a real result and is not merely occurring by chance. It is a number between 0 and 1. Since the p-value is calculated in relation to the null hypothesis, to determine whether you should accept your actual hypothesis, you need to subtract the observed p-value from 1 to give you the percentage likelihood that your hypothesis should be accepted. A p-value of 0.1 thus indicates that there is a 90 percent chance ($1 - 0.1$) that you are seeing a real relationship.

In most scientific circles, a p-value of .05 (equal to a 95 percent chance that you are not making a mistake rejecting the null hypothesis) is required before you can assert with some confidence that the effect is *significant* and not due to chance. In doing project monitoring, however, it may be very difficult to get p-values that are this high, especially if you have small sample sizes.

Categorical Data: Comparing Expected and Observed Values in Grouped Data (■)

When dealing with categorical data (either original data or continuous data that have been categorized), the most common way of testing hypotheses about two or more variables is to use a *chi-square test*. This technique tests the basic null hypothesis that a set of *observed values* in a frequency or contingency table will match *expected values* predicted by some theoretical model. If this null hypothesis can be rejected, then the observed values significantly differ from the expected values. This hypothesis can be tested through the calculation of the test statistic chi-square (χ^2) as outlined in the example below.

Chi-square tests are useful when you want to see how frequencies in actual groups compare to what your theory might predict. They are the most commonly used technique with the time-series monitoring strategies presented in chapter 6. They can also be used to explore relationships between variables as shown in the box below.

Process Hint: If you are using a Microsoft Excel spreadsheet, you can use the "Chitest" function. Enter an observed values table and an expected values table. Go to the cell where you want to display the result and enter <=Chitest("Actual Range","Expected Range")> where "Actual Range" equals the cells containing your observed values and "Expected Range" equals the cells containing your expected values. The computer will return the p-value for the chi-square test when you hit enter. Other software programs have similar types of functions—consult the manual for specific instructions.

Example: Chi-Square Analysis

Suppose that you are interested in testing the hypothesis:
> Wealthy households are more likely to use sustainable agriculture techniques than poor households.

In your research, you construct a contingency table as shown in the example stated earlier. Note that household income was originally a continuous variable that was categorized, while sustainable technique use is a pure categorical variable.

Table of Observed Values

Household Income	Sustainable Agriculture Use			
(Pesos/Year)	None	Partial	Full	Total
Poor (0–1999)	18	13	11	42
Middle (2000–3999)	24	14	20	58
Rich (4000+)	7	7	6	20
Total	49	34	37	120

Based on these data, it is hard to tell whether they support your hypothesis. You thus decide to try a chi-square test of the null hypothesis that:
> Wealthy households are no more likely to use sustainable agricultural techniques than poor households.

In effect, this null hypothesis implies that poor, middle income, and rich households will be equally distributed among the sustainable agricultural use categories in direct proportion to their overall number in the sample. We can calculate expected frequencies for this null hypothesis by taking the row totals from the Table of Observed Values and dividing them by 3 (the number of columns) to get the proportion of households that we would expect to get if there was no effect. The expected frequencies are:

Table of Expected Values

Household Income	Sustainable Agriculture Use			
(Pesos/Year)	None	Partial	Full	Total
Poor (0–1999)	14.0	14.0	14.0	42
Middle (2000–3999)	19.3	19.3	19.3	58
Rich (4000+)	6.6	6.6	6.6	20
Total	40	40	40	120

To calculate the test statistic χ^2 you can either use a computer statistical package or the following procedure illustrated in the table below.

1. List the data point from each cell of the table of observed values as shown in column A.
2. List the corresponding data point for each cell from the table of expected values as shown in column B.
3. Subtract the expected value from the observed value for each cell as shown in column C.
4. Take each number in column C and square it (multiply it by itself) as shown in column D.
5. Divide each value in column D by the expected value as shown in column E.
6. Add up all the values in column E to get the value for the chi-squared test statistic. In this case, $\chi^2 = 4.58$.
7. Take the total number of rows (R) in the observed values table and subtract 1 from it. In this case, $(R - 1) = 2$.
8. Take the total number of columns (C) in the observed values table and subtract 1 from it. In this case, $(C - 1) = 2$.
9. Multiply $(R - 1)$ by $(C - 1)$. In this case, $2 \times 2 = 4$. This is the *degrees of freedom* (df) for the test.
10. Using a chi-square table from a statistics book, look up the value of the test statistic for the given level of degrees of freedom. In this case for $\chi^2 = 4.58$ and df = 4, you find that p = 0.3325. Because your p-value is not less than 0.05, you cannot reject the null hypothesis, meaning there is no statistically significant difference between the observed and expected values.

(continues)

The *degrees of freedom* for a statistical test is the number of independent parameters and values. It is calculated in different ways for different tests. The probability of a given test statistic being significant varies according to the number of degrees of freedom. You therefore look up the value of the test statistic in a table for the given number of degrees of freedom.

As a rule, the more degrees of freedom that you have, the more likely it is that you will be able to detect a true difference between two samples. Statisticians refer to the ability to detect a true difference between two samples as the *power* of your test. If the power of your test is too low, then there is little chance you'll detect a difference in your results, even if there are real differences between the variables you're studying. A small sample size is almost always the root cause of low power.

A Observed Value (O)	B Expected Values (E)	C (O − E)	D (O − E)²	E
18	14.0	4.0	16.00	1.14
13	14.0	−1.0	1.00	0.07
11	14.0	−3.0	9.00	0.64
24	19.3	4.7	22.09	1.15
14	19.3	−5.3	28.09	1.46
20	19.3	0.7	0.49	0.03
7	6.6	0.4	0.16	0.02
7	6.6	0.4	0.16	0.02
6	6.6	−0.6	0.36	0.05

Chi-Squared Statistic	$\chi^2 = 4.58$
Number of Rows (R) − 1	3 − 1 = 2
Number of Columns (C) − 1	3 − 1 = 2
df = (R − 1) x (C − 1)	2 x 2 = 4
p-value	$p = 0.3325$

Suppose, however, that in another village you conduct a similar survey. Now you find that there is an observed distribution:

Table of Observed Values

Household Income (Pesos/Year)	Sustainable Agriculture Use			
	None	Partial	Full	Total
Poor (0–1999)	25	12	5	42
Middle (2000–3999)	21	20	17	58
Rich (4000+)	2	6	12	20
Total	48	38	34	120

Using the same expected values as before, you again compute χ^2 which in this case is equal to 22.84. When you compare this to a chi-square table, you find that $p = 0.0001$ and therefore you are able to reject the null hypothesis. You can therefore conclude with a good deal of certainty in this case that adoption of sustainable harvesting techniques is higher for wealthier households. Note, however, that this test says nothing about why this relationship exists.

Continuous Data: Comparing Averages with Census Data Drawn from All Units in a Population (●)

As stated earlier in this section, when you are not sampling but rather measuring entire populations, then comparisons are relatively easy. The basic procedure, as illustrated in the following example, is merely to calculate the desired descriptive statistic (such as average number of households or variance in household income) for the populations in question, compare them, and see if the result is meaningful in the context of the project goals and objectives. This is most commonly used with the pre-test/post-test, strict control, and comparison group monitoring strategies in the cases where you can obtain complete census data.

Example: Comparing Two Populations When You Measure All Units

In the Tropical Forest Scenario, you are interested in assessing changes in income in a village over time, looking at the hypothesis:

Average income of households from Umoja Village participating in the enterprise at the end of the project is greater than average income for these households during the initial year of the project.

There are 20 households in Umoja Village and it is fairly easy to survey each of them. You survey all 20 households at the start of the project and find that they have an average income of 1843 pesos/year and then survey all 20 households at the end of the project and find that they now have an average income of 3123 pesos/year. You compare these by subtracting 3123 – 1843 to get a net increase in income of 1280 pesos/year. You have clearly shown that your results support your hypothesis.

Note, however, that merely proving this hypothesis does not make it meaningful. If your project's objective was to raise average income by 5000 pesos/year, then you have not met your objective. Alternatively, if your objective was to raise income by 500 pesos/year, then you have met your objective.

Continuous Data: Comparing Averages from Samples Drawn from a Single Population over Time (■)

The averages of samples drawn from a population over time are most commonly compared using a *paired t-test*. A paired t-test compares an average calculated from a sample drawn at time 1 (usually before the intervention) to an average calculated from a second sample drawn at time 2 (usually after an intervention)—in effect, testing the hypothesis:

Average at time 1 = Average at time 2

When it can be assumed that the samples are drawn from normally distributed populations with equal variances, then the test statistic t can be calculated as shown in the example below. It is important to remember that this t-test only needs to be done when you are comparing samples from the two time periods (as opposed to censuses of the entire population). If you can calculate the averages for the entire population at the two times directly, you do not need to use a t-test and can simply make direct comparisons as in the previous section.

A paired t-test is most useful when you are using a pre-test/post-test monitoring strategy in which you want to compare the units influenced by your project to themselves before and after the project intervention. For instance, you might want to compare the household income in a village before and after the project, as shown in the following example.

When a population is not normally distributed, then nonparametric statistics such as the Mann–Whitney U Test need to be calculated (see any good statistics book for the procedure to do this).

Process Hint: To calculate a paired t-test using a Microsoft Excel spreadsheet, enter your data in two columns. Under the "Tools" menu, select "Data Analysis." You will then get a menu of different analyses—select the one that says "t-test: Paired Two Sample for Means." Select this analysis and follow the directions. You can also use the "TTest" function, but this will not give you the same level of detail in the output. Other software programs have similar types of analyses.

Example: Conducting a Paired t-Test to Compare a Population to Itself over Time

As an example, assume an objective for a project is:

> By the end of the fifth year of the project, families in Bikuna Village involved in NTFP harvesting will increase their income by 15 percent from NTFP harvesting and processing enterprises.

To monitor this objective, you need to track changes in amount earned from NTFPs over time ("amount earned from NTFPs" is your indicator). You thus want to test the hypothesis that:

> Average household income from NTFPs in Bikuna Village at the end of the project is greater than average household income from NTFPs at the start of the project.

You sample 20 percent ($n = 16$) of the households in the village involved in the enterprise at the beginning of the project (T_1) and sample the same 16 households at the end of the project (T_2). You calculate the descriptive statistics for both samples and come up with average incomes from NTFPs of 2307.5 pesos per household for the initial year of the project and 2428.1 pesos per household for the final year of the project (an average net increase of 120.6 pesos per household). This result seems to support your hypothesis that income from NTFPs is increasing over the life of the project.

However, since you only sampled some of the households in the total village in each period, this difference could be due to chance. You therefore want to use a paired t-test to determine the probability that this difference is due to chance, testing the null hypothesis:

> Average household income from NTFPs at end of project = Average household income from NTFPs at start of project.

To calculate the test statistic t you can either use a computer program or the procedure illustrated in the table below.

1. List the units sampled in column A. In this case, there were 16 households sampled.
2. List the observed data point for each unit for the initial time period (T_1) in column B and for the final time period (T_2) in column C.
3. Subtract the value for T_1 from the value for T_2 as shown in column D.
4. Calculate the average and standard deviation for the values in column D. Note that while average (T_2) – average (T_1) = average ($T_2 - T_1$), the same relationship does not hold true for the standard deviation.
5. Take the total number of pairs sampled and take the square root of this number. In this case, $n = 16$ and $\sqrt{16} = 4$.
6. Divide the average for the values in column D by the standard deviation for the values in column D and then multiply this number by the square root of the number of pairs to get the test statistic t In this case:
$$t = (120.6/201.8) \times 4 = 2.39$$
7. Take the total number of pairs sampled and subtract 1 to get the degrees of freedom (df) for the test. In this case, $16 - 1 = 15$.
8. Using a t-table from a statistics book, look up the value of the test statistic for the given level of degrees of freedom (a one-tailed test). In this case, $t = 2.39$, df = 15, $p = 0.015$.

A Household Sampled	B Value for T_1	C Value for T_2	D $T_2 - T_1$
1	1940	2130	190
2	2430	2690	260
3	2340	2350	10
4	2210	2360	150
5	1460	1200	−260
6	3450	3870	420
7	2340	2620	280
8	2880	3200	320
9	1570	1530	−40
10	2670	2980	310
11	1790	1640	−150
12	2940	3150	210
13	2230	2430	200
14	1940	1800	−140
15	2230	2150	−80
16	500	2750	250

Average $(T_2 - T_1)$	120.6
Std. Dev. $(T_2 - T_1)$	201.8
Number of Pairs (n)	$n = 16$
Square Root of n	$\sqrt{16} = 4$
Test statistic (t)	$\left(\dfrac{120.6}{201.8}\right) \times 4 = 2.39$
df $= (n - 1)$	$16 - 1 = 15$
p-value (p)	$p = 0.015$

You then look at these results and based on the p-value can conclude with 98.5 percent (1.00 − 0.015) certainty that you can reject the null hypothesis and thus be reasonably sure that average income from NTFPs at end of the project is greater than average income from NTFPs at the start of the project.

It is reassuring to see that the project has led to an increase in income over the past five years. However, you still need to check to see if you have reached your objective. In the objective, you stated that based on group discussions with community members, they need to increase their income from NTFPs by 15 percent to reduce the threat posed by their overharvesting. The average cash need for families that were sampled during the baseline period (T_1) was 2307.5 pesos/year. Your objective was to increase income by 346 pesos (15 percent of 2307.5) and yet your average increase was only 120.6 pesos, which works out to be about 5.2 percent of total needs. Thus, in this case, even though the results of this analysis are statistically significant, this change is not programmatically significant as it does not meet your objective.

Continuous Data: Comparing Averages from Samples Drawn from Two Different Populations (■)

The averages of samples drawn from two different populations are most commonly compared using a *two sample t-test*. This t-test compares an average calculated from a sample from one population to an average calculated from a sample drawn from a second population—in effect, testing the hypothesis:

Average of population 1 = Average of population 2

When it can be assumed that the samples are independently drawn from normally distributed populations with equal variances, then the test statistic t can be calculated as shown in the following example. As in the case of the paired t-test, this test only needs to be done when you are comparing two samples (as opposed to complete populations).

A two sample t-test is most useful when you are using a strict control or comparison group monitoring strategy in which you want to compare the units influenced by your project to a control or comparison group. For instance, you might want to compare the household income in a village that is part of the project to a village that is not part of the project as shown in the box below.

Here again, if the assumptions of normality do not hold, you will need to use nonparametric tests, such as the Mann–Whitney U Test or the Kolmogorov–Smirnov test. These tests tend to have less power to resolve subtle differences, but are perfectly valid to use.

Also, if you are interested in testing hypotheses involving three or more populations, you cannot use a t-test but instead need to employ a single-factor Analysis of Variance (ANOVA)—consult any good statistics book as to how to do this test.

Although this t-statistic is similar to the paired t-test, there are some differences in the calculations.

Process Hint: To calculate a two sample t-test using a Microsoft Excel spreadsheet, enter your data in two columns. Go under the "Tools" menu and select "Data Analysis." You will then get a menu of different analyses—select the one that says "t-test: Two-Sample Assuming Equal Variances." Select this analysis and follow the directions. You can also use the "TTest" function, but this will not give you the same level of detail in the output. Other software programs have similar types of analyses.

Example: Conducting a Two Sample t-Test to Compare Two Populations

Suppose that the hypothesis that you want to test is:
    Income in Bikuna Village (part of the project) is greater than income in Umjoa Village (not part of the project).

To test this hypothesis, you measure income in samples drawn from the two villages. You sample 20 percent ($n = 16$) of the households in Bikuna village and 20 percent ($n = 20$) households from Umjoa village. You calculate the descriptive statistics for both samples and come up with average incomes from NTFPs of 2428 pesos per household for Bikuna and 2098 pesos per household for Umjoa (an average of 330 pesos per household more than Bikuna households). These results seem to support your hypothesis that income from NTFPs has increased in the village where the project took place.

However, since you only sampled some of the households in each village, this difference could be due to chance. It is easily possible that your sample of households in Bikuna only included those with higher incomes. You thus want to use a t-test to determine the probability that this difference is due to chance, testing the null hypothesis:
    Average income from NTFPs in Bikuna = Average income from NTFPs in Umjoa.

To calculate the two sample test statistic t you can either use a computer program or the procedure illustrated in the table below.

1. List the number of units sampled in column A. In this case, there were 16 households sampled in Bikuna and 20 in Umjoa.

2. List the measured data point for each unit for sample 1 in column B and for sample 2 in column C.
3. Calculate the average for each sample as shown in line D.
4. Subtract the average from the second sample from the first sample as shown in line E.
5. Calculate the variance for each sample as shown in line F.
6. List the number of observation in each sample as shown in line G and then subtract 1 as shown in line H.
7. Multiply the variance for each sample (line F) by $n - 1$ (line H) as shown in line I.
8. Add the numbers of observations for the two samples and subtract 2 as shown in line J.
9. Compute the "pooled variance" for the sample according to the following formula: $\dfrac{(n_1 - 1)\text{Var}_1 + (n_2 - 1)\text{Var}_2}{n_1 + n_2 - 2}$

   In this case, the values are $\dfrac{481136 + 221585}{34} = 336093$ as shown in line K.
10. Take each sample size and divide it into 1 (line L) and then add them together (line M).
11. Multiply line K by line M and take the square root as shown in line N.
12. Divide the line E by line N to get the value for t as shown in line O. In this case, $t = 1.698$.
13. Take the sum of the observations for the two samples and subtract 2 to get the degrees of freedom (df) for the test as shown in line P. In this case, $16 + 20 - 2 = 34$.
14. Using a t-table from a statistics book, look up the value of the test statistic for the given level of degrees of freedom (a one-tailed test). In this case, $t = 1.698$, df $= 34$, $p = 0.0493$.

If the sequence of steps may seem confusing, it is because the formula for calculating a two sample t is complex. If you look at it piece by piece as we do here, however, it is not difficult—for those of you who prefer seeing formulas, it is:

$$t = \frac{\text{Avg}_1 - \text{Avg}_2}{\sqrt{\dfrac{1}{n_1} + \dfrac{1}{n_2} \times \dfrac{(n_1 - 1)\text{Var}_1 + (n_2 - 1)\text{Var}_2}{n_1 + n_2 - 2}}}$$

A	B	C
Household Sampled	Bikuna (Sample 1)	Umjoa (Sample 2)
1	2130	1940
2	2690	2430
3	2350	2100
4	2360	2970
5	1200	1810
6	3870	1420
7	2620	2390
8	3200	1650
9	1530	2450
10	2980	2110
11	1640	1400
12	3150	1730
13	2430	2900

(continues)

A Household Sampled	B Bikuna (Sample 1)	C Umjoa (Sample 2)		
14	1800	2560		
15	2150	1840		
16	2750	2410		
17		1700		
18		2220		
19		2470		
20		1460		
Average (Avg)	2428	2098		D
$Avg_1 - Avg_2$			330.1	E
Variance (Var)	481136	221585		F
n	16	20		G
$(n-1)$	15	19		H
Var x $(n-1)$	7217044	4210120		I
$n_1 + n_2 - 2$			34	J
Pooled Variance			336093	K
$1/n$	0.0625	0.05		L
$1/n_1 + 1/n_2$			0.1125	M
$\sqrt{\text{Line M} + \text{Line K}}$			194.45	N
$t = $ Line E $\div$ Line N			1.698	O
df $= (n_1 + n_2 - 2)$			34	P
p-value			0.0493	Q

You then look at these results and based on the p-value can conclude with about 95 percent (1.00 – 0.049) certainty that you can reject the null hypothesis and thus be reasonably sure that average income from NTFPs in Bikuna is greater than average income in Umjoa.

Continuous Data: Graphical Analyses of Correlation Between Variables (●)

Correlation refers to the relationship between two variables without implying a cause-and-effect relationship between the two.

Using continuous data, simple relationships between two variables are generally depicted by drawing *scatterplots*, which show the relationship between two variables. As shown in the example below, these plots can visually depict the degree of *correlation* between the two variables, although it does not tell you the direction of causality in the relationship.

Example: Using a Scatterplot to Examine Relationships Between Variables

Suppose that you are interested in exploring the relationship between education levels and income. In your survey, you have collected data on the number of years of schooling completed by the head of each household and annual household income. These data are as follows:

Obs.	Years in School	Annual Income
1	5	2800
2	7	3100
3	3	1800
4	0	1200
5	0	1400
6	5	1600
7	10	5200
8	0	900
9	3	2200
10	4	1900
11	6	2700

The data are then plotted as below, showing that as education increases, income generally increases as well, indicating that education is correlated with income.

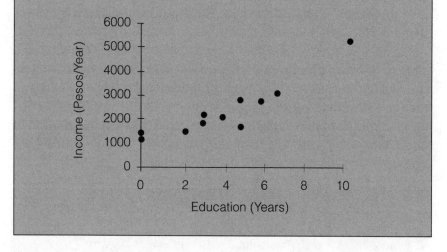

Continuous Data: Statistical Analyses of Causal Relationships Between Variables (◆)

To look at causal relationships between variables, we need to divide them into one or more *independent variables* and one *dependent variable*. When both the independent and dependent variables are continuous data, relationships between the variables are typically analyzed using *linear regression analysis*. Regression analyses are basically testing the hypothesis:

Change in variable 1 is linearly linked to change in variable 2

Independent variables are those factors that predict the effect—they are traditionally plotted along the horizontal or *x*-axis.

A *dependent variable* is the measurement of the effect itself—it is traditionally plotted along the vertical or *y*-axis.

In the scenarios presented in this

book, the target conditions can be considered dependent variables and the factors can be seen as independent variables. A given factor, however, can also be a dependent variable in relation to other factors that affect it.

If your dependent variable is categorical and your independent variables are either categorical or continuous, you must use a statistical procedure known as logistic regression.

If your dependent variable is continuous and your independent variables are categorical, then you can use either regression analysis with "dummy variables" or ANOVAs.

Consult any advanced statistics book for information on how to conduct these analyses.

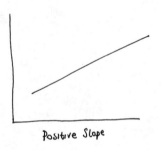

Positive Slope

Negative Slope

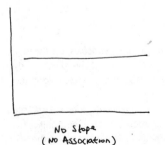

No Slope
(No Association)

For instance, in the education/income example shown earlier, it seems that as the level of education increases, income also increases. Linear regression involves measuring how strong this association is by fitting a line that is mathematically calculated to come as close as possible to all the points in a scatterplot. This line can be used both to describe the existing relationship and to predict what future observations might look like.

In terms of describing the relationship, there are two numbers that are important. The *linear correlation coefficient* (which is represented by r) is related to how well the line that is drawn fits the observed data points. This number thus serves as a measurement of how well change in the independent variable explains change in the dependent variable. If $r = 1$, then there is a perfect linear relationship between the x and y variables—the regression line includes all the points. If $r = 0$, then there is no relationship—the data points are randomly scattered. In many cases, r^2 is used instead of r.

The *slope* of the regression line (which is represented by b) determines how "steep" the line is. If, in our example, the slope is positive, then this means that as education increases, income also increases. If the slope is negative, then as education increases, income decreases. One of the most important hypotheses that can be tested with regression analysis is the null hypothesis $b = 0$. If you can reject this hypothesis, then you can demonstrate that there is a significant slope to the line, thus supporting the hypothesis that an effect exists.

Once you have established a regression line, then it is also possible to use this line to predict future observations. To do so, you can locate the value of the desired input along the x- or y-axis and then use it to read off the graph as shown in the box. This prediction technique is more reliable as you move toward the middle of your data—it is difficult to make predictions at one end of the graph.

Example: Regression Analysis

Suppose that you are interested in testing the hypothesis:

Household income increases with increasing education of the head of the household.

You enter the data from the preceding example into a computer spreadsheet or statistical package and use it to calculate a regression analysis. From this analysis, you get a print-out that looks something like:

Parameter	Coefficient	Std Err	t	p
Intercept (Constant)	915.94	259.17	3.534	0.0063
X Variable (Slope = b)	342.43	52.41	6.533	0.0001

Regression of education on income, $r^2 = 0.8258$

In addition, the computer draws a graph of the regression that looks like:

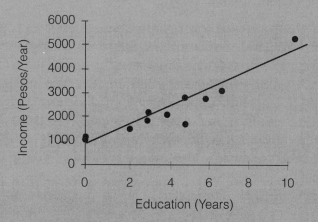

So what does all this mean? The two key factors are the values for *r* and *b*. In this case, $r^2 = 0.8258$, indicating that 82 percent of the variation in income can be explained by change in income. Generally, if you have an r^2 value above 0.6 (60 percent), then this indicates that your independent variable does a fairly good job of predicting your dependent variable. The estimate of the slope of the line *b* is listed in the table as being 342.43 ± 52.41. This number means that for every year of increasing education, you can expect a 342 peso increase in income. The t-test that is shown in the table is testing the null hypothesis:

> The slope of the regression line = 0 (there is no effect of education on income).

In this case, the p-value computed for this t-test is 0.0001, which indicates that you can be very sure that the slope of this line is significantly greater than 0.

Finally, even though you did not sample any people with 8 years of education, you might be interested in trying to predict what someone's income might be if they did indeed have this amount of schooling. As shown below, you can draw a vertical line (a) on the graph up from 8 years on the *x*-axis to where it touches the regression line. You then draw a horizontal line (b) from this point to the *y*-axis to get a measurement of the predicted income, which in this case, is about 4000 pesos/year.

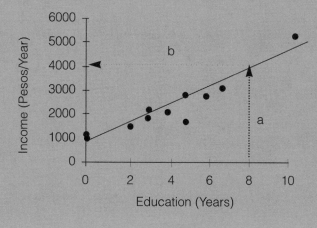

Analyzing Qualitative Data

Describing Qualitative Data

In the focus group sessions and key informant interviews you conducted in the Wetlands Scenario, you might want to know what the most common perceptions are among users of the Everson Watershed regarding the effects of pollution. You also might want to know if there is general agreement among key informants about which locations are most important for recreation or if they have a wide range of opinions. In each case, describing your data enables you to both better understand them and present them to other people.

When dealing with data collected using qualitative methods there are several techniques that can be used that are rough analogues to the descriptive techniques used for data collected using quantitative methods. The techniques that we present here include classifying responses (similar to looking at frequencies) and determining levels of agreement among responses (similar to looking at central tendency and variance).

Grouping Responses (●)

A common technique for analyzing data collected using qualitative methods is to group common responses. This classification can be done with data collected from some techniques but not others. In general, grouping analyses are difficult to do within focus groups since the group itself is supposedly a homogenous unit. It is possible, however, to classify data between focus groups or to roughly group data collected via techniques like key informant interviews or matrix rankings. For instance, in the birdwatching key informant interview example described earlier, you may group respondents based on where they live or based on their age. As is generally the case with data from qualitative methods, when you begin to quantify them, you need to be careful not to imply a sense of *false precision*.

False precision occurs when data are presented as being more accurate than they actually are. It is particularly important to be on the lookout for this type of error when you are using qualitative data. For instance, it may be tempting to take data gathered through a focus group interview and divide the answers into different categories and then make inferences about the variance. The problem here, however, is that the selection of your focus group is deliberately biased and thus cannot be used for this type of analysis.

Example: Classifying Results of a Key Informant Study

In your research you have conducted interviews with six key informants regarding the importance of different threats to different wetland habitats used for birdwatching. In your database you have compiled the following comments regarding this topic:

Interview Number	Position	Major Threats Identified
1	County Env. Supervisor	Road noise, pollution, habitat loss
2	Birdwatcher	Crowds, pollution
3	Resident	Crowds, power boats
4	Head of Local NGO	Habitat destruction, feral house cats, pollution
5	Resident	Hunters leaving litter
6	State Wildlife Biologist	Habitat loss, organic chemical pollution

Looking at these responses, you can state that "almost all respondents identified pollution as a major threat to the habitats used for birdwatching." You can also classify the responses based on the position that people hold into those respondents who porfessionally deal with environmental issues in the watershed (Interviews 1, 4, and 6) and those who do not (Interviews 2, 3, and 5). You can then say that "all of the professional environmentalists viewed habitat destruction as a major threat while none of the others did."

Determining Level of Agreement Among Responses (●)

Another common technique for analyzing data collected using qualitative methods is to look at the level of agreement in responses. The level of agreement among responses in a sample can most easily be described by determining which answers to questions are most commonly given by respondents. Researchers use words like "all," "almost all," or "none" to describe the degree of agreement. For instance, in the focus group example from the Wetlands Scenario, you might have found that in the initial focus group interview, almost none of the respondents reported that they thought that pollution was a problem in the Everson Watershed. In a follow-up focus group interview held at the end of the project, you might have found that almost all of the respondents believed that pollution was a problem.

If you find it easy to define the response to a certain question using words like "all" or "none," then there is not a great deal of variability among the responses. If, however, you find it difficult to identify a consistent response in your group, then there is a high degree of variation for that response. For instance, in the key informant example looking at preferred birdwatching sites, you might find that most people agreed about a few of the most prominent sites, but that for smaller and lesser known sites there was very little agreement.

> **Example: Examining Levels of Agreement in Focus Group Responses**
>
> You have conducted four focus groups (two from urban areas and two from rural areas) looking at citizens' perceptions of pollution in the Everson Watershed. Going through your transcripts of the sessions, you can conclude that for the two groups from rural areas, there was a high level of agreement in which you can further conclude that "almost all respondents were unaware of pollution problems." In the two urban groups, however, there was not much consensus, and instead you can only conclude "there was a great deal of variation in response. Some people felt that pollution is a problem while others are unaware of a problem."
>
>   Note that when interpreting the results of these transcripts, in addition to analyzing the transcribed interviews for the focus group sessions, you can also incorporate the moderator and observer's notes on nonverbal cues such as tone or volume of the person's voice. For instance, one person might say "Pollution was a *big* problem," meaning that she felt that pollution was the biggest threat, while another person might say "Pollution *was* a big problem," meaning that the threat had now been solved. Unless you have the contextual information, your analyses of the statements could easily be biased.

Testing Hypotheses with Qualitative Data

Although the concept of hypothesis testing has traditionally been applied primarily to data collected using quantitative methods, it can be relatively straightforward with data collected using qualitative methods as well. For instance, in the Wetlands Scenario, you might want to test the hypothesis:

> Community members' knowledge about the threats posed by pollution in the Everson Watershed has increased over time due to our project's intervention.

You can measure change in knowledge over time that is attributable to your project's intervention by conducting a series of focus group interviews at the start and at the end of the project and directly comparing the results. You can also use your key informant interview data from the Wetlands Scenario to see if certain bird species are more visible from bird blinds than others. Or you might want to look at what factors lead to an enjoyable birdwatching experience.

We consider two techniques for testing hypotheses with data collected using qualitative methods: comparing responses and testing relationships in interview responses.

Comparing Responses (●)

Using data from qualitative methods, you can examine hypotheses by comparing answers from different respondents. This process involves formulating the idea that you want to test and then look-

---

Example: Testing Comparison Hypotheses with Qualitative Data

Suppose that you are interested in using the results of a key informant interview study to test the hypothesis:

Herons are more likely to roost near bird blinds than hawks.

To test this idea, you might group responses from the informants into a rough table showing those who believe the hypothesis holds and those who don't. You could then get some sense of whether your hypothesis holds.

---

ing at the results to see whether or not they support your hypothesis. In the key informant example from the Wetlands Scenario cited earlier, you might be interested in testing a hypothesis about heron roosting behavior as shown in the box above.

Testing Relationships in Interview Responses (●)

Using data from qualitative methods, relationships between variables can also be described. For instance, you might be interested in knowing which factors affect a person's decision to go birdwatching. You might thus use preference ranking to determine which factors people find most important as shown in the following box.

Example: Testing Relationships with Qualitative Data

Suppose that you are interested in using the results of preference ranking to examine the question:

What factors most influence people's enjoyment of birdwatching?

The factors that respondents identified in the preference ranking exercise include:

- Number of birds sighted
- Number of species sighted
- Number of rare species sighted
- Proximity of site to their house
- Proximity of site to parking lot
- Degree of solitude
- Lack of water pollution at sight

Using the approach described in chapter 6, you determine that the most important factor identified by your respondents is the number of species sighted. The least important factor is the proximity of the site to the parking lot. Here again you cannot generalize the results to the broader population but can only consider them relevant to the type of people that you interviewed. For instance, in our sample you purposefully sampled only young avid birdwatchers. If you had done the exercise with senior citizens, you might have found proximity of the site to the parking lot was the most important factor.

Communicate Results to Your Internal and External Audiences (Step E2)

For the purposes of this guide, we use the word *presentation* to refer to any communications product, including spoken, written, and multi-media products.

The next step in the process is to develop and give *presentations* of the results from your analyses to your internal and external audiences, including project partners, other stakeholders in and around the project site, and outside audiences.

Selecting a Presentation Format for Your Audience

The first step in developing a presentation is to pick a format that best suits the information that you want to convey and the specific audience that you are trying to reach. As discussed in chapter 5, there are many different potential audiences for the information being generated by your project and monitoring efforts. Each of these audiences, may require that information be packaged in a separate way for it to reach them most effectively. Specific types of communication tools that we describe include:

- Oral presentations

- Discussion sessions

- Informal contacts

- Reports

- Press and media releases

- Brochures and pamphlets

- Formal (academic) papers and books

- Visual presentations (posters, slide shows, films)

- Internet and world wide web

For each format, we discuss what it is, the type of audience that it is best suited for, the types of information that it is useful and not useful for conveying, and its cost, both in terms of money and other resources.

Oral Presentations

What are they? Speaking directly to your audience, often using handouts, charts, slides, or other visual aids to supplement your message. Presentations can be formal (a lecture at a conference) or informal (a five-minute talk during a staff meeting).

Who will they reach? Presentations generally only reach a live audience, unless videotaped or broadcast on television or radio. If handouts are provided to accompany the presentation or people take good notes, then some information may be retained and

passed on to other people. As a rule, however, you do not get a substantial *multiplier effect*.

When are they useful? When you can directly access your target audience and need to provide them with specific information that you have and that they do not have. Presentations can also be useful when combined with discussions or to introduce people to the highlights of complex written materials. Oral presentations are particularly useful with audiences who can't read.

When are they not useful? When your audience is not locally accessible or when you have substantial amounts of information to convey that cannot be quickly absorbed. Long formal speeches are almost never effective ways to communicate information. Presentations are generally not very effective (compared to discussions or written materials) in cases where the audience is not fluent in the language being used.

What do they cost? Generally, presentations don't cost much.

What other resources are required? You need to have a comfortable location for people attending the presentation—although not so comfortable that people fall asleep. You also need to prepare both the presentation itself and any handouts or visual aids in advance. Make sure that you practice your presentation a few times so your are comfortable with it. Finally, you may need to have slide projectors, overhead projectors, or other equipment ready if required for your presentation. Be prepared, however, to give your presentation without your slides or overheads in case the machine breaks or the power goes out.

A *multiplier effect* is when people who receive your information pass it on to other people and so on, thus expanding the number of people that you reach.

Example. In the Tropical Forest Scenario, the project team presents the results of the formal survey to community leaders and to local government officials. They design a 20-minute presentation for the community leaders that focuses on their findings regarding the numbers of households that have adopted sustainable farming techniques and some of the constraints to wider adoption of these methods. In addition, they design a 10-minute summary presentation focusing on the impacts that the project has achieved and the expected effects of the pending dam that they present to the government officials. This presentation includes a number of slides.

Discussion Sessions

As discussed in chapter 2, *facilitation* involves guiding a discussion so that it stays on track and covers the necessary issues. A good facilitator will enable a group of people to make progress without dominating the discussion or imposing his or her own views.

What are they? Meetings during which monitoring analyses can be presented and then discussed by all relevant parties. Discussions generally need to be *facilitated* by one of the participants or an outside party. They can be formal (at a conference) or informal (telling stories around a fire).

Who will they reach? Discussions only reach live audiences. They tend to have a limited multiplier effect unless people get so excited about the discussion that they talk to other people about what they learned.

When are they useful? When you have information to share with small groups of people from whom you would like to get input on the topic. Discussions can also be an effective way to present information in the sense that people often retain things they discuss better than things they merely hear. Finally, they can be useful when you want people to work together to take action based on the information presented.

When are they not useful? When you are working with large groups (more than 10 people). As with presentations, they also do not work with an audience that is not locally accessible.

What do they cost? Generally fairly cheap.

What other resources are required? None beyond preparing the format and materials, deciding who will facilitate the discussion, and locating an adequate meeting place. Effective facilitation is an art and requires significant investments of time and energy to prepare.

Example. In the Tropical Forest Scenario, the project team meets with key community leaders to discuss the results of the participatory mapping exercise and uses the outcome of the discussion to decide where to concentrate sustainable agriculture project efforts. The discussion session is facilitated by one of the project staff.

Informal Contacts

What are they? Conversations in person, on the phone, or by mail with various people.

Who will they reach? Informal contacts are generally restricted to people that you know or people who contact you.

When are they useful? When you need to provide information to people who you know can use it.

When are they not useful? When you want to communicate detailed information with informal contacts.

What do they cost? Generally very cheap—often just the cost of a local phone call.

What other resources are required? None.

Example. In the Wetlands Scenario, a project staff member telephones one of the State Wildlife Officers to discuss potential gov-

ernmental responses to an alarming decrease in marsh hawk populations that has been documented through analysis of bird census data. In the Tropical Forest Scenario, one of the community members on the project staff meets with his neighbor (who happens to be the one of the important village chiefs) to regularly discuss project matters.

Reports

What are they? Written documents that focus on one or more topics. These documents can range from a handwritten paper outlining analysis findings to a glossy printed annual report.

Who will they reach? Reports obviously only reach audiences who can read. Reports will be used by researchers and by other people who use written documents. They also have the potential to be stored in libraries and other collections and thus made accessible to people you do not know who might be interested in the topic. Unfortunately, they also have a tendency to sit on people's shelves gathering dust and never being read.

When are they useful? When you have large amounts of information that you need to share with many people. Reports are also useful for getting your findings out into the "public record."

When are they not useful? When you are working with illiterate people. Reports also do not work very well with busy people who do not have time to read detailed documents.

What do they cost? Moderately to very expensive, depending on the size and quality of the final product.

What other resources are required? Reports require significant investments of time and skill to write and produce. In particular, attention should be focused on ensuring that the report is well structured, written, and formatted so that it is both attractive and easy to use.

Example. In the Wetlands Scenario, the NGO implementing the project produces an annual report that is distributed to its members, funding sources, government officials, other advocacy groups, and other interested parties. This report focuses on using the results from the monitoring work to document the impact that the NGO has had in achieving its project goals and objectives.

Press and Media Releases

What are they? News and human interest oriented stories that are sent to newspapers, radio, and television journalists with the hope that the media source will then use the story as the basis to publicly report on the results of your project.

Who will they reach? If they are picked up by the media, press releases will reach various sections of the general public depending on which medium is being used (for example, the audience listening to a popular radio program will be different from an audience reading an academic magazine). Press releases can also be effective in reaching policy makers and decision makers.

When are they useful? When you have newsworthy findings that you want to make widely and rapidly available.

When are they not useful? When you have detailed findings that are not of interest to the general public. In addition, you often do not have control over how the final article or story appears in the media. As a result, the final story may be altered from the message

you intended to convey. Press releases may thus have unintended results if not managed carefully.

What do they cost? Press releases are generally fairly inexpensive as the costs are borne by the media outlet.

What other resources are required? Press releases require substantial writing skill to ensure that they get picked up by journalists and convey the intended message without being changed. The trick is to make them interesting and yet focused on the core message that you wish to get across. You may also need to develop long-term relationships with media people so that they will be more willing to use your materials.

Example. In the Savannah Scenario, the government agency issues a press release outlining how wildlife poaching has dropped by 85 percent since the beginning of the project.

Brochures and Pamphlets

What are they? Printed items that are generally produced in large quantities and distributed to many people. These documents tend to be short and contain highlights as opposed to more detailed information.

Who will they reach? These documents tend to be less targeted than others. There is some potential for a multiplier effect.

When are they useful? When you want to provide an overview of findings to a wide range of people. Brochures and pamphlets should be regarded as a "teaser" that people can skim and decide if they want to learn more about the subject. To this end, a brochure should contain explicit instructions on how to obtain more detailed information. They are also useful in reaching busy people (like politicians) who will not read more detailed documents.

When are they not useful? When you need to provide detailed information.

What do they cost? The cost of brochures and pamphlets varies greatly depending on the quality of the final product. At their simplest (a few photocopied pages stapled together) they can be fairly cheap. At their most complex (color glossy photos and fancy paper) they can be very expensive.

What other resources are required? Significant time is required to plan and write the brochure, making sure that it contains only the most essential bits of information.

Example. In the Wetlands Scenario, the NGO implementing the project produces a brochure on project successes which is distributed to the general public to recruit new members.

Formal (Academic) Papers and Books

What are they? Documents produced by established scientific journals and publishing houses. Articles and books go through a formal *peer review* process. Presentations given at formal scientific conferences are also included in this category.

Who will they reach? Formal papers and books generally only reach technical or academic audiences. Even more than reports, papers and books will be used by researchers and by other people who are accustomed to using written documents. These documents also have the potential to be stored in libraries and other collections and can thus be made accessible to all people who might be interested in the topic.

When are they useful? When you want to make your findings available to a select audience of people who are particularly interested in a certain field of knowledge. In addition, since peer reviewed documents have a certain credibility, they can be used to support other presentations based on the same topic (a brochure or press release that is based on the findings presented in a formal paper).

When are they not useful? When you are trying to reach non-specialist audiences who usually do not read academic journals and who can be discouraged by the technical language typical of peer reviewed publications.

What do they cost? Publishing costs are generally covered by either the journal or the publisher (although some journals levy page charges), so it can be relatively cheap in financial terms unless you have to purchase large numbers of reprints to give to people.

What other resources are required? Formal papers and books require extensive investments of time and energy to attain a quality stan-

Peer review is a process that involves having an editor send a draft manuscript to experts in the field (whose identity is generally not revealed to the authors) to decide whether it meets professional standards and to determine if any revisions need to be made.

Process Hint: While formal papers and books require high standards, you should not feel intimidated by this format—chances are good that anyone who can follow and implement the ideas in this book can also write a formal paper or book.

dard sufficient to pass the peer review process. In addition, once you have completed the manuscript, it can often take months or even years before the final paper is published.

Example. In the Tropical Forest Scenario, the project enterprise specialist works with other team members to draft a paper describing the results of project activities. He presents this paper to a scientific conference on "Methods for Sustainable Use of Rainforests" and also sends the paper to an applied forestry journal for publication.

Visual Presentations (Posters, Slide Shows, Films)

What are they? Presentations that combine pictures with text (written or narrated). Visual presentations can range from a small poster put up in a hallway explaining monitoring results to a play put on by a community theater group to an elaborate video production.

Who will they reach? Visual presentations can be very effective in reaching people who either can't read or are very busy. Simple forms (posters, theater) can be used to reach a wide-ranging audience, whereas the more technology-dependent forms (films, slide shows) require people who have access to the necessary audiovisual equipment.

When are they useful? When you have powerful images that you want to communicate. Like pamphlets and brochures, visual presentations can be good ways to introduce people to a topic. As stated earlier, they can be very effective with illiterate people.

When are they not useful? When you need to convey detailed information. In addition, they often depend on technology that may not be available.

What do they cost? Effective visual presentations are usually (but not always) much more expensive than written presentations. In particular, film and video presentations are very expensive to produce.

What other resources are required? Video presentations generally require extensive investments of time and skill to develop quality products.

Example. In the Tropical Forest Scenario, the project team develops a slide show that illustrates the success that they have had in helping communities increase crop yields by using sustainable agriculture techniques. They then take this slide show to other villages in the Indah Biosphere Reserve using a small portable generator to power the slide projector.

Internet and World Wide Web

What are they? The Internet is a system by which computers around the world are linked together through telephone lines. Most Internet sites are restricted to sending text files. The worldwide web is a part of the Internet that allows the transmission of text, graphics, video, and sound. Within the Internet, common ways of transferring information include using e-mail (sending messages to specific people), listservs (sending messages to people who have subscribed to be on a list related to a specific topic), and setting up web sites (specific arrangements of linked pages of information that people can access).

Who will they reach? The Internet is restricted to people who have computers that are connected to central computers. This means that it is generally limited to well-educated urban dwellers.

When are they useful? When you have information that you want to make available cheaply to many people.

When are they not useful? When you want to reach people who do not have access to the necessary technology and telephone connections. In addition, the unfiltered nature of the Internet means that people have to know how to find the information that they want.

What do they cost? It is fairly expensive to acquire the hardware and software and the physical connection necessary to access Internet files. Once you have Internet access, sending e-mail is generally very cheap. For people who have the necessary skills, setting up web sites is relatively cheap.

What other resources are required? Computers in general and the Internet in particular can use up vast amounts of time. It also requires substantial time to create and maintain web sites—it is important to provide people with new information over time, updating your site.

Example. In the Wetlands Scenario, project staff members create a web site to provide updates on analysis results to the NGO members who live in the Everson Watershed.

Preparing and Delivering Presentations

Once you have selected the appropriate format or formats, the next step is to prepare the presentation and deliver it to your intended audience. For any of the presentation options described above, you should use the following series of steps to help you prepare it. In the following example, these steps are outlined for a report on the success of a nontimber forest product enterprise being prepared by the NGO in the Tropical Forest Scenario.

- *Prepare an Outline of the Presentation.* Sketch out the ideas that you wish to present. Arrange them in an order that makes sense. Identify any visual aids or other types of information that you would like to include in the document (see example below). In developing your presentation, keep in mind the 10 commandments listed later in this section.

- *Assign Tasks to People and Draft the Presentation.* Carry out assignments necessary to complete a draft of the document.

- *Review Presentation with Team and Key Individuals.* Send the draft presentation around to other team members and to key informants to get their input.

- *Revise the Presentation.* Discuss suggestions from reviewers and make any changes that you feel are necessary. You do not have to accept all changes that reviewers make—only the ones that you think will improve the document.

- *Produce the Presentation.* Print or otherwise produce the presentation.

- *Deliver the Presentation.* Deliver the presentation to the target audience.

Example: Outline for a Report

A Report on Birdwatching in the Everson Watershed
Cover *[Photo of birdwatcher at one of the sites]*

Executive Summary
1. Introduction: Discussion of the need for this report and what it covers.
2. Location: Overview of the Everson Watershed and the specific project area. *(Include map of Watershed and close-up map of project area)*
3. Methods and Data: Discussion of the key informant interview methods used and the selection of key informants to be interviewed. *(Show sample questionnaire)*
4. Findings: Discussion of the results of the study
    4.1. Important Sites: List of sites identified by respondents. *(Include map showing key locations)*
    4.2. Threats: Discussion of key threats identified by respondents.
5. Recommendations: Summary of results and recommendations for further project work and monitoring.

These commandments are modified from Theis and Grady (1991).

As you go through the steps in developing a presentation, there are 10 basic commandments to keep in mind regarding effective communication:

1. Remember your audience at all times and focus on the information that they want and need.

2. Keep your presentation within time and space limits. In general, the shorter and simpler the presentation, the better it is.

3. Make use of figures, charts, diagrams, and other visual aids.

4. Make your presentation interesting and entertaining—where appropriate, humor can help if done correctly.

5. Prepare in advance. If it is an oral presentation, rehearse it. If it's written, edit it repeatedly.

6. Anticipate what information will be controversial and be sure to justify it.

7. Get input from the entire project team during the development of the presentation.

8. Pay attention to content, structure, and form of your presentation—they are all important in helping your audience understand what you have to say.

9. Be timely—don't delay for months to produce a 100 percent perfect final product.

10. Avoid jargon.

Assessing the Effectiveness of Communication Efforts

After you have completed and delivered your presentation, you may want to follow up with your audience either informally or with a formal survey in a pre-test/post-test design as discussed in chapter 6. In particular, you need to find out:

• Did they get the message that you hoped they would?

• What could you have done to improve the presentation?

• What additional information do they need?

With this follow-up, you can improve both your existing presentation and future ones.

Sources and Further Readings

Explanations of and details about most of the analytical techniques described in this chapter can be found in any good statistics textbook. The statistics references that we used include the following:

Kleinbaum, David G., and Lawrence L. Kupper (1978). *Applied Regression Analysis and Other Multivariable Methods.* Duxbury Press, Boston, Massachusetts. A detailed discussion of regression analysis.

Kosecoff, Jacqueline, and Arlene Fink (1982). *Evaluation Basics: A Practitioner's Manual.* Sage Publications, Beverly Hills, California. A good overview of monitoring and evaluation including a brief discussion of various tools with education-based examples.

Miles, Matthew B., and A. Michael Huberman (1984). *Qualitative Data Analysis: A Sourcebook of New Methods.* Sage Publications, Newbury Park, California. A basic overview of qualitative data analysis.

Philip, Michael S. (1994). *Measuring Trees and Forests,* 2nd Edition. CAB International, Wallingford, United Kingdom. A detailed overview of statistical principles as they are applied to forestry problems.

Rice, Janet (1997). *Biostatistics.* Information available on the Internet at http://www.Tulane.edu/~bioscdc/. A good basic description of different statistical tools with many examples that are primarily drawn from the health sciences.

Rosner, Bernard (1982). *Fundamentals of Biostatistics.* Duxbury Press, Boston, Massachusetts. A good basic statistics book with health and biological examples.

Theis, Joachim, and Heather M. Grady (1991). *Participatory Rapid Appraisal for Community Development: A Training Manual Based on Experiences in the Middle East and North Africa.* International Institute for Environment and Development, London, United Kingdom. A clear and simple overview of how to analyze and use data.

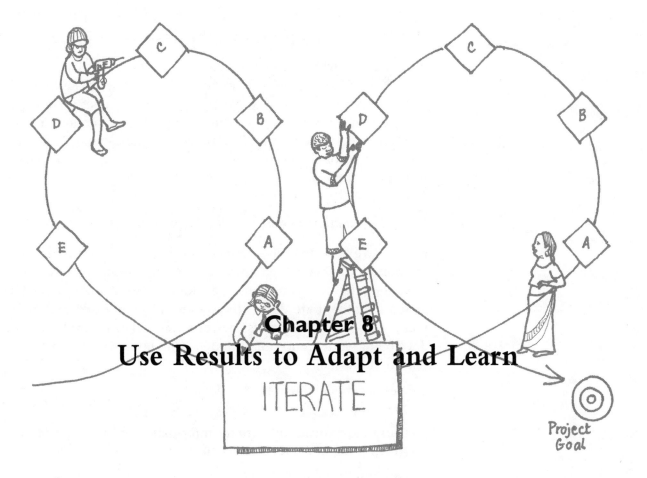

Chapter 8
Use Results to Adapt and Learn

ITERATE

Project
Goal

You have now worked your way through the entire project cycle. You have developed a Project Conceptual Model, written and implemented Management and Monitoring Plans, analyzed your data, and communicated your results to your internal and external audiences. After all your hard work, you may want to just sit back and relax, thinking your work is done. But wait a minute. In one sense you are done, but in another sense you have only just begun.

In the first chapter, we said that one of the basic principles behind this guide is applying the concept of adaptive management to community-based conservation and development projects. Adaptive management has three main components: testing assumptions, adaptation, and learning. In the previous steps in the project cycle, you have established the framework and obtained the information that will enable you to do adaptive management.

Your challenge now is to use this framework and information to improve your project and the world's knowledge. To do so, you will need to revisit the cycle many times, each time testing new assumptions, adapting your project according to what you have learned, and sharing the results with other practitioners working on conservation and development projects. This process of repeating the steps in the project cycle again and again, each time coming closer to your goal, is called iteration.

Using the information presented in this chapter, you should be able to:
- Put your assumptions to the test (Step I1).
- Adapt your project based on your monitoring results (Step I2).
- Share what you have learned about your project (Step I3).

Put Your Assumptions to the Test (Step I1)

The choice of which project activities you undertake at your project site is based on your experience and a series of assumptions. The first component of adaptive management involves systematically testing your assumptions to see which interventions work and which do not and why. The process in *Measures of Success* is designed to provide you with a framework that you can use to test these assumptions.

Using Information Throughout the Steps in the Project Cycle

By now, we hope that you understand that you should make use of information that you gain throughout the project cycle. At each step along the way, you should be taking a critical and systematic look at what you are doing (the content of your work) and how you are doing it (the process of your work). For example, while developing your Conceptual Model, you should be asking yourself questions like:

- Does our model illustrate the major threats to biodiversity at the project site?

- Is our model consistent with the information obtained from local stakeholders, key informants, and other sources?

- Does our model make sense?

- Have we included all relevant stakeholders necessary to develop an accurate model?

  Similarly, when designing your Management Plan, you should be asking questions like:

- Are our objectives linked to the key threat factors in the model?

- Do our goal, objectives, and activities meet the appropriate criteria?

- Will implementation of our activities lead to realization of our project's objectives which in turn will lead to realization of our project's goal?

- Is our Management Plan feasible?

  Finally, when developing your Monitoring Plan, you should be asking questions like:

- Is our monitoring strategy appropriate for what we want to learn?

- Are we using the appropriate indicators for a given goal or objective?

- Are we using the appropriate methods to measure each indicator?

- Are we using the most cost-effective methods for measuring each indicator?

Asking and, more importantly, answering these questions will give you important insights into whether your project is working or not.

Testing Assumptions

By following the process outlined in *Measures of Success*, you have also been testing your project and underlying assumptions in an experimental fashion. You first identified these assumptions in your Initial Conceptual Model—they are represented by the boxes and arrows that show causal relationships between different factors affecting your target condition. These assumptions were then further clarified in your Management Plan as you defined each objective. Next, your Monitoring Plan was set up to get the data needed to test these assumptions. Implementing your Management and Monitoring Plans should have generated these data. And finally, your analysis and communications work should have transformed these data into information about these assumptions.

So now that you have gone through all this work, what have you found? Were your assumptions right? Were they wrong? Or, do you not yet have sufficient information to say for sure? In particular, given that your project was designed under the Threat Reduction Assessment (TRA) approach to reduce threats to your target condition, you need to consider whether you have been successful in this regard. Were the threats that you initially identified the important ones? Did you succeed in reducing or eliminating their impact? Are there other threats that you overlooked or that weren't present at the start of your project that are now important? At this point, you should take the time to formally revisit each of the assumptions that you made and each threat that you identified and think about these questions.

For example, in the Tropical Forest Scenario, based on your assessment of local site conditions, you initially made the assumption that rattan collectors who received a 25 percent increase in their income would not continue to use destructive harvesting methods. Your initial monitoring work shows, however, that although average family income from rattan collection has increased 32 percent, most families are still using destructive methods. Clearly the assumptions inherent in your objective were wrong.

On the other hand, in the Coastal Scenario, you made the assumption that by holding meetings with community members and working with the Council of Elders, you could get people to respect and maintain marine sanctuary areas. This project assumption was further based on the underlying assumption that community members would respect the sanctuary areas once they learned about them. In this case, both these assumptions seem to have been correct because your monitoring results show that there are no incidents of community members fishing in sanctuary areas.

For more detail on the TRA Index, see Salafsky and Margoluis (1998).

Both of the preceding examples demonstrate a relatively informal way of assessing whether your initial objectives were sufficient to significantly reduce the identified direct threats to your target condition. To assess your success in meeting threats in a more systematic way, you can follow the procedure for calculating the TRA index outlined in the following box. The TRA index can be used to measure your success in reducing threats at your site over time. It can also be used to compare your project to projects at other sites (assuming that all groups use it in the same way). As shown in the example, the TRA index indicates that although the project team had some success in meeting external threats such as Big game hunting and Tourism, they had less success in meeting internal threats such as Cattle grazing and Community hunting.

Calculating the TRA Index

This example is based on the Savannah Scenario.

1. *Review your original list of all direct threats.* Revisit the list that you made when you were designing your project of direct threats to biodiversity at the project site (see the section on identifying and ranking threats in chapter 3). Examples of direct threats for the Savannah Scenario are presented in column A of the table below.

2. *Copy the rankings of each threat.* Write down the rankings you assigned for each threat under the headings Area, Intensity, and Urgency (columns B–D).

3. *Define what fully meeting each threat involves.* For each threat, define what would have to happen for this threat to be met completely as outlined in the explanations beneath the table. In defining what meeting the threat entails, try to think about the threat as you did back when you did the original ranking, not with your current knowledge.

4. *Add up the score across the three criteria.* Add up columns B–D to get the total ranking shown in column E.

5. *Determine the degree to which each threat has been met.* At the end of the assessment period, work with your project team to determine the degree to which each threat has been met. These assessments can be made either quantitatively or qualitatively, depending on the type of threat and the data that are available. As shown in column F, in either case the reduction in threat should be expressed as the percentage change in the original threat identified at the start of the project.

6. *Calculate the raw score for each threat.* Multiply the point total by the percentage to get the raw score for each threat, as shown in column G.

7. *Calculate the final Threat Reduction Assessment index score.* Add up the total raw scores for all threats and divide by the total number of possible points and multiply by 100 percent to get the final score for the project, as shown in column H.

(continues)

A Threat	B Area Ranking	C Intensity Ranking	D Urgency Ranking	E Total Ranking	F Threat Met	G Raw Score	H TRA Index
Big game hunting	2	2	3	7	80%	5.6	
Foreign hunters	4	4	5	13	50%	6.5	
Community hunting	3	3	4	10	10%	1.0	
Tourism	5	7	7	19	50%	9.5	
Fire	6	5	2	13	30%	3.9	
Cattle grazing	7	6	6	19	0%	0.0	
Diseases from cattle and dogs	1	1	1	3	0%	0.0	
Total	28	28	28	84		26.5	32%

Explanation of Threats

Big game hunting: Hunting by wealthy foreigners seeking trophies; 100 percent reduction requires no incidents of illegal hunting inside the park and WMAs.

Foreign hunters: Hunting by poachers crossing the border from a neighboring country; 100 percent reduction requires no illegal hunting inside the park.

Community hunting: Hunting by local people for their own consumption; 100 percent reduction requires no hunting in the park and having community members follow hunting regulations in the WMAs.

Tourism: Degradation of resources, disturbance to wildlife, and pollution caused by tourist visits; 100 percent reduction requires having tour operators follow guidelines for game viewing and using approved systems for disposing of waste.

Fire: Fires set by local residents to promote the growth of new grass; 100 percent reduction requires eliminating human-caused fires.

Cattle grazing: Degradation of grassland habitats by grazing cattle; 100 percent reduction requires eliminating cattle grazing inside the park boundaries.

Diseases from cattle and dogs: Transfer of diseases from domestic animals to wild ones; 100 percent reduction requires eliminating cattle grazing inside the park boundaries.

Adapt Your Project Based on Your Monitoring Results (Step I2)

Once you have formally considered your assumptions, the second component of adaptive management is to use the information that you have obtained to adapt and improve your project. To do so, you need to revisit the steps in the project cycle again and again. If you are working with an existing project, you can use the steps in the project cycle in order to refine and improve it.

Beginning Again?

Fundamentally, adaptive management is about *iteration*. Iteration means to repeat a process or sequence of steps which brings you

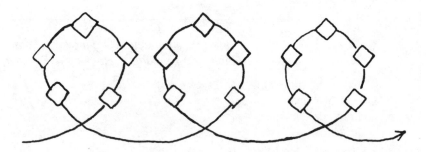

successively closer to a desired result. By using this word in describing the project cycle, we are hoping to make clear that we are not advocating getting stuck in an endless loop. Instead, as illustrated in the diagram above, we are hoping that by revisiting the various steps in the cycle, you will also move forward each time. Each iteration should help you make progress in reaching your goals and objectives.

Iteration involves using the results of your monitoring to improve your project. As you look at your results, you may find that the project is going as planned and that only a few changes or adaptations need to be made to keep it on track. On the other hand, you may find that things are not going at all as you expected and you'll need to make some big changes. The extent to which you go back through the project cycle step by step and the degree to which you focus on modifying the outputs of each step will be determined by your analysis of the monitoring results.

Returning to the Tropical Forest Scenario, after realizing that harvesters are continuing their destructive harvesting behaviors despite obtaining a 25 percent increase in income, you might ask yourself "What happened?"

At this point, you have a couple options. Your first impulse might be to "pretend that the monitoring findings didn't surface and declare victory everywhere else." As tempting as this step might be, it's ultimately not going to help you achieve your goal. Your next impulse might be to "claim the data were not accurate or that the analysis was too superficial." This could well be true—you need to think about your monitoring work and make sure that it is giving you accurate results. If, however, your monitoring and analysis seem okay, then chances are you've made a significant finding regarding income and harvesting. You must then have your project team "scrutinize your findings and your beliefs" and "fine tune your theories and assumptions." In other words, you have to go back through the steps in the project cycle and see what went wrong.

One possibility is that your Project Conceptual Model was wrong. For instance, you may have thought that income levels

The quotations in this section are from Renzi (1998).

would influence the way that people value resources and thus higher income levels would lead to sustainable harvesting. In looking at the results of your monitoring, however, it might be the case that a small group of harvesters who worked with university researchers on developing sustainable harvesting techniques were more likely to practice sustainable harvesting themselves. As a result, you conclude that in addition to raising income, it may also be necessary to inform people about sustainable harvesting techniques in order to change their behavior. So you would need to go back and add a training component to your Management Plan that conveys to the harvesters the results of the sustainable harvest studies you conducted in conjunction with university staff.

Or perhaps your objective was wrong. For instance, you may have thought that increasing income by 25 percent was sufficient, but perhaps income really has to be increased by 50 percent for families to stop harvesting rattan destructively. So you would need to go back and revise the objective based on your analysis of the data on the relationship between income and harvesting behavior. According to your analyses, does harvesting behavior become more sustainable as income levels rise? At what level does this behavorial change occur?

Or perhaps your project assumption was correct but other contextual factors in the world changed. For instance, if village residents lost their other main source of income due to falling prices for agricultural products, then the 25 percent increase would not adequately compensate for this other loss. So you would have to figure out a way to increase income to compensate for the agricultural losses. Or you would have to develop a nonincome related objective for changing the "overharvesting of products" factor, such as developing harvesting rules and enforcement systems.

Or perhaps your monitoring or analysis work was wrong. For instance, you might have measured income using a proxy indicator, such as the average amount of rice consumed per household per month. But perhaps you later discover that rice consumption is not a sensitive indicator of income and as a result, your monitoring results are biased. So you would have to redesign your monitoring plan to use a better indicator for income.

Whatever the problem is, you need to figure it out and try to alter your Management Plan to fix it. You will then also have to alter your Monitoring Plan to understand the impacts of your new activities. If they work, great. If they don't, then you have to revisit the project cycle yet again and come up with still other ideas. This iteration process can be difficult. But the monitoring work that you've done should give you guidance in doing it.

Entering the Project Process at Other Points in the Cycle

We have written this book to cover design, management, and monitoring from the very beginning of a project. We have assumed that you need to go through the entire process and construct your Project Plan (Project Conceptual Model, Management Plan, and Monitoring Plan) from the ground up.

The process presented in this book can be used, however, almost as easily with an ongoing project as it can with a new one. We refer to this process as *retrofitting*. To retrofit an existing project, you first need to take stock of the work that has been done. Maybe you have already completed an action plan, logistical framework (logframe), threat analysis, or project map for your project. If you have any of these pieces, you may want to develop a Project Plan based on this previous work.

In doing so, you may find that while some of the earlier interventions make sense, others may not and should be discontinued. In addition, you may have to adapt these pieces into your plan by making sure that they are consistent with the criteria for goals, objectives, activities, and indicators outlined in this guide. The point is to use the process presented here to help think about your project in a structured fashion to develop and monitor successful interventions.

The process presented in this book can even be used to help you understand or evaluate some other project with which you may not be working directly. In this case the process can be used to provide a framework for organizing your review. For instance, you may want to sketch out a Conceptual Model of the project in question to get a basic understanding of what it's trying to do—the assumptions of the people who designed the project. Ideally, you should do this review in conjunction with project staff and local stakeholders—it might also be a way in which you can introduce them to the use of a more systematic approach to improving their project.

Document and Share What You Have Learned About Your Project

The final component of adaptive management involves documenting what you have learned about your project and sharing it with other people in the broader conservation and development community.

Promoting Learning in Your Group

Conservation and development projects can take years or even decades to demonstrate their impact. In many ways, conservation can be seen as a perpetual process. In almost all cases, conservation projects will need to last far longer than the involvement of any one person. As a result, it is critical that the work you do and the knowledge you gain be captured in some form of *institutional knowledge*.

As you go through the steps in the project cycle, you may want to consider keeping careful records of your work. These records should clearly document what you learned from each iteration through the project cycle—the assumptions that you tested and their results. In addition, you should also document the process of how you arrived at the decisions that you made and what steps you took to implement them.

These records will enable other members of your group to learn from your experience. If you don't write these things down, then the knowledge you have acquired through all your hard work will leave when you leave the group. If, on the other hand, you write your insights down and communicate them to your colleagues, then they will be able to benefit from your insights in the future.

In documenting project outcomes, a common mistake is to focus only on success and to ignore or hide failures. The title of this book is *Measures of Success*, and we certainly hope that by following the systematic approach outlined in this book you will achieve project success. At the same time, however, you shouldn't feel like you need to hide the difficulties you've encountered—you and other people can often learn more from your failures than from your successes.

If we were always 100 percent sure that our project activities were going to be completely successful, then there would be no need to design and put into place a Monitoring Plan. The key to a truly successful project lies in learning from what you are doing whether it works or not. With this experience, you and your group will grow and will be able to take on new and bigger challenges in the future.

Improving Global Knowledge

Conservation and development projects do not occur in a vacuum. Instead, they are affected by conservation efforts taking place throughout the world. Hopefully, at the start of your project, you were able to benefit from other people's knowledge about how to develop and implement effective conservation and development projects. Now that you have your own experience, it is time to give something back.

In addition to helping you improve your specific project, the learning that you have experienced can improve the world's knowledge of how to develop and implement conservation and development projects. If you've made it all the way through the project cycle, then you are bound to have learned something along

Institutional knowledge refers to the learning accumulated by a group. In general, this knowledge has to be captured in a permanent form, such as a written document or (in the case of illiterate people) a story handed down as part of an oral tradition.

Process Hint: You can use the different communication tools presented in chapter 7 to help reach different audiences.

the way. Write it down and share it with other people. We want to learn from your experiences.

For a whole variety of reasons, including lack of time or a feeling that no one is really interested anyway, conservation practitioners at all levels tend not to share information about their projects with their colleagues who are working on similar projects. The challenges that conservation practitioners face around the world are many, but it is surprising how similar they are across regions. It is, therefore, essential that we take the learning process beyond our own specific projects and into the greater arena of conservation so that others may learn from our successes and mistakes. Adaptive management needs to start locally, but its greatest impact, perhaps, is the application of local lessons to global issues.

Some Parting Advice

We'd like to end with a few final hints about using an adaptive management approach with conservation and development projects.

Maintain Flexibility and Be Prepared to Change Your Project

In most conservation projects, the work is never really done. Changing conditions at your site and unexpected outcomes of project activities mean that you must always be prepared to respond to new situations to keep your project on track. Adaptation is a constant process. In order to reach your project goals and objectives, you must continuously change and modify your Project Plan according to available information.

The operative word here is "change." If something in your Project Plan is not working, change it! If you do not, chances are your project will not be successful. Everything described in *Measures of Success*—your Project Conceptual Model, your Management Plan, and your Monitoring Plan—can be adapted. In fact, we encourage you to adjust your Project Plan as often and as much as you think is required. Success is usually a moving target. You will find that the only way to attain it is by being flexible and open to change.

Be Receptive to Unexpected Results

No matter how well you plan your project, it will never go exactly as you intended it to. This uncertainty is not necessarily a bad thing. In many ways, the most interesting results—the findings that lead to true advances in understanding—are the ones you never expected to get. You will only benefit from these unexpected results, however, if you are ready to look for them, learn from them, and act on them. To borrow a phrase from Albert Einstein, "chance favors the prepared mind." Being genuinely curious and willing to learn from both success and failure will ultimately strengthen your skills as a project manager.

Don't Wait for Complete Information to Take Action

No matter how well you develop your Monitoring Plan, it will never provide you with all the information about a given situation. In fact, we have designed *Measures of Success* to help you collect only the information that is most essential—not all possible information about your project and project site. Thus, although in an ideal world you would have all the information that you need to make a decision with complete confidence, in the real world this will rarely if ever happen.

Management of conservation and development projects requires making decisions with incomplete information. It requires you to use your common sense, your past experience, and the information available to you to do the best you can. But don't be paralyzed by indecision. Make the best choice you can, move forward with it, monitor the results, and change the decision if necessary.

You Can Manage Adaptively

Many conservation practitioners feel that they are too overwhelmed by their management tasks or lack the technical knowhow to manage their projects adaptively. We believe, however, that by using the ideas and tools in this book in conjunction with your common sense, experience, and hard work, you can use adaptive management to help your project achieve success. We look forward to learning from the results of your projects.

Sources and Further Readings

Gunderson, Lance, C. S. Holling, and S. S. Light (1995). *Barriers and Bridges to the Renewal of Ecosystems and Institutions*. Columbia University Press, New York, New York. A volume of case studies exploring adaptive management in the context of ecosystem-scale natural resource use decisions.

Lee, Kai N. (1993). *Compass and Gyroscope: Integrating Science and Politics for the Environement*. Island Press, Washington, D.C. A very readable and poetic description of adaptive management.

Renzi, Mark (1998). The Miner's Canary: Applying Multi-Disciplinary Monitoring and Evaluation to Integrated Conservation and Development Programs. In *Measuring Conservation Impact: An Interdisciplinary Approach to Project Monitoring and Evaluation*. Biodiversity Support

Program, Washington, D.C. A good discussion of using monitoring results in a conservation and development project.

Salafsky, Nick, and Richard Margoluis (1998). The Threat Reduction Assessment (TRA) Approach to measuring conservation success. Manuscript submitted to *Conservation Biology*. An explanation of the TRA approach.

Salafsky, Nick, and Richard Margoluis, with Kent Redford, Barbara Dugelby, and Jonathan Adams (in press). *Adaptive Management: A Primer on Its Application and Use for Conservation and Development Projects*. The Nature Conservancy, Arlington, Virginia. A discussion of some of the theoretical concepts underlying *Measures of Success*.

Appendix A
Project Plans for Scenarios

Project Plan for the Tropical Forest Scenario*

Scenario Description

Suppose you are the manager of a nongovernmental organization (NGO) that is responsible for managing the Indah Biosphere Reserve. The core area of the reserve contains approximately 100,000 hectares of tropical moist forest which includes a mixture of primary and secondary forests. The 80,000 hectare buffer zone around the core area contains 30 small villages whose residents include native and migrant peoples. Residents of the villages are primarily subsistence farmers who grow grains, other food crops, and a few cash crops in small shifting agricultural plots in the forest. Residents also collect timber and nontimber forest products (NTFPs) which they use in their homes and sell in local markets. From what you can tell, it appears that the major threats to the forest include expansion of farms into forest areas, local overharvesting of forest products, commercial logging, expansion of cattle ranches, and the development of a large dam for hydro-electric power generation. At this point, the NGO that you are working for is planning a project that will involve working with community members to develop a few of the forest products for national and international sale and other interventions.

Project Details

Funding for the project is from a large international environmental NGO, local donations, and bilateral government assistance. The project is currently scheduled to last for five years. Core NGO staff members involved with this project include the NGO executive director, the reserve director, the agronomist, the ecologist, and the project community enterprise specialist.

Group's Mission

The implementing NGO's mission is: We seek to conserve our country's tropical forests by developing long-term integrated conservation and development projects and supporting policies in partnership with the local community members who live in and around these forests and with appropriate government officials. In doing so, we strive to maintain open, transparent, and democratic relationships with our partners and among ourselves.

---

*The information on this page is not part of the Project Plan but is provided as background information about the scenario.

Initial Conceptual Model Summary

The target condition this project will address is the primary forest in the Indah Biosphere Reserve. This area is defined by the abundant plant and animal life that is found in the reserve. Although some small-scale subsistence hunting occurs, animals in the Indah forest are relatively safe. The biggest threat to fauna is the wholesale destruction of habitat through deforestation. Deforestation also directly affects the primary forest found in the core area of the reserve.

Deforestation of the reserve is caused by a number of direct threats, including fire, cattle ranching, and commercial logging. There is a proposed hydropower dam that will cause massive destruction of some of the most heavily forested areas of the reserve if it is built. The Ministry of Infrastructure has planned the construction of the dam with financing from multi-lateral banks, but many stakeholders hope that the plans will be abandoned. Commercial logging is a direct function of the amount of timber concessions that have been awarded to private companies by the Ministry of Agriculture and Forestry. Likewise, the policies of this ministry influence cattle ranching in and around the reserve.

Another threat to the primary forests in the reserve is the overharvesting of nontimber forest products (NTFPs). This comes about from a general lack of knowledge, lack of land and resource tenure rights, and the need for cash to cover health and education

Tropical Forest Scenario

Initial Conceptual Model

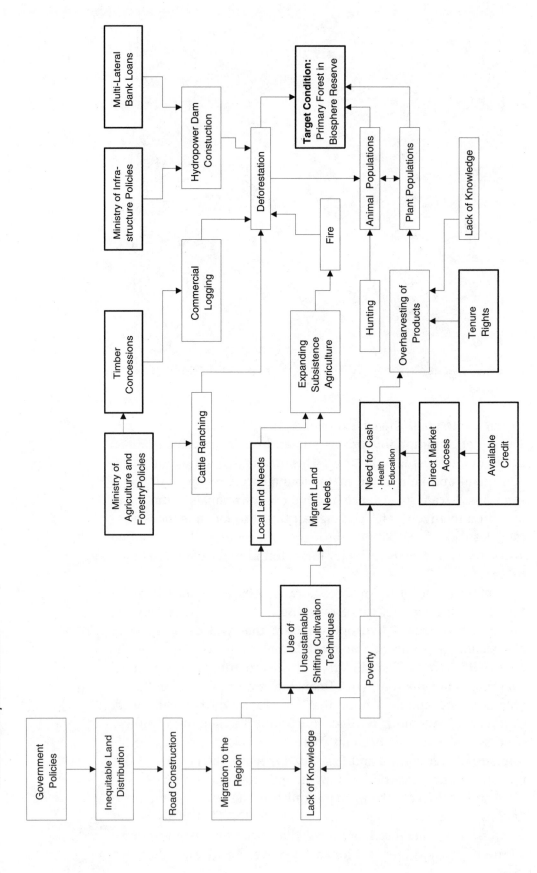

needs. A general lack of cash results from a lack of access to markets and credit and from the general state of poverty that is found in the communities around the reserve.

Most fires that directly affect the reserve come from escaped agricultural burning that result from the ever-expanding agricultural frontier. The advancement of the agricultural frontier is the result of migrants and local community members' needs for more land and the application of unsustainable shifting cultivation techniques.

A lack of knowledge of appropriate agriculture strategies results from the lack of opportunity to get an education because of the absence of economic resources to go to school and from the fact that new immigrants are unaware of proper techniques. Road construction, inadequate land distribution, and inadequate government policies all combine to adversely affect the way the natural resources in the Indah Biosphere Reserve are used.

Management Plan

Project goal: To conserve the forests in the Indah Biosphere Reserve for future generations.

Objective 1. Income Generation (from NTFPs)

By the end of the fifth year of the project, 10 percent of the families in the buffer zone cover 25 percent of their annual cash needs from NTFP harvesting and processing enterprises.

Factor(s) in Conceptual Model targeted by objective. Factor #1: Need for cash; Factor #2: Market access; Factor #3: Available credit.

Project assumptions. Factor #1: Group discussions during initial visits by the project team to the community to assess local site conditions revealed that community members believe that they would need to cover about 25 percent of their annual cash needs in order to participate in the project activities. It is assumed that by providing project participants the means to cover 25 percent of their household needs, they will value the NTFP resource enough to conserve it for long-term use. Factor #2: Community residents complain that most of the money generated from NTFPs goes to middlemen who currently buy the products. It is assumed, therefore, that by providing direct market access for NTFPs, project participants will be able to earn more money from less NTFP volume. Factor #3: During key informant interviews, leaders identified the absence of available credit as the main obstacle to organizing NTFP collectors and processors. It is assumed that by providing small amounts of credit at the beginning of the project, NTFP collectors and processors will be able to cover short-term household needs for cash and will, therefore, be more likely to participate in the enterprise.

Underlying assumptions. (1) Project can adequately determine family cash level needs. (2) Cash generated through enterprises will be equitably distributed throughout the household. (3) Changing the income of 10 percent of families will demonstrate benefits to other households in the project site causing a "multiplier effect." (4) There is local interest in participating in an NTFP enterprise.

Activities for Objective 1

• **Activity 1. Conduct Study of Sustainable Yields.** Conduct a study to determine sustainable harvest yields for rattan and bamboo for NTFP enterprises.

Why do this activity? In order to figure out the quantity of NTFPs that can be sustainably extracted annually, project managers and community members must understand the biology of the NTFPs. At present, community members harvest NTFPs without considering the long-term effects of their harvesting or the effects of other harvesters.

How will the activity be carried out? Ecologist will organize National University faculty and students who have expressed interest in doing research in the reserve to conduct study.

Who is responsible for the activity? Ecologist.

When will the activity take place? Preliminary results will be made available by the end of the first year of the project. Study will continue for the five years of the project to refine results and make recommendations for improved management of resources.

Where will the activity take place? Study to be coordinated out of the reserve field office. Study to be conducted at 5 permanent field plots, various randomly positioned transects, and at sites where local harvesters collect raw materials in the reserve.

Underlying assumptions. (1) Adequate analysis of sustainable harvest yields can be made within the first year in order to start enterprises. (2) National University faculty and staff will make a long-term commitment to the study. (3) Local NTFP harvesters will be willing to cooperate with researchers.

Prerequisites. Director of NGO must talk to National University faculty to arrange for University involvement.

• **Activity 2. Conduct Market Study for Products.** Conduct a market study to determine demand for and prices of rattan, and bamboo mats and baskets.

Why do this activity? Before NGO gets involved in assisting NTFP harvesters and processors, it must understand true demand for NTFPs in regional, national, and international markets.

How will the activity be carried out? Community enterprise specialist will organize National University faculty and students who have expressed interest in doing market research for NTFPs from the reserve.

Who is responsible for the activity? Community enterprise specialist.

When will the activity take place? Results will be made available by the end of the first year of the project.

Where will the activity take place? Study to be coordinated out of the reserve field office. Study to be conducted at regional markets and with national and international buyers.

Underlying assumptions. (1) Adequate market analysis can be completed by the end of the first year. (2) National University faculty and staff can do the study. (3) National and international buyers will be willing to cooperate with researchers.

Prerequisites. Director of NGO must talk to National University faculty to arrange for University involvement.

- **Activity 3. Organize Rattan Central Marketing Units.** Organize central marketing units (CMUs) to collect rattan from family-owned micro-enterprises and sell rattan to urban-based buyers.

Why do this activity? During community assessments, it was revealed that NTFP collectors and processors spend on average between 50 and 60 percent of their net cash returns on transportation costs to sell their products in urban markets. Project managers considered organizing community cooperatives, but community members reported that they have had very negative experiences with co-ops in the past. Community members said that what they needed was someone to help them market their products more effectively and efficiently.

How will the activity be carried out? CMUs will be organized with a management committee consisting of the enterprise specialist and three representatives of the rattan collectors. The CMU will purchase rattan at market prices from harvesters, grade it, and then sell it to contacts in urban areas. Grading, transportation, and marketing costs will be deducted on a per unit basis before profits are distributed back to harvesters.

Who is responsible for the activity? Project community enterprise specialist.

When will the activity take place? CMUs will be formally inaugurated during second year of project, after preliminary results of sustainable harvest yields and market studies are made available. Initial organization of CMUs, however, will be discussed with rattan collectors during the first year of the project.

Where will the activity take place? Initially in the four communities where rattan collection presently takes place. Other communities may be included later if they express interest.

Underlying assumptions. (1) Rattan collectors want to organize their marketing practices. (2) Organizing CMUs will reduce the per unit transportation and market costs of rattan. (3) CMU managers will be able to effectively and efficiently market rattan and return profits to individual collectors. (4) Rattan collectors will continue to trust and cooperate with CMU management committee.

Prerequisites. (1) Results of the sustainable harvest yields and market studies must first be analyzed. (2) Enterprise Specialist will consult with rattan collectors to decide the best way to establish CMUs. (3) Specific buyers must be identified before CMUs are established.

- **Activity 4. Organize Bamboo Mat and Basket CMUs.** Organize bamboo mat and basket weaving CMUs to collect finished products from family-owned micro-enterprises and sell these products to urban-based buyers.

Why do this activity? Same reasons as in activity 3. Also, support of this activity will benefit both women and men in the communities. Family micro-enterprises are usually composed of two clear divisions of labor: collection and preparation of raw bamboo is usually done by men, while women weave the bamboo into mats and baskets.

How will the activity be carried out? CMUs will have a management committee that will consist of the enterprise specialist, two representatives of the bamboo collectors (men), and two representatives of the mat and basket weavers (women). Transportation and market costs will be deducted on a per unit basis before profits are distributed back to family micro-enterprises.

Who is responsible for the activity? Project community enterprise specialist.

When will the activity take place? CMUs will be formally inaugurated during second year of project, after preliminary results of sustainable harvest yields and market studies are made available. Initial organization of CMUs, however, will be discussed with bamboo collectors and weavers during the first year of the project.

Where will the activity take place? In six of the ten communities where bamboo collection and mat and basket weaving presently take place. Because of their small size, the family micro-enterprises of four communities will be incorporated into other larger community CMUs.

Underlying assumptions. (1–4) Same as in activity 3, except applied to bamboo collectors and mat and basket weavers. (5) Family micro-enterprise participants from the smaller communities will not be marginalized in the CMUs.

Prerequisites. (1) Results of the sustainable harvest yields and market studies must first be analyzed. (2) Enterprise specialist will consult with bamboo collectors and mat and basket weavers to decide the best way to establish CMUs. (3) Specific buyers must be identified before CMUs are established.

- **Activity 5. Develop Quality Control Measures.** Develop quality control measures for rattan and weaving family micro-enterprises.

  Why do this activity? Higher quality products demand higher prices. During initial interviews with regional buyers, some reported that the quality of rattan, mats, and baskets from the communities around the reserve is variable. Some of the products, according to some buyers, are not marketable in regional or national markets.

  How will the activity be carried out? Enterprise specialist will work with family micro-enterprise participants to establish objective quality standards and the CMU management committee will evaluate each unit of product before it is accepted to be sold.

  Who is responsible for the activity? Project community enterprise specialist.

  When will the activity take place? During years two through five of the project.

  Where will the activity take place? At each of the sites of the CMUs.

  Underlying assumptions. (1) Management committees will be able to self-monitor the quality of the products that participants are producing. (2) Participants will cooperate fully with management committee.

  Prerequisites. Enterprise specialist to consult with buyers to begin to develop criteria for quality control.

- **Activity 6. Provide Credit for Enterprise Participants.** Provide credit for participants in rattan and bamboo micro-enterprise CMUs.

  Why do this activity? During initial community assessment, collectors and processors expressed the need to receive a small amount of cash to cover their needs while their products are being marketed by the CMU management committees. This request was made for the first year of operation of the CMUs only.

  How will the activity be carried out? Very small loans will be made to family micro-enterprises. The exact amount of these loans will be determined after further consultation with participants.

  Who is responsible for the activity? Project community enterprise specialist.

When will the activity take place? During the second year of the project (CMUs are to be established in second year of the project).

Where will the activity take place? Credit will be secured from the micro-enterprise fund of the regional offices of the Ministry of Development.

Underlying assumptions. (1) Family micro-enterprises will be able to repay loans when payments are due. (2) Ministry of Development will cooperate in granting small credit loans.

Prerequisites. Enterprise specialist to contact Ministry of Development to facilitate granting of credit to family micro-enterprises.

- **Activity 7. Develop Community Monitoring System for NTFPs.** Develop a system to self-monitor the amount of NTFPs being extracted from the reserve.

Why do this activity? The initial sustainable yield study will project the total allowable amount of annual NTFP harvest from the reserve. In order to remain within these limits, participants must monitor the quantity of NTFP extraction.

How will the activity be carried out? Enterprise specialist will work with project participants to set up a two-pronged monitoring system: monitoring of rattan and bamboo extraction will occur in areas of the reserve where collection takes place and monitoring of the quantities of final products collected by the CMU will occur. National University students will be recruited to assist in periodic resource evaluations.

Who is responsible for the activity? Project community enterprise specialist.

When will the activity take place? Throughout years two through five of the project. Status of collection sites will be evaluated with the help of National University students twice a year.

Where will the activity take place? At collection sites and CMUs.

Underlying assumptions. (1) CMUs and local participants can effectively self-monitor extraction activities. (2) Participants can learn some very simple monitoring techniques that they can use in the field. (3) University students will be willing to participate.

Prerequisites. Enterprise specialist must talk to National University students to arrange for their involvement.

Objective 2. Stop Dam Construction

Within three years, current Ministry of Infrastructure plans to build a hydro-electric dam immediately adjacent to the Biosphere Reserve have been abandoned.

Factor(s) in Conceptual Model targeted by objective. Factor #1: Ministry of Infrastructure policies; Factor #2: Multi-lateral bank loans.

Project assumptions. Factors #1 and #2: The proposed dam will inundate approximately 50,000 hectares of the reserve including about 20,000 hectares (or one-fifth) of the core area. Although the reserve is an officially registered protected area, there is little co-operation between ministries ensuring its protection. Because the actual construction site will be situated outside of the reserve, the Ministry of Infrastructure planned the construction and solicited international donor funds without consulting the National Commission of Protected Areas (CPA), part of the Ministry of Natural Resources. The effects of the dam, however, will be most dramatic within the reserve. It is assumed that government officials and representatives of the multi-lateral development banks can be convinced to abandon construction plans.

Underlying assumptions. (1) Alternative sources of power can be found elsewhere to meet the electricity demands that prompted the Ministry of Infrastructure to plan the dam in the first place (or demand can be reduced).

Activities for Objective 2

- **Activity 1. Convene Meeting with Government Officials.** Convene a meeting of representatives of the Ministries of Infrastructure, Natural Resources, Development, and Finance; representatives of the CPA; and the executive director of the NGO to convince the Ministry of Infrastructure to abandon dam construction plans.

  Why do this activity? The first step to halt construction of the dam may be simply to explain the impact of the proposed dam on the reserve. The NGO believes that the Ministry of Infrastructure must be given the chance to reverse its decision to build the dam without a lot of publicity and public pressure.

  How will the activity be carried out? Executive director and president of the NGO board of directors will request the meeting with the relevant representatives.

  Who is responsible for the activity? Executive director of the NGO.

  When will the activity take place? Within the first six months of the project.

  Where will the activity take place? The meeting will take place at the National Palace.

  Underlying assumptions. (1) Relatively high-level officials from the ministries and the CPA will attend the meeting. (2) The Ministry of Infrastructure is politically able to reverse its decision to build the dam.

Prerequisites. The president of the board of directors will person-ally contact the Ministers of Infrastructure, Natural Resources, Development, and Finance and the director of the CPA to inform them of the purpose of the meeting and request they send appro-priate representatives, if they do not attend the meeting them-selves.

- **Activity 2. Lobby National Assembly.** Lobby National Assem-bly to pass legislation prohibiting major infrastructure that threatens protected areas.

  Why do this activity? At present, there is no legislation to prevent the construction of large public works that adversely affect pro-tected areas. The National Assembly was very instrumental in establishing the Biosphere Reserve, and protection of the envi-ronment has been one of its priorities for the past five years. The NGO believes the National Assembly will be willing to act quickly to pass legislation to guard protected areas from the neg-ative environmental impacts of large public works.

  How will the activity be carried out? The executive director, repre-sentatives of the board of directors, and the reserve director will meet with staff members of key deputies to ask them to draft, introduce, and support the required legislation.

  Who is responsible for the activity? The executive director of the NGO.

  When will the activity take place? Legislation to be passed in the assembly by the end of the first year of the project.

  Where will the activity take place? The activity will be coordinated out of the central offices of the NGO with frequent visits to the offices of National Assembly deputies.

  Underlying assumptions. Deputies will be willing to introduce and support legislation.

  Prerequisites. None.

- **Activity 3. Lobby Multi-Lateral Development Banks.** Lobby multi-national development banks to withdraw funding for the dam project.

  Why do this activity? Without the financing to do the project, the Ministry of Infrastructure will not carry it forward. Multi-national development banks must be made aware that this pro-ject would have serious adverse environmental and social effects in and around the reserve.

  How will the activity be carried out? Executive director and mem-bers of the board of directors of the NGO will meet with the country representatives of the multi-national banks that have agreed to finance the dam project. Executive director will pre-pare a complete briefing for the NGO's presentation to the coun-try representatives.

Who is responsible for the activity? Executive director of the NGO.

When will the activity take place? Within the first year of the project.

Where will the activity take place? In the offices of the multi-national banks.

Underlying assumptions. Representatives of the multi-national banks will be willing to listen to the NGO's presentation and reasons for withdrawing funding.

Prerequisites. Results of the meeting in activity 1 must be known first. If that meeting is successful, then there will be no need to do this activity.

Objective 3. Commercial Logging

To stop all timber extraction in the core area of the reserve by the end of the third year of the project.

Factor(s) in Conceptual Model targeted by objective. Factor #1: Ministry of Agriculture and Forestry policies; Factor #2: Timber concessions.

Project assumptions. Factors #1 and #2: Although the reserve gained protected status two years ago, individuals and private companies still hold legal concessions to extract timber from within the core area of the reserve and timber harvesting continues. These concessions have been granted by the Ministry of Agriculture and Forestry (MAF). Since concession permits last only three years, all existing concessions will end not later than the end of the third year of the project. Although declaration of the reserve disallowed the granting of new concessions, MAF has continued to provide them to some individuals. It is assumed that by enforcing existing policies, concessions can be phased out.

Underlying assumptions. (1) MAF will be willing to comply with existing laws that prohibit the granting or renewal of forestry concessions inside protected areas. (2) Concession holders will obey the law by extracting only what their concession permit allows and by ceasing extraction activities on or before the expiration dates of their permits.

Activities for Objective 3

- **Activity 1. Implement Policies to Phase Out Concessions.** Work with MAF and the National Commission of Protected Areas (CPA) to implement existing policy legislation designed to phase out concessions in biosphere reserves.

  Why do this activity? To date, little pressure has been put on MAF to discontinue the issuing of concessions within the core area of the reserve. MAF is legally bound to phase out concessions in the core area, and with some public attention, the NGO believes that MAF will comply.

How will the activity be carried out? Executive director and president of the board of directors of the NGO will meet with the MAF and the director of CPA to report on concession activities within the core area of the reserve. The executive director will prepare a briefing using current aerial photography of the reserve to demonstrate the impact of recent concession activities. The NGO will offer data and technical support to assist MAF in the phasing out of concessions in the core area of the reserve.

Who is responsible for the activity? Executive director of the NGO.

When will the activity take place? Within the first six months of the project.

Where will the activity take place? In the offices of the MAF.

Underlying assumptions. The provision of concessions to some individuals and private companies has occurred because of a lack of communication and organization within MAF; once the minister is informed of the situation, he will ensure that MAF complies with the law.

Prerequisites. Most recent aerial photography of reserve must be compiled and analyzed.

- **Activity 2. Hire Forestry Specialist to Monitor Concessions.** Hire a forestry specialist to make sure that concession holders abide by the terms of their concession permits.

Why do this activity? Although MAF is responsible for monitoring concession activities throughout the country, it is severely understaffed to do so effectively. A forestry specialist working for the NGO would enable it to more effectively monitor concession activities in the reserve.

How will the activity be carried out? Director of the reserve will place an announcement in the newspaper and at the National University, interview candidates, and make the final selection in consultation with the executive director.

Who is responsible for the activity? Director of the reserve.

When will the activity take place? Within the first six months of the project.

Where will the activity take place? Central offices of the NGO.

Underlying assumptions. (1) Competent and honest candidates will be relatively easy to find. (2) Selected candidate will be willing to accept salary that will be offered. (3) Forestry specialist will be in no danger from potentially hostile concession permit holders.

Prerequisites. Prepare job description and calculate salary range for the position.

- **Activity 3. Hire or Secund Staff Members to Man Checkpoints.** Hire and secund two staff members to MAF to man checkpoint on road leading from reserve.

  Why do this activity? Almost all timber harvesting occurs in one area of the reserve that is accessible by only one road. Tighter control of this access route will help to ensure compliance of concession permits. Staff can monitor permit use and species of timber being extracted. MAF has already requested assistance from the NGO to help man the checkpoint.

  How will the activity be carried out? As in activity 2, the director of the reserve will hire the appropriate personnel. These new staff members will be secunded to MAF and stationed at the checkpoint for two years. They will work closely with MAF staff already stationed at the checkpoint.

  Who is responsible for the activity? Director of the reserve.

  When will the activity take place? Staff will be hired within the first six months of the project.

  Where will the activity take place? Selection will take place at the central offices of the NGO, and new staff will be stationed at the checkpoint.

  Underlying assumptions. (1) Staff will be able to man checkpoints 24 hours a day. (2) Private staff hired by the NGO will work well and effectively with MAF staff. (3) NGO staff will be in no danger from potentially hostile concession permit holders.

  Prerequisites. Work out terms of the agreement with MAF.

Objective 4. Improved Subsistence Agriculture

Within five years, 20 percent of the local families in communities bordering the core area of the reserve have switched from shifting cultivation to permanent plots.

Factor(s) in Conceptual Model targeted by objective. Factor #1: Local land needs; Factor #2: Use of unsustainable shifting cultivation techniques.

Project assumptions. Factor #1: During the initial assessment of the communities surrounding the core area of the reserve, residents almost unanimously expressed the desire and need to have title over the lands they cultivate. It is assumed that by securing titles residents will be more likely to protect their land and use it sustainably. Factor #2: With expanding human populations around the reserve, subsistence farming, primarily in the form of small shifting agricultural plots, has begun to seriously threaten the reserve core area. Comparison of the last two aerial surveys of the reserve revealed that advancement of the agricultural frontier as a result of newly cleared small family plots is the leading cause of forest area coverage loss in the reserve. At present, there are basically two options for family farmers to maintain or increase production levels: they can either increase their area planted or they can increase their productivity per unit of area. Most farmers do little to intensify per-area productivity and instead adhere to traditional shifting agricultural practices that guide them to clear new lands every three to four years. It is assumed that by teaching farmers new sustainable agricultural techniques productivity per unit of area will increase, and there will be less need to increase the amount of area planted, therefore slowing the acceleration of the clearing of new lands for family plots.

Underlying assumptions. (1) Intensifying productivity of family plots can be achieved while maintaining or reducing family labor inputs required to meet basic needs. (2) As new families are established, instead of having to clear forest to establish new plots, they will be able to use other fallow lands, thereby reducing the pressure on primary forest areas. (3) The initial 20 percent of farmers who establish permanent rather than shifting plots will generate a multiplier effect, which will prompt other farmers in the region to adopt similar practices.

Activities for Objective 4

- **Activity 1. Work with IAR to Issue Titles to Family Farmers.** Work with the National Institute of Agrarian Reform (IAR) to issue titles to family farmers living around the reserve for lands in the buffer zone that they have traditionally cultivated.

  Why do this activity? By establishing tenurial rights for local farmers, they will be more likely to invest in their plots for long-term and sustainable yields.

  How will the activity be carried out? Director of the reserve will contact representatives of IAR to begin the process of titling lands in communities immediately adjacent to the core area of the reserve. The director will facilitate meetings between the IAR and community members to initiate the process.

  Who is responsible for the activity? Director of the reserve.

  When will the activity take place? For the entire five years of the project.

  Where will the activity take place? In the relevant communities and the central offices of the NGO and IAR.

Underlying assumptions. (1) There will be relatively little disagreement within communities over boundaries of traditional family lands. (2) By providing greater land security to local farmers, they will be more likely to better care for their land. (3) Titling will prompt family farmers to discontinue establishing new agricultural plots in the reserve.

Prerequisites. (1) NGO will organize communities into three lists of priorities for land titling, with the highest priority given to those communities immediately adjacent to the core area of the reserve. (2) Agronomist will work with community members to prepare them for IAR meetings. (3) Family plots must be surveyed and demarcated by IAR representatives.

- **Activity 2. Promote Soil Erosion Control.** Intensify family plot production through the use of traditional and enhanced soil erosion control methods.

Why do this activity? Most family farmers do not practice soil erosion prevention. As a result much of the productive topsoil in shifting family plots is washed away by the third year of cultivation.

How will the activity be carried out? Agronomist will work intensively with selected family farmers in key communities to establish demonstration plots. Agronomist will hold community meetings to discuss and demonstrate benefits of soil erosion prevention techniques. Upon request, the agronomist will advise other farmers who wish to learn the soil erosion prevention techniques.

Who is responsible for the activity? Agronomist.

When will the activity take place? Demonstration plots will be established within the first two years of the project. Community meetings will occur throughout the five years of the project, as will technical assistance from the agronomist.

Where will the activity take place? In the communities.

Underlying assumptions. (1) Family farmers will be willing to adopt new practices. (2) Differences between the old and new techniques of cultivation will be noticeable within the first three years of the project. (3) New techniques will actually decrease the amount of labor invested per unit of production, thus inducing family farmers to adopt them.

Prerequisites. (1) Identify family farmers who have adopted some sustainable agricultural techniques in the past, and consult with them about which techniques seemed to work and which did not. (2) Take community leaders and some particularly interested family farmers to other sites in the country where farmers have adopted similar techniques and where the positive results are readily observable.

- **Activity 3. Promote Intercropping.** Promote traditional practices of intercropping grain crops with nitrogen fixing crops to enrich soil fertility and reduce weeding labor requirements.

  Why do this activity? Intercropping is a practice that many farmers, especially those that have lived in the reserve for many generations, have employed to increase yields. Weeding requires the majority of labor inputs in agricultural plots between planting and harvesting. Experience from other parts of the country has identified some promising crops that help fix nitrogen, reduce weeding labor inputs and soil erosion (as they act as ground cover), and are edible.

  How will the activity be carried out? Same method as for activity 2, but for intercropping varieties.

  Who is responsible for the activity? Agronomist.

  When will the activity take place? Throughout the five years of the project.

  Where will the activity take place? In the communities.

  Underlying assumptions. Same assumptions as for activity 2.

  Prerequisites. Same prerequisites as for activity 2.

- **Activity 4. Reinforce Traditional Composting Practices.** Reinforce traditional practices of increasing soil fertility through composting.

  Why do this activity? Some farmers, mostly outside of the reserve where good agricultural land is more difficult to find, have used composting to enrich the soils of their fields. By using these traditional techniques as opposed to chemical fertilizers, farmers can maintain healthy soils that will require minimal inputs over the long run.

  How will the activity be carried out? Same method as for activity 2, but for composting.

  Who is responsible for the activity? Agronomist.

  When will the activity take place? Throughout the five years of the project.

  Where will the activity take place? In the communities.

  Underlying assumptions. Same assumptions as for activity 2.

  Prerequisites. Same prerequisites as for activity 2.

- **Activity 5. Introduce IPM Techniques.** Introduce family farmers to integrated pest management (IPM).

  Why do this activity? One of the biggest reasons, other than loss of soil fertility, that family farmers change plots so frequently is pest damage. After a few years of working the same plot, farmers can no longer successfully combat insects and other plant pests that decrease yields. IPM has gained widespread support among family farmers in other parts of the country. Local farmers have been impressed that they can control pests naturally without expensive and dangerous pesticides.

How will the activity be carried out? Same method as for activity 2, but for IPM.

Who is responsible for the activity? Agronomist.

When will the activity take place? Throughout the five years of the project.

Where will the activity take place? In the communities.

Underlying assumptions. Same assumptions as for activity 2.

Prerequisites. Same prerequisites as for activity 2.

- **Activity 6. Enhance Use of Fire.** Work with family farmers to use fire more appropriately and effectively to clear fallow lands, control pests and weeds, and provide soil nutrients.

  Why do this activity? Fire has been used by generations to clear fallow lands, control pests and weeds, and provide soil nutrients (through the production of ash). Recent experience from other parts of the country, however, suggests that pest and weed control and soil productivity can be improved without the use of fire. Agricultural fires that have escaped control of farmers have caused extensive damage to forests in the buffer and core areas of the reserve.

  How will the activity be carried out? Agronomist will work with family farmers to demonstrate the use of other techniques that do not require the use of fire but increase soil fertility and protect crops against pests (see activities 2, 3, 4, and 5). Agronomist will present slide show and film that explains the proper use and control of fire and demonstrates benefits of not burning fields.

  Who is responsible for the activity? Agronomist.

  When will the activity take place? Throughout the five years of the project.

  Where will the activity take place? In the communities.

  Underlying assumptions. (1) Family farmers will not use fires as much once they see the benefits of using other techniques. (2) Family farmers will be more cautious in their use of fire once they understand how to better control it. They will also be less likely to let fires get out of control once they realize how it can have negative effects on the reserve and the country as a whole.

  Prerequisites. (1) Get the slide show and film from the MAF. (2) Buy a small portable gas-powered generator to provide electricity for the projection of the slide show and film in the communities.

Tropical Forest Scenario

Project Conceptual Model

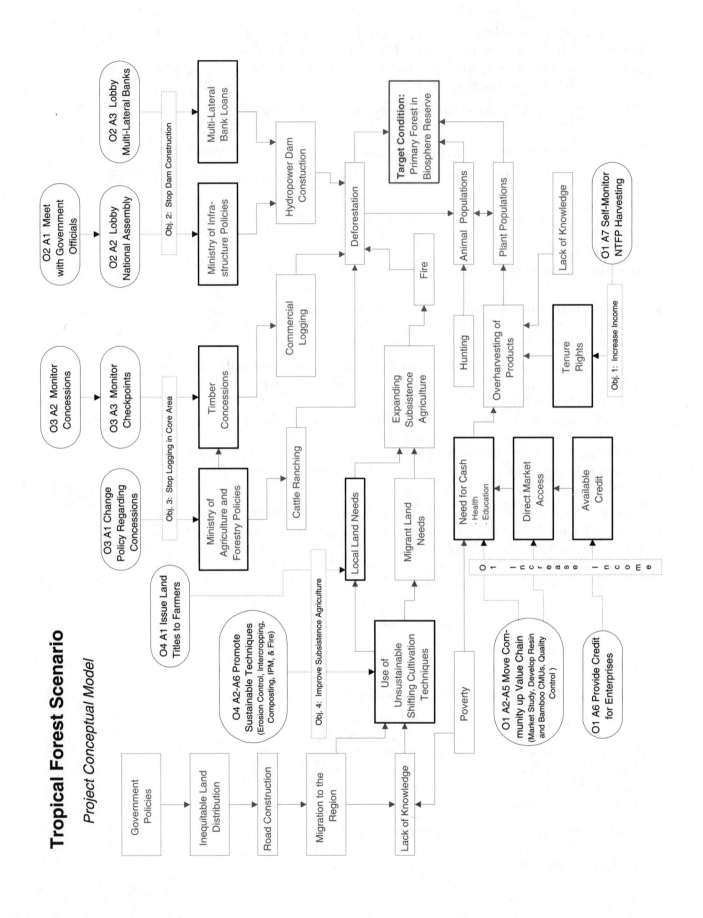

Project Management Timeline

Project Management Timeline—Indah Biosphere Reserve																					
Management Tasks / Project Year / Quarter	**1**				**2**				**3**				**4**				**5**				**People Responsible**
	1	2	3	4	1	2	3	4	1	2	3	4	1	2	3	4	1	2	3	4	
Goal: To conserve forests in the Indah Biosphere Resource for future generations																					
O1. Income generation (from NTFPs)																					
– A1. Conduct study of sustainable yields				X	X	X	X	X	X	X	X	X	X	X	X	X	X	X	X	X	Ecologist
– A2. Conduct market study for products				X																	Enterprise specialist
– A3. Organize rattan CMUs					X	X	X	X													Enterprise specialist
– A4. Organize bamboo mat/basket CMUs					X	X	X	X													Enterprise specialist
– A5. Develop quality control measures					X	X	X	X	X	X	X	X	X	X	X	X	X	X	X	X	Enterprise specialist
– A6. Provide credit for enterprise participants					X	X	X	X													Enterprise specialist
– A7. Develop community monitoring system for NTFPs					X	X	X	X	X	X	X	X	X	X	X	X	X	X	X	X	Enterprise specialist
O2. Stop dam construction																					
– A1. Convene meeting with gov. officials		X																			Executive director
– A2. Lobby national assembly	X	X	X	X																	Executive director
– A3. Lobby multilateral development banks	X	X	X	X																	Executive director
O3. Commercial logging																					
– A1. Implement policies to phase out concessions	X	X																			Executive director
– A2. Hire forestry specialist to monitor concessions	X	X																			Reserve director
– A3. Hire staff to man checkpoints	X	X																			Reserve director
O4. Improved subsistence agriculture																					
– A1. Work with IAR to issue land titles	X	X	X	X	X	X	X	X	X	X	X	X	X	X	X	X	X	X	X	X	Reserve director
– A2. Promote soil erosion control	X	X	X	X	X	X	X	X	X	X	X	X	X	X	X	X	X	X	X	X	Agronomist
– A3. Promote intercropping	X	X	X	X	X	X	X	X	X	X	X	X	X	X	X	X	X	X	X	X	Agronomist
– A4. Reinforce composting practices	X	X	X	X	X	X	X	X	X	X	X	X	X	X	X	X	X	X	X	X	Agronomist
– A5. Introduce IPM techniques	X	X	X	X	X	X	X	X	X	X	X	X	X	X	X	X	X	X	X	X	Agronomist
– A6. Enhance use of fire	X	X	X	X	X	X	X	X	X	X	X	X	X	X	X	X	X	X	X	X	Agronomist

Monitoring Plan

Goal, Objective, or Additional Information

Goal. To conserve the forests in Indah Biosphere Reserve for future generations.

Monitoring Strategy 1: Measure changes over time in area of primary forest in core area of reserve.
Monitoring Strategy 2: Measure changes over time of rattan density.
Monitoring Strategy 3: Determine regeneration rates of rattan species within reserve core area.
Monitoring Strategy 4: Measure changes over time of bamboo density.

What (Indicators)	How (Methods & Tasks)	When	Who	Where	Comments
Area (ha) of forest in the reserve core area	Mapping • Obtain aerial photographs of reserve area	Annually	Ecologist	Capital city	Assumes that maps are available on a yearly basis from government. Since hunting is not prevalent in the area, it is not necessary to survey animal populations (including seed dispersers).
	• Digitize maps to show vegetative cover	Annually	Ecologist	Project office	
	• Ground truth maps	Annually	Ecologist	Reserve area	
Density of rattan species (canes/ha)	Transects • Use vegetation maps (produced above) to determine potential rattan habitat	By month 6 of project	Ecologist	Project office	According to the implementation plan, data collection and analysis will be conducted by National University faculty and students in coordination with the ecologist.
	• Walk random 5m × 500m transects in potential rattan habitats counting rattans	Annually	Ecologist	Reserve core area	
Regeneration of rattan species (seedlings/ha)	Biological plots • Establish 20 10m × 10m plots in rattan habitats	By end of first year	Ecologist	Reserve core area	Same as above.
	• Count seedlings in plots	Annually	Ecologist	Reserve core area	
Density of bamboo species (plants/ha)	Transects • Use vegetation maps (produced above) to determine potential bamboo habitat	By month 6 of project	Ecologist	Project office	Same as above.
	• Walk random 5m × 500m transects in potential rattan habitats counting bamboo	Annually	Ecologist	Reserve core area	

254

Goal, Objective, or Additional Information

Objective 1: Income generation (from NTFPs). By the end of the fifth year of the project, 10 percent of the families in the buffer zone cover 25 percent of their annual cash needs from NTFP harvesting and processing enterprises.

Monitoring Strategy 1: Determine change over time in percentage of families in buffer zone who earn income from NTFPs.
Monitoring Strategy 2: Measure change in income from NTFPs in project participants compared to nonparticipants over time.
Monitoring Strategy 3: Monitor change in household cash needs over time among project participants.

What (Indicators)	How (Methods & Tasks)	When	Who	Where	Comments
Percentage of families in project area (buffer zone) earning income from NTFPs	Review of secondary data • Obtain regional census data	Project start and end	University staff	Village governments	Because there are differences in household size, we need to calculate the ratio of cash from NTFP work to total household needs for each individual household and then take the average of all households in the project area.
	Review of enterprise records • Determine number of participating households	Annually	Enterprise specialist	Project headquarters	
Amount (pesos/year) earned by households involved in the project from NTFPs	Review of enterprise records • Determine income earned by participating households	Annually	Enterprise specialist	Project headquarters	
	Household survey • Determine income earned by nonparticipating households	Annually	Enterprise specialist	Nonparticipant households	
Annual cash needs per household	Household survey • Determine size of and cash needs for participating households	Year 2 and every year thereafter	Enterprise specialist	Participants' households	To calculate the amount of cash needs met by the project's income generating activities, we must first determine annual household cash needs.

Activities for Objective 1	*Person Responsible for Monitoring the Activity*	*Target Date(s) for Obtaining Information*
Activity 1. Conduct study of sustainable yields	Ecologist	By end of first year of project
Activity 2. Conduct market study for products	Enterprise specialist	By end of first year of project
Activity 3. Organize rattan central marketing units (CMUs)	Enterprise specialist	Operative by end of second year of project
Activity 4. Organize bamboo mat and basket weaving CMUs	Enterprise specialist	Operative by end of second year of project
Activity 5. Develop quality control measures	Enterprise specialist	During years 2–5 of the project
Activity 6. Provide credit for CMU participants	Enterprise specialist	Once CMUs have been established
Activity 7. Develop community monitoring system for NTFPs	Enterprise specialist	During years 2–5 of the project

Goal, Objective, or Additional Information

Objective 2. Stop dam construction. Within three years, current Ministry of Infrastructure plans to build a hydro-electric dam immediately adjacent to the Biosphere Reserve have been abandoned.

Monitoring Strategy 1: Monitor changes in laws affecting conservation of the Indah Biosphere Reserve.
Monitoring Strategy 2: Determine if status of dam construction plans changes over time.

What (Indicators)	How (Methods & Tasks)	When	Who	Where	Comments
Legislation passed by National Assembly	Key informant interview • Talk with allies in the assembly	Throughout first year	Executive director	At capital building and via phone	Target dates for monitoring may have to shift contingent upon success of project activities.
	Review of secondary data • Read newspapers for stories on dam construction	Throughout first year	Executive director	NGO headquarters	
Dam construction plans status	Key informant interview • Talk with contacts in Ministry of Infrastructure • Confirm findings with contacts in multilateral banks	Throughout first year / Throughout first year	Executive director / Executive director	Meetings in capital city / Meetings in capital city	Contacts with bank staff are to triangulate information obtained from ministry.

Activities for Objective 2	Person Responsible for Monitoring the Activity	Target Date(s) for Obtaining Information
Activity 1. Convene meeting with government officials	Executive director	Held within first six months of project
Activity 2. Lobby National Assembly	Executive director	Completed by end of first year of project
Activity 3. Lobby multilateral development banks	Executive director	Operative by end of first year of project

Goal, Objective, or Additional Information

Objective 3. Commercial logging. To stop all timber extraction in the core area of the reserve by the end of the third year of the project.

Monitoring Strategy 1: Determine changes over time in number of active concessions in the reserve.
Monitoring Strategy 2: Measure changes over time in new logging.
Monitoring Strategy 3: Measure changes over time in amount of logs being removed from the reserve core area.

What (Indicators)	How (Methods & Tasks)	When	Who	Where	Comments
Number of active concessions in reserve core area	Review of secondary data • Using MAF Registry, determine current concession areas	Every six months	Forest specialist	MAF Provincial Office	Assumes that records are current and accurate. This number should decrease over time since MAF is not supposed to issue new licenses.
Number of new stumps in forest areas	Ecological census • Conduct periodic censuses of active concessions in core area to count fresh stumps	Every six months	Forest specialist	Core areas of the reserve	Assumes that stumps can be easily found and dated
Number of truckloads of timber coming from reserve core area	Direct observation • Count trucks leaving reserve	Continuously once staff are hired	Checkpoint guards	Sole road access point to core area	Accuracy depends on no new access routes being developed to extract timber from the reserve core area.

Activities for Objective 3	Person Responsible for Monitoring the Activity	Target Date(s) for Obtaining Information
Activity 1. Implement policies to phase out concessions	Executive director	Held within first six months of project
Activity 2. Hire a forestry specialist to monitor concessions	Reserve director	Hired within first six months of project
Activity 3. Hire/second staff members to man checkpoints	Reserve director	Hired within first six months of project

Goal, Objective, or Additional Information:

Objective 4. Improved subsistence agriculture. Within five years, 20 percent of the local families in communities bordering the core area of the reserve have switched from shifting cultivation to permanent plots.

Monitoring Strategy 1: Measure changes over time in proportion of families farming permanent plots.
Monitoring Strategy 2: Measure changes over time of farmers who legally own their land.
Monitoring Strategy 3: Measure changes over time in percentage of farmers who practice "sustainable agriculture."

What (Indicators)	How (Methods & Tasks)	When	Who	Where	Comments
Percentage of families farming on permanent plots	Household survey • Conduct survey of farmers to determine farming practices	Annually	Agronomist	In communities in buffer zone	Project team expects there to be a multiplier effect and thus need to survey all households in the communities.
Percentage of families holding titles to farm plots	Review secondary data • Review information in village land registry books	Annually	Agronomist	In village government offices	
Percentage of families using soil erosion control, intercropping, nitrogen fixing, composting, and IPM techniques (separate measurements for each)	Household survey • Conduct survey of farmers to determine farming practices	Annually	Agronomist	In communities in buffer zone	

Activities for Objective 4	Person Responsible for Monitoring the Activity	Target Date(s) for Obtaining Information
Activity 1. Work with IAR to issue titles to family farmers	Reserve director	Monitor titles issued over life of project.
Activity 2. Promote soil erosion control	Agronomist	Monitor production over life of project.
Activity 3. Promote intercropping	Agronomist	Monitor intercropping over life of project.
Activity 4. Reinforce traditional composting practices	Agronomist	Monitor composting over life of project.
Activity 5. Introduce IPM techniques	Agronomist	Monitor use of IPM over life of project.
Activity 6. Enhance use of fire	Agronomist	Monitor use of fire over life of project.

Goal, Objective, or Additional Information:

Additional Information Needed to Assess Project Impact

What (Indicators)	How (Methods & Tasks)	When	Who	Where	Comments
Related to goal— secondary effects of NTFP harvesters: Amount of products other than rattan and bamboo harvested by species	Key informant interviews • Interview NTFP harvesters	Annually	Enterprise specialist	Harvester households	Although preliminary reports suggest that harvesters focus almost exclusively on rattan or bamboo while in the forest, project staff are concerned that the increased intensity of harvesting could lead to damaging effects on other biological resources.
	Direct observations • Accompany harvesters during NTFP trips	Annually	Enterprise specialist	Harvesting camps	
Related to Obj. 1— relative importance of NTFP harvesting in household economy: Rank of NTFPs to other economic activities	Wealth ranking • Interview residents in project communities to determine ranking criteria	Month 4	Enterprise specialist	Project communities	Monitoring for Objective 1 only focuses on income generation from the core enterprise itself—this information is needed to ensure that the NTFP enterprises provide sufficient return to labor relative to other economic activities to motivate local involvement in the project.
	• Select sample across three socioeconomic groups	Month 4	Enterprise specialist	Project communities	
	Matrix ranking • Interview 10 representatives of each socioeconomic group	Month 4 and end of project	Enterprise specialist	Project communities	
Related to Obj. 4— effects of market forces: Price of cash crops	Key informant survey • Interview vendors in regional markets	Monthly	Enterprise specialist	Regional markets	Fluctuations in cash crop prices are a major factor influencing the amounts of new forest land cleared for production.
	Seasonal calendar/sentinel site • Interview five selected vendors in regional markets	Monthly	Enterprise specialist	Regional markets	

(continues)

Additional Information Needed to Assess Project Impact (*continued*)

What (Indicators)	How (Methods & Tasks)	When	Who	Where	Comments
Related to cattle ranching factor—expansion of pasture areas: Area (ha) of pasture land in reserve	Mapping • Use aerial photographs from goal monitoring • Determine pasture area • Ground truth maps	Every 2 years Every 2 years Every 2 years	Agronomist Agronomist Agronomist	Capital city Project office Reserve area	Although they initially decided not to focus on cattle ranching based on the threat ranking exercise, project staff want to track this factor to see if it becomes necessary to redesign the project to address this potential threat.
Related to hunting factor—prevalence of illegal hunting in reserve: Number of families involved in hunting	Direct observation • Record observations of hunting evidence during regular visits to villages Key informant interviews • Discuss with contacts in communities	Ongoing Annually	All project staff Ecologist	Project communities Project communities	During initial assessments, the project staff determined that hunting was not a major threat to animal populations in the region. Staff, however, want to ensure that hunting does not become a major problem. The quantity of animals hunted cannot be determined directly, but numbers of hunting families provides a rough check of hunting intensity in the area.
New factors—new factors at the site that affect project success	Direct observation • Observe changes at the project site	Ongoing	All project staff	All locations	Project staff need to be constantly aware of potential changes in the project site that would require a revision of the Project Conceptual Model and Management Plan.

260

Project Management Timeline

Project Monitoring Timeline—Indah Biosphere Reserve

Monitoring Tasks	Y1 Q1	Q2	Q3	Q4	Y2 Q1	Q2	Q3	Q4	Y3 Q1	Q2	Q3	Q4	Y4 Q1	Q2	Q3	Q4	Y5 Q1	Q2	Q3	Q4	People Responsible
Goal: To conserve the forests in the Indah Biosphere Reserve for future generations																					
– Area (ha) of forest in the reserve core area	X							X				X				X				X	Ecologist
– Density of rattan species (canes/ha)		X						X				X				X				X	Ecologist
– Regeneration of rattan species (seedlings/ha)		X						X				X				X				X	Ecologist
– Density of bamboo species (plants/ha)		X						X				X				X				X	Ecologist
O1. Income generation (from NTFPs)																					
– Percentage of families in project area (buffer zone) earning income from NTFPs	X							X				X				X				X	University staff/Enterprise specialist
– Amount (pesos/year) earned by households involved in the project from NTFPs	X							X				X				X				X	Enterprise specialist
– Annual cash needs per household	X							X				X				X				X	Enterprise specialist
– A1. Conduct study of sustainable yields		X			X																Ecologist
– A2. Conduct market study for products					X				X												Enterprise specialist
– A3. Organize rattan CMUs									X												Enterprise specialist
– A4. Organize bamboo mat/basket CMUs									X												Enterprise specialist
– A5. Develop quality control measures						X	X	X	X	X	X	X	X	X	X	X	X	X	X	X	Enterprise specialist
– A6. Provide credit for participants										X		X									Enterprise specialist
– A7. Develop community monitoring system					X	X	X	X	X	X	X	X	X	X	X	X	X	X	X	X	Enterprise specialist
O2. Stop dam construction																					
– Legislation passed by National Assembly	X					X															Executive director
– Dam construction plans status	X					X															Executive director
– A1. Convene meeting with government officials		X																			Executive director
– A2. Lobby National Assembly	X	X	X	X																	Executive director
– A3. Lobby multilateral development banks								X													Executive director
O3. Commercial logging																					
– Number of active concessions in reserve core area	X			X	X			X	X			X	X			X	X			X	Forest specialist
– Number of new stumps in forest areas	X			X	X			X	X			X	X			X	X			X	Forest specialist
– Number of truckloads of timber coming from reserve core area	X			X	X			X	X			X	X			X	X			X	Checkpoint guards
– A1. Implement policies to phase out concessions			X					X				X									Executive director
– A2. Hire forestry specialist to monitor concessions			X																		Reserve director
– A3. Hire/secund staff to man checkpoints			X																		Reserve director

(continues)

Project Monitoring Timeline—Indah Biosphere Reserve (continued)

Monitoring Tasks	1				2				3				4				5				People Responsible
Quarter	1	2	3	4	1	2	3	4	1	2	3	4	1	2	3	4	1	2	3	4	
O4. Improved subsistence agriculture																					
– Percentage of families farming on permanent plots	X	X	X					X				X				X				X	Agronomist
– Percentage of families holding titles to farm plots	X	X	X					X				X				X				X	Agronomist
– Percentage of families using erosion control, intercropping, nitrogen fixing, composting, IPM techniques	X	X	X					X				X				X				X	Agronomist
– A1. Work with IAR to issue land titles to family farmers			X	X	X	X	X	X	X	X	X	X	X	X	X	X	X	X	X	X	Reserve director
– A2. Promote soil erosion control			X	X	X	X	X	X	X	X	X	X	X	X	X	X	X	X	X	X	Agronomist
– A3. Promote intercropping			X	X	X	X	X	X	X	X	X	X	X	X	X	X	X	X	X	X	Agronomist
– A4. Reinforce composting practices			X	X	X	X	X	X	X	X	X	X	X	X	X	X	X	X	X	X	Agronomist
– A5. Introduce IPM techniques			X	X	X	X	X	X	X	X	X	X	X	X	X	X	X	X	X	X	Agronomist
– A6. Enhance use of fire			X	X	X	X	X	X	X	X	X	X	X	X	X	X	X	X	X	X	Agronomist
Additional Information																					
– Amount of products other than rattan and bamboo harvested by species								X				X				X				X	Enterprise specialist
– Rank of NTFPs to other economic activities			X																	X	Enterprise specialist
– Price of cash crops	X	X	X	X	X	X	X	X	X	X	X	X	X	X	X	X	X	X	X	X	Enterprise specialist
– Area (ha) of pasture land in reserve								X				X				X				X	Agronomist
– Number of families involved in hunting				X				X				X				X				X	Ecologist
– New factors at the site that affect project success	X	X	X	X	X	X	X	X	X	X	X	X	X	X	X	X	X	X	X	X	All project staff

Project Plan for the Savannah Scenario★

Scenario Description

Suppose you are a wildlife biologist working for the local office of the Government Park Service to coordinate a project to design and implement a conservation plan for Karimara National Park. The park is 750,000 hectares (ha) of savannah and grasslands in a semi-arid, subtropical setting with an additional 500,000 ha of land in Wildlife Management Areas (WMAs) around the park. Outside of the WMAs are a number of settlements inhabited by semi-nomadic livestock herders who graze their cattle in the WMAs and occasionally in the park. Residents of the settlements depend on their livestock and limited hunting and gathering of wild animals and plants for subsistence. Major threats to the park include over-grazing, overhunting, and poaching of large mammal species, and the effects of a rapidly increasing and unregulated foreign tourism industry. The Park Service is considering taking a number of steps to protect the park against these threats.

Project Details

The initial phase of this project is scheduled to last for seven years, but it is anticipated that the project will then continue for the fore-seeable future using funds from the Park Service. Formal project staff include the project coordinator and the project assistant. Other staff available include park guards, park inspectors, and other Government Park Service staff.

Group's Mission

The mission of the National Park Service is: To protect the natural heritage and beauty of our country through a system of parks and reserves for the benefit and enjoyment of all our citizens. NPS is dedicated to the belief that a healthy environment is the basis of a healthy society.

★The information on this page is not part of the Project Plan but is provided as background information about the scenario.

Initial Conceptual Model Summary

In Karimara National Park our target condition is grassland and savannah ecosystems. It can be described in terms of grassland and savannah dynamics and the animal populations that are found in the park. The grasslands and savannah are degraded by tourism, cattle grazing, and fire.

As Karimara is a popular tourist destination, commercial tour hotels and tour operators are usually booked to capacity. Large numbers of tourists and the vehicles they use for game viewing damage extensive tracts of fragile grasslands and savannah. Vehicle traffic also disturbs the normal reproductive and migration cycles of many of the animal species found in the park. Tourism is also responsible for polluting the park because of improper disposal of sewage and solid wastes.

The intensity of cattle grazing in the park is influenced by the number of cattle owned by herders who reside in the communities around the park. At the end of the dry season, herders burn large tracts of grasslands to promote growth of new pasturage for their animals. Fires occur more frequently and increase in intensity during drought years.

Cattle, and the dogs that are used to herd them, have been known to transmit diseases to wild ungulates and wild dogs, respectively, in the past. The number of cattle (and correspondingly the number of dogs) families own is a function of their economic situation. As milk production is one of the only sources of income in the area, and social status is determined by the number of animals a family owns, most families strive to have as many cat-

Savannah Scenario

Initial Conceptual Model

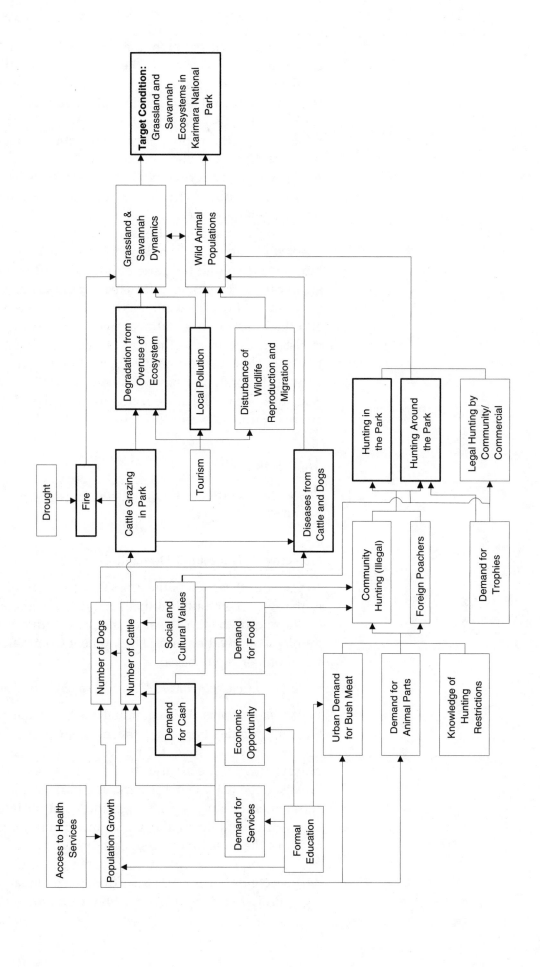

tle as possible. Increasing human population around Karimara has caused a parallel increase in the population of cattle.

The demand for cash is a function of the need to cover expenses such as food and basic services (for instance, school and medical services). It is also related to how many other economic opportunities exist in the region. Formal education influences these economic factors as well as population growth in the area. Family heads with more formal education tend to have fewer children. Access to health services for women and children also have an impact on family size.

Wild animal populations in and around the park are directly affected by hunting. Cash demands force community members to hunt in and around the park, although this does not appear to be significant at the moment. Poachers from the neighboring country also hunt highly prized animals to sell their meat in urban markets and their parts to international traders. Big game trophy hunting is also present around the park. Community members complain that they have little knowledge of hunting restrictions in and around the park and have expressed a willingness to cooperate with the National Park Service to curb illegal hunting in and around Karimara National Park.

Management Plan

Project goal. Conserve the grassland and savannah ecosystems of Karimara National Park.

Objective 1. Household Demand for Cash

To provide 20 percent of the gross revenue from park entrance fees to the seven communities that surround Karimara National Park by the end of the third year of the project (disbursement to community Conservation and Development Committees (CDCs) provided on per capita basis).

Factor(s) in Conceptual Model targeted by objective. Demand for cash.

Project assumptions. During initial visits by the project team to the communities bordering the national park, discussions with residents revealed that their need for cash was a major factor causing them to keep large herds of livestock, one of the major threats to the wildlife of the park. The park is currently generating substantial revenues from foreign and domestic tourists who come to see the wildlife in the park, and community members are aware of the large amounts of cash being generated. The national government is currently undertaking a series of initiatives to devolve control over local issues from the national level to the local level. Project staff assume that they can affect local demand for cash (and thus the number of cattle) by providing for revenue sharing of funds from tourism in the national park with local residents.

Underlying assumptions. (1) Twenty percent of gross revenues from the park will be sufficient to motivate community members to protect the park. (2) Funds will be transferred from NPS account to the community accounts on a timely basis. (3) Communities find it acceptable to have CDCs receive, manage, and use the money. (4) Communities will spend the money equitably and wisely.

Activities for Objective 1

- **Activity 1. Produce Revenue Sharing Accord.** Produce an official government accord that provides for communities to share in the revenues generated by national parks and gives the NPS the authority to manage such arrangements.

  Why do this activity? In order for communities to receive revenues generated from national parks, national legislation must be enacted to permit this type of revenue-sharing arrangement.

  How will the activity be carried out? NPS negotiates with Ministries of Tourism, Natural Resources, and Finance.

  Who is responsible for the activity? NPS director.

  When will the activity take place? By the end of the first year of the project.

  Where will the activity take place? Central offices of NPS in the capital.

  Underlying assumptions. (1) Support for this type of legislation exists in the national government. (2) Passage of this legislation will be relatively easy.

  Prerequisites. NPS director contacts key government officials.

- **Activity 2. Conduct Community Meetings to Explain Benefits.** Conduct a series of community meetings to explain and demonstrate the benefits that communities can receive from helping to conserve the Karimara National Park.

  Why do this activity? (1) To keep community members involved in the project. (2) To continually gauge community interest in and support for conservation efforts in the national park.

  How will the activity be carried out? NPS Department of Community Outreach helps project coordinator prepare audiovisual materials for meetings.

  Who is responsible for the activity? Project coordinator and assistant (project team) for NPS.

  When will the activity take place? Every six months for the first two years of the project.

Where will the activity take place? In each of the seven communities surrounding the park.

Underlying assumptions. None.

Prerequisites. Arrange convenient meeting times with community leaders.

- **Activity 3. Organize Communities.** Organize community (CDCs) that include all sectors of the communities (especially women) and that will be responsible for managing the funds generated by the revenue-sharing program.

  Why do this activity? (1) Formal community structure is required to manage funds received through revenue-sharing accord. (2) For the project to be effective in meeting threats, CDCs need to represent all sectors of the community.

  How will the activity be carried out? NPS project team contacts community leaders and holds an open forum in each of the seven communities to form CDCs.

  Who is responsible for the activity? NPS project team.

  When will the activity take place? During second year of project.

  Where will the activity take place? In each of the seven communities surrounding the park.

  Underlying assumptions. Community leaders will be willing to include representation of normally marginalized groups.

  Prerequisites. Informal meetings with community leaders to explain purpose of CDCs and gauge interest in the process.

- **Activity 4. Establish Community Bank Accounts.** Establish community accounts with the national bank to which revenue-sharing proceeds will be deposited and from which the CDCs may withdraw funds.

  Why do this activity? (1) Disbursements will be by bank transfer. (2) Processing payments through a bank account will make it easier to monitor disbursements.

  How will the activity be carried out? NPS team works with each community's CDC and accompanies representatives to national bank to set up accounts.

  Who is responsible for the activity? NPS project team.

  When will the activity take place? After CDCs have been organized, during second and third years of project.

  Where will the activity take place? Set up accounts in district capital at regional offices of national bank.

  Underlying assumptions. (1) CDC representatives will be able to manage bank accounts effectively and equitably. (2) Proceeds from NPS will be deposited into CDC accounts as planned.

Prerequisites. CDC representatives whose names will be on the accounts must have all their personal registration documents in order.

- **Activity 5. Develop Revenue Sharing Plans.** Develop plans for spending funds generated by revenue-sharing program for each community.

  Why do this activity? (1) Plans need to be developed to ensure that communities spend the money they receive in a mutually agreed upon fashion. (2) Formal plans will allow community members to monitor CDC use of funds.

  How will the activity be carried out? NPS project team, in collaboration with representatives of the Ministry of Development, and each CDC develop plans.

  Who is responsible for the activity? NPS project team.

  When will the activity take place? During second and third years of project.

  Where will the activity take place? In each of the seven communities surrounding the park.

  Underlying assumptions. CDCs adequately represent all community members.

  Prerequisites. None.

Objective 2a. Tourism Waste Management

By the end of the project (December 2001), all local commercial hotel and tour operators dispose of wastes in ways that do not contaminate the park and its surrounding areas.

Factor(s) in Conceptual Model targeted by objective. Local pollution.

Project assumptions. In initial assessment of local site conditions, project staff found that hotels, restaurants, and other tourist operations are major sources of solid waste and sewage that impact the land, rivers, and wildlife within the national park. It is assumed that by educating operators and developing and enforcing a waste management plan this problem can be overcome.

Underlying assumptions. Hotel and tour operators feel that it is in their own best interest to maintain clean environments in and around Karimara National Park.

Activities for Objective 2a

- **Activity 1. Training in Waste Disposal.** Educate commercial operators who work in and around the park regarding how to properly manage and dispose of solid and sewage wastes.

Why do this activity? There are currently no standards for dealing with wastes.

How will the activity be carried out? Hold training and information workshops that include management and staff of the four commercial hotel and tour operators.

Who is responsible for the activity? Karimara National Park chief warden and NPS project team.

When will the activity take place? Twice a year for the first two years, then once a year for the last three years of the project.

Where will the activity take place? Workshops to take place at hotels on a rotating basis.

Underlying assumptions. (1) Hotel and tour operators will want to cooperate with NPS to support and attend training sessions. (2) Inadequate waste disposal is due to a lack of knowledge of proper disposal methods.

Prerequisites. Karimara National Park chief warden and project coordinator need to negotiate with commercial hotel and tour owners to sponsor rotating workshops and ensure that staff and management will attend training sessions.

- **Activity 2. Develop Waste Disposal Plan.** Develop an enforcement plan for local commercial hotel and tour operations' waste disposal that includes self-policing, periodic site visits by park officials, and a schedule of fines for violations.

Why do this activity? Mechanism is needed to ensure compliance with waste management plans.

How will the activity be carried out? NPS project team works, in collaboration with local commercial tour and hotel operators, to draft plan. Final plan is approved by park chief warden, NPS central office, and tour and hotel owners.

Who is responsible for the activity? NPS project team.

When will the activity take place? By the end of the first year of the project.

Where will the activity take place? Karimara National Park headquarters.

Underlying assumptions. Local commercial tour and hotel operators will be willing to cooperate with enforcement efforts.

Prerequisites. Park chief warden needs to talk to hotel and tour owners to explain the activity and get their endorsement.

- **Activity 3. Inspect Hotel and Tour Operators.** Random inspections of local commercial hotel and tour operations to check for compliance to waste disposal plan.

Why do this activity? Outside inspections will provide operators with incentives for compliance.

How will the activity be carried out? NPS project team will schedule visits two days in advance with park inspectors.

Who is responsible for the activity? Karimara Park inspectors.

When will the activity take place? Twice a year, during the third, fourth, and fifth years of the project.

Where will the activity take place? All hotel and tour operators' permanent and temporary lodging and camping sites.

Underlying assumptions. None.

Prerequisites. None.

Objective 2b. Tourism Game Viewing

By the end of the project, all local commercial hotel and tour operators adhere to Karimara National Park guidelines for game viewing and other park use.

Factor(s) in Conceptual Model targeted by objective. Factor #1: Disturbance of wildlife reproduction and migration; Factor #2: Degradation from overuse of ecosystem.

Project assumptions. Factors #1 and #2: In initial assessment of local site conditions, project staff found tour operations have negative effects on plant and animal populations throughout the Karimara National Park. For example, vehicles driving off designated highways cause erosion and high levels of habitat degradation. Improper game viewing disrupts wildlife feeding and reproductive behavior. Park staff assume that by developing guidelines for and training operators in proper wildlife viewing these problems can be avoided.

Underlying assumptions. Use of proper game viewing techniques can minimize disruption while not significantly reducing tourism opportunities.

Activities for Objective 2b

- **Activity 1. Develop Game Viewing Guidelines.** Develop guidelines for game viewing and park use that will include regulations on keeping vehicles in designated areas and on designated roads, keeping visitors inside vehicles at all times while in the park, and maintaining adequate distance from game while viewing.

Why do this activity? Developing standardized, acceptable guidelines in conjunction with tour operators will increase the likelihood that they will be accepted and followed.

How will the activity be carried out? The NPS project team will work with local commercial hotel and tour operators to develop the guidelines.

Who is responsible for the activity? NPS project team.

When will the activity take place? Within the first year of the project.

Where will the activity take place? Park headquarters.

Underlying assumptions. Present tour operations are disruptive to wildlife in the park.

Prerequisites. Research guidelines used in other national parks and other countries.

- **Activity 2. Develop Penalties.** Develop a system of fines for infractions of guideline regulations.

  Why do this activity? By developing a mutually accepted system of sanctions, operators will be more willing to comply with the guidelines.

  How will the activity be carried out? NPS project team, in consultation with local commercial hotel and tour operators, prepares schedule of fines.

  Who is responsible for the activity? NPS project team.

  When will the activity take place? Within first year of the project.

  Where will the activity take place? Park headquarters.

  Underlying assumptions. Fines will act as an effective deterrent to disruptive game viewing practices.

  Prerequisites. Park chief warden needs to talk to hotel and tour owners to explain activity and get their endorsement.

- **Activity 3. Conduct Training for Wildlife Viewing.** Hold training and information workshops with all local commercial hotel and tour operator managers and guides on adherence to the guidelines.

  Why do this activity? Guideline information needs to be communicated to all operators.

  How will the activity be carried out? NPS project team coordinates park wardens and guards to give workshops.

  Who is responsible for the activity? NPS project team.

  When will the activity take place? Annually, once the guidelines and schedule of fines are complete.

  Where will the activity take place? Workshops to take place at hotels on a rotating basis.

  Underlying assumptions. These workshops will provide the

opportunity for operators to provide feedback to the park service on the guidelines.

Prerequisites. None.

Objective 3a. Eliminate Escaped Fires

By the end of the project, there will be no more uncontrolled fires set by local residents within the wildlife management areas (WMAs) around the park to generate pasturage for cattle.

Factor(s) in Conceptual Model targeted by objective. Fire.

Project assumptions. Fires set by local residents to promote the growth of new grass shoots for their cattle cause widespread burning of grassland and savannah areas during the dry season, especially from fires that escape from controlled burn areas. Although the savannah is a fire adapted ecosystem, the intentional fires are more frequent than naturally occurring fires and thus disrupt the natural ecosystem patterns. It is assumed that intentionally set fires can be controlled by educating residents.

Underlying assumptions. (1) Most fires in the region are set by humans. (2) Alternative range management systems can provide sufficient fodder for cattle. (3) Simple cost-effective techniques are available to promote controlled burns.

Activities for Objective 3a

- **Activity 1. Conduct Community Meetings to Explain Benefits.** Hold meetings with the residents of the seven communities around the park to discuss the benefits of the park and the need to protect it.

  Why do this activity? Based on information collected during the initial local site assessment, the project team learned that local residents do not fully understand the ecological benefits provided by the park.

  How will the activity be carried out? NPS project team organizes meetings in consultation with community leaders.

  Who is responsible for the activity? NPS project team.

  When will the activity take place? Twice a year in conjunction with meetings described under activity 2 for objective 1.

  Where will the activity take place? In each of the seven communities.

  Underlying assumptions. Local residents are willing to attend meetings.

  Prerequisites. (1) Arrange convenient meeting times with

community leaders. (2) Prepare materials to present at the meetings.

- **Activity 2. Train Herders in Fire Management.** Train local herders in safe fire use and control practices for improving pastures.

  Why do this activity? To teach local herders how to do controlled burns.

  Who is responsible for the activity? NPS project team.

  How will the activity be carried out? NPS project team works with the Ministry of Agriculture to develop training materials and plan. Ministry of Agriculture trainers facilitate workshop.

  When will the activity take place? During first and second years of project.

  Where will the activity take place? In each of the seven communities.

  Underlying assumptions. (1) NPS will be able to get Ministry of Agriculture to participate. (2) Herders will be interested in attending training sessions. (3) Herders are unaware of safe fire use and control practices for improving pastures.

  Prerequisites. Develop materials for the training.

- **Activity 3. Show Herders the Park and WMA Boundaries.** Community leaders and herders are taken on field visits to learn the park and WMA boundaries.

  Why do this activity? During the local site assessment, local herders explained that they were unaware of where the park and WMA boundaries were and thus were unable to respect them.

  How will the activity be carried out? NPS project team coordinates with park guards.

  Who is responsible for the activity? Karimara Park guards.

  When will the activity take place? During first year of project.

  Where will the activity take place? All seven communities and around perimeter of park.

  Underlying assumptions. Community members are not familiar with park and WMA boundaries.

  Prerequisites. None.

Objective 3b. Eliminate Cattle Grazing Inside Park

Within the last two years of the project, there are no reported incidents of herders grazing their cattle inside the park boundaries.

Factor(s) in Conceptual Model targeted by objective. Factor #1: Cattle grazing in park; Factor #2: Disease from cattle and dogs.

Project assumptions. Factors #1 and #2: Currently, local herders will graze their cattle inside park and WMA boundaries during certain times of the year. There is some scientific evidence that shows that certain diseases (hoof and mouth disease from cattle and distemper from domestic dogs used to herd cattle) are transmitted to wild animal populations within the park. It is assumed that by reducing the number of cattle and dogs in the park the project will be able to reduce the prevalence of these diseases in wild animal populations.

Underlying assumptions. Herders will be willing to graze their cattle outside of the park.

Activities for Objective 3b

- **Activity 1. Designate Pasture Areas.** Work with local herders of the seven communities to establish areas of the WMAs that will be accessible for cattle grazing at specific times of the year.

  Why do this activity? By limiting pasture to selected areas within the WMAs, the project will reduce contact between domestic and wild animal populations.

  How will the activity be carried out? NPS project team will work with Ministry of Agriculture personnel and herders from the seven communities to determine what areas inside the park are suitable to cattle grazing.

  Who is responsible for the activity? NPS project team.

  When will the activity take place? Within first year of the project.

  Where will the activity take place? Site visits to areas that NPS, Ministry of Agriculture, and local herders believe are suitable for cattle grazing.

  Underlying assumptions. (1) Herders will graze only in mutually agreed upon designated areas. (2) Suitable areas exist inside the WMAs where wildlife do not graze so that cattle to wildlife contacts are minimized.

  Prerequisites. (1) NPS reviews aerial photo and wildlife census records to determine possible cattle grazing sites within the WMAs. (2) Through wildlife census data, NPS staff will determine times of the year when cattle can safely graze in specific areas inside the WMAs.

- **Activity 2. Conduct Community Meetings to Explain Boundaries.** As above, community meetings are held to discuss the benefits of the park, and leaders and herders are shown the park and WMA boundaries.

  Why do this activity? Based on information collected during the initial local site assessment, the project team learned that local residents do not fully understand the ecological benefits provided by the park or where the boundaries are located.

How will the activity be carried out? NPS project team organizes meetings in consultation with community leaders.

Who is responsible for the activity? NPS project team.

When will the activity take place? Twice a year in conjunction with meetings described under activity 2 for objective 1.

Where will the activity take place? In each of the seven communities.

Underlying assumptions. Local residents are willing to attend meetings.

Prerequisites. (1) Arrange convenient meeting times with community leaders. (2) Prepare materials to present at the meetings.

Objective 4. Reduce Illegal Hunting

To reduce by 90 percent incidents of illegal hunting inside the park and WMAs by the end of the project.

Factor(s) in Conceptual Model targeted by objective. Factor #1: Hunting in the park; Factor #2: Hunting around the park; Factor #3: Legal hunting by community/commercial.

Project assumptions. Factors #1, #2, and #3: In discussions with local residents during the initial site visits, project staff learned that there are three kinds of hunters who are taking animals from the park: local residents who are unaware of the restrictions and park boundaries, poachers from the neighboring country who hunt large game to sell in urban markets and for wild animal parts to sell to the international market, and big game trophy hunters who come from the capital city and from abroad to hunt large animals. It is assumed that trophy hunters and their guides will comply with hunting restrictions once they are understood and a monitoring system is put in place. It is also assumed that community members will respect park boundaries once they are shown to them and will feel they have more control over the use of the resources of the park once they have been empowered to police community hunting.

Underlying assumptions. (1) Trophy hunting operators will respect hunting restriction and will not attempt to corrupt park officials. (2) Community members will participate in monitoring illegal hunting activities in the park.

Activities for Objective 4

• **Activity 1. Meet with Trophy Hunting Operators.** Hold meetings with local trophy game hunting operators to clarify park boundaries, hunting restrictions (both inside park and in WMAs), and penalties for unlawful hunting.

Why do this activity? To inform local trophy hunting operator of park boundaries and regulations.

How will the activity be carried out? NPS project team in collaboration with park guards.

Who is responsible for the activity? NPS project team.

When will the activity take place? Within first year.

Where will the activity take place? Local trophy game hunting operators' offices.

Underlying assumptions. (1) Some local trophy game hunting occurs illegally inside the park and in the WMAs. (2) Some local trophy game hunting operators are unaware of hunting regulations in and around the park.

Prerequisites. Arrange suitable meeting times with operators.

- **Activity 2. Monitor Trophy Game Hunts.** Provide NPS guards to accompany and monitor all trophy game hunts.

Why do this activity? To ensure that trophy game hunters comply with NPS regulations.

How will the activity be carried out? NPS Karimara Park Guards will be coordinated through park headquarters office. Expenses of guards will be paid by operators.

Who is responsible for the activity? NPS Karimara Park guard corps.

When will the activity take place? For the last four years of the project.

Where will the activity take place? Guards will be coordinated out of the park headquarters.

Underlying assumptions. (1) By having a representative of the NPS with them during hunts, local trophy game hunting operators will be less likely to hunt illegally. (2) Local trophy game hunting operators will not attempt to bribe guards to be able to hunt illegally. (3) Local trophy game hunting operators will be willing to pay the expenses of guards who accompany hunts.

Prerequisites. Park chief warden needs to talk to local trophy game hunting operators to explain the activity and get their endorsement.

- **Activity 3. Meet with Communities to Discuss Hunting Restrictions.** Hold community meetings to discuss hunting restrictions in the park and WMAs and penalties for unlawful hunting.

Why do this activity? Based on information collected during the initial local site assessment, the project team learned that local residents do not fully understand the current legal hunting restrictions in the park.

How will the activity be carried out? NPS project team organizes meetings in consultation with community leaders.

Who is responsible for the activity? NPS project team.

When will the activity take place? During the first year of the project.

Where will the activity take place? In each of the seven communities.

Underlying assumptions. Community members are unaware of hunting restrictions in and around the park.

Prerequisites. Set up meetings with community leaders.

- **Activity 4. Show Community Members the Park and WMA Boundaries.** Take all community men on field visits to learn the park and WMA boundaries.

   Why do this activity? During the local site assessment, community members explained that they were unaware of where the park and WMA boundaries were and thus were unable to respect them.

   How will the activity be carried out? NPS project team coordinates with park guards.

   Who is responsible for the activity? Karimara Park guards.

   When will the activity take place? During first year of project in conjunction with similar visits described above for activity 3 in objective 3a.

   Where will the activity take place? All seven communities and around the perimeter of the park.

   Underlying assumptions. (1) Community members are not familiar with park and WMA boundaries. (2) Only men are responsible for hunting. (3) Local residents, and not outsiders, are responsible for illegal hunting in and around the park.

   Prerequisites. None.

- **Activity 5. Develop Community Policing System.** Work with local community leaders to develop a community-based self-policing system for monitoring illegal hunting in the park and WMAs.

   Why do this activity? To control illegal hunting in the park by foreign poachers and community members.

   How will the activity be carried out? NPS project team coordinates with park guard corps to work with community leaders to set up a system to monitor hunting activities and inform NPS staff of illegal hunting activities in a timely fashion.

Who is responsible for the activity? Karimara Park guards and community members.

When will the activity take place? By the end of the second year.

Where will the activity take place? In each of the seven communities.

Underlying assumptions. Communities will be willing and able to self-police hunting practices.

Prerequisites. (1) Establish channels of communication for reporting infractions. (2) Set up schedule of fines.

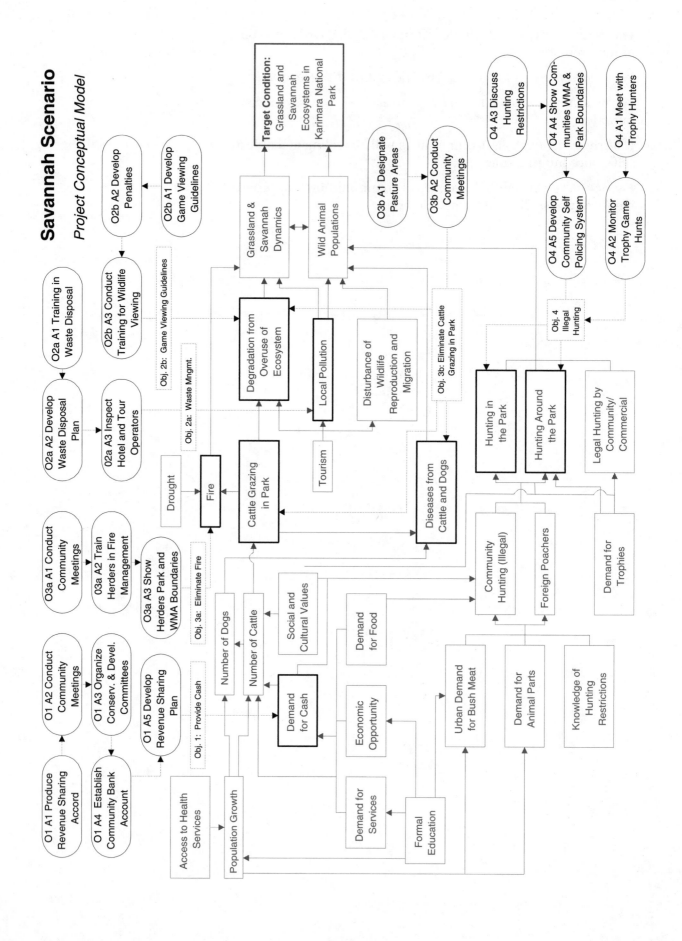

Savannah Scenario

Project Conceptual Model

Project Management Timeline

Management Tasks / Project Year Quarter	1 Q1	1 Q2	1 Q3	1 Q4	2 Q1	2 Q2	2 Q3	2 Q4	3 Q1	3 Q2	3 Q3	3 Q4	4 Q1	4 Q2	4 Q3	4 Q4	5 Q1	5 Q2	5 Q3	5 Q4	People Responsible
Goal: To conserve the grassland and savannah ecosystems of Karimara National Park																					
O1. Household demand for cash																					
– A1. Produce revenue sharing accord	X	X	X	X																	NPS director
– A2. Conduct community meetings	X		X		X		X														Project coordinator/assistant
– A3. Organize communities					X	X	X	X													NPS project team
– A4. Establish community bank accounts							X	X	X	X											NPS project team
– A5. Develop revenue sharing plans							X	X	X	X	X	X									NPS project team
O2a. Tourism waste management																					
– A1. Training in waste disposal		X		X		X		X			X				X					X	NPS project team
– A2. Develop waste disposal plan		X	X	X																	NPS project team
– A3. Inspect hotels/tour operators										X		X		X		X		X		X	Park inspectors
O2b. Tourism game viewing...																					
– A1. Develop game viewing guidelines		X	X	X																	NPS project team
– A2. Develop penalties		X	X	X																	NPS project team
– A3. Conduct training for wildlife viewing						X				X				X				X			NPS project team
O3a. Eliminate escaped fires...																					
– A1. Conduct community meetings	X		X		X		X														NPS project team
– A2. Train herders in fire management	X		X		X		X														NPS project team
– A3. Show herders boundaries	X		X																		Park guards
O3b. Eliminate cattle grazing inside park																					
– A1. Designate pasture areas	X	X	X	X																	NPS project team
– A2. Conduct community meetings	X		X		X		X														NPS project team
O4. Reduce illegal hunting...																					
– A1. Meet with trophy hunting operators	X	X																			NPS project team
– A2. Monitor trophy game hunts					X	X	X	X	X	X	X	X	X	X	X	X	X	X	X	X	Park guards
– A3. Meet with communities	X	X																			NPS project team
– A4. Show community members boundaries	X		X																		Park guards
– A5. Develop policing system					X	X	X	X													Park guards and community members

Monitoring Plan

Goal, Objective, or Additional Information

Goal. To conserve the grassland and savannah ecosystems of Karimara National Park.

Monitoring Strategy 1: Monitor change over time in area of degraded grasslands and savannah.
Monitoring Strategy 2: Monitor change over time of key species, including elephants and rhinos.

What (Indicators)	How (Methods & Tasks)	When	Who	Where	Comments
Area (ha) of grasslands and savannah in the park and WMA burned or degraded	**Mapping** • Use aerial surveys to determine areas affected	Annually	Project coordinator	Park and WMAs	The National Park Service routinely does annual aerial surveys and we expect to use this information to monitor the habitats.
	Direct observation • Ground truth results of surveys	Ongoing	Project coordinator	Park and WMAs	Direct observations done as part of monitoring work for objectives 3a and 3b described below
Population size of rhinos, elephants, and other key species	**Census** • Use aerial surveys to determine population size	Annually	Project coordinator	Park and WMAs	The National Park Service routinely does annual aerial surveys and we expect to use this information to monitor the animal populations.

Goal, Objective, or Additional Information

Objective 1. Household demand for cash. To provide 20 percent of the gross revenue from park entrance fees to the seven communities that surround Karimara National Park by the end of the third year of the project (disbursement to community Conservation and Development Committees (CDCs) provided on per capita basis).

Monitoring Strategy 1: Measure change over time in park revenues flowing to the seven communities receiving benefits.

What (Indicators)	How (Methods & Tasks)	When	Who	Where	Comments
Percentage of gross park revenues going to seven communities (by community)	Review of records • Determine gross revenue and disbursement to communities from National Park Service (NPS) records	Every six months	Project assistant	Village governments	Two indicators are being measured to cross-check the official NPS data with the amount received by community members.
	Key informant interviews • Interview CDC members	Every six months	Project assistant	Park headquarters	

Activities for Objective 1	Person Responsible for Monitoring the Activity	Target Date(s) for Obtaining Information
Activity 1: Produce revenue sharing accord	Project coordinator	By end of first year of project
Activity 2: Conduct community meetings to explain benefits	Project coordinator	Every six months in first two years of project
Activity 3: Organize communities	Project coordinator	At end of second year of project
Activity 4: Establish community bank accounts	Project coordinator	At end of second and third years of project
Activity 5: Develop revenue sharing plans	Project coordinator	At end of second and third years of project

Goal, Objective, or Additional Information

Objective 2a. Tourism waste management. By the end of the project (December 2001), all local commercial hotel and tour operators dispose of wastes in ways that do not contaminate the park and its surrounding areas.

Monitoring Strategy 1: Observe change in number of open garbage pits over time.
Monitoring Strategy 2: Observe change over time in compliance with waste disposal plan by hotel and tour operators.

What (Indicators)	How (Methods & Tasks)	When	Who	Where	Comments
Number of open garbage pits in and around Karimara National Park	Direct observations • Inspect sites around key tourism areas	Ongoing	Park inspectors	Near heavily used tourist sites	This information can be easily collected during normal park inspector patrols.
Number of hotel and tour operators disposing of sewage in compliance with accepted disposal plan	Direct observations • Inspect sewage disposal systems at hotels and tour sites	Every six months	Park inspector	Hotels and tour camps	

Activities for Objective 2a	Person Responsible for Monitoring the Activity	Target Date(s) for Obtaining Information
Activity 1: Training in waste disposal	Project assistant	Annually
Activity 2: Develop waste disposal plan	Project assistant	End of first year of project
Activity 3: Inspect hotel and tour operators	Park inspectors	Every six months after second year

Goal, Objective, or Additional Information

Objective 2b. Tourism game viewing. **By the end of the project, all local commercial hotel and tour operators adhere to Karimara National Park guidelines for game viewing and other park use.**

Monitoring Strategy 1: Compare number of citations issued for violation of game viewing guidelines in Karimara to a neighboring park.
Monitoring Strategy 2: Observe change over time in number of vehicle tracks encountered off of designated game viewing roads.

What (Indicators)	*How (Methods & Tasks)*	*When*	*Who*	*Where*	*Comments*
Number of citations issued for infractions of game viewing guidelines	Review of records • Review park guard weekly reports to count numbers of infractions in Karimara and Masamba National Parks	Annually	Project assistant	Karimara and Masamba Park headquarters	Masamba National Park is very similar to Karimara National Park. Commercial game viewing in Masamba is as heavy as in Karimara.
Evidence of vehicle use away from designated roads	Direct observation • Count vehicle tracks in sensitive habitat areas	Ongoing	Park guards	Sensitive areas in park	Indicator will have to be adjusted for sensitivity levels in dry and rainy seasons.

Activities for Objective 2b	*Person Responsible for Monitoring the Activity*				*Target Date(s) for Obtaining Information*
Activity 1: Develop game viewing guidelines	Project coordinator				By end of first year of project
Activity 2: Develop penalties	Project coordinator				By end of first year of project
Activity 3: Conduct training for wildlife viewing	Project coordinator				Annually

285

Goal, Objective, or Additional Information:

Objective 3a. Eliminate escaped fires. By the end of the project, there will be no more uncontrolled fires set by local residents within the wildlife management areas (WMAs) around the park to generate pasturage for cattle.

Monitoring Strategy 1: Over time, measure amount of land outside of designated pasture lands that is burned.
Monitoring Strategy 2: Monitor reports of escaped fires that were intentionally set to promote new pasture.

What (Indicators)	*How (Methods & Tasks)*	*When*	*Who*	*Where*	*Comments*
Area (ha) of land outside of designated pasture areas that is burned	Direct observation • Census areas around designated pasture areas	Annually following dry season	Park guards	Around designated pasture areas	This information by itself is not sufficient to measure the objective since it does not distinguish between naturally and human started fires.
Number of reports of escaped fires around designated pasture areas	Key informant interviews • Interview village leaders	Annually following dry season	Project assistant	Villages	Preliminary surveys indicate that leaders have a good idea of what areas have burned and who burned them.

Activities for Objective 3a		*Person Responsible for Monitoring the Activity*		*Target Date(s) for Obtaining Information*
Activity 1. Conduct community meetings to explain benefits		Project assistant		Every six months
Activity 2. Train herders in fire management		Project coordinator		End of first and second years of project
Activity 3. Show herders the park and WMA boundaries		Project assistant		By end of first year of project

Goal, Objective, or Additional Information

Objective 3b. Eliminate cattle grazing inside park. Within the last two years of the project, there are no reported incidents of herders grazing their cattle inside the park boundaries.

Monitoring Strategy 1: Compare number of times herders encountered grazing cattle in park over time.

What (Indicators)	How (Methods & Tasks)	When	Who	Where	Comments
Number of incidents of cattle grazing inside the park	Direct observation • Count numbers of encounters with herders inside park boundaries	Ongoing as part of routine patrols	Park guards	Throughout park and WMAs	Park staff initially wanted to measure "number of wild animals that have died from domestic animal diseases" as the best indicator for the negative impact of cattle grazing in the park. They found, however, that it was too difficult and expensive to measure. They thus elected to use this indicator as a proxy.

Activities for Objective 3b	*Person Responsible for Monitoring the Activity*	*Target Date(s) for Obtaining Information*
Activity 1. Designate pasture areas	Project assistant	By end of first year of project
Activity 2. Conduct community meetings to explain boundaries	Project coordinator	Every six months

287

Goal, Objective, or Additional Information

Objective 4. Reduce illegal hunting. To reduce by 90 percent incidents of illegal hunting inside the park and WMAs by the end of the project.

Monitoring Strategy 1: Compare the number of elephants and rhinos killed before and after project interventions.
Monitoring Strategy 2: Measure the change in number of encounters with hunters inside the park over time.
Monitoring Strategy 3: Compare levels of illegal hunting by trophy hunting operators in Karimara National Park to a neighboring park.

What (Indicators)	*How (Methods & Tasks)*	*When*	*Who*	*Where*	*Comments*
Number of elephant and rhino carcasses found within the park and WMAs (by species)	Direct observation • Count numbers of carcasses inside park and WMA boundaries	Ongoing as part of routine patrols	Park guards	Throughout park and WMAs	This indicator is primarily targeted at the threat posed by foreign poachers who hunt elephants and rhinos to sell ivory, meat, and horns to various markets.
Number of encounters with hunters inside park boundaries	Direct observation • Count number of hunters encountered inside park and WMA boundaries	Ongoing as part of routine patrols	Park guards	Throughout park and WMAs	This indicator is targeted primarily at subsistence by local people inside the park and WMAs.
Number of citations issued for illegal hunting to trophy hunting operators	Direct observation • Record number of violations of hunting regulations in Karimara and Masamba National Parks	Ongoing as part of routine monitoring	Park guards assigned as monitors	Throughout Karimara and Masamba National Parks and WMAs	This indicator is targeted at trophy hunting.

Activities for Objective 4	*Person Responsible for Monitoring the Activity*	*Target Date(s) for Obtaining Information*
Activity 1. Meet with trophy hunting operators	Project coordinator	By end of first year of project
Activity 2. Monitor trophy game hunts	Project coordinator	Annually
Activity 3. Meet with communities to discuss hunting restrictions	Project coordinator	By end of first year of project
Activity 4. Show community members the park and WMA boundaries	Project assistant	By end of first year of project
Activity 5. Develop community policing system	Project coordinator	By end of second year of project

Goal, Objective, or Additional Information

Additional Information Needed to Assess Project Impact

What (Indicators)	How (Methods & Tasks)	When	Who	Where	Comments
Related to social and cultural values factor—change in attitudes about cattle: Relative importance of numbers of cattle in determining social status	Focus group discussion • Discuss with community members attitudes about the social importance of the numbers of cattle Matrix ranking • Use preference ranking to look at importance of cattle	Annually Annually	Project coordinator Project coordinator	Seven villages around park Seven villages around park	Changing attitudes about the relationship between the number of cattle owned by a household and social status will influence the number of cattle per household and therefore the number of cattle grazing in the project area.
Related to urban demand for bush meat factor—meat demand: Price (per kg) of bush meat in provincial capital	Key informant interviews • Interview meat sellers to determine price	Monthly	Project coordinator	Provincial capital	Urban demand for bush meat is one of the major factors driving illegal hunting in the park. Allows project to take into account this effect in measuring its success in reducing illegal hunting.
Related to population factor—population growth: Number of people living in villages in the project area	Key informant interviews • Interview local village chiefs to get their population information	Annually	Project assistant	Local villages	Increasing population leads to increasing demands on natural resources in the park and WMA. The project needs to track this growth using the chief's records so that its effect can be accounted for.
Related to drought factor—rainfall (mm rainfall per month): Comparison of rainfall levels in the region to the historical record	Review records • Collect rainfall data for five sites in and around the park from Department of Meteorology records	Monthly	Project coordinator	Provincial office	The park ecosystems are extremely sensitive to changes in rainfall. It is thus important to measure rainfall to assess the direct impacts of the project. Even if fire control efforts succeed, natural fires may confound the indicator during droughts.
New factors: New factors at the site that affect project success	Direct observation • Observe changes at the project site	Ongoing	All project staff	All locations	Project staff need to be constantly aware of changes in the project site that might require a revision of the Project Plan.

Project Management Timeline

Project Monitoring Timeline—Karimara National Park

Monitoring Tasks	Y1 Q1	Y1 Q2	Y1 Q3	Y1 Q4	Y2 Q1	Y2 Q2	Y2 Q3	Y2 Q4	Y3 Q1	Y3 Q2	Y3 Q3	Y3 Q4	Y4 Q1	Y4 Q2	Y4 Q3	Y4 Q4	Y5 Q1	Y5 Q2	Y5 Q3	Y5 Q4	People Responsible
Goal: To conserve the grassland and savannah ecosystems of Karimara National Park.																					
– Area (ha) of grasslands/savannah in the park and WMA burned or degraded	X	X	X	X	X	X	X	X	X	X	X	X	X	X	X	X	X	X	X	X	Project coordinator
– Population size of rhinos, elephants, and other key species				X				X				X				X				X	Project coordinator
O1. Demand for cash																					
– Percentage of gross park revenues going to seven communities						X				X				X			X				Project assistant
– A1. Produce revenue sharing accord	X	X																			Project coordinator
– A2. Conduct community meetings to explain benefits	X	X			X																Project coordinator
– A3. Organize communities				X																	Project coordinator
– A4. Establish community bank accounts				X								X									Project coordinator
– A5. Develop revenue sharing plans				X								X									Project coordinator
O2a. Tourism waste management																					
– Number of open garbage pits in and around Karimara National Park					X	X	X	X	X	X	X	X	X	X	X	X	X	X	X	X	Park inspectors
– Number of hotel and tour operators practicing proper sewage disposal techniques					X				X				X				X				Park inspectors
– A1. Training in waste disposal						X			X				X				X				Project assistant
– A2. Develop waste disposal plans				X	X																Project assistant
– A3. Inspect hotel and tour operators						X			X				X				X				Park inspectors
O2b. Tourism game viewing																					
– Number of citations issued for infractions of game viewing guidelines								X	X	X	X	X	X	X	X	X	X	X	X	X	Project assistant
– Evidence of vehicle use away from designated roads					X	X	X	X	X	X	X	X	X	X	X	X	X	X	X	X	Park guards
– A1. Develop game viewing guidelines				X																	Project coordinator
– A2. Develop penalties				X																	Project coordinator
– A3. Conduct training for wildlife viewing				X								X				X				X	Project coordinator
O3a. Eliminate escaped fires																					
– Area (ha) of land outside of designated pasture areas that is burned				X		X		X		X		X		X		X		X			Park guards
– Number of reports of escaped fires around designated pasture areas				X		X		X		X		X		X		X		X			Project assistant
– A1. Conduct community meetings to explain benefits				X	X	X		X	X					X				X			Project assistant
– A2. Train herders in fire management				X		X															Project coordinator
– A3. Show herders the park and WMA boundaries				X	X	X															Project assistant

290

O3b. Eliminate cattle grazing inside park

Indicator / Activity													Responsible party
–Number of incidents of cattle grazing inside the park	X	X	X	X	X	X	X	X	X	X	X	X	Park guards
–A1. Designate pasture areas	X												Project assistant
–A2. Conduct community meetings to explain boundaries		X		X		X		X		X		X	Project coordinator

O4. Reduce illegal hunting

Indicator / Activity													Responsible party
–Number of elephant and rhino carcasses found within the park and WMAs	X	X	X	X	X	X	X	X	X	X	X	X	Park guards
–Number of encounters with hunters inside park boundaries	X	X	X	X	X	X	X	X	X	X	X	X	Park guards
–Number of citations issued for illegal hunting to trophy hunting operators	X	X	X	X	X	X	X	X	X	X	X	X	Park guards (assigned as monitors)
–A1. Meet with trophy hunting operators	X												Project coordinator
–A2. Monitor trophy game hunts		X		X		X		X		X		X	Project coordinator
–A3. Meet with communities to discuss hunting restrictions	X												Project coordinator
–A4. Show community members the park and WMA boundaries	X												Project assistant
–A5. Develop community policing system	X												Project coordinator

Additional Information

Indicator / Activity													Responsible party
–Relative importance of numbers of cattle in determining social status												X	Project coordinator
–Price (per kg) of bush meat in provincial capital	X	X	X	X	X	X	X	X	X	X	X	X	Project coordinator
–Number of people living in villages in the project area												X	Project assistant
–mm of rain per month: Comparison of rainfall levels to the historical record	X	X	X	X	X	X	X	X	X	X	X	X	Project coordinator
–New factors at the site that affect project success	X	X	X	X	X	X	X	X	X	X	X	X	All project staff

291

Project Plan for the Coastal Scenario*

Scenario Description

Suppose you are the formally educated son or daughter of the traditional leader of a coastal village who has been chosen by your people to help them find the best way to maintain their resources for future generations. Your village is located at the mouth of a river flowing from upland forests through mangrove forests into Bocoro Bay. The residents of your village get most of their food from fishing and gathering shellfish in the river and coral reefs surrounding the bay. Residents cook their food and build their houses using wood from the mangrove forests growing along the coast. Over the past few years, you and your neighbors have noticed that residents of neighboring villages are increasingly coming into your village's traditional fishing grounds. In addition, large fishing boats from other countries have begun operating in the same area. The elders of the community have noticed over time that local fishermen have to go farther away from the community to catch enough fish to eat and sell and that they are catching smaller fish. In addition, silt and pollution coming down the river have ruined many of the reefs. Furthermore, it is becoming harder to find shrimp in coastal areas near small rivers where the mangroves have been cut down. The elders are now proposing to enhance your people's traditional resource management systems to conserve the plant and animal resources in the bay for future generations.

Project Details

The activities and monitoring described for this scenario are the result of this community's (Bocoro Village) perceived need to do something about decreasing yields from their traditional fishing grounds. After unsuccessfully soliciting assistance from the regional government and a local community development non-governmental organization (NGO), the residents of Bocoro Village decided to try to resolve their problems on their own. The community has a long and strong tradition of cohesiveness and unity that serves to make communal decisions respected and honored. Upon finishing their secondary education at the regional school, some Bocoro children have gone to the Provincial University, and the Council of Elders counts on their help in dealing with government and NGO officials and for technical support in planning project activities and measuring their success. The community has chosen the university-educated eldest son of the village chief to

*The information on this and the following page is not part of the Project Plan but is provided as background information about the scenario.

serve as the project coordinator. The chief's son has demonstrated leadership and a desire to help the community. He will provide general oversight of the project for planning, management, and monitoring. Although the community has virtually no cash funds to devote to implementing a project or monitoring it, community members have agreed to invest their time and efforts into taking action to ensure there will be sufficient natural resources for generations to come.

Group's Mission

During a community meeting called by the Council of Elders, residents formulated the following declaration that can be considered a mission statement: We, the residents of Bocoro Village, wish to promote our own health and well-being by finding ways to better manage the natural resources upon which our lives and economy depend. We are convinced that, by working together with a common purpose and common vision, we can provide a safe and productive future for our children and their children.

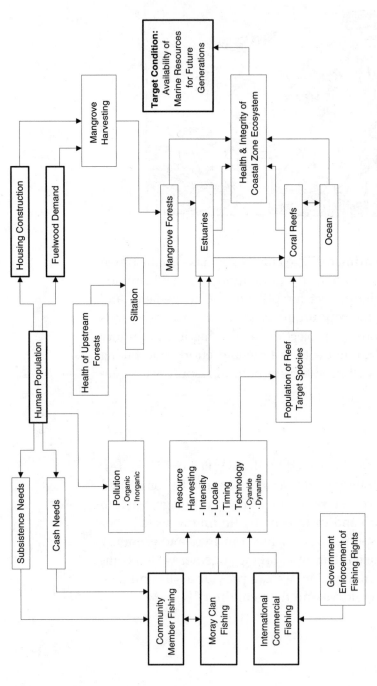

Coastal Scenario

Initial Conceptual Model

Initial Conceptual Model Summary

The target condition at our site, Bocoro Bay, is the availability of marine resources for future generations. In this area, the availability of marine resources is directly related to the health and integrity of the coastal zone ecosystem, which is made up of mangrove forests, estuaries, coral reefs, and open ocean.

Mangrove forests close by our village are affected by the extent to which we harvest wood for building materials (for housing construction) and to meet our demand for fuelwood. The mangrove forests are important not only for the wood they provide us but also because they keep the estuaries (where most of the fish that live in Bocoro Bay reproduce) healthy and clean. We have found that the estuaries are also greatly affected by the silt that is carried by the river, which empties into the shallow inlet. Siltation of the river is caused by people cutting down the forest in the mountains. This deforestation leads to the washing away of the soil that ends up in our river, so the health of the upstream forests determines how much silt gets washed down into the estuary. We have noticed that the estuaries are also very sensitive to pollution—both organic pollution, such as human waste, and inorganic pollution, such as pesticides.

The quantity and quality of the fish and other marine species we harvest from the reef is related to the population of the various species we value. To some extent, the population of fish found on the reef is a result of their success in multiplying in the estuaries that we just mentioned. The population of these fish has changed a lot over the past 10 years, and we believe it is primarily because of the way we and others have been harvesting these resources. When we talk about resource harvesting we mean the intensity, place (locale), and timing of fishing and the technology used. In the last couple of years, some fishing families have used cyanide and bombs for fishing; these new techniques have been very destructive to our fish.

In addition to our village, there are other people who take fish from Bocoro Bay. These include neighboring villages and big international commercial fishing boats that come and fish in areas where they are supposedly not allowed to be. These commercial boats come and fish on our traditional fishing grounds only because the government does not do anything to support our traditional claims to the areas or to enforce no-commercial-fishing limits.

In our community, our fathers and our fathers' fathers fished so that their families could eat. The fish we catch and the shellfish we gather are used to feed our families and to sell to buyers that come from the city so we can earn some money to buy things we need to live. We have seen over the years that the increasing numbers of people in our village and in other villages in the area have made marine resources scarcer. This is probably due to the fact that as the population has increased and more and more people needed to catch fish to eat and sell in the market, the fish just could not reproduce fast enough to keep up with the pressure we were putting on them. Also, as the village has grown, more and more mangrove wood has been cut for housing construction and fuelwood. We have also noticed that as the population grew, pollution got worse and worse. It seems that one of the biggest problems we have is balancing the number of people in our village with the amount of resources we have to feed ourselves and earn some money.

Management Plan

Project goal. To ensure the availability of marine resources for our grandchildren and our grandchildren's grandchildren.

Objective 1a. Restrict Location of Resource Harvesting

During the second year of the project there are no incidents of community members fishing in sanctuary areas.

Factor(s) in Conceptual Model targeted by objective. Resource harvesting.

Project assumptions. Based on past experience, the Council of Elders assumes that if community members are involved in establishing the sanctuary and are responsible for its success, then there will be no violations in the future.

Underlying assumptions. (1) Setting up and maintaining sanctuary areas on the reef will enable populations of marine organisms to maintain themselves and recover. (2) Community members will respect and maintain the sanctuary areas.

Activities for Objective 1a

- **Activity 1. Hold Meetings with Community Members.** Hold meetings with community members to discuss declaring part of the traditional fishing grounds to be sanctuary areas.

   Why do this activity? No major decisions are taken in the community by the Council of Elders without full participation of all community members.

   How will the activity be carried out? Elders will hold meetings with all community residents to explain and get agreement on sanctuary principle.

Who is responsible for the activity? Chief and Council of Elders.

When will the activity take place? Second month of the project.

Where will the activity take place? Chief's house.

Underlying assumptions. None.

Prerequisites. None.

- **Activity 2. Designate Sanctuary Areas.** Convene meeting of Council of Elders to designate, map, and mark sanctuary areas based on traditional fishing practices.

    Why do this activity? In past community meetings, some residents have strongly supported the idea of setting aside sanctuary areas where fish can safely grow and reproduce. At present, however, there are no areas in the Bocoro Bay area where there are restrictions on fishing.

    How will the activity be carried out? The Chief will convene a meeting of the Council of Elders and solicit suggestions (based on results of the community meeting) as to which areas should be designated sanctuaries and how they should be marked.

    Who is responsible for the activity? Chief.

    When will the activity take place? Fourth month of the project.

    Where will the activity take place? Chief's house.

    Underlying assumptions. Elders will be able to agree on sanctuary principle and locations.

    Prerequisites. Discuss with Elders prior to meeting.

- **Activity 3. Initiate Community Policing Mechanisms.** Develop and implement the policing mechanisms that will be used to enforce the sanctuary policies.

    Why do this activity? Community members feel that they can effectively enforce sanctuary policies on their own. However, they want clear guidelines that everyone knows in order to avoid future conflicts.

    How will the activity be carried out? Elders will discuss the policing system and decide on methods and sanctions that will be imposed for violations.

    Who is responsible for the activity? Council of Elders.

    When will the activity take place? Fourth month of the project.

    Where will the activity take place? Chief's house.

    Underlying assumptions. (1) Elders can agree on policies. (2) Community can enforce policing mechanisms.

    Prerequisites. Review techniques used in other villages.

Objective 1b. Restrict Timing of Resource Harvesting

By the end of the second year of the project, village elders do not hear any substantiated reports or find evidence of community members fishing for taboo species during their critical breeding periods.

Factor(s) in Conceptual Model targeted by objective. Resource harvesting.

Project assumptions. The Council of Elders assumes that if community members are made aware of the need to suspend fishing during critical breeding periods, they will respect taboo periods.

Underlying assumptions. (1) Setting up and maintaining taboo periods for resource harvesting during critical breeding periods will enable populations of marine organisms to maintain themselves. (2) Sufficient information is available on marine species' life cycles to be able to determine appropriate breeding periods.

Activities for Objective 1b

- **Activity 1. Designate Taboo Periods.** Convene village elders to agree on taboo periods for harvesting critical species.

  Why do this activity? In past community meetings, some residents have strongly supported the idea of establishing taboo periods when fish can breed and reproduce. At present, however, there are no taboo periods for marine resources harvesting in the Bocoro Bay.

  How will the activity be carried out? The Chief will convene a meeting of the Council of Elders and solicit suggestions as to what the taboo periods should be for different species.

  Who is responsible for the activity? Chief and Council of Elders.

  When will the activity take place? Third month of the project.

  Where will the activity take place? Chief's house.

  Underlying assumptions. Elders will be able to agree on taboo periods.

  Prerequisites. Research traditional taboo periods and scientific knowledge of breeding cycles.

- **Activity 2. Develop Seasonal Fishing Calendar with Community Members.** Hold meetings with community members to discuss taboo periods and develop seasonal fishing calendar.

  Why do this activity? To complement the information that is available about the life cycles of various marine species.

  How will the activity be carried out? Elders will hold meetings with family heads within the village to explain and get agreement on sanctuary principle.

Who is responsible for the activity? Chief and Council of Elders.

When will the activity take place? Fourth month of the project.

Where will the activity take place? Elders' houses.

Underlying assumptions. There is abundant local knowledge on the life cycles of various marine species.

Prerequisites. None.

Objective 1c. Promote the Use of Nondestructive Technology

By the end of the second year of the project, no fishermen are using either cyanide or bombs for capturing fish.

Factor(s) in Conceptual Model targeted by objective. Resource harvesting.

Project assumptions. It is assumed that by making fishermen aware of the damage that cyanide and bomb fishing cause and by getting them to agree to clear fishing guidelines they will cease fishing with these destructive techniques.

Underlying assumptions. (1) Cyanide and dynamite fishing destroys the reef and ultimately will reduce the fish population. (2) Alternative technologies are available and will be adopted by clan members.

Activities for Objective 1c

• **Activity 1. Visit Damaged Sites.** Council of Elders organizes visit of the head of each family group to bombed and cyanide-impacted reef sites.

Why do this activity? To demonstrate to community fishermen the destructive impacts of bombing and cyanide.

How will the activity be carried out? Heads of families go with Elders to visit sites on designated dates.

Who is responsible for the activity? Chief and Council of Elders.

When will the activity take place? Fifth month of the project.

Where will the activity take place? Bombed out reef sites in Wide Bay.

Underlying assumptions. (1) Most fishermen do not really know the damage that bombing and cyanide cause. (2) By showing fishermen the damage, they will be motivated to stop it.

Prerequisites. Locate suitable reef sites.

- **Activity 2. Develop Policing Mechanisms.** Develop more formal community policing mechanisms to enforce existing restrictions on cyanide and bomb fishing.

  Why do this activity? Community members feel that they can effectively enforce prohibition of bombing and cyanide use. However, they want clear guidelines that everyone knows in order to avoid future conflicts.

  How will the activity be carried out? Elders will hold meetings with family heads within the village to explain and get agreement on fishing restrictions.

  Who is responsible for the activity? Chief and Council of Elders.

  When will the activity take place? Sixth month of the project.

  Where will the activity take place? Elders' houses.

  Underlying assumptions. None.

  Prerequisites. None.

Objective 1d. Reduce Fishing Intensity

By the end of the third year, reduce incidents of harvesting snappers, groupers, and conch in violation of community council defined size limits to fewer than 15 per month.

Factor(s) in Conceptual Model targeted by objective. Resource harvesting.

Project assumptions. Based on past experience, the Council of Elders assumes that if community members are involved in defining size limits and are responsible for self-monitoring their catch, then limits will be honored.

Underlying assumptions. (1) Capture of immature fish damages the reproductive potential of the fish populations. (2) Fishermen in the Bocoro Bay area are catching fish that are too young and small.

Activities for Objective 1d

- **Activity 1. Define Size Limits.** Council of Elders organize and hold meeting to discuss size limits.

  Why do this activity? Council of Elders must include community members in discussions on size limits.

  How will the activity be carried out? Meeting called and organized.

  Who is responsible for the activity? Chief and Council of Elders.

  When will the activity take place? Fifth month of the project.

  Where will the activity take place? Chief's house.

Underlying assumptions. None.

Prerequisites. Elders discuss appropriate limits.

- **Activity 2. Develop Measuring Devices.** Community members produce measuring devices that fishermen and women can use in their boats to assess catch size.

  Why do this activity? Fishing families need some objective way to determine whether their catch is within the established limits.

  How will the activity be carried out? Once size limits have been set, the local blacksmith will produce the measuring devices.

  Who is responsible for the activity? Community members designated to produce devices.

  When will the activity take place? Sixth month of the project.

  Where will the activity take place? Blacksmith's shop.

  Underlying assumptions. None.

  Prerequisites. Same as activity 1.

- **Activity 3. Develop Monitoring System.** Council of Elders develop a system of monitoring daily catches to ensure compliance with established size guidelines.

  Why do this activity? By monitoring daily catches, the community can determine to what extent other residents are adhering to established size limits.

  How will the activity be carried out? Elders arrange schedule by which one of them will meet all incoming boats in the evening to inspect catches.

  Who is responsible for the activity? Council of Elders.

  When will the activity take place? After the sixth month of the project.

  Where will the activity take place? At the community dock.

  Underlying assumptions. None.

  Prerequisites. Same as activity 1.

Objective 1e. Reduce Fishing by Moray Clan

Within three years of the project start date, no more than one incident per month occurs in which Moray Clan members are found fishing in village traditional fishing grounds.

Factor(s) in Conceptual Model targeted by objective. Resource harvesting.

Project assumptions. The Moray Clan has access to a much larger area to fish than the residents of Bocoro Village. They are also notorious for overfishing fragile areas are using destructive techniques. In the past, Bocoro Village has done little to prevent Moray Clan members from fishing on traditional Bocoro fishing grounds. The Council of Elders assumes that if it can prevent Moray Clan members from fishing in traditional Bocoro Village fishing grounds, then more marine resources will be available in the future.

Underlying assumptions. Negotiation with the Moray Clan is possible.

Activities for Objective 1e

- **Activity 1. Discuss Issue with Moray Clan.** The Council of Elders organizes a delegation to discuss the purpose and status of sanctuaries and traditional fishing grounds with the Moray Clan.

  Why do this activity? Council of Elders wishes to negotiate a quiet settlement to disputes they've had with Moray Clan Elders for the past 20 years.

  How will the activity be carried out? Meeting called and organized.

  Who is responsible for the activity? Chief and Council of Elders.

  When will the activity take place? Tenth month of the project.

  Where will the activity take place? Moray Clan Chief's house.

  Underlying assumptions. None.

  Prerequisites. Contact Moray Clan and set up meeting.

- **Activity 2. File Complaint with Provincial Ministry.** If activity 1 above fails, the Council of Elders contacts the Provincial Ministry of Marine Resources to enlist their assistance in enforcing traditional resource claims.

  Why do this activity? Council of Elders sees no other options to resolve the conflict if their direct negotiations fail.

  How will the activity be carried out? Council of Elders will go with the project coordinator to meet the appropriate government officials.

  Who is responsible for the activity? Council of Elders.

  When will the activity take place? Twelfth month of the project.

  Where will the activity take place? Provincial capital.

  Underlying assumptions. Government officials will be willing to entertain the complaint and will be able to enforce restrictions on the Moray Clan.

  Prerequisites. Determine results of above activity.

Objective 2. Keep Foreign Fishing Vessels Out of Bocoro Bay

By the end of five years, numbers of foreign fishing vessels operating in community fishing grounds have been reduced by 75 percent.

Factor(s) in Conceptual Model targeted by objective. International commercial fishing.

Project assumptions. Foreign fishing vessels are using sophisticated technology to unsustainably and illegally overfish marine resources in Bocoro Village traditional fishing grounds. It is assumed that these commercial fishing vessels can be controlled by publicizing their violations.

Underlying assumptions. Government officials are willing to stand up to the foreign governments.

Activities for Objective 2

- **Activity 1. Document Fishing Violations.** Train key observers to document sightings of illegal foreign fishing activities (including ship identification numbers) and report sightings to provincial authorities.

  Why do this activity? As it is theoretically the government's job to control illegal hunting, this information can help it to identify and penalize ships in violation of the law.

  How will the activity be carried out? Local villagers will be trained by the project coordinator to write down observations of foreign fishing vessels operating in traditional waters (including taking pictures with small pocket cameras). These reports will be compiled and sent to the provincial government authorities.

  Who is responsible for the activity? Project coordinator.

  When will the activity take place? Starting in the first month of the project.

  Where will the activity take place? Traditional fishing grounds.

  Underlying assumptions. Information will get to those in government with decision-making power related to the control of illegal commercial fishing, and enforcement will occur.

  Prerequisites. (1) Identify and interview government officials who would be interested in the information and will be able to act on it. (2) Purchase small cameras and film.

- **Activity 2. Publicize Violations.** Contact sympathetic NGOs in the national capital city for assistance in obtaining media coverage of the violations.

  Why do this activity? Sympathetic NGOs have helped in the past to publicize important issues.

How will the activity be carried out? Project coordinator will contact the appropriate NGOs.

Who is responsible for the activity? Project coordinator.

When will the activity take place? Sixth month of the project.

Where will the activity take place? Provincial and national capitals.

Underlying assumptions. (1) Public awareness of the situation in Bocoro Bay will mobilize broad support for the local communities. (2) Government officials will be willing to entertain the complaints and can enforce the international treaties.

Prerequisites. None.

Objective 3a. Reduce Use of Mangrove Firewood

By the end of two years, all households will use one-third less mangrove firewood (measured by weight) than they did at the start of the project.

Factor(s) in Conceptual Model targeted by objective. Factor #1: Mangrove harvesting; Factor #2: Fuelwood demand.

Project assumptions. Factors #1 and #2: It is assumed that by educating village residents and demonstrating more efficient cooking methods, residents will reduce the amount of mangrove they use for firewood.

Underlying assumptions. (1) Firewood need is one of the major reasons for cutting down mangroves which provide habitat for critical marine resources. (2) Women in the village will be willing to adopt new stove technology.

Activities for Objective 3a

- **Activity 1. Increase Clan Knowledge.** Hold community education meetings to discuss the importance of mangroves for maintenance of the estuarine food chain.

   Why do this activity? Most community residents are unaware of the relationship between estuary production and the amount of fish found on the reefs.

   How will the activity be carried out? Project coordinator and Council of Elders call a meeting of all men and women in the community.

   Who is responsible for the activity? Project coordinator and Council of Elders.

   When will the activity take place? Starting in the second year of the project.

   Where will the activity take place? Chief's house.

Underlying assumptions. A community education campaign will be successful in changing knowledge and behavior regarding mangrove firewood use.

Prerequisites. Presentation needs to be developed.

- **Activity 2. Make Improved Cook Stoves.** Consult with local government authorities for assistance in obtaining plans for building improved cook stoves that reduce fuelwood consumption and then assist families to make their own stoves.

  Why do this activity? Construction of these stoves has been shown to reduce the amount of fuelwood consumption. Another benefit of these stoves is that smoke is vented through a chimney, thus reducing the amount of smoke in the house.

  How will the activity be carried out? Project coordinator will contact the appropriate NGOs to obtain plans and will work with each family to assist them in building the improved stoves.

  Who is responsible for the activity? Project coordinator.

  When will the activity take place? Second year of the project.

  Where will the activity take place? Provincial capital and community.

  Underlying assumptions. Provincial NGOs have plans for the stoves.

  Prerequisites. None.

Objective 3b. Eliminate Use of Mangrove Wood for Construction

By the end of seven years, all new buildings constructed in the community use no mangrove wood and substitute other materials.

Factor(s) in Conceptual Model targeted by objective. Factor #1: Mangrove harvesting; Factor #2: Housing construction.

Project assumptions. Factors #1 and #2: The Council of Elders assumes that by identifying and promoting the use of alternative construction materials, residents will stop using mangrove wood in the future.

Underlying assumptions. (1) Housing construction is the other major reason for cutting down mangroves which provide habitat for critical marine resources. (2) People in the village will be willing to adopt new construction technology.

Activities for Objective 3b

- **Activity 1. Identify Substitute Materials.** Hold community meetings to discuss other building materials that could be used for housing (e.g., bamboo).

Why do this activity? In order to eliminate reliance on mangrove for construction material, other readily available alternative sources must be identified.

How will the activity be carried out? Project coordinator and Council of Elders meet with various family heads.

Who is responsible for the activity? Project coordinator and Council of Elders.

When will the activity take place? Twice during the second year of the project.

Where will the activity take place? Elders' houses.

Underlying assumptions. None.

Prerequisites. Find information about other building options used in the Bocoro Bay area.

- **Activity 2. Produce Substitute Materials.** Plant bamboo and other fast-growing species to provide long-term supplies of building materials.

  Why do this activity? To meet local demands the community will have to plant substitution species that can be used for construction.

  How will the activity be carried out? Materials will be distributed to families to plant in their fallow garden plots.

  Who is responsible for the activity? Appointed members of the community.

  When will the activity take place? Second year of the project.

  Where will the activity take place? In fallow lands around Bocoro Village.

  Underlying assumptions. Plant materials can be obtained and will grow in local conditions.

  Prerequisites. Find information about tree species that can be grown in plantations and that are useful for building construction.

Objective 4a. Promote Family Planning

By the end of three years, 75 percent of families in the community are knowledgeable about and have access to contraceptive options.

Objective 4b. Increase Birth Spacing

By the end of ten years, average birth spacing for the community has doubled.

Note: The following section applies to Objectives 4a and 4b.

Factor(s) in Conceptual Model targeted by objectives. Human population.

Project assumptions. The Council of Elders assumes that by promoting family planning and birth spacing average family size will decrease leading to a greater likelihood that there will be enough resources for everyone in the future.

Underlying assumptions. (1) Population growth is a major factor that will affect use of marine resources and ultimately the welfare of the community. (2) Residents of the village are willing to adopt family planning methods.

Activities for Objectives 4a and 4b

- **Activity 1. Hold Education Meetings.** Arrange with Ministry of Health officials to hold monthly education meetings that discuss family planning benefits and options.

  Why do this activity? The Ministry of Health has an effective education program for family planning and are willing to work in Bocoro Village.

  How will the activity be carried out? Village chief contacts Ministry of Health officials to arrange calendar of meetings.

  Who is responsible for the activity? Project coordinator, village chief, and Ministry of Health officials.

  When will the activity take place? Starting in the second year of the project.

  Where will the activity take place? Village chief's house.

  Underlying assumptions. None.

  Prerequisites. Council of Elders talk privately to each head of household to discuss the substance of the meetings.

Note: Cultural sensitivities preclude setting directly measurable impact objectives such as contraceptive acceptance and prevalence in this community. This objective, although weak in this regard, is the best one possible.

- **Activity 2. Train Traditional Birth Attendants.** Arrange with Ministry of Health officials to train traditional birth attendants (TBAs) in family planning and well-baby care.

  Why do this activity? The TBAs are the most consulted health care providers for child birth, neonatal, and infant care.

  How will the activity be carried out? Village chief contacts Ministry of Health.

Who is responsible for the activity? Ministry of Health officials.

When will the activity take place? Starting in the second year of the project.

Where will the activity take place? Village health clinic.

Underlying assumptions. Working with TBAs will have the greatest impact on child health in Bocoro Village.

Prerequisites. None.

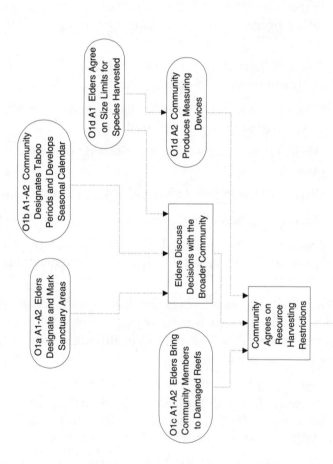

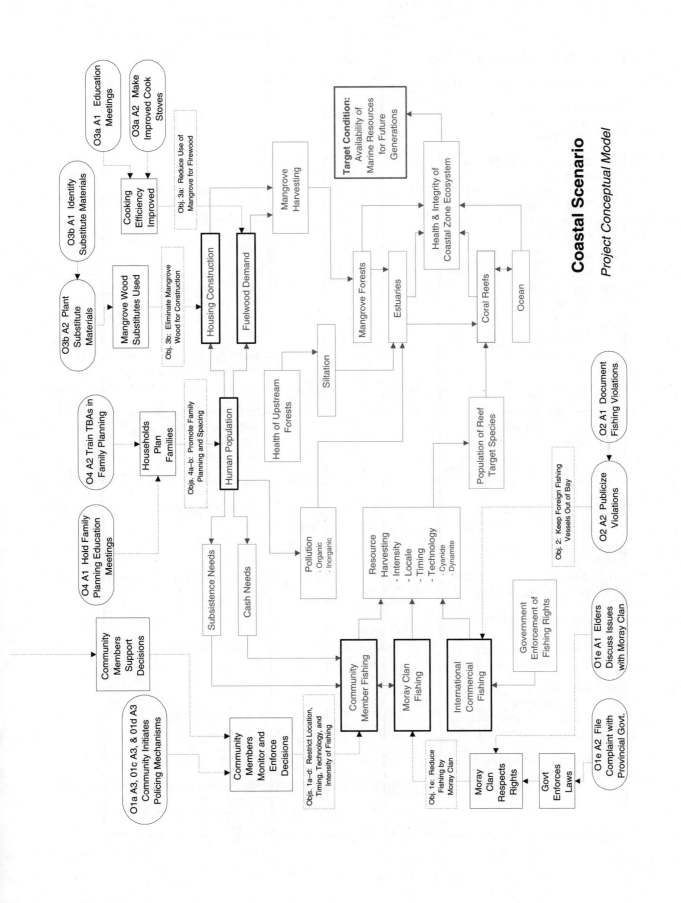

Coastal Scenario

Project Conceptual Model

Project Management Timeline

Management Tasks	Project Year Quarter	1 Q1	2	3	4	2 Q1	2	3	4	3 Q1	2	3	4	People Responsible

Project Management Timeline—Bocoro Bay (first three years)

Management Tasks	Y1 Q1	Q2	Q3	Q4	Y2 Q1	Q2	Q3	Q4	Y3 Q1	Q2	Q3	Q4	People Responsible
Goal: To ensure the availability of marine resources for our grandchildren and our grandchildren's grandchildren													
O1a. Restrict location of resource harvesting													
– A1. Hold community meetings	X												Chief/Council of Elders
– A2. Designate sanctuary areas		X											Chief
– A3. Initiate community policing mechanisms		X											Council of Elders
O1b. Restrict timing of resource harvesting													
– A1. Designate taboo periods	X												Chief/Council of Elders
– A2. Develop fishing calendar		X											Chief/Council of Elders
O1c. Promote the use of nondestructive technology													
– A1. Visit damaged sites		X											Chief/Council of Elders
– A2. Develop policing mechanisms			X										Chief/Council of Elders
O1d. Reduce fishing intensity													
– A1. Define size limits		X											Chief/Council of Elders
– A2. Develop measuring devices			X										Community members
– A3. Develop monitoring system			X										Council of Elders
O1e. Reduce fishing by Moray Clan													
– A1. Discuss issues with Moray Clan				X									Chief/Council of Elders
– A2. File complaint with Provincial Ministry					X								Council of Elders
O2. Keep foreign vessels out of Boroco Bay													
– A1. Document fishing violations	X												Project coordinator (PC)
– A2. Publicize violations		X											PC
O3a. Reduce use of mangrove firewood													
– A1. Increase clan knowledge					X	X			X	X			PC/Council of Elders
– A2. Make improved cook stoves					X	X	X	X					PC
O3b. Eliminate use of mangrove for construction													
– A1. Identify substitute materials					X	X							PC/Council of Elders
– A2. Produce substitute materials						X	X	X	X	X	X	X	Community members
O4a. Promote family planning													
O4b. Increase birth spacing													
– A1. Hold education meetings					X	X	X	X	X	X	X	X	Chief/PC/Ministry of Health officials
– A2. Train TBAs					X		X		X		X		Chief and Ministry of Health officials

Monitoring Plan

Goal, Objective, or Additional Information

Goal. To ensure the availability of marine resources for our grandchildren and our grandchildren's grandchildren.

Monitoring Strategy: Compare amount of captured marine resources by species over time.

What (Indicators)	How (Methods & Tasks)	When	Who	Where	Comments
Total number of individuals of target species (snapper, grouper, and conch) brought to shore per day	*(below are for both indicators)* Key informant interviews • Designated council member interviews fishermen	Daily	Designated council member	Community dock	See monitoring information for Objective 1d and "Additional Information." All fisherman return to the community dock at the same time each afternoon where they unload their catch.
Total number of individuals of nontarget species brought to shore per day	Direct observation • Designated council member reviews daily catches (notes species and weights)	Daily	Designated council member	Community dock	It is expected that as community management of marine resources becomes routine, fisherman will catch fewer but larger fish. If this is shown to be true, then it can be presumed that fish species will be allowed to reach reproductive maturity before being harvested. A reflection of species health will be the abundance of adult individuals.

These indicators will be analyzed and compared on a yearly basis to control for natural seasonal differences. |

311

Goal, Objective, or Additional Information

Objective 1a. Restrict location of resource harvesting. During the second year of the project, there are no incidents of community members fishing in sanctuary areas.

Monitoring Strategy: Compare the number of sanctuary fishing violations over time.

What (Indicators)	*How (Methods & Tasks)*	*When*	*Who*	*Where*	*Comments*
Number of reports of violations	Key informant interviews • Interview chief and members of Council of Elders, which receives reports of violations.	Monthly, at meetings of Council of Elders	Project coordinator in collaboration with one council member	Traditional meeting place: Chief's house	Incidents of violations of community norms are traditionally reported to Council of Elders.

Activities for Objective 1a	*Person Responsible for Monitoring the Activity*	*Target Date(s) for Obtaining Information*
Activity 1: Hold meetings with community members	Project coordinator	By third month of the project
Activity 2: Designate sanctuary areas	Project coordinator	By the fifth month of the project
Activity 3: Initiate community policing mechanisms	Project coordinator	By the sixth month of the project

Goal, Objective, or Additional Information

Objective 1b. Restrict timing of resource harvesting. By the end of the second year of the project, village elders do not hear any substantiated reports or find evidence of community members fishing for taboo species during their critical breeding periods.

Monitoring Strategy: Compare frequency of fishing during taboo periods over time.

What (Indicators)	How (Methods & Tasks)	When	Where	Who	Comments
Number of reports of fishing in which taboo species are caught and kept	Key informant interviews • Interview members of Council of Elders, which receives reports of violations.	Monthly, at meetings of Council of Elders	Traditional meeting place: Chief's house	Project coordinator in collaboration with one council member	Incidents of violations of community norms are traditionally reported to Council of Elders

Activities for Objective 1b	Person Responsible for Monitoring the Activity	Target Date(s) for Obtaining Information
Activity 1: Designate taboo periods	Project coordinator	Fourth month of project
Activity 2: Develop seasonal fishing calendar with community members	Project coordinator	Fifth month of project

313

Goal, Objective, or Additional Information

Objective 1c. Promote the use of nondestructive technology. By the end of the second year of the project, no fishermen are using either cyanide or bombs for capturing fish.

Monitoring Strategy 1: Monitor the number of reports of destructive fishing over time.
Monitoring Strategy 2: Observe the changes over time of the amount of reef area affected by destructive fishing techniques.

What (Indicators)	How (Methods & Tasks)	When	Who	Where	Comments
Reports of cyanide fishing Reports of bomb fishing	Key informant interviews • Interview members of Council of Elders, which receives reports of violations.	Monthly, at meetings of Council of Elders	Project coordinator in collaboration with one council member	Traditional meeting place: Chief's house	Incidents of violations of community norms are traditionally reported to Council of Elders. Especially in the cases of these types of fishing, community tolerance for violations is very low so reporting will be good.
Reef area damaged by cyanide fishing Reef area damaged by bomb fishing	Direct observation • Sentinel site monitoring of high risk areas	Ongoing	Project coordinator with members of the community	Areas of the reef that are at highest risk of destructive fishing practices	Only certain areas of the reef have been destroyed by cyanide or bombs in the past. These are areas that are farthest from and most inaccessible to the community. These are the areas that will be included as sentinel sites.

Activities for Objective 1c	*Person Responsible for Monitoring the Activity*	*Target Date(s) for Obtaining Information*
Activity 1: Visit damaged sites	Project coordinator	By sixth month of project
Activity 2: Develop policing mechanisms (in conjunction with Objective 1a)	Village chief	By sixth month of project

Goal, Objective, or Additional Information

Objective 1d. Reduce fishing intensity. By the end of the third year, for snappers, groupers, and conch there are no incidences of harvesting in violation of size limits as defined by the community council for each species.

Monitoring Strategy: Measure the change over time in the amount of undersized individuals brought to shore for key species.

What (Indicators)	How (Methods & Tasks)	When	Who	Where	Comments
Number of snappers below permissible size brought to shore	Key informant interviews • Designated council member interviews fishermen	Daily	Designated council member	Community dock	All fisherman return to the community dock at the same time each afternoon where they unload their catch.
Number of groupers below permissible size brought to shore	Direct observation • Designated council member reviews daily catches	Daily	Designated council member	Community dock	
Number of conch below permissible size brought to shore					

Activities for Objective 1d	Person Responsible for Monitoring the Activity	Target Date(s) for Obtaining Information
Activity 1. Define size limits	Designated council member	By sixth month of project
Activity 2. Develop measuring devices	Project coordinator	By seventh month of project
Activity 3. Develop monitoring system	Project coordinator	By seventh month of project

315

Goal, Objective, or Additional Information

Objective 1e. Reduce fishing by Moray Clan. Within three years of the project start date, no more than one incident per month occurs in which the Moray Clan are found fishing in village traditional fishing grounds.

Monitoring Strategy: Monitor the change over time of the frequency with which Moray Clan members are found in Bocoro Village fishing grounds.

What (Indicators)	*How (Methods & Tasks)*	*When*	*Who*	*Where*	*Comments*
Number of incidents per month in which members of the Moray Clan are found fishing in Bocoro Village traditional fishing grounds	Key informant interviews • Designated council member interviews fishermen	Monthly	Designated council member	Community dock	The Council of Elders expect fisherman to report trespassing by Moray Clan members as soon as it occurs. The council, however, wants to interview fisherman monthly just to make sure that no violations go unreported.

Activities for Objective 1e	*Person Responsible for Monitoring the Activity*	*Target Date(s) for Obtaining Information*
Activity 1. Discuss issue with Moray Clan	Designated council member	By end of first year of project
Activity 2. File complaint with Provincial Ministry	Project coordinator	After end of first year of project

316

Goal, Objective, or Additional Information

Objective 2. *Keep foreign fishing vessels out of Bocoro Bay.* By the end of five years, numbers of foreign fishing vessels operating in community fishing grounds have been reduced by 75 percent.

Monitoring Strategy: Monitor presence of foreign fishing vessels in Bocoro Bay over time.

What (Indicators)	How (Methods & Tasks)	When	Who	Where	Comments
Number of sightings of foreign fishing vessels per month	Key informant interviews • Designated council member interviews fishermen	Ongoing	Designated council member	Community dock	
	Direct observation • Count number of foreign fishing vessels sighted	Ongoing	Designated "Key Observers" from community	Throughout Bocoro Bay	

Activities for Objective 2	Person Responsible for *Monitoring the Activity*	Target Date(s) for *Obtaining Information*
Activity 1. Document (foreign) fishing violations	Project coordinator	Monthly
Activity 2. Publicize violations	Village chief	Monthly, as needed

317

Goal, Objective, or Additional Information

Objective 3a. Reduce use of mangrove firewood. By the end of two years, all households will use one-third less mangrove firewood (measured by weight) than they did at the start of the project.

Monitoring Strategy 1: Compare amounts of household consumption of mangrove for firewood over time.
Monitoring Strategy 2: Track percentage of households that adopt improved cook stoves over time.

What (Indicators)	How (Methods & Tasks)	When	Who	Where	Comments
Kilograms of mangrove wood used for firewood per household on a weekly basis	Formal survey (household) • Project coordinator and community volunteers will approximate family consumption of fuelwood using Salter scales borrowed from the Health Post	Twice each year	Project coordinator	Community households	By looking at how much mangrove wood each household is using and how many households have improved cook stoves, it can be determined how effective the stoves are in reducing mangrove firewood demand.
Percentage of households using improved cook stoves	Direct observation • During visits to household for the formal survey, volunteers will observe presence or absence of improved stove	Twice each year	Project coordinator	Community households	

Activities for Objective 3a	Person Responsible for Monitoring the Activity	Target Date(s) for Obtaining Information
Activity 1. Increase clan knowledge	Project coordinator	Semiannually, after second year of project
Activity 2. Make improved cook stoves	Project coordinator	Semiannually, after second year of project

Goal, Objective, or Additional Information

Objective 3b. Eliminate use of mangrove wood for construction. By the end of seven years, all new buildings constructed in the community use no mangrove wood and instead substitute other materials.

Monitoring Strategy: Compare building construction materials over time.

What (Indicators)	How (Methods & Tasks)	When	Who	Where	Comments
Number of new building projects using mangrove wood	Direct observation • Count number of new building projects using mangrove wood	Ongoing	Project coordinator	In community wherever new construction occurs	As the community is relatively small, it will be easy to observe when new construction projects use mangrove wood.

Activities for Objective 3b	Person Responsible for Monitoring the Activity	Target Date(s) for Obtaining Information
Activity 1. Identify substitute materials	Project coordinator	By the end of the second year of the project
Activity 2. Produce substitute materials	Project coordinator	Ongoing, after second year of project

319

Goal, Objective, or Additional Information:

Objective 4a. Promote family planning. By the end of three years, 75 percent of families in the community are knowledgeable about and have access to contraceptive options. (*Note:* Cultural sensitivities preclude setting more directly measurable impact objectives such as contraceptive acceptance and prevalence in this community. This objective, although weak in this regard, is the best one possible.)

Monitoring Strategy 1: Measure change in knowledge of village residents regarding family planning over time.
Monitoring Strategy 2: Observe change over time of availability of family planning methods.

What (Indicators)	How (Methods & Tasks)	When	Who	Where	Comments
Percentage of women 15–45 years of age knowledgeable about family planning options	Formal survey (household) • Project coordinator will work with community traditional birth attendants (TBAs) and Ministry of Health technicians to collect data	Once annually	Project coordinator	Community households	
Percentage of men 15–45 years of age knowledgeable about family planning options	Formal survey (household) • Project coordinator will work with community TBAs and Ministry of Health technicians to collect data	Once annually	Project coordinator	Community households	
Number of sites in community where contraceptives are available	Direct observation • Count number village dispensaries and homes of TBAs where contraceptives are available	Ongoing	Project coordinator	Throughout community	

Activities for Objective 4a	*Person Responsible for Monitoring the Activity*	*Target Date(s) for Obtaining Information*
Activity 1. Hold education meetings	Project coordinator	Ongoing, after second year of project
Activity 2. Train traditional birth attendants	Project coordinator	Ongoing, after second year of project

320

Goal, Objective, or Additional Information

Objective 4b. Increase birth spacing. By the end of 10 years, average birth spacing for the community has doubled.

Monitoring Strategy: Measure average time between births in Bocoro Village families over time.

What (Indicators)	How (Methods & Tasks)	When	Who	Where	Comments
Average time in months between births for all families	Formal survey (household) • Project coordinator will work with community traditional birth attendants (TBAs) and Ministry of Health technicians to collect data	Once annually	Project coordinator	Community households	

Activities for Objective 4b	Person Responsible for Monitoring the Activity	Target Date(s) for Obtaining Information
Activity 1. Hold education meetings	Project coordinator	Ongoing, after second year of project
Activity 2. Train traditional birth attendants	Project coordinator	Ongoing, after second year of project

Goal, Objective, or Additional Information

Additional Information Needed to Assess Project Impact

What (Indicators)	How (Methods & Tasks)	When	Who	Where	Comments
Related to availability of marine resources for future generations—overall pressure on fishing resources:					Although data will be gathered daily when fishermen bring in their catch to the community dock, analysis will be based on yearly catch to control for natural differences in seasonality.
Number of different species brought to shore per day	Key informant interviews • Designated council member interviews fishermen	Daily	Designated council member	Community dock	If the number of different species brought to shore increases, it may be a reflection of fishermen seeking nontarget species to substitute for the initial reduced catch that may result from target species fishing restrictions.
Average weight of fish brought to shore by species by day	Direct observation • Designated council member reviews daily catches (notes species and weights)	Daily	Designated council member	Community dock	If the size of different fish species brought to shore is increasing and the number of species caught remains the same over time, then chances are biodiversity is being conserved.
Related to mangrove harvesting—area affected:					Mangrove harvesting for construction is traditionally regulated by the village chief and the Council of Elders who give permission to community residents
Number of 20m × 20m mangrove plots given out by the Council of Elders for construction per year	Key informant interviews • Interview chief and members of Council of Elders, which receives reports of violations	Monthly, at meetings of Council of Elders	Project coordinator in collaboration with one council member	Traditional meeting place: Chief's house	to cut specific 20m × 20m plots of mangrove forest. Residents who want to cut mangrove wood must petition the council at one of its monthly meetings. If the number of petitions diminishes or stops, it can be presumed that mangrove harvesting is likewise reduced.

322

Indicator	Method	Frequency	Who	Location	Comments
Number of new 20m × 20m plots cleared per year	Direct observation • Inspections made during walks through area where red mangrove is usually harvested for construction	Once a month	Project coordinator in collaboration with one council member	Traditional harvesting areas near community	Monitoring the extent to which mangrove harvesting for construction has occurred is relatively easy as community members only harvest from one area where red mangrove is found. Also, as harvesters clear-cut an entire plot that has been given to them by the Council of Elders, it is easy to observe when this occurs.
Related to human population factor—population size: Number of new families established in Bocoro Village	Key informant interviews • Council of Elders keeps census registry for the community. Each time a new family is established (that is, builds a new house), this is recorded in the community registry.	Once a year	Project coordinator in collaboration with one council member	Traditional meeting place: Chief's house	Population increases in Bocoro Village can be measured by how many new houses are built for new families—from either village children who get married and establish their own family or newly arrived immigrants. If population increases greatly during the life of the project, it will be difficult to reduce pressure on marine resources. It is, therefore, very important to keep track of this indicator.
New factors: New factors at the site that affect project success	Direct observation • Observe changes at the project site	Ongoing	All project staff	All locations	Project staff need to be constantly aware of potential changes in the project site that would require a revision of the Project Conceptual Model and Management Plan.

Project Monitoring Timeline

Project Monitoring Timeline—Bocoro Bay (first five years)

Monitoring Tasks	Year 1 Q1	Q2	Q3	Q4	Year 2 Q1	Q2	Q3	Q4	Year 3 Q1	Q2	Q3	Q4	Year 4 Q1	Q2	Q3	Q4	Year 5 Q1	Q2	Q3	Q4	People Responsible
Goal: To ensure availability of marine resources																					
– Total number of individuals of target species brought to shore per day	X	X	X	X	X	X	X	X	X	X	X	X	X	X	X	X	X	X	X	X	Designated council member
– Total number of individuals of nontarget species brought to shore per day	X	X	X	X	X	X	X	X	X	X	X	X	X	X	X	X	X	X	X	X	Designated council member
O1a. Restrict location of resource harvesting																					
– Number of reports of violations	X	X	X	X	X	X	X	X	X	X	X	X	X	X	X	X	X	X	X	X	Project coordinator (PC)/council member
– A1. Hold community meetings	X																				PC
– A2. Designate sanctuary areas		X																			PC
– A3. Initiate community policing mechanisms			X																		PC
O1b. Restrict timing of resource harvesting																					
– Number of reports of fishing taboo species	X	X	X	X	X	X	X	X	X	X	X	X	X	X	X	X	X	X	X	X	PC/council member
– A1. Designate taboo periods	X																				PC
– A2. Develop fishing calendar	X																				PC
O1c. Promote use of nondestructive technology																					
– Reports of cyanide fishing	X	X	X	X	X	X	X	X	X	X	X	X	X	X	X	X	X	X	X	X	PC/council member
– Reports of bomb fishing	X	X	X	X	X	X	X	X	X	X	X	X	X	X	X	X	X	X	X	X	PC/council member
– Reef area damaged by cyanide fishing	X	X	X	X	X	X	X	X	X	X	X	X	X	X	X	X	X	X	X	X	PC/community members
– Reef area damaged by bomb fishing	X	X	X	X	X	X	X	X	X	X	X	X	X	X	X	X	X	X	X	X	PC/community members
– A1. Visit damaged sites		X																			PC
– A2. Develop policing mechanisms			X																		Chief
O1d. Reduce fishing intensity																					
– Number of snappers below permissible size brought to shore	X	X	X	X	X	X	X	X	X	X	X	X	X	X	X	X	X	X	X	X	Designated council member
– Number of groupers below permissible size brought to shore	X	X	X	X	X	X	X	X	X	X	X	X	X	X	X	X	X	X	X	X	Designated council member
– Number of conch below permissible size brought to shore	X	X	X	X	X	X	X	X	X	X	X	X	X	X	X	X	X	X	X	X	Designated council member
– A1. Define size limits	X																				Designated council member
– A2. Develop measuring devices		X																			PC
– A3. Develop monitoring system		X																			PC

324

O1e. Reduce fishing by Moray Clan
- Number of incidents/month in which Moray Clan fishing in Bocoro fishing grounds — Designated council member
  - A1. Discuss issue with Moray Clan — Designated council member
  - A2. File complaint with Provincial Ministry — PC

O2. Keep foreign vessels out of Bocoro Bay
- Number of sightings of foreign fishing vessels per month — Designated council member
  - A1. Document fishing violations — PC
  - A2. Publicize violations — Chief

O3a. Reduce use of mangrove firewood
- Kg of mangrove wood used for firewood per household on a weekly basis — PC
- Percentage of households using improved cook stoves — PC
  - A1. Increase clan knowledge — PC
  - A2. Make improved cook stoves — PC

O3b. Eliminate mangrove for construction
- Number of new building projects using mangrove wood — PC
  - A1. Identify substitute materials — PC
  - A2. Produce substitute materials — PC

O4a. Promote family planning
O4b. Increase birth spacing
- Percentage of women 15–45 years old knowledgeable about family planning options — PC
- Percentage of men 15–45 years old knowledgeable about family planning options — PC
- Number of sites in community where contraceptives are available — PC
- Average time in months between births for all families — PC
  - A1. Hold education meetings — PC/council member
  - A2. Train TBAs — PC

Additional Information
- Number of different species brought to shore per day — Designated council member
- Average weight of fish brought to shore by species — Designated council member
- Number of 20m × 20m mangrove plots given out for construction per year — PC/council member
- Number of new 20m × 20m plots cleared per year — PC/council member
- Number of new families established in Bocoro Village — PC/council member
- New factors at the site that affect project success — All project staff

Project Plan for the Wetlands Scenario[*]

Scenario Description

Suppose you are the manager of a local chapter of a conservation advocacy group whose members live near the Everson Watershed. The wetlands in the watershed serve as important habitats for migratory birds and for a number of fish and game species. These species support extensive recreational uses of the area including birdwatching, canoeing, fishing, and hunting. The wetlands are also part of the water supply system for major urban areas in the watershed. The wetlands are threatened by growing development and urbanization including road construction and dredging. They are also affected by water pollution (especially from agricultural chemicals) and invasions of exotic plant and animal species. You are planning to work with local landowners and governments to purchase or obtain conservation easements on lands containing critical wetland and upstream habitat. In addition, your organization is hoping to work to educate the public about the importance of the upstream habitats in maintaining the wetlands. Finally, you are hoping to devise a management plan to help control some of the impacts of exotic species.

[*]The information on this and the following page is not part of the Project Plan but is provided as background information about the scenario.

Project Details

The Friends of the Everson Watershed (FOEW) is an advocacy group that was developed to protect the Everson Watershed against encroaching development. The group was originally founded to manage several nature preserves. Over the past decade or so, however, the group has been expanding both in terms of its core membership and the scope of the activities it is undertaking. FOEW has about 1000 committed members who are organized into chapters around the watershed. Today, the FOEW has more than 10 full-time staff members.

The project is currently scheduled to last for five years. Staff members involved in this project include two scientists (a biologist and a hydrologist), an acquisitions manager who handles land purchases, a data specialist who works especially with mapping information, a community outreach officer, and a legislative outreach coordinator. In addition, for this project the group is looking to hire an agricultural outreach officer and one or two interns. FOEW works closely with several state agencies, including the Department of Environment and the Department of Agriculture. In addition, for this project FOEW will be working with researchers from Everson State University, who will be hired on a contract basis.

Group's Mission

The mission of FOEW is: To protect the natural areas in our state to maintain their value as habitat and for human use. We attempt to accomplish this by integrating science, policy, advocacy, and education while working with local constituencies and lawmakers. We believe that our society's health and well-being are inextricably linked to the health of the natural environment in which we live.

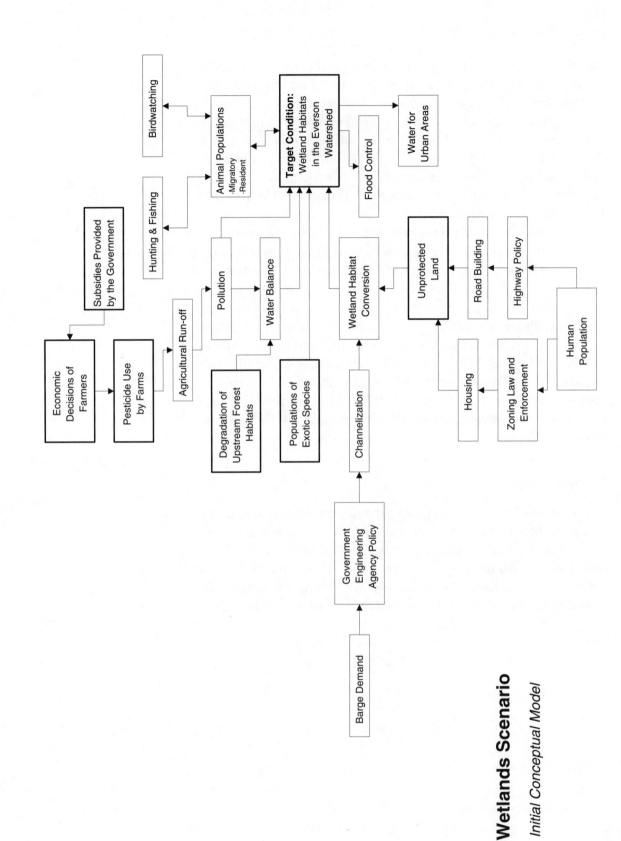

Wetlands Scenario

Initial Conceptual Model

Initial Conceptual Model Summary

Our target condition is focused on the wetland habitats in the Everson Watershed. These habitats include deep river and shallows habitats in the river itself and freshwater and brackish marshes and swamps alongside the river. These habitats provide food and shelter to many different plant and animal species, including a number of different birds and animals that provide hunting and nature watching opportunities to local residents. In addition, the wetland habitats help control the hydrological balance in the watershed, providing flood control and drinking water for downstream cities.

One major threat to the wetlands habitat is direct conversion for houses, roads, marinas, and other forms of development. Although current federal and state law prohibits any net loss of wetlands from development, privately held parcels of wetlands can be converted if other areas of wetland are created within the watershed. Growing human populations in the watershed are increasing the pressure on these lands for conversion, and there is some movement from landowners to change the laws and zoning regulations.

Wetlands, including in particular the river and shallows habitats, are also directly affected by dredging that occurs to keep boat traffic channels in the river open. Current dredging policies maintained by the Federal Engineering Agency do not pose a great threat to the wetlands at the moment because they are limited to maintaining already existing channels.

Another major threat to the wildlife in the Everson Watershed are inorganic pesticides that enter the streams and rivers through soil erosion and run-off from farms. These pesticides are affecting large fish, fish-eating birds and mammals, humans, and other organisms that are high on the food chain. Pesticide use has increased in recent years. This increase has been driven by economic decisions of farmers which are in turn influenced by the state tax code which subsidizes pesticide use by allowing large agribusinesses to deduct the cost of pesticides as an operating expense.

A third major threat comes from exotic plant and shellfish species that have been introduced into the watershed in recent decades. These species, which originally come from other continents, generally have no natural predators and thus are able to proliferate, choking out native species through direct competition and by creating eutrophic conditions in which the rotting materials reduce oxygen levels in the water, thus killing fish and other species. Specifically, one species of water hyacinth has been identified as a particular problem.

The last major threat comes from degradation of dry forests in the upper reaches of the Everson Watershed. The continuing population growth and development in the region coupled with a lack of knowledge of environmental issues by township and county zoning commissioners means that forests are being cut down and paved over, affecting the water balance in the streams and other wetland habitats.

Management Plan

Project goal. To maintain healthy wetlands in the Everson Watershed in order to provide water to nearby urban areas and wildlife-based recreational opportunities for residents and visitors.

Objective 1. Habitat Conversion Reduced in Critical Sites

Within five years, 80 percent of identified privately owned priority wetland and adjacent natural habitat areas have been legally protected against conversion.

Factor(s) in Conceptual Model targeted by objective. Unprotected land.

Project assumptions. Although federal and state laws prohibit a net loss of wetland areas, privately owned wetland sites can still be developed if the loss of wetland areas is offset by the creation of other wetland areas. Therefore, it is necessary to identify the key wetland areas currently in private hands and then protect them. In addition, since wetland habitats depend on the health of adjacent forest and other habitats in the watershed, these also need to be protected. It is assumed that legal protection will mean that these priority habitats are indeed safe from degradation and destruction.

Underlying assumptions. (1) State and federally owned lands are legally protected against development. (2) Key wetland and adjacent areas can be identified. (3) Identified areas can be protected.

Activities for Objective 1

- **Activity 1. Map Critical Wetland Areas.** Identify critical wetland and adjacent habitat areas in the Everson Watershed using existing base maps combined with ground-truthing field visits.

  Why do this activity? In order to determine the total pool of sites where the project could work.

  How will the activity be carried out? The Friends of the Everson Watershed (FOEW) biologist and data specialist will work with existing habitat maps and property ownership maps to identify potential sites for protection. The biologist will then visit the sites in conjunction with local chapter representatives and the State Environmental Agency mapping staff.

  Who is responsible? FOEW biologist.

When will the activity take place? Starting in the third month of the project and to be completed by the ninth month.

Where will the activity take place? Mapping will cover the Everson Watershed. Ground truthing will focus on key areas that have been identified.

Underlying assumptions. (1) State Environmental Agency can contribute staff and computer time to do necessary mapping work. (2) Permission can be obtained from property owners to do ground-truthing field work.

Prerequisites. Need to compile existing map information.

- **Activity 2. Select Priority Habitat Parcels.** Develop a list of biological criteria (e.g., conservation importance, degree of connection to other sites) for ranking habitat parcels and then apply criteria to develop a list of priority sites.

  Why do this activity? The project cannot work everywhere but must focus on the most important sites.

  How will the activity be carried out? FOEW staff (biologist and data specialist) develop criteria and then apply them.

  Who is responsible? FOEW data specialist.

  When will the activity take place? Starting in the ninth month of the project and ending by the twelfth month.

  Where will the activity take place? In FOEW offices.

  Underlying assumptions. Sufficient information exists for all sites.

  Prerequisites. FOEW staff must compile existing information about sites.

- **Activity 3. Develop Interventions and Rank Costs.** For each parcel identified here, develop potential interventions such as conservation easements, brokering sales of land to the state, or outright purchase. Select which interventions will be most cost-effective in relation to the conservation importance of the site.

  Why do this activity? The project has limited resources and must use them on the most important sites.

  How will the activity be carried out? FOEW staff (acquisitions manager and data specialist in conjunction with local chapter members) research each site and develop interventions. Sites will then be ranked in terms of conservation importance relative to the cost of the intervention. The staff will also produce a timetable for various interventions.

  Who is responsible? FOEW acquisitions manager.

  When will the activity take place? Starting in the twelfth month of the project and ending by the fifteenth month.

  Where will the activity take place? In FOEW offices.

Underlying assumptions. Sufficient information exists for all sites concerning ownership.

Prerequisites. FOEW staff must compile existing information about sites and, wherever possible, survey current owners regarding their plans and preferences.

- **Activity 4. Enact Conservation Interventions.** Implement conservation interventions identified for sites in roughly the order outlined during the ranking exercise.

  Why do this activity? By implementing interventions in the determined order, staff can most efficiently address priority conservation needs.

  How will the activity be carried out? FOEW staff and chapter members will enact appropriate interventions.

  Who is responsible? FOEW acquisitions manager.

  When will the activity take place? According to the timetable developed in the preceding step.

  Where will the activity take place? Townships throughout the Everson Watershed.

  Underlying assumptions. Rankings and data will have to be updated over time to reflect changes in the ownership, changes in state and FOEW budgets, and other factors.

  Prerequisites. None.

Objective 2. Inorganic Water Pollution Reduced

Within 10 years, levels of inorganic pesticides in water and wildlife in the Everson Watershed are reduced by 75 percent.

Factor(s) in Conceptual Model targeted by objective. Factor #1: Pesticide use by farms; Factor #2: Subsidies provided by the government.

Project assumptions. Factor # 1: According to recent studies, inorganic pesticides enter the Everson Watershed from agricultural run-off and accumulate in the fatty tissues of fish, birds, people, and other organisms that are high on the food chain through the process of bioconcentration. These pesticides also contaminate the drinking water supplies for major urban areas in the region and are possibly linked to health problems including cancer and sterility in the human population. It is assumed that inorganic pesticides in water and wildlife can be reduced by identifying major pollution sources and developing pollution reduction strategies with farmers. Factor #2: Tax subsidies to large commercial farmers indirectly encourage pesticide use as those crops that are subsidized generally require more pesticide use. It is assumed that by reducing subsidies for these pesticide-dependent crops, pesticide use will decline and the amount of inorganic pesticides found in water and wildlife will be reduced.

Underlying assumptions. (1) Pesticide use by farmers is a function of the economic decisions that they make. (2) Pesticides trapped in existing sediments are relatively stable and will not be disturbed and released, thus confounding monitoring efforts.

Activities for Objective 2

- **Activity 1. Identify Areas of High Pesticide Concentration.** Work with State Environment Department officials and Everson State University researchers to identify areas of the river with high pesticide concentrations.

  Why do this activity? In order to determine which parts of the watershed are most in need of remedial action. (Note that this activity will also provide baseline information that can be used to monitor the effectiveness of the project.)

  How will the activity be carried out? Fish and water samples will be drawn from major rivers and streams throughout the watershed. Samples will be analyzed at the university labs in conjunction with State Environment Department officials.

  Who is responsible? FOEW hydrologist.

  When will the activity take place? During the spring and fall of the first year of the project.

  Where will the activity take place? Major rivers and streams throughout the watershed.

  Underlying assumptions. Cost-effective assays exist for all key pesticides.

  Prerequisites. Hydrological flow patterns have already been mapped.

- **Activity 2. Identify Potential Pesticide Sources.** Once areas of high pesticide levels have been identified and mapped, identify potential sources in the local watershed using land-use maps and field surveys.

  Why do this activity? The project team can more effectively contact farmers if it first identifies where the most likely problem sites are located.

  How will the activity be carried out? Compare watershed maps with land-use maps to identify potential sources. These sources will then be surveyed by the outreach officer to determine pesticide uses. In addition, where available, records of pesticide use at the local State Agricultural Office will also be consulted.

  Who is responsible? FOEW agricultural outreach officer.

When will the activity take place? Year 2 of the project.

Where will the activity take place? Areas of high pesticide levels.

Underlying assumptions. (1) Records are available. (2) State officials will cooperate with outreach officer.

Prerequisites. Hire agricultural outreach officer who can liaise comfortably with state officials.

- **Activity 3. Develop Pesticide Reduction Strategies.** Work with farmers who are using high levels of pesticide to reduce or eliminate their use.

  Why do this activity? Pesticides can best be controlled by working in partnership with farmers.

  How will the activity be carried out? Where the farmers are receptive, the FOEW agricultural outreach officer in conjunction with local chapter community leaders and State Agricultural Extension agents will work with them to develop integrated pest management (IPM) and contour plowing methods and techniques that reduce the need for pesticides and the amount that runs off fields.

  Who is responsible? FOEW agricultural outreach officer.

  When will the activity take place? Years 2–5 of the project.

  Where will the activity take place? Farms identified in activity 2.

  Underlying assumptions. (1) Farmers will be receptive to working to reduce pesticide use. (2) Farm profitability can be maintained with reduced or eliminated pesticide use. (3) A price premium can be developed for pesticide-free farm products.

  Prerequisites. Completing activities 1 and 2.

- **Activity 4. Promote Pesticide Reduction Legislation.** Lobby federal and state legislators to end subsidies to large agribusinesses operating in the Everson Watershed that use high levels of pesticides.

  Why do this activity? One of the major reasons behind the use of pesticides is the set of tax subsidies that the state government provides to large agribusinesses in the state who tend to use higher amounts of pesticides.

  How will the activity be carried out? Meet with legislators and organize letter writing campaigns. If appropriate, organize consumer boycotts of key products.

  Who is responsible? FOEW legislative relations officer.

  When will the activity take place? Years 1–5 of the project.

  Where will the activity take place? State capital.

  Underlying assumptions. (1) Pesticide use is linked to tax code subsidies. (2) Citizen action and boycotts can influence legislative policy.

Prerequisites. Identify critical legislators (allies, opponents, and fence-sitters) and determine the appropriate strategy for each one.

Objective 3. Exotic Species Controlled

Within three years of the project start date, coverage of water hyacinth in critical wetland habitats has been reduced by 50 percent.

Factor(s) in Conceptual Model targeted by objective. Populations of exotic species.

Project assumptions. Water hyacinth, an exotic species introduced into the Everson Watershed in the 1960s, covers wetland areas, displacing native plants and eliminating habitat for game fish species. It is assumed that this exotic can be controlled by removing it from canals and other waterways.

Underlying assumptions. Effective control efforts are possible; physical removal will be sufficient to prevent immediate reinfestation of the water hyacinth.

Activities for Objective 3

- **Activity 1. Identify Areas of Infestation.** Work with State Environment Department to identify areas with high levels of infestation.

  Why do this activity? To effectively target removal efforts.

  How will the activity be carried out? FOEW will send out information to local chapter members for them to survey the water in their areas. Their information will then be mapped by the FOEW data management specialist working with local chapter members.

  Who is responsible? FOEW hydrologist.

  When will the activity take place? Year 1 of the project.

  Where will the activity take place? Local chapters throughout the watershed.

  Underlying assumptions. Chapter members willing to volunteer exist in all areas of the watershed.

  Prerequisites. Prepare information letters to send out.

- **Activity 2. Conduct Periodic Removal of Plants.** Organize community teams that will remove plants from designated areas on a semi-annual basis.

Why do this activity? To remove the plants.

How will the activity be carried out? Local chapter leaders will organize teams to mechanically remove water hyacinth plants from the surface on a semi-annual basis. Plant material will be composted in designated areas.

Who is responsible? FOEW community outreach coordinator.

When will the activity take place? In spring and fall on dates to be set by local chapters.

Where will the activity take place? Sites identified in the preceding step.

Underlying assumptions. Insurance questions will not be a problem.

Prerequisites. Completion of activity 1.

Objective 4. Local Community Knowledge Increased

Within three years, 15 percent of the community members and 45 percent of the relevant government officials in the Everson Watershed have knowledge about the importance of and threats to upstream forest areas that support wetland habitats.

Factors(s) in Conceptual Model targeted by objective. Degradation of upstream forest habitats.

Project assumptions. Wetlands in the watershed depend on the health of upstream forests and other habitats in the watershed to maintain their water balance. Long-term conservation of these habitats will only occur if the general public understands their importance for both ecosystem and human health and welfare. It is assumed that outreach and education activities will lead to a significant change in knowledge of those exposed to the messages.

Underlying assumptions. (1) If people learn about the importance of priority habitats, they will take actions to conserve them. (2) Different materials are required to reach the general public and government officials.

Activities for Objective 4

• **Activity 1. Research and Write Guidebook.** Work with State Environment Department officials to write a simple community-oriented guidebook to the functions, values, and protection of the wetlands in the Everson Watershed and the links to the upstream habitats.

Why do this activity? There are currently no materials that are available to present to the public the importance of the wetlands and upstream habitats in the watershed.

How will the activity be carried out? FOEW biologist, community outreach coordinator, data specialist, and intern will research basic information. Research specific sites in the watershed and prepare detailed maps outlining special features and threats.

Who is responsible? FOEW biologist.

When will the activity take place? Years 1–2 of the project.

Where will the activity take place? FOEW offices and field visits as needed.

Underlying assumptions. Information exists on all relevant sites.

Prerequisites. (1) Compile base maps of key sites. (2) Hire intern.

- **Activity 2. Hold Community Outreach Sessions.** Conduct information sessions and meetings in towns throughout the watershed.

  Why do this activity? To provide information to community members.

  How will the activity be carried out? Schedule meetings in conjunction with local chapter members.

  Who is responsible? FOEW community outreach coordinator.

  When will the activity take place? Years 1–5 of the project.

  Where will the activity take place? Towns throughout the watershed.

  Underlying assumptions. Community members will be receptive to the information sessions.

  Prerequisites. Prepare materials for presentations.

- **Activity 3. Hold Political Outreach Sessions.** Conduct information sessions and meetings in towns throughout the watershed with local town councils.

  Why do this activity? To provide information to politicians and decision makers.

  How will the activity be carried out? Schedule meetings in conjunction with local chapter members.

  Who is responsible? FOEW community outreach coordinator.

  When will the activity take place? Years 1–5 of the project.

  Where will the activity take place? Towns throughout the watershed.

  Underlying assumptions. Town councils will be receptive to the presentations.

  Prerequisites. Prepare materials for presentations.

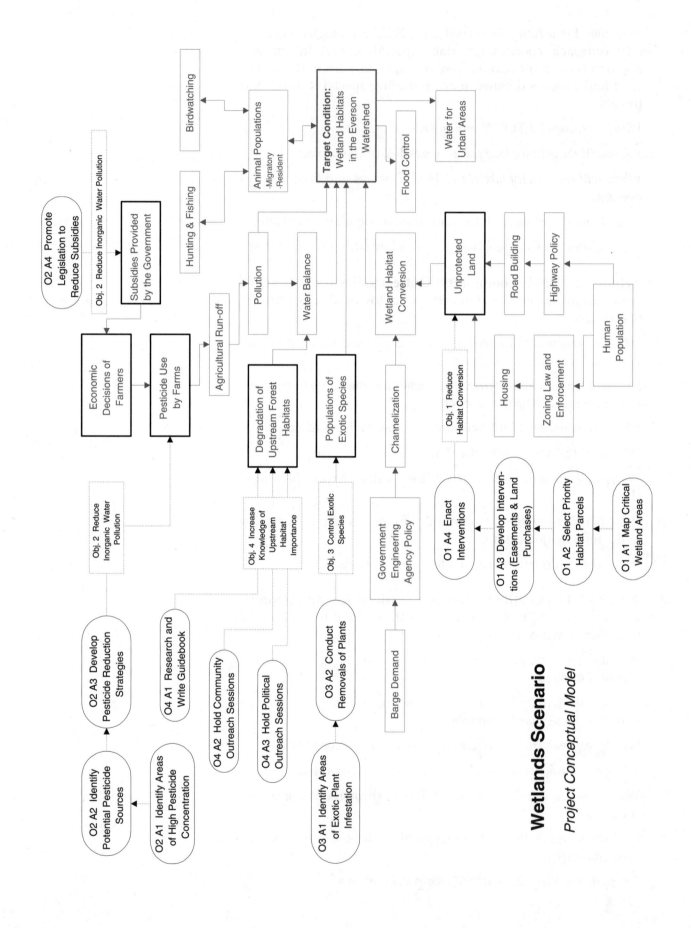

Wetlands Scenario

Project Conceptual Model

Project Management Timeline

Management Tasks	Y1 Q1	Y1 Q2	Y1 Q3	Y1 Q4	Y2 Q1	Y2 Q2	Y2 Q3	Y2 Q4	Y3 Q1	Y3 Q2	Y3 Q3	Y3 Q4	Y4 Q1	Y4 Q2	Y4 Q3	Y4 Q4	Y5 Q1	Y5 Q2	Y5 Q3	Y5 Q4	People Responsible
Goal: To maintain healthy wetlands in Everson in order to provide water to nearby urban areas and wildlife-based recreational opportunities for residents and visitors.																					
O1. Habitat conversion reduced in critical sites																					
– A1. Map critical wetland areas		X	X																		Biologist
– A2. Select priority habitat parcels				X																	Data specialist
– A3. Develop interventions and rank costs					X																Acquisitions manager
– A4. Enact conservation interventions						X	X	X	X	X	X	X	X	X	X	X	X	X	X	X	Acquisitions manager
O2. Inorganic water pollution reduced																					
– A1. Identify areas of high pesticide concentration		X	X	X																	Hydrologist
– A2. Identify potential pesticide sources					X	X	X	X													Agricultural officer
– A3. Develop pesticide reduction strategies					X	X	X	X	X	X	X	X	X	X	X	X	X	X	X	X	Agricultural officer
– A4. Promote pesticide reduction legislation	X	X	X	X	X	X	X	X	X	X	X	X	X	X	X	X	X	X	X	X	Legislative officer
O3. Exotic species controlled																					
– A1. Identify areas of infestation		X	X	X																	Hydrologist
– A2. Conduct periodic removals of plants					X		X		X		X		X		X		X		X		Community outreach coordinator
O4. Local community knowledge increased																					
– A1. Research and write guidebook		X	X	X	X	X	X	X													Biologist
– A2. Hold community outreach sessions	X		X		X		X		X		X		X		X		X		X		Community outreach coordinator
– A3. Hold political outreach sessions			X				X				X				X					X	Community outreach coordinator

Monitoring Plan

Goal, Objective, or Additional Information

Goal. To maintain healthy wetlands in the Everson Watershed in order to provide water to nearby urban areas and wildlife-based recreational opportunities for residents and visitors.

Monitoring Strategy 1: Measure changes over time in the populations of key species.
Monitoring Strategy 2: Measure changes in degree of satisfaction in those who use the Everson Watershed for recreation over time.

What (Indicators)	How (Methods & Tasks)	When	Who	Where	Comments
Numbers of green and blue heron nests per ha of wetland habitat (by species)	Formal surveys • Map habitats where these birds are found • Count active nests in heron breeding sites	By month 6 of the project Annually	Dept. of Env. and biologist Dept. of Env. and biologist	Project office Identified sites	These species were selected because it was determined that they were especially sensitive to both loss of wetland habitat and to pesticide levels in the ecosystem. Monitoring work will be done by State Environmental Department Biologists, but will be overseen by The Friends of the Everson Watershed (FOEW) Biologist.
Densities (nesting pairs/sq. km) of fish eagles in wetland habitat	Formal surveys • Map habitats where birds are found • Conduct line transects of eagle sightings	By month 6 of the project Annually	Dept. of Env. and biologist Dept. of Env. and biologist	Project office Identified sites	Same as above.
Hunter and birdwatcher satisfaction	Focus groups • Draft guide • Organize groups • Conduct sessions	By month 6 By month 12 Annually	Community outreach coordinator Community outreach coordinator Community outreach coordinator	Office Hunting sites Hunting sites	

Goal, Objective, or Additional Information

Objective 1. Habitat conversion reduced in critical sites. Within five years, 80 percent of identified privately owned priority wetland and adjacent natural habitat areas have been legally protected against conversion.

Monitoring Strategy: Monitor change over time in area of priority land under protected status.

What (Indicators)	How (Methods & Tasks)	When	Who	Where	Comments
Percentage of identified critical sites that are legally protected	Review of project records • Identify critical sites	By month 9 of project	Data specialist	Project office	This indicator is very straightforward and the data should be readily available.
	• Review documents to determine percentage that are protected	Annually	Data specialist	Project office	

Activities for Objective 1	Person Responsible for Monitoring the Activity	Target Date(s) for Obtaining Information
Activity 1. Map critical wetland areas	Data specialist	By end of ninth month of project
Activity 2. Select priority habitat parcels	Data specialist	By end of first year of project
Activity 3. Develop interventions and rank costs	Data specialist	By end of fifteenth month of project
Activity 4. Enact conservation interventions	Acquisitions manager	Yearly basis

Goal, Objective, or Additional Information

Objective 2. Inorganic water pollution reduced. Within 10 years, levels of inorganic pesticides in Everson Watershed are reduced 75 percent.

Monitoring Strategy 1: Compare changes over time in pesticide levels in key species in Everson to a control site.
Monitoring Strategy 2: Compare changes over time in pesticide levels in water and sediment in Everson to a control site.
Monitoring Strategy 3: Monitor changes in inorganic pesticide use by farmers over time.
Monitoring Strategy 4: Monitor changes in legislation that affect pesticide use.

What (Indicators)	*How (Methods & Tasks)*	*When*	*Who*	*Where*	*Comments*
Levels of commonly used pesticides in bass and crab tissues (by type of pesticide)	Formal surveys • Identify sites and sampling protocol • Collect and analyze specimens	By month 6 of project Annually	Biologist Biologist	Project office Identified sites	The laboratory analyses will be conducted by researchers from the Environmental Studies Toxicology Lab at Everson State University who will be hired as consultants by the project.
Levels of commonly used pesticides found in water and sediment samples (by type of pesticide)	Formal surveys • Identify sites and sampling protocol • Collect samples and run assessments	By month 6 of project Every three months	Hydrologist Hydrologist	Project office Designated points	Same as above. For both of these indicators, control sites will be identified in the Hudglades Watershed where no intervention is occurring for comparison to the Everson Watershed.
Percentage of farms identified as using high levels of pesticides that reduce their usage by at least 50 percent	Key informant interviews • Identify critical sites • Interview with farmers to determine percentage reduction in use	By year 2 Annually	Ag. officer Agricultural officer	Project office Project office	Need to have a good working relationship with farmers.
Passage of legislation reducing subsidies for pesticides	Key informant interviews • Interview staff of important members of state legislature agricultural committees	Every six months	Legislative relations officer	State capital	The legislative relations officer should have a working knowledge of whether the legislation has been passed, but we include this point to make sure to record this information periodically.

Activities for Objective 2

	Person Responsible for Monitoring the Activity	*Target Date(s) for Obtaining Information*
Activity 1. Identify areas of high pesticide concentration	Hydrologist	By end of sixth month of project
Activity 2. Identify potential pesticide sources	Hydrologist	By end of second year of project
Activity 3. Develop pesticide reduction strategies	Agricultural Outreach Officer	Yearly basis

Goal, Objective, or Additional Information

Objective 3. Exotic species controlled. Within three years of the project start date, coverage of water hyacinth in critical wetland habitats has been reduced by 50 percent.

Monitoring Strategy: Monitor changes over time in amount of area covered by water hyacinth.

What (Indicators)	How (Methods & Tasks)	When	Who	Where	Comments
Percentage of area of identified wetlands covered by water hyacinth	Formal survey • Identify critical areas • Survey sites to determine level of infestation	By end of first year of project Every six months	Hydrologist Hydrologist	Project office Project office	Monitoring should be fairly straightforward since the water hyacinth plants are very visible on the surface.

Activities for Objective 3		Person Responsible for Monitoring the Activity	Target Date(s) for Obtaining Information
Activity 1. Identify areas of infestation		Hydrologist	By end of first year of project
Activity 2. Conduct periodic removal of plants		Hydrologist	Annually

343

Goal. Objective, or Additional Information

Objective 4. Local community knowledge increased. Within three years, 15 percent of the community members in the watershed and 45 percent of the government officials in the Everson Watershed have knowledge about the importance of and threats to upstream forest areas that support wetland habitats.

Monitoring Strategy: Measure changes over time in knowledge of community members and government officials.

What (Indicators)	How (Methods & Tasks)	When	Who	Where	Comments
Percentage of community members in the watershed who demonstrate knowledge of the importance of and threats to upstream habitats to wetlands	Formal survey • Develop and pre-test questionnaire • Administer questionnaire to approximately 10 percent of population between 18–45 years of age	By month 6 of project Baseline at month 6 and final at end of project	Community outreach coordinator Community outreach coordinator	Project office Public grocery stores	Although surveying people in grocery stores may contain some bias compared to conducting house-to-house or telephone surveys, it is cheaper and the team decided that it was sufficiently accurate for their purposes.
Percentage of government officials who demonstrate knowledge of the importance of and threats to upstream habitats to wetlands	Direct observation • Develop and pre-test observation checklist • Apply checklist during meetings with relevant government officials	By month 6 of project Baseline at month 6 and final at end of project	Community outreach coordinator Community outreach coordinator	Project office Government offices	Monitoring will be conducted informally as the coordinator meets with various officials.

Activities for Objective 4	Person Responsible for Monitoring the Activity	Target Date(s) for Obtaining Information
Activity 1. Research and write guidebook	Community outreach coordinator	By end of second year of project
Activity 2. Hold community outreach sessions	Community outreach coordinator	Annually
Activity 3. Hold political outreach sessions	Community outreach coordinator	Annually

Goal, Objective, or Additional Information

Additional Information Needed to Assess Project Impact

What (Indicators)	How (Methods & Tasks)	When	Who	Where	Comments
Related to wetland habitat conversion factor—highway policy: Number of new highway miles planned	Key informant interviews • Interview state highway officials to determine plans for highway construction	Annually	Legislative outreach coordinator	Highway department offices	Although the project is currently not undertaking any interventions related to this factor, staff members want to keep abreast of planned changes in highways that might affect the wetlands.
Related to zoning law factor—changes in zoning policy: Changes in the zoning policy at the state or federal level that affect wetland areas	Secondary data review • Read newspaper accounts to determine if changes in legislation are pending	Weekly	Legislative outreach coordinator	Project offices	Current laws protect wetland areas from many types of conversion. As part of his or her normal duties, the legislative outreach coordinator will see if there are proposed changes in zoning policy that might affect this process in the future.
Related to government engineering agency policy—frequency of channel dredging: Incidents of dredging in critical areas	Key informant interviews • Interview Federal Engineering Agency staff members to determine location and frequency of dredging	Annually	Hydrologist	Engineering agency offices	Current dredging policy was judged not to be a significant threat. The project will monitor dredging to make sure that it does not change in intensity.
Related to human population factor—population growth: Number of people living in Everson Watershed	Secondary data review • Collect records from municipalities in the watershed	Annually	Community outreach coordinator	Township offices	Population is one of the major factors affecting the watersheds in the region.
New factors: New factors at the site that affect project success	Direct observation • Observe changes at the project site	Ongoing	All project staff	All locations	Project staff need to be constantly aware of potential changes in the project site that would require a revision of the Project Conceptual Model and Management Plan.

345

Project Monitoring Timeline

Project Monitoring Timeline—Everson Watershed

Monitoring Tasks	Y1 Q1	Y1 Q2	Y1 Q3	Y1 Q4	Y2 Q1	Y2 Q2	Y2 Q3	Y2 Q4	Y3 Q1	Y3 Q2	Y3 Q3	Y3 Q4	Y4 Q1	Y4 Q2	Y4 Q3	Y4 Q4	Y5 Q1	Y5 Q2	Y5 Q3	Y5 Q4	People Responsible
Goal: To maintain healthy wetlands in the Everson Watershed in order to provide water to nearby urban areas and wildlife-based recreational opportunities for residents and visitors.																					
– Numbers of green and blue heron nests per ha of wetland habitat	X	X			X	X			X	X			X	X			X	X			Dept. of Environment and biologist
– Densities (nesting pairs/sq. km) of fish eagles in wetland habitat	X	X			X	X			X	X			X	X			X	X			Designated council member
– Hunter and birdwatcher satisfaction			X				X				X				X				X		Community outreach coordinator
O1. Habitat conversion reduced in critical sites																					
– Percentage of identified critical sites that are legally protected	X	X						X				X				X				X	Data specialist
A1. Map critical wetland areas	X	X																			Data specialist
A2. Select priority habitat parcels			X																		Data specialist
A3. Develop interventions and rank costs				X																	Data specialist
A4. Enact conservation interventions					X			X				X				X				X	Acquisitions manager
O2. Inorganic water pollution reduced																					
– Levels of pesticides in bass and crab tissues		X				X				X				X				X			Biologist
– Levels of pesticides found in water and sediment samples	X	X	X	X	X	X	X	X	X	X	X	X	X	X	X	X	X	X	X	X	Hydrologist
– Percentage of farms identified as using pesticides that reduce usage			X					X				X				X				X	Agricultural officer
– Passage of legislation reducing subsidies for pesticides						X				X				X			X				Legislative relations officer
A1. Identify areas of high pesticide concentration		X																			Hydrologist
A2. Identify potential pesticide sources			X																		Hydrologist
A3. Develop pesticide reduction strategies							X				X				X						Agricultural outreach officer
A4. Promote pesticide reduction legislation							X				X				X						Legislative outreach officer
O3. Exotic species controlled																					
– Percentage of area identified as wetlands covered by water hyacinth		X				X				X				X			X				Hydrologist
A1. Identify areas of infestation		X																			Hydrologist
A2. Conduct periodic removal of plants						X				X				X			X				Hydrologist
O4. Local community knowledge increased																					
– Percentage of community members who demonstrate knowledge	X											X				X				X	Community outreach coordinator
– Percentage of government officials who demonstrate knowledge	X											X				X				X	Community outreach coordinator
A1. Research and write guidebook		X																			Community outreach coordinator
A2. Hold community outreach sessions						X				X				X			X				Community outreach coordinator
Additional Information																					
– Number of new highway miles planned	X				X				X				X				X				Legislative outreach coordinator
– Changes in zoning policies at state or federal level	X	X	X	X	X	X	X	X	X	X	X	X	X	X	X	X	X	X	X	X	Legislative outreach coordinator
– Incidents of dredging in critical areas	X	X	X	X	X	X	X	X	X	X	X	X	X	X	X	X	X	X	X	X	Hydrologist
– Number of people living in the Everson Watershed	X	X	X	X	X	X	X	X	X	X	X	X	X	X	X	X	X	X	X	X	Community outreach coordinator
– New factors at the site that affect project success	X	X	X	X	X	X	X	X	X	X	X	X	X	X	X	X	X	X	X	X	All project staff

Appendix B
Glossary of Select Terms

This appendix contains a list of many of the terms defined in this book. These definitions are not based on a dictionary but instead refer to how the term is used in the context of this guide.

Activity. A specific action or set of tasks undertaken by project staff designed to reach each of the project's objectives. A good activity meets the criteria of being: linked, focused, feasible, and appropriate. An activity is also sometimes called an intervention. In a Conceptual Model, an activity is represented by an oval.

Adaptation. Systematically using the information resulting from monitoring to improve your project. One of the three components of adaptive management in a project context.

Adaptive management. A process that integrates project design, management, and monitoring to provide a framework for testing assumptions, adaptation, and learning. It was originally developed to manage natural resources in large-scale ecosystems.

Analysis. The process of studying data to extract information from them.

Association. A term used in statistical inference that is a measurement of the extent to which two or more variables are found to be related or connected.

Assumption. See *Project assumption* or *Underlying assumption.*

Audience. See *Internal audiences* and *External audiences.*

Average. See *Mean.*

Baseline data. Data collected at the beginning of a project. They provide a benchmark against which change that occurs during the project period can be assessed.

Bias. A tendency in making a measurement to produce results that are systematically lower or higher than the true value.

Biodiversity. The variety and variability of life on earth. It is an abbreviation for biological diversity.

Budget. A table that outlines the predicted expenses for the Management and Monitoring Plans.

Categorical variable. A variable recorded in discrete intervals or as groups.

Cause and effect. The extent to which one factor in a Conceptual Model influences another. See *Relationship.*

Census. A measurement of all of the individuals in a population. See also *Sampling.*

Chi-square test. An analytical technique that tests the basic null hypothesis that a set of observed values in a frequency or contingency table will match expected values predicted by some theoretical model. It is used for categorical variables.

Codebook. A reference guide that lists each question or piece of information to be collected, the possible responses for each question or piece of information, and the codes assigned to each possible response. It is used primarily for quantitative data.

Coding. See *Data coding.*

Coding guide. A reference guide that represents an outline of how data and information will be recorded and organized for analysis. It is used primarily for qualitative data.

Comparison group. A group that is used for comparison to another group that has received some intervention. Unlike a control group, a comparison group is not randomly selected.

Comparison group monitoring design. Monitoring in which a sample is deliberately selected and "matched" to a treatment group influenced by the project to determine whether the project had an effect. Selection of treatment and control groups is not done randomly.

Conceptual Model. A diagram of a set of relationships between certain factors that are believed to impact or lead to a target condition. The foundation of project design, management, and monitoring. It is developed in two stages—an Initial Conceptual Model and a Project Conceptual Model. It is the first part of a complete Project Plan.

Conservation and development projects. Projects that have as their primary goal the conservation of natural ecosystems and species. They are based on the philosophy that in order to maintain economic and community development a healthy and viable natural resource base must be sustained. They operate by involving and addressing the needs of human stakeholders who have an interest in the natural resources of the project site.

Constraints. Problems that a project encounters that keep it from succeeding, such as lack of time, lack of money, lack of trained personnel, and lack of social or political opportunities.

Contingency table. An analytical technique that is used to show the association between two or more variables.

Continuous variable. A variable measured along a measurable scale.

Contributing factors. Factors in a Conceptual Model that are not classified as indirect or direct threats but that somehow affect the target condition.

Control group. A group of randomly selected individuals that have not been subject to project activities.

Correlation. An analytical technique that shows the relationship between two variables without implying a cause-and-effect relationship between the two.

Cost-effectiveness. The ratio of impact to cost of a given activity or monitoring approach. An activity that is highly cost-effective will have a high degree of impact relative to the amount of money required.

Criteria. Attributes of various parts of Management and Monitoring Plans. (Singular is *criterion.*)

Data. A set of observations collected through monitoring and research efforts. Information is derived from data through analysis. (Singular is *datum.*)

Data coding. The process of defining how you want to represent and record your data. Each piece of data you collect should be recorded using a consistent and specific code that represents each characteristic you are measuring.

Data collection instrument. A standardized format developed and used for obtaining data under a certain method, such as a questionnaire, topic guide, checklist, or record form.

Degrees of freedom. The number of independent parameters and values in a statistical test. It is calculated in different ways for different tests. The probability of a given test statistic being significant varies according to the number of degrees of freedom. You therefore look up the value of the test statistic in a table for the given number of degrees of freedom. As a rule, the more degrees of freedom that you have, the more likely it is that you will be able to detect a true difference between two samples.

Dependent variable. A variable that is a function of other variables. Generally graphed on the *y*-axis. See *Target condition* and *Independent variable*.

Diamond. One of the five stages (A–E) in the overall project cycle.

Direct observation. A data collection method in which a team systematically observes individuals, groups, animals, plants, objects, events, processes, or relationships and then records the observations.

Direct ranking. A form of matrix ranking that allows project teams to evaluate factors against specific criteria or attributes.

Direct threats. Factors in a Conceptual Model that immediately impact biodiversity (the target condition) or physically cause its destruction.

Error. The uncertainty in a measurement made using a given method.

Existing information. Information from data that have already been collected for some purpose other than designing and monitoring your project.

External audiences. People interested but not directly involved in the project, including donors, policy makers in government and other agencies, other members of the conservation and development community, and the broader public.

Extrapolate. A process of taking the results from a sample and applying them proportionately to an overall population.

Facilitator. A person who helps members of a group conduct a meeting in an efficient and effective way but who does not dictate what will happen.

Factors. The specific events, situations, conditions, policies, attitudes, beliefs, or behaviors that you believe affect the target condition in a Conceptual Model. Some of the most important factors that you must consider in model building for conservation and development projects are direct and indirect threats to biodiversity. Factors correspond roughly to predictors or independent variables in evaluation research.

False precision. A mistake that occurs when data are presented as being more accurate than they actually are. It is particularly important to be on the lookout for this type of error when you are using qualitative data.

Focus group discussion. A data collection method that involves bringing together a group of people to talk about a specific topic. It takes advantage of group dynamics and allows respondents to be guided by a skilled moderator into increasing levels of depth on key issues included in the Monitoring Plan. Focus groups are ideally fairly homogenous groups of between six and eight participants.

Formal survey. A data collection method that uses a standardized approach to collect data on individuals (including people, plants, and animals) or groups (households or organizations) through structured measurement or the questioning of systematically identified samples.

Frequency table. An analytical technique used to show the distribution or range of values of a single variable.

Goal. A general summary of the desired state that a project is working to achieve. A good goal meets the criteria of being visionary, relatively general, brief, and measurable.

Group. (Project implementation) The organization or collection of people implementing a project.

Group. (Sampling) A specific subset of the population that you choose to consider in your monitoring efforts—for example, households participating in a project or rattan collectors not participating in the project.

Habitat mapping. A data collection and presentation method that combines biological, ecological, and physical data to form maps illustrating natural area and human land-use pattern boundaries. In monitoring, this technique is used most often to determine the impacts of different human activities on natural areas and to represent changes over time of species distribution and density.

Histogram. An analytical technique that uses graphical representation of groups of data or information in the form of bars, also referred to as a bar chart.

Homogenous. Characteristic of a group in which all members are similar.

Hypothesis. A formal statement proposed about the population or populations being sampled.

Hypothesis testing process. A statistical technique for formally testing a statement comparing two or more samples drawn from one or more populations.

Impact. The results you are trying to accomplish within a project.

Independent variable. A variable that is used, possibly in conjunction with other variables, to describe a given outcome or dependent variable. Usually shown on the *x*-axis.

Indicator. A unit of information measured over time that documents changes in a specific condition. A given goal, objective, or additional information need can have multiple indicators. A good indicator meets the criteria of being measurable, precise, consistent, and sensitive.

Indirect threats. Factors in a Conceptual Model that underlie or lead to the direct threats.

Information. Knowledge that is extracted from data through the process of analysis.

Information need. What a specific audience wants to know about the project.

Initial Conceptual Model. The first stage of a Conceptual Model that shows what is going on at your project site before you begin the project. This model describes the site's target condition, factors, and relationships prior to the start of your project.

Institutional knowledge. The learning accumulated by a group. In general, this knowledge has to be captured in a permanent form, such as a written document or (in the case of illiterate people) a story handed down as part of an oral tradition.

Instrument. See *Data collection instrument.*

Internal audiences. People directly involved in the project, including project staff, the local community members with whom your project is working, other groups that are collaborating with you, and other stakeholders in the project.

Intervention. See *Activity.*

Iteration. To repeat a process or sequence of steps that brings you successively closer to a desired result.

Key informant interview. A data collection method that involves semi-structured, in-depth consultations with knowledgeable individuals in which only some of the questions are predetermined. Instead of using a formal survey questionnaire, an informal topic guide is generally used, also called "informal interviews."

Learning. Systematically documenting the process that your team has gone through and the results you have achieved. One of the three components of adaptive management in a project context.

Linear regression analysis. An analytical technique that measures the association between two or more variables. Linear regression involves measuring how strong a linkage is by fitting a line that is mathematically calculated to come as close as possible to all the points in a scatterplot. This line can be used both to describe the existing relationship and to predict what future observations might look like.

Local stakeholder participation. Active involvement in the design, management, and monitoring of the project. It does not just involve notifying local community members about your new project. Instead, full participation requires active efforts on your part to ensure that representatives of all the stakeholder groups at the project site—men and women, young and old, rich and poor, those with power and those without power—become involved.

Local stakeholders. Residents of the project site who have a vested interest in the natural resources of the area (who are often called "community members") as well as other people who potentially will be affected by project activities.

Management Plan. An outline for the interventions you will undertake. It contains a project's goal, objectives, and activities. It is the second part of a complete Project Plan.

Matrix ranking. A data collection method that uses tables to order and determine the relative importance of particular items, conditions, or perceptions.

Mean. A descriptive statistic that is the sum of all the observations in a population or sample divided by the total number of observations.

Median. A descriptive statistic that measures central location as calculated by arranging observations in order of size and taking the middle one such that there is an equal number of sample points on both sides.

Method. A specific technique used to collect data to measure an indicator. Methods vary in their accuracy and reliability, cost-effectiveness, feasibility, and appropriateness.

Mission statement. A written description of your group's mission. Your mission statement should include the purpose, strategies, and values of your group.

Model. A simplified representation of reality, often presented in the form of a picture.

Monitoring. The periodic collection and evaluation of data relative to stated project goals, objectives, and activities. Many people often also refer to this process as monitoring and evaluation (M&E).

Monitoring Plan. An outline for the steps you will undertake to ensure that the project is on track. It lists a project's audience, their information needs, the strategies that will be used for data collection, the indicators, the methods that will be used to collect data, and when, by whom, and where data will be collected. It is the third part of a complete Project Plan.

Monitoring strategy. The broad plan for getting data needed to meet each information need. It generally describes the specific comparison that you will be making with your monitoring efforts.

Noncontact. A term in survey methodology that indicates when a potential respondent refuses to be interviewed.

Nonprobability sampling. A form of sampling in which the chance of a given individual within the population being selected is not known or is unequal compared to the chance of other individuals being selected. It is most often associated with qualitative data collection and analysis. Nonprobability sampling is frequently used because it is usually less time consuming, less costly, and less complicated than probability sampling. Two popular forms of nonprobability sampling are purposeful sampling (also known as "convenience" or "judgmental" sampling) and quota sampling.

Nonresponse. A term in survey methodology that indicates when a person being interviewed refuses to give an answer to a particular question.

Null hypothesis. A hypothesis opposite the one that you are trying to support. You try to reject the null hypothesis in order to prove your hypothesis.

Objective. A specific statement detailing the desired accomplishments or outcomes of a project. If the project is well conceptualized and well designed, realization of a project's objectives should lead to the fulfillment of the project's goal. A good objective meets the criteria of being impact oriented, measurable, time limited, specific, and practical.

Opportunities. Factors in a Conceptual Model that potentially have a positive effect on your target condition.

Outcome. See *Target condition* and *Dependent variable.*

Outlier. A data point that is outside of the expected range for a particular variable. An outlier is not necessarily an error, but it should be carefully checked to ensure that it represents a true value.

Paired t-test. An analytical technique that compares an average calculated from a sample drawn before the intervention to an average calculated from a second sample drawn after an intervention. A paired t-test is most useful when you are using a pre-test/post-test monitoring strategy in which you want to compare the units influenced by your project to themselves before and after the project intervention. See *Two sample t-test.*

Pairwise ranking. A data collection method that is a form of matrix ranking used to determine the main problems or preferences of individual community members, identify their ranking criteria, and easily compare the priorities of different individuals.

Participation. See *Local stakeholder participation.*

Population. The collection of all sampling units that you could potentially observe. All units in a population must share at least one characteristic—for example, households in a community, rattan collectors, or trees of a certain species.

Power. The ability of a test statistic to detect a true difference between two samples. If the power of a test is too low, then there is little chance of detecting a real difference in the results, even if there is one. A small sample size is almost always the root cause of low power.

Practitioners. Managers, researchers, and local stakeholders who are responsible for designing, managing, and monitoring conservation and development projects.

Predictor. See *Factors* and *Independent variable.*

Preference ranking. A data collection method that is a form of matrix ranking that allows a field team to quickly determine the main problems or preferences of individuals in a given site and enables the priorities of different individuals to be easily compared. This method allows the team to incorporate the viewpoints of a number of local stakeholders in the assessment. It is very similar to voting but is done individually as the team talks to different residents.

Presentation. Any communications product, including spoken, written, and multi-media ones.

Pre-test/post-test monitoring design. A monitoring approach in which a team measures a sample or population before an intervention to establish a baseline, implements the intervention, and then remeasures the sample or population to see how it has changed.

Primary information. Information drawn from data that you specifically collect while designing and monitoring your project.

Probability sampling. A form of sampling in which every individual in the population has an equal chance of being selected for the sample. It is most often associated with quantitative data collection and analysis. Two of the most commonly used types of probability sampling are simple random sampling and stratified random sampling. See *Nonprobability sampling*.

Probing. A technique used in many qualitative data collection methods for following up on a specific point and asking as many questions as necessary to get a good understanding of the issue.

Process. How you are going to achieve impact within a project.

Project. Any set of actions undertaken by any group of managers, researchers, or local stakeholders interested in achieving certain defined goals and objectives.

Project assumption. A causal chain of project activities and factors that affect a target condition. In scientific terms, it is equal to a hypothesis.

Project Conceptual Model. A complete version of a Conceptual Model that adds project activities to the Initial Conceptual Model to show how you expect your project will influence the situation at your site.

Project cycle. The steps involved in developing and implementing a Management and Monitoring Plan and analyzing the results.

Project overhead. Items in a project budget that are not directly attributable to any one objective of the project. It includes things like the time that staff spend planning the project and administrative costs like supplies and rent.

Project Plan. The blueprint for your project. It is composed of a Project Conceptual Model, Management Plan, and Monitoring Plan.

Proxy indicator. A substitute for an indicator that cannot be directly measured or assessed.

Purpose. Part of a mission statement that describes what your group is seeking to accomplish.

Purposeful sampling. A form of sampling in which there is deliberate selection of information-rich cases or key informants for monitoring. See *Nonprobability sampling* and *Sentinel site*.

p-Value. The probability that a test statistic represents a real result and is not merely occurring by chance. It is a number between zero and one.

Qualitative methods. Techniques for collecting data that are not easily summarized in numerical form, such as minutes from community meetings and general notes from observations. Qualitative data normally describe people's knowledge, attitudes, or behaviors.

Quantitative methods. Techniques for collecting data that are easily represented as numbers, such as answers to formal surveys and enterprise financial records. Quantitative data generally describe formal measurements of variables such as income, crop production, or animal population densities.

Quota sampling. A form of sampling in which there is selection of a fixed and predetermined number of units that possess some particular characteristic of interest to be included in the monitoring work. These cases are compared to an equal number of units that are similar except in that they lack the particular characteristic of interest. Quota sampling is generally only used with the comparison group monitoring design.

Range. A descriptive statistic that measures the difference between the smallest and largest observations in a sample or population.

Rapid Appraisal (RA). A variety of qualitative social methods that are presented as a package of techniques designed to encourage maximum community involvement and consultation in data collection, analysis, and use. Rapid Appraisal techniques are especially useful for assessing local site conditions. Generally, however, most Rapid Appraisal techniques are too descriptive and open ended in nature to be used as the only tool for rigorous and long-term project monitoring efforts.

Relationship. An effect that one factor or variable has on another. In a Conceptual Model they are represented by arrows. These arrows usually point in one direction. See *Cause and effect.*

Resources. Items that a project has or needs, such as staff time, managerial time, local knowledge, money, equipment, the presence of trained personnel, and sociopolitical opportunities.

Retrofitting. Applying the process presented in this book to an already existing project.

Sampling. Measurement of a subset of individuals in a population.

Sampling frame. A description of the set of all the possible individuals that a project team can sample.

Scale. A set of evenly spaced numbers, like markings on a ruler or rankings between 1 and 10, that is used to measure things.

Scatterplot. An analytical technique that involves graphical representation of the relationship between two continuous variables.

Scenarios. Fictional examples of projects used in this guide that show the many challenges of managing conservation and development projects around the world.

Sentinel site. A form of sampling that involves selecting sampling units based on some characteristic of particular importance to your team's monitoring. A sentinel site is also particularly sensitive to some condition in which you are most interested.

Significant. A result from a statistical test that is greater than a defined probability (usually 95 percent) of not being due to chance.

Simple random sampling. A form of sampling in which each individual in a population has an equal chance of being selected. See *Probability sampling* and *Stratified random sampling.*

Social (or participatory) mapping. A data collection and recording method that involves having community members draw or assist in drawing maps.

Social transects or land-use profiles. A data collection and recording method that involves maps that represent cross-sections of human or natural landscapes. These maps are drawn from a side-view perspective and may or may not be drawn to scale.

Stakeholders. See *Local stakeholders.*

Standard deviation. A descriptive statistic that measures the spread or the distance of data from the mean. It is the square root of the variance.

State. The condition of an object or system in a Conceptual Model at one point in time.

Statistics. The science of analyzing data drawn from samples to make inferences about populations.

Strategies. Part of a mission statement that describes the general activities or programs your group chooses to undertake to pursue its purpose.

Strategic planning. A process for defining the general purpose of your group and then deciding what types of activities you will carry out to achieve your group's ends.

Stratified random sampling. A form of sampling that is similar to simple random sampling, except the population is first divided into different subgroups, or strata, based on some characteristic, such as age, sex, tribal group in a household survey, or habitat type in a botanical survey, and then a random sample is selected within each stratum. See *Probability sampling* and *Simple random sampling.*

Strict control monitoring design. A monitoring approach that is also referred to as "experimental design." It involves taking all units in the population and randomly dividing them into two groups. Individuals in the treatment group will be subject to the project intervention whereas individuals in the control group will not. The monitoring involves comparing the treatment group with the control group to determine whether the project had an effect.

Target condition. The situation you intend to

influence through your project activities. It is akin to the outcome or dependent variable in scientific analysis or evaluation research—it is the condition you are trying to explain, predict, or modify.

Tasks. The set of specific actions that need to be undertaken to implement each method or monitoring plan.

Testing assumptions. Systematically trying different interventions to achieve a desired outcome. One of the three components of adaptive management in a project context.

Test statistic. A number calculated from sample data according to a certain formula and then compared to an established distribution to test a statistical hypothesis.

Threat Reduction Assessment (TRA) approach. A method for project design, management, and monitoring that can simplify your work by enabling you to focus on the key threat factors. If you can be confident that you have identified all the threats to biodiversity at a site and that you have addressed all of these threats, then you can assume that conservation has occurred or will occur in the future. One of the two main principles underlying this book.

Threats. See *Direct threats* and *Indirect threats*.

Timeline. A bar graph that lists the major activities and tasks involved in a Management or Monitoring Plan. It also shows how long the various activities are supposed to last and the relationship between different activities over time.

Time-series monitoring design. A monitoring approach that involves collecting data multiple times before, during, and after a project is implemented. Because it tracks trends, the time-series monitoring design can provide more reliable results than the pretest/post-test monitoring design. It is also, however, more expensive to do since it requires collecting and analyzing greater amounts of data.

Topic guide. A list of topics to be covered in a key informant interview or focus group session. It is used for probing respondents. Questions are generally open ended, meaning that they leave space for the respondent to answer in different ways.

Tracking records. A data collection method that involves designing a form that is used to systematically collect quantitative data, such as a business's profit and loss, levels of community participation, and production figures over time.

Transcription. The process of typing or writing out the results of recorded focus group sessions or key informant interviews.

Treatment group. A group of randomly selected individuals who have been subjected to project activities.

Triangulation. Use of a variety of sources, methods, or field team members to cross-check and validate data and information. See *Validation*.

Two sample t-test. An analytical technique that compares an average calculated from a sample from one population to an average calculated from a sample drawn from a second population. It is most useful when you are using a strict control or comparison group monitoring strategy in which you want to compare the units influenced by your project to a control or comparison group. See *Paired t-test*.

Underlying assumption. The effects that other conditions and factors could potentially have on the causal chain of a project assumption.

Unit. A single item or individual that you are interested in observing. Depending on the type of monitoring that you are doing, units can be, for example, a community, a household, a person, a garden plot, or a tree.

Validation. The process of cross-checking to ensure that the data obtained from one monitoring method are confirmed by the data obtained from a different method. See *Triangulation*.

Values. Part of a mission statement that describes the beliefs that the members of your group have in common and try to put into practice while implementing the group's strategies.

Variable. A particular characteristic of a unit that an observer is interested in measuring.

Variance. A descriptive statistic that calculates the mean difference between each observation in a sample or population and the mean for the group, with the differences being squared to avoid problems with positive and negative signs. Like standard deviation, it is a measurement of spread or the distance of data from the mean.

Wealth ranking. A data collection method that is a form of matrix ranking that is used to determine the relative socioeconomic level of community members within a project area. For monitoring, wealth ranking is most useful to see whether the socioeconomic status of project participants improves over time compared to those who do not participate in the project.

Index

About the Authors

RICHARD MARGOLUIS is the director of the Biodiversity Support Program's (BSP) Analysis and Adaptive Management (AAM) Program. BSP is a consortium of World Wildlife Fund, The Nature Conservancy, and World Resources Institute funded by the U.S. Agency for International Development (USAID). Richard is responsible for managing BSP's portfolio of applied conservation and development research projects and its strategic planning, monitoring, and evaluation technical assistance component. AAM works in collaboration with BSP's regional programs and consortium member organizations in Asia, Africa, Latin America, and the Caribbean.

Before coming to BSP, Richard worked primarily with local nongovernmental organizations in Latin America and Africa to improve the design, management, and monitoring of their conservation and development initiatives. While living and working in Guatemala, Richard served as the assistant director of the Sierra de las Minas Biosphere Reserve. While in Sudan, North Africa, Richard assisted local organizations in developing low-cost drought and famine early warning information systems.

Richard received his B.A. from Northwestern University and his master's in public health (MPH) and Ph.D. from Tulane University. His academic training has been in Latin American studies, international public health, epidemiology, and project planning and evaluation. Richard is on the faculty at Tulane University.

NICK SALAFSKY is currently working as senior program officer/scientist for the Biodiversity Support Program in Washington, D.C. Nick is working with BSP's Biodiversity Conservation Network (BCN), which is evaluating the feasibility of enterprise-oriented community-based approaches to biodiversity conservation across the Asia/Pacific Region. In particular, Nick is responsible for helping BCN and its grantees develop monitoring and evaluation programs that will feed into a systematic analytical framework and for working with grantees to implement these programs. With BCN, Nick travels regularly to visit projects throughout South and Southeast Asia and the Pacific.

Previously, Nick spent several years conducting interdisciplinary research in West Kalimantan, Indonesia, studying the forest gardens, a locally developed agroforestry system, from economic, ecological, soil science, and agroforestry perspectives. In addition, in the same region of Kalimantan, Nick has done interdisciplinary research on nontimber forest products, economic research on the effects of a transmigration program and El Niño–Southern Oscillation–linked droughts on village economies, and primatological studies on the red-leaf monkey. Nick has also researched and written a management guide for the endangered freshwater tidal habitats in the Hudson River Estuary in New York State.

Nick's background is in the interface of ecology and economics. He received a B.A. in biological anthropology/behavioral ecology from Harvard University and an M.A. in resource economics and an interdisciplinary Ph.D. in environmental studies from Duke University. Nick has published scientific papers on a wide range of subjects and also has extensive experience with training programs.